THE COMMUNIST IDEAL IN HEGEL AND MARX

One reader has called this study 'easily the best book on the relation of Hegel to Marx.' With spirited argument, MacGregor demonstrates that Hegelian logic suited Marx's purpose so well because it already contained the unique elements that later appeared in Marx's social theory, including the notions of surplus value and the transition to communism. The most exciting thing about the book is the clear demonstration that the mature Marx gets ever closer to Hegel, and is *increasingly* indebted to him. In short, the author gives us a new Hegel and a new Marx.

In a manner both original and penetrating, MacGregor shows that dialectical logic is pre-eminently social logic, a reconstruction in thought of social relationships and social structure. Central to the work is an examination of the *Philosophy of Right*, in which Hegel delineated a theory of modern capitalist society. MacGregor provides a compelling analysis of Hegel's importance for Lenin and a strong caveat that contemporary Marxism ignores Hegel to its own peril. MacGregor establishes that Hegel's absolute idealism is founded on a theory of the dialectics of labour similar to Marx's historical materialism. Another significant discovery elucidates Hegel's concept of property as the missing link which joins Marx's formulation to classical liberal theory. A major contribution to Marxist and Hegelian theory, this inquiry will stimulate debate for some time to come.

DAVID MACGREGOR is an Associate Professor of Sociology at King's College, University of Western Ontario.

To Patricia

The Communist Ideal
in Hegel and Marx

DAVID MACGREGOR

UNIVERSITY OF TORONTO PRESS

TORONTO and BUFFALO

CANADIAN CATALOGUING IN PUBLICATION DATA

MacGregor, David, 1943–
The Communist Ideal in Hegel and Marx

Includes bibliographical references and index.
ISBN 0-8020-5616-4
1. Marx, Karl, 1818–1883. 2. Hegel, Georg Wilhelm
Friedrich, 1770–1831. 3. Hegel, Georg Wilhelm
Friedrich, 1770–1831 — Influence. I. Title.
B3305.M74M32   1984   C83-098411-9

43,372

Contents

Preface

Theoretical work is lonely by nature and thus the community and encouragement of friends and mentors is doubly important. I welcome the opportunity to thank Patricia Bishop without whose intelligent and perceptive criticism this book could not have been completed. I am also pleased to acknowledge the guidance and interest of Donald G. MacRae, Professor of Sociology at the London School of Economics, who supervised the PhD dissertation that forms the basis of this book. R.I.K. Davidson, my editor at the University of Toronto Press, offered his cheerful and generous support at all the arduous stages of the publication process and made my life considerably easier and happier than it otherwise would have been. C.B. Macpherson at the University of Toronto read an early version of the manuscript and helped it along to publication; and John Keane gave valuable comments and advice.

This is the place to express my appreciation for the insightful criticism and patient editing of the anonymous reader at the University of Toronto Press. In addition I would like to acknowledge the helpful comments of the reviewer at the Social Science Federation of Canada.

My friends Lesley De Pauw, Mark De Pauw, Stan Marshall, Gerry Nixon, and Sheila Zurbrigg gave me support and confidence in the long days of writing this book. My colleagues at King's College, Bernie Hammond, Kathy Kopinak, and Alan Pomfret, read and commented on the manuscript; Al Koop, David Flynn, and Dante Lenardon extended important assistance. At the University of Western Ontario, Tom Sea provided helpful advice on the historical context of the writings of Hegel and Marx, and James Rinehart gave me lots of arguments on Marxism. Sean O'Hegarty read the various drafts of this study and offered useful suggestions. The debt I owe to my sister Betty is immense.

The Research Grants Committee at King's College provided crucial financial assistance, and the Dean and the Principal of the College have been most supportive. My years at the LSE were amply funded by the Canada Council. This book has been published with the help of a grant from the Social Science Federation of Canada, using funds provided by the Social Sciences and Humanities Research Council of Canada.

I would like to thank David Boudreau and Cathy Mendler for their assistance in editing the manuscript. Jean Fyfe, Jean Murphy, Lynda Laird, Miff Lysaght, and Cathy Mendler have all at one time or another and with great forbearance and skill transformed my awkwardly typed pages into a legible product.

A special acknowledgment goes to my friend who sees in black and white; Patricia will know whom I mean.

D.M.

The Communist Ideal
in Hegel and Marx

He: You are right. The main thing is that you and I should exist, and that we should be you and I. Apart from that let everything go as it likes. The best order of things, to my way of thinking, is the one I was meant to be part of, and to hell with the most perfect of worlds if I am not of it. I would rather exist, even as an impudent argufier, than not exist at all.

I: There is nobody who doesn't share your opinion and criticize the existing order of things without realizing that he is thereby denying his own existence.

Diderot, *Rameau's Nephew*

What is rational is actual and what is actual is rational. On this conviction the plain man like the philosopher takes his stand, and from it philosophy starts in its study of the universe of mind as well as the universe of nature. If reflection, feeling, or whatever form subjective consciousness may take, looks upon the present as something vacuous and looks beyond it with the eyes of superior wisdom, it finds itself in a vacuum, and because it is actual only in the present, it is itself mere vacuity.

G.W.F. Hegel, *Philosophy of Right*

Introduction

Lenin was among the first to realize that a profound understanding of Marx demands a thorough knowledge of Hegel. Marx uses Hegelian categories throughout his work, and he assumes in his readers some familiarity with dialectical logic. An attempt to read Marx on the Hegelian terms through which he meant to be interpreted forms one aspect of this book. My major argument is that Hegelian logic suited Marx's purpose so well because it already contains the unique elements that later appeared in his own social theory, including the notions of surplus value and the transition to communism. Dialectical logic is pre-eminently social logic, a reconstruction in thought of social relationships and social structure. Logic's implications for social analysis are brought home by Hegel himself in the *Philosophy of Right* where he presents a theory of modern capitalist society which parallels that of Marx and throws even greater light on our contemporary situation than the richly textured analysis of *Capital*.

Marx acknowledged that employment of Hegelian dialectic is what separates his work from the mainstream of bourgeois thought. Yet he also helped create the myth of Hegel the idealist who had everything upside down. By challenging his view of Hegel, this study reveals a new Marx, a thinker intensely aware of the contradictory character of capitalism, the system's infinite capacity not only to degrade the human spirit but also to contribute to the liberation of all men and women. As he grew older Marx's expanding sensitivity to the nuances of the bourgeois epoch sent him back again and again to the work of Hegel.[1]

Marx's misinterpretation of the Hegelian Idea set him against Hegel's theory of the state and may have prevented him from coming fully to grips with the contradictory reality of liberal democracy only now being seriously confronted by his latter-day followers (who have much to learn from Hegel).

This book points to an understanding of the liberal democratic state that tempers Marx's critique with the insights of Hegel's political theory.

No attempt to do justice to the complexities surrounding the relationship of Hegel and Marx can avoid confronting the thinker who deeply influenced them both and whose doctrine is the quintessential expression of the bourgeois spirit – Immanuel Kant. Considerable space is also devoted in this study to Ludwig Feuerbach, who attains nothing like the status of Kant in the history of philosophy but is nevertheless a vital part of the intellectual connection between Marx and Hegel. Another key figure in my account is V.I. Lenin.

In 1914, just after the declaration of war in Europe, Lenin spent three arduous months studying Hegel's *Science of Logic*; the brilliant Conspectus that resulted from this effort and which constitutes over a hundred pages in the famous 'Philosophical Notebooks'[2] has proven even more of a puzzle to scholars than Marx's transformation of Hegelian dialectic. Anti-Hegelian Marxists like Althusser and Colletti have struggled to show that Lenin either completely alchemized Hegel or simply misunderstood him, while Hegelian Marxists such as Marcuse have proven unable to use the Conspectus to support their own interpretation of Hegel. But what Lenin stumbled upon that fall in the elegant Bern library is that Hegelian logic is nothing less than a theoretical analysis of human social activity. 'When Hegel endeavours – sometimes even huffs and puffs – ' Lenin remarks (p. 190) 'to bring man's purposive activity under the categories of logic, saying that this activity is the "syllogism" ... that the subject (man) plays the role of a "member" in the logical "figure" of that "syllogism", and so on, – THEN THAT IS NOT MERELY STRETCHING A POINT, A MERE GAME, THIS HAS A VERY PROFOUND, PURELY MATERIALISTIC CONTENT.'

The implications of Lenin's commentary were never seriously considered by later theorists. Although he counselled Marxists to adopt the Hegelian theory of knowledge and abandon that of Feuerbach and Kant, his advice was ignored. The 'Philosophical Notebooks' along with *Materialism and Empirio-Criticism* (which presented a philosophical position utterly at variance with the Conspectus) were hailed as 'an outstanding achievement of Lenin's creative genius'[3] by theorists of orthodox dialectical materialism, but there was hardly any question of a critical understanding of Hegel's impact on Marx from this quarter.

The Hegelian influences which operated a few years after Lenin's study in the writings of the young Lukács, Karl Korsch, and Antonio Gramsci anticipated many later developments but did not offer, as did Lenin, a radical interpretation of Hegel's ontology. A more searching evaluation had to await

5 Hegel and Marx

Georg Lukács' *The Young Hegel* (written in 1938 but unpublished until ten years later) and Herbert Marcuse's *Reason and Revolution* (published in 1941) which owed much to Lukács' and Marcuse's acquaintance with Marx's *Paris Manuscripts* and Hegel's early system, the *Jenenser Realphilosophie* (both of which were unpublished until the early 1930s). At about the same time the French theorists Alexandre Kojève and Jean Hyppolite were developing a novel reading of the *Phenomenology* which emphasized the centrality of Hegel's master-servant dialectic for the work of Marx.

The writings of Lukács and Marcuse, Kojève and Hyppolite indicated that the seeds of historical materialism were gleaned by Marx from his youthful reading of the *Phenomenology*. According to these theoreticians, Marx returned often to the early Hegel for his substantive arguments, only consulting the master's mature works for the mysteries of dialectic method. Associated with this version of the Hegel-Marx relationship was the idea that Hegel considerably modified his radical views as he grew older, producing in the end a pseudo-religious system that glorified Protestantism and the Prussian state. While Lukács and the others assumed that Marx's intellectual development followed a consistent pattern, an alternative account suggested that the change in Hegel had its later co-ordinates in Marx. Like most members of the Young Hegelians in the early 1840s Marx was struck by the seductive rhythm of the *Phenomenology* which clashed so desperately with the authoritarian progress of the *Philosophy of Right*. His encounter with the early Hegel spawned the Young Marx, for some a humanist with a special message for the twentieth century, and for others (most notably Louis Althusser in *For Marx*[4]) a woolly liberal who would only later come down firmly to the materialist earth.

Despite Althusser's influential notion of the epistemological break which divides the humanist from the scientific Marx, there are good reasons to consider the *Phenomenology* a founding text of Marxism. Yet not a single reference to it appears in *Capital*, while there are numerous citations for volumes belonging to Hegel's allegedly reactionary later period, including the *Philosophy of Right* and both versions of *Logic*. Moreover, the quasi-Hegelian language of the *Grundrisse* owes more to the *Encyclopaedia* than to the *Phenomenology*. It was inevitable therefore that the debate about Marx's relation to Hegel would eventually focus on Hegel's later writings. In 1963 Robert Heiss pointed to the remarkable parallels between *Capital* and the section on civil society in the *Philosophy of Right*.[5] Shlomo Avineri, Raymond Plant, and Charles Taylor among others have also referred to the similarities between the mature work of Hegel and Marx. None of them, however, has gone far enough in connecting Hegel's social theory with the ontology of *Logic* even though Hegel insists in the Preface (p. 3) to the *Philosophy of Right* that 'it will be obvious from the work itself that the whole, like the formation of its parts, rests on the logical spirit. It is also from this point of view above all that I should like my book to be taken and judged.'

Apart from some considerable surface changes the debate on Hegel and Marx has practically stood still since Lenin opened the *Science of Logic* in 1914. Almost all commentators would agree with Lukács's orthodox assessment that Hegel's 'general view of history and society prevented him from grasping the importance of class antagonisms as a motive force, to say nothing of making any general inferences from their observed laws of motion.' Lacking these essential Marxist insights his 'understanding of society loses itself in the miasma of mysticism.'[6] However, the inferences to be drawn from Lenin's Conspectus could not have been clearer: the premises of Hegelian logic were the same as those that informed the work of Marx, and they help explain the mysterious resemblance between Marx's and Hegel's critique of bourgeois society.

An objection may be raised to my account of the Hegel-Marx relationship that I should like to anticipate. How could two theorists who lived in such different historical periods possibly draw identical conclusions about the character and fate of capitalist society? The industrial revolution was stalled in Germany during Hegel's lifetime and had barely gained momentum when Marx entered studies in law, history, and philosophy at Berlin in 1836, five years after Hegel's death. The brief experience of power in Paris and elsewhere during the revolutions of 1830 and 1848 greatly altered the objectives and consciousness of the European working class and split it apart from its erstwhile allies among the bourgeoisie. Thus the economic and political landscape Marx had before him while writing *Capital* contrasted strongly with the society Hegel analyses in the *Philosophy of Right*.

Although the economic take-off in Germany was delayed until the mid 1830s, long after the industrial transformation of England, its foundations had been laid at least a decade before. Even the earliest years of the nineteenth century found Germany in the throes of an immense bourgeois revolution, and if industrial development lagged behind, agriculture was modernized and rationalized after Prussia's devastating defeat in 1806 by Napoleon, so that 'only profit and loss determined the fortunes of the landowners.'[7] The upheavals in rural Germany that attended the dismantling of feudal privilege and emancipation of the peasantry created a landless proletariat whose conditions could not have been much better than those of the poverty-stricken Manchester workers Engels studied in 1844.

'Propertyless, uprooted, homeless, belonging neither to the state nor an estate, almost half the inhabitants of the German territories lived in poverty and misery.'[8]

In any case the primary model followed by Hegel and Marx in their respective social and political theories was never Germany. Both writers believed that Great Britain showed Germany 'the image of its own future,'[9] and employed the British example for their interventions in economics and politics. As early as 1799 Hegel studied Steuart's *Inquiry into the Principles of Political Economy*,[10] and the last work he published was an expert critical survey of the social and economic factors surrounding the introduction of the English Reform Bill in 1831. His account of civil society and the state in the *Philosophy of Right* is based more closely on the English system than the German one.

Nevertheless, differences in the historical context of their writings may help explain the importance of the state for Hegel and its comparative neglect by Marx. Germany was one of the first countries to harness the tremendous economic power of the state and the relatively enlightened Prussian bureaucracy of Hegel's time was strongly committed to a program of industrialization.[11] Hegel could not have missed the interventionist role of the state since it was a leading element in Germany; exiled in London, Marx was absorbed by the English experience of capitalist development in which government played only a limited part.

The expansion of the state's role in economic affairs created a new professional stratum in Germany that may have influenced Hegel's conception of the bureaucracy or universal class. Recruited from the educated middle class, Hegel's bureaucracy is an expanding social stratum whose rising power must eventually come into conflict with that of other major groups. Here again, Marx ignored Hegel's insights, dismissing his theory of bureaucracy as mostly illusion (*CPR* 51). Another Hegelian element that has no equivalent in Marx is the place of the corporation in civil society and the state. Hegel's corporation is a hybrid that borrows equally from the feudal craft and trade guilds that still existed in his Germany and the modern joint stock companies that made their first appearance in England around the end of the eighteenth century. For Hegel the corporation and the interventionist state are twin poles of stability in an otherwise atomized and anarchic civil society.

For theoretical rather than historical reasons, the concepts of working class or proletariat and class consciousness do not have exactly the same status in Hegel as in Marx. Hegel sees the *business class* as a dialectical unity that includes the opposites, capitalists and workers. What these conflicting classes *share* is a self-contradictory world view in terms of which (e.g., property, liberty, and equality) they carry out their struggle for power in the corporations and the state. However, the dynamics of this struggle are much the same for Hegel and Marx. Both argue that the bourgeois property relation is exploitative and both insist that it will be replaced by a different concept of property through the class-conscious political action of the proletariat. But whereas Marx located his ideal of communism in the revolutionary consciousness of the working class, Hegel postulated that the rational state could only emerge from social and political struggles within the business class and between it and the middle-class bureaucracy. Consciousness could never sink into an abstract universal of the kind Marx envisions except at the cost of life and liberty in the state; and classes as functional entities rather than structures of inequality must continue to endure if the individual is to have an effective presence in government. Consequently Hegel's state grows from the tension between the universal consciousness of the bureaucracy and the particular consciousness of the business class.

It is arguable that the working class Marx examined in *Capital* was fundamentally different in its social position and class consciousness from the one studied earlier by Hegel in the *Philosophy of Right*. As a result, Hegel could not have foreseen the proletariat's struggle for control in the corporation and the state, as I claim he did. A fully class-conscious workers' movement did not emerge in England or anywhere else until 1830 when 'in France and England the bourgeoisie ... conquered political power,'[12] and a general utopian socialist program was not conceived prior to that year. There were, however, many examples of trade-union agitation and working-class revolt long before 1830, certainly enough to capture the attention of the philosopher of self-consciousness, Hegel. Thus the British Combination Acts of 1799-1800 that forbade the formation of trade unions also indicated the presence of at least a section of militant workers, and by the end of the Napoleonic Wars Britain experienced 'the high wind of social discontent which blew ... in successive gusts [until] the middle forties: Luddite and Radical, trade unionist and utopian-socialist, Democratic and Chartist.'[13]

In his lectures at Jena in 1805-06, Hegel had already declared that 'industrialists and manufacturers base their very existence on the misery of a class.'[14] Nor was he the only German to notice this British phenomenon. Some years later the Romantic writer Mueller wrote that in England 'capital and labour, which ought everywhere to support and sustain each other as material and tool, show themselves to be divided into large and naturally hostile masses.'[15] The eventual political consequences of this conflict, its impact on power relations on the factory floor and in the state itself, were clear to Hegel. After all, by the early years of the nineteenth century followers of Saint-Simon, Robert Owen, and later of David Ricardo were preparing the socialist programs which would grow so rapidly after 1830. These ideas took their first purely theoretical form in the pages of the *Philosophy of Right* where Hegel outlines the conflicting logic that would eventually enlarge the influence of organized workers in the affairs of the corporation and in the running of government. Accordingly, a recent study of German theories of the state and the corporation suggests that 'in the vast range of speculation on the "social question" in nineteenth century Germany, no writer matched the profundity of Hegel, one of the earliest observers, although many aped his conclusions.' Hegel, therefore, 'illuminates most profoundly our understanding of modern Germany.'[16]

A final even more intractable problem afflicts the argument that history totally divides the theoretical universe of Hegel and Marx. Its subtitle makes clear that *Capital* is not so much an empirical study as it is a *critique of political economy*, and for Marx the last classic contribution to that discipline was made by David Ricardo in 1817, four years before publication of the *Philosophy of Right*. Moreover, as Marx notes (*Cap., I*, 96), criticism of political economy actually began 'in Ricardo's lifetime, and in opposition to him ... in the person of Sismondi.' Writing in 1819, Sismondi 'denounced the crises in industry, which he attributed (and was probably the first to do so) as much to the abuses of competition as to underconsumption by the workers. The basic evil in the social sphere seemed to him to be the division of society into two antagonistic classes, one of which was the "exploiter" of the other ... He had the merit of defining property as a "social right" and of strongly advocating State intervention.'[17] If Sismondi could undertake the critique of bourgeois political economy in 1819, there is no reason to suppose that it was beyond the reach of Hegel. Along with Ricardo, Adam Smith and J.B. Say are among the very few authors actually cited in the *Philosophy of Right* and there is no doubt that Hegel critically appropriated their writings in his discussion of civil society just as Marx did several decades later.

Kant advises that, once completed, theoretical research that appeared very dubious when half-finished, 'is at last found to be in an unexpected way completely harmonious with [what went before] provided this dubiousness is left out of sight for a while and only the business at hand is attended to until finished ... writers would save themselves many errors and much labour lost (because spent on delusions) if they could only resolve to go to work with a little more ingenuousness.'[18] The form of this study is the form of its content. It is by no means the result of a pre-established intent. It began as an investigation of the relationship between Hegel and Marx, and this indeed is what it is; but most of the views about Hegel criticized in these pages are ones I also used to hold. The movement of the form of this book is also the movement of my own discoveries and of a developing appreciation not only of Hegel but also of a deeper, more subtle Marx. To say that I consciously employed dialectic method would be false; but in retrospect the method is really contained in it. For dialectic is above all a method of discovery.

1

Hegel and Marx

1 INTRODUCTION

This study is an attempt to rescue Hegel's thought from the interpretation imposed on it by Marx. I will argue against Marx's claim that the Hegelian dialectic 'must be inverted, in order to discover the rational kernel within the mystical shell.' There is no 'mystificatory side'[1] to the Hegelian dialectic: Hegel's use of the dialectic is identical with that of Marx.

In *Capital*, Marx openly declares himself a pupil of Hegel – and he is certainly Hegel's foremost exponent and student. As I will show, Marx's theory of modern capitalist society owes much more to Hegel than is generally recognized; but there are also many aspects of Hegel's social and political thought which Marx fails to explore or develop. Some of these aspects are illuminated in the chapters which follow, including Hegel's sociology of religion and his theory of the state. 'Hegel,' notes Mehring, 'is alleged to have said on his death bed about his pupils: only one of them understood me, and he misunderstood me.'[2] With hindsight it appears that Hegel might almost have been thinking of his intellectual heir, Marx.

'The mystification which the dialectic suffers in Hegel's hands,' states Marx, 'by no means prevents him from being the first to present its general form of motion in a comprehensive and conscious manner.'[3] Paradoxically, however, few writers in the Marxist tradition have made a serious effort to reveal the rational side of the Hegelian dialectic.[4] Usually the main effort goes in the opposite direction, and Marxist commentators on Hegel are generally distinguished by their negative and captious approach to his thought. Here – as in many other respects – they resemble their bourgeois counterparts. Nor is this resemblance accidental. The prevailing consciousness or ideology of Marxism shares much the same categories and an identical structure of thought with its bourgeois opponent. And Hegel's dialectic method is from start to finish the enemy and destroyer of what he refers to as the understanding (or bourgeois) mind. As Marx himself insists, 'the dialectic ... is a scandal and an abomination to the bourgeoisie and its doctrinaire spokesmen ... being in its very essence critical and revolutionary.'[5]

Dialectic concerns 'the *relation of consciousness to the object*'[6]; false or 'finite' consciousness (ideology in the pejorative sense of the term) appears when consciousness conceives itself to be *external* to its object. What Marx would call communist consciousness, and what Hegel terms Reason, is a form of thought which perceives itself to be *identical* with its object. 'The Idea in its *subjectivity*,' writes Hegel, 'is the Notion that is active in the object, relates itself to itself therein, and by giving itself its reality in the object finds *truth*.'[7] Both Marxist and bourgeois thinkers, however, conceive of thought as separate from its object. For the understanding consciousness, there is a finished world existing outside, and independent of thought, and the problem of knowledge is simply to gain access to this external world. 'The general error of the Understanding,' notes Hegel, consists in the belief 'that what is metaphysical is only a "thought-thing" *alongside*, i.e. *outside* actuality.'[8] This view, as I will argue, is the root of all ideology or false consciousness; it forms the dominant structure of thought in capitalist society – a structure which both Marxist and bourgeois have in common. According to the Understanding, 'truth is the agreement of thought with the object, and in order to bring about this agreement – for it does not exist on its own account – thinking is supposed to adopt and accommodate itself to the object.'[9]

The notion that thought is identical with the external world is, of course, dismissed by Marxist and bourgeois positivist alike as 'wild idealism' 'sheer metaphysics,' and so forth. It is also opposed by the subjective idealist Kant, who argues, according to Hegel, that 'in its relation to the object ... thinking does not go out of itself to the object; this, as a thing-in-itself, remains a sheer beyond of thought.'[10] According to the accepted notion of logic, thought can deal only with the empty *form* of things, while the *content* of the external world remains independent of thinking. Nevertheless, Hegel's suggestion that thought is identical with its object does not entail a belief in the non-reality of the material world. The categories of thought are *identical* with the external world, but they are also *distinct* from it. Thus the subject matter of logic or the system of categories 'is not *things* but their *import*, the Notion of them.'[11] Like Marx, Hegel does not deny the autonomous reality of the external world, of nature, of objectivity as given by the senses: 'In man's *practical* approach to Nature,' he states, 'the latter is, for him, something immediate and external; and he himself is an external and therefore sensuous individual.'[12]

2 WORK AND THE SOCIAL INDIVIDUAL

That knowledge is identical with its object is the fundamental thesis of dialectic method as employed by Hegel and Marx. Dialectic concerns the concept which Marx refers to as 'revolutionizing practice,' and which Hegel calls 'ideality.' Ideality refers to theoretical and practical *activity*, the effort through which men and women create their ideas and translate them into concrete reality. The notion of revolutionizing practice or ideality is best illustrated by a relation familiar to everyone: *work*. As Hegel remarks, 'work and effort [are] the middle term between the subjective and the objective.'[13]

Work is a social relationship – a collective enterprise – whereby nature is subordinated and made a *means* to the diverse ends of men and women. Precisely because labour transforms natural objects into instruments and expressions of human will, work is also a chief aspect of the transcendental, creative quality of consciousness. 'Man's practical approach to nature,' notes Hegel, discloses 'the correct presupposition that nature does not itself contain the absolute, final end.'[14] The same point is stressed by Marx: 'nature becomes one of the organs of [the worker's] activity, which he annexes to his own bodily organs, adding stature to himself in spite of the Bible.'[15]

Hegel argues that there are three moments or phases in the process he variously calls finite teleology, work, or external purposiveness. The first appears as the *subjective end* or *purpose* of the individual. Purposiveness of any sort, he observes, implies 'an *intelligence* ... as its author,'[16] and in the form of subjective end, human intelligence manifests itself as a universal, as an infinite range of self-relation and possibility. Seen from this side, the subjective end reflects the inner unity and reach of consciousness – the ground not only of all technical production, but also of art and the highest realms of science. But the subjective end must also direct itself outwards and find a *concrete object* in the external world. The necessity for the subjective end to absorb the detail of the objective world and relate its activity 'as to something *already there*,' constitutes the finitude of the subjective end. 'Finite things are finite because they do not possess the complete reality of their Notion within themselves, but require other things to complete it.'[17]

The second moment of finite teleology is the *means* (of production) through which the activity of the worker is communicated to the object. The means is external to the purpose and also to the object of labour, and thus appears as 'a merely *mechanical* object,' i.e., a tool or machine. The acting subject takes advantage of the mechanical and chemical properties of the means and the object of labour in order to transform the object into the desired end. 'The negative attitude of purposive activity towards the object is thus not an *external* attitude, but the alteration and transition of objectivity in its own self into the end.' In the process of external purposiveness, the subject 'puts forward an object as means, allows it to wear itself out in its stead, exposes it to attrition and shields itself behind it from mechanical violence.'[18]

The final moment of finite teleology is the *realized end*, the object as transformed by labour. Hegel argues that the realized end of finite teleology is a flawed product because it is not an end in itself, but 'again becomes a Means or material for other Ends, and so on for ever.'[19] A house or a clock, for example, 'may appear as ends in relation to the tools employed for their production; but the stones and beams, or wheels and axles, and so on, which constitute the actuality of the end fulfil that end only through the pressure that they suffer, through the chemical process with air, light, and water to which they are exposed and that deprive man of them by their friction and so forth.'[20] Hegel distinguishes between production and consumption goods, and accords to the former a much higher position than to objects destined for immediate consumption. In a passage which must have made a deep impression on Marx, Hegel writes:

Since the end is finite it has a finite content; accordingly it is not an absolute, nor simply something that in its own nature is *rational*. But the *means* is the external middle term of the syllogism which is the realization of the end; in the means, therefore, the rationality in it manifests itself as such by maintaining itself in *this external other*, and precisely *through* this externality. To this extent the *means* is *superior* to the *finite* ends of *external* purposiveness: the *plough* is more honourable than are immediately the enjoyments procured by it and which are ends. The *tool* lasts, while the immediate enjoyments pass away and are forgotten. In his tools man possesses power over external nature, even though in respect of his ends he is, on the contrary, subject to it.[21]

Work is an aspect of theoretical and practical human activity, ideality, or revolutionizing practice. But the chief element in work, as in all ideality, is *thought* or human consciousness. Only the *action of thought* separates human activity from that of other animals.[22] As Marx puts it in a passage from *Capital* which owes much to Hegel:

We presuppose labour in a form in which it is an exclusively human characteristic. A spider conducts operations which resemble those of a weaver, and a bee would put many a human architect to shame by the construction of its honeycomb cells. But what distinguishes the worst architect from the best of bees is that the architect builds the cell in his mind before he constructs it in wax. At the end of every labour process, a result emerges which had already been conceived by the worker at the beginning, hence already existed ideally. Man not only effects a change of form in the materials of nature; he also realizes ... his own purpose in those materials. And this is a purpose he is conscious of, it determines the mode of his activity with the rigidity of a law, and he must subordinate his will to it. This subordination is no mere momentary act. Apart from the exertion of the working organs, a purposeful will is required for the entire duration of the work.[23]

The concept of ideality or revolutionizing practice as expressed in work is deceptively simple. But the process of negativity or human effort is precisely what cancels the distinction between thought and external reality. In the labour process, notes Hegel, 'the distinction between a content, which is explicit *for* consciousness only *within consciousness itself*, and an intrinsic reality outside it, no longer exists.'[24] The notion of ideality lies behind all the passages in Hegel which critics decry as 'metaphysical,' 'abstruse,' 'monstrous,' and so forth. Hegel points out, for example, that the process of finite teleology itself – the simplest form of ideality – overthrows virtually all the categories of the Understanding:

It can ... be said of the teleological activity that in it the end is the beginning, the consequent the ground, the effect the cause, that it is a becoming of what has become, that in it only what already exists comes into existence, and so forth; which means that in general all the determinations of relationship belonging to the sphere of reflection or of immediate being have lost their distinctions, and what was enunciated as an *other*, such as end, consequent, effect, etc., no longer has in the end relation the determination of an other, but on the contrary is posited as identical with the simple Notion.[25]

Ideality or revolutionizing practice is the means whereby mind or human consciousness shows itself to be 'the absolutely concrete.' The absolutely concrete for Hegel, is something which in every respect is *identical with itself even in its distinction of itself from itself*. The mind of an artist, for example, remains a self-identical thing even while it distinguishes an aspect of itself – the work of art – from itself, through thought and practical activity. Hegel refers to the thinking individual as 'the Notion,' (the notion is 'the freedom and self-subsistence of the self-conscious subject'; it is 'none other than the *I* or pure self-consciousness,') and the notion is 'absolutely concrete ... when it *exists* as notion distinguishing itself from its objectivity, which notwithstanding the distinction still continues to be its own. Everything else which is concrete, however rich it be, is not so intensely identical with itself and therefore not so concrete on its own part.'[26] The essence of mind or consciousness, argues Hegel, is the capacity and need for its own *duplication* through the active union of theoretical and practical activity. 'The universal need for art,' he remarks in the *Aesthetics*,

is man's rational need to lift the inner and outer world into his spiritual consciousness as an object in which he recognizes again his own self. The need for this spiritual freedom he satisfies, on the one hand, within by making what is within him explicit to himself, but correspondingly by giving outward reality to this his explicit self, and thus in this duplication of himself by bringing what is in him into sight and knowledge for himself and others. This is the free rationality of man in which all acting and knowing, as well as art too, have their basis and necessary origin.[27]

According to Hegel, finite teleology provides access to a kind of *truth* which goes beyond the form of mere *correctness* that is the Understanding's version of truth. Correctness – the agreement between an object and the mental representation of it – is certainly an important moment or aspect of truth, but it assumes that ideas must passively conform to the pattern of the external world.[28] Work, however, displays the sort of truth achieved whenever men and women build a community out of the savagery of nature, or the truth people marvel at in the work of a fine artisan. 'Truth,' says Hegel, 'is the positive as the knowing that agrees with the object; but it is only this likeness to itself in so far as the knower has put himself into a negative relation with the other, has penetrated the object and sublated the negation which it is.'[29]

The concept of work or finite teleology provides a ready example of two essential aspects of dialectic: *contradiction*, and *sublation* or *transcendence*. The accepted notion of dialectic is the dull formula, 'thesis, antithesis, synthesis.' This dialectic triad appears rarely in the work of either Hegel or Marx, and, as it stands, says less than nothing about dialectic. Moreover, its misuse, as Hegel observes, 'has made the said form tedious and given it a bad name.' He adds, however, that 'the triteness of this use of it cannot detract from its inner worth and we must always value highly the discovery of the shape of the rational, even though it was at first uncomprehended.'[30] In the labour process, the purpose or end of the working subject is the thesis, the objective reality on which that purpose is exercised is the antithesis, and the product of the labour process is the synthesis.

The object confronting the individual represents a *contradiction* between his or her ideal notion of what the object *should be* and what it actually *is*. And the activity of the worker is directed at surmounting this antithesis. The result of the labour process, like that of all dialectic movement, is sublation or transcendence (*Aufheben* in Hegel's terminology). The negative activity of labour – an activity which confronts, opposes and transforms external reality – has a positive or constructive result which contains in itself all the moments or aspects of the process which joined together in its creation. The positive aspect of dialectic in the labour process is also, of course, emphasized by Marx:

A machine which is not active in the labour process is useless. In addition, it falls prey to the destructive power of natural processes. Iron rusts; wood rots. Yarn with which we neither weave nor knit is cotton wasted. Living labour must seize on these things, awaken them from the dead, change them from merely possible into real and effective use-values. Bathed in the fire of labour, appropriated as part of its organism, and infused with vital energy for the performance of the functions appropriate to their concept and to their vocation in the process, they are indeed consumed, but to some purpose, as elements in the formation of new use-values, new products, which are capable of entering into individual consumption as means of subsistence or into a new labour process as means of production.[31]

In the rather abstract terminology of his *1844 Manuscripts*, Marx alludes to the supreme importance of Hegel's dialectics of labour, calling it 'the outstanding achievement' and 'final outcome' of the *Phenomenology*. Hegel, he suggests, 'grasps the essence of *labour* and comprehends objective man – true, because real man – as the outcome of man's *own labour*.'[32] The young Marx does not examine the role of the dialectics of labour in Hegel's writings after the *Phenomenology*, and later commentators such as Marcuse in *Reason and Revolution*[33] assume that the concept plays no part in Hegel's mature system. In fact, however, the concept is fundamental to Hegelian theory. Thus in both versions of Hegel's *Logic*, the dialectics of labour introduces the loftiest realm of pure thought, the Idea.[34] Moreover, the notion of work, as I will demonstrate, is fundamental to the structure of the *Philosophy of Right*, where in a significant passage (§56, 47) Hegel remarks, 'To impose a form on a thing is the mode of taking possession most in conformity with the Idea to this extent, that it implies a union of subject and object, although it varies endlessly with the qualitative character of the objects and the variety of subjective aims.'

The crucial role of the dialectics of labour in Hegel's thought reveals the central focus of his social and political theory. For many critics, including Marx, this focal point is *Geist* or Spirit, understood as a supra-historical, supra-individual cosmic divinity which accomplishes its own self-realization through the process of history.[35] Accordingly, the passages devoted to finite teleology in *Logic* have often been held to refer to the relationship between *Geist* and world historical individuals who appear as *means* to the realization of the larger goal of Reason. In fact, Hegel does employ the concept of finite teleology to explicate the workings of his famous 'cunning of reason' in the *Lectures on the Philosophy of World History* (76), giving as an example Caesar's usurpation of power which secured the ascendency of Rome in world history. On Hegel's interpretation, Caesar's own self-aggrandizing action thus served as a means to the greater rational goal of Spirit.[36] But Hegel goes on to assert that the category of means is inadequate to the real nature of human individuals which is precisely to be *ends in themselves*, rather than mere vehicles of a celestial puppeteer.[37] I will return to this argument in a later chapter, but for the moment it is necessary merely to assert that the crowning element in Hegel's system is the rational human individual as his or her capacities and abilities, i.e. self-consciousness, are developed through work and practical action in society.

The conception of the individual – the ego or the 'I' – as the supreme universal reality is one which Hegel drew from the Christian religion as well as from the transcendental idealism of Kant. In Kant's philosophy, however, the individual appears as an abstraction, existing almost entirely as a form of thought, a theoretical rather than a practical social being. Similarly, in Christianity the infinite quality of the individual takes only pictorial form as the figure of Christ; and until the advent of Protestantism, where work is seen as a calling in the service of God, the mundane social world was kept strictly separate from the sphere of the sacred. Hegel's unique achievement is to link the abstract idealism of Kant with the active principle of individual work and effort in society first articulated by Martin Luther.

If Hegel's focus is the individual, his concern is not with the isolated individual who dominated Enlightenment philosophy and lingered in the pages of Kant. Instead Hegel conceives the individual as primarily a social being. He insists that a person cannot exist apart from society but must necessarily reflect and be a part of his or her social world. 'Separate individuals,' he writes, 'are and always remain only incidental, and outside the reality of the state they have no substantiality in themselves. For substantiality is no longer merely the *particular* property of this or that *individual*, but is stamped upon him on its own account and in a *universal* and *necessary* way in all his aspects down to the tiniest detail.'[38] This emphasis on the social quality of the individual explains why Hegel's *Geist* always takes a national or socio-historical form. The spirit of even a world historical individual is also the spirit of his or her society. 'Whatever happens,' says Hegel, 'every individual is a child of his time.'[39]

The dialectics of labour, in Hegel's view, expresses and constitutes an essential linkage between the individual and society. Work and practical action are the *means*, the locus of the particular, through which the individual realizes his or her capabilities and becomes identical with the social or the universal. For Hegel, this dialectical process of unity and differentiation may be expressed in the syllogistic form he calls 'absolute mechanism' in the *Encyclopaedia Logic*. A fully articulated society, he suggests,

is a system of three syllogisms. (1) The Individual or person, through his particularity or physical or mental needs (which when carried out to their full development give *civil* society), is coupled with the universal, i.e. with society, law, right, government. (2) The will or action of the individuals is the intermediating force which procures for these needs satisfaction in society, in law, etc., and which gives to society, law, etc., their fulfilment and actualization. (3) But the universal, that is to say the state, government, and law, is the permanent underlying mean in which the individuals and their satisfaction have and receive their fulfilled reality, intermediation, and persistence. Each of the functions of the notion, as it is brought by intermediation to coalesce with the other extreme, is brought into union with itself and produces itself: which production is self-preservation.[40]

Hegel's concern with the role of the individual in society is shared by Marx, although Marx's social theory is usually construed exclusively as a theory of class and class struggle. I will argue in this book, however, that the notion of social class for both thinkers is indispensable to their concept of the social individual, the person who is at once *identical with* and *distinct from* his or her social world.[41] If work constitutes the node of the particular through which the individual enters social life, the dialectics of labour in modern society is possible and only makes sense as the co-operative labour of the individual united with others in a social class. Only by being a member of a specific social class, states Hegel, can a person become a 'somebody.' Social class is the solid ground on which the personal identity of the individual is founded and stabilized. Thus what membership in a social class represents above all, states Hegel, is 'the disposition to make oneself a member of one of the moments of civil society by one's own act, through one's energy, industry, and skill, to maintain oneself in this position, and to fend for oneself only through this process of mediating oneself with the universal, while in this way gaining recognition both in one's own eyes and in the eyes of others.'[42]

3 THE HEGELIAN IDEA

The dialectics of labour and the concept of the social individual are vital components of Hegel's social and political thought, just as they are in that of Marx. Yet in the 1873 postface to the second German edition of *Capital* – where Marx seeks to defend himself from charges of 'Hegelian sophistry' by outlining the difference between his own and Hegel's use of dialectic method – there is no reference to these peculiarly Hegelian notions. This absence not only distorts Hegel, it also helps to conceal Marx's considerable debt to him. Writes Marx (102),

My dialectical method is, in its foundations, not only different from the Hegelian, but exactly opposite to it. For Hegel, the process of thinking, which he even transforms into an independent subject, under the name of 'the Idea', is the creator of the real world, and the real world is only the external appearance of the Idea. With me the reverse is true: the ideal is nothing but the material world reflected in the mind of man, and translated into forms of thought.

Marx's estimate of Hegelian method, which is given qualified endorsement in a recent study by Charles Taylor,[43] restates a position he reached thirty years earlier while still a youthful scholar and an enthusiastic disciple of Ludwig Feuerbach.[44] The young Marx was particularly influenced by the analysis of Hegel offered in two of Feuerbach's works. *Preliminary Theses on the Reform of Philosophy,* and *Principles of the Philosophy of the Future,* both published in 1843.[45] Feuerbach argued in these studies that the truth of Hegel could be revealed merely by transposing the central terms of his philosophy. If Hegelian logic, for example, vests the Idea with supreme power and views men and women as servants of divine Reason, then reality must be the opposite: the Idea is actually the product and instrument of real, living human beings. Thus Hegel mystifies the relationship between humanity and the Absolute, alienating men and women from their own creative powers. Demystifying Hegel meant turning him upside down. 'We need only turn the *predicate* into the *subject*,' wrote Feuerbach, 'that is, *reverse* speculative philosophy. In this way we have the unconcealed, pure, and untarnished truth.'[46]

Applying Feuerbach's transformative critique to the *Philosophy of Right*, the young Marx argued that Hegel's 'logical, pantheistic mysticism' gives 'the Idea ... the status of a subject, and the actual relationship of family and civil society to the state is conceived to be its inner imaginary activity.' The real relationship, he contended, is the reverse of the one put forward by Hegel. 'The fact is that the state issues from the mass of men existing as members of families and of civil society; but speculative philosophy expresses this fact as an achievement of the Idea, not the idea of the mass, but rather as the deed of an Idea-Subject which is differentiated from the fact itself.' Precisely in this Feuerbachian transposition of Hegel the young Marx felt he had solved 'the entire mystery of the *Philosophy of Right* and of Hegelian philosophy in general.'[47] Marx, it seems, never changed his opinion.

Unfortunately, even tragically, the ingenious transformative critique of Hegel pioneered by Feuerbach was simply wrong. Later I will show that Feuerbach's deep misunderstanding of Hegel had an impact on Marx that was little short of disastrous. In any case, the Hegelian Idea bears no resemblance to the omniscient creator envisioned by Marx. Rather it expresses the dialectical identity of the individual with society and the 'absolutely valid laws and institutions' which emerge from this identity.[48] According to Hegel, the Idea is the 'essence, aim, and object' of every individual; it is 'the actuality of men – not something which they have, as men, but which they *are*.' Like any human production, whether it be an automobile or a code of law, the Idea constitutes a practical unity of fact and theory. And it is the will and self-conscious action of individuals which form the link between the Idea as mere concept and its concrete existence in society. Human will, Hegel observes, 'is the *existential* side of reason ... the act of developing the Idea, and of investing its self-unfolding content with an existence which, as realizing the Idea, is *actuality*.'[49]

The 'self-unfolding content of the Idea' is the subject matter of Hegel's *Science of Logic* and the condensed and powerful version of *Logic* in the *Encyclopaedia of the Philosophical Sciences*. These works provide the deep structure for the social and political theory of the *Philosophy of Right*. In a sense, therefore, Hegel had performed his own transformative critique long before it occurred to Feuerbach and the young Marx. The social logic of the *Philosophy of Right* is the inverted, material side of the logic of pure thought.[50]

This leads to another aspect of the relationship between Hegel's social theory and dialectical logic. If, as Hegel informs us, logic concerns 'knowledge which is in the element of pure thought alone,'[51] its content is also the thought process as it occurs or could occur in the mind of any rational individual. The tortuous ascent from Being to the Absolute Idea traced by *Logic* follows the one encountered by the human mind when it gives itself up to its own self-contemplation. Similarly, the social logic studied in the *Philosophy of Right* is the concrete product of the ideality of each member of society. 'All the aims of society and the State,' notes Hegel, 'are the private aims of the individuals.'[52]

There is an understandable resistance to the Hegelian notion that the structure and evolution of society conform to a rational pattern, a resistance remarked on by Hegel himself in the famous preface to the *Philosophy of Right*. Men and women are willing to grant there is logic in the movement of the heavens or the migration patterns of the Canada goose. Human social arrangements, however, are supposed to be the product of chance and caprice leavened, perhaps, with a modicum of reason. Even less attractive is the conception that society and the state, with all their faults and perversions, could be related in any way to one's own thought and action. Yet everyone agrees that human language and its grammar constitute a rational system, even though language, like society itself, arises from practical and accidental circumstance. Nor is there much mystery involved in the active identity (and distinction) between the thinking individual and his or her language. But if words, phrases, and even grammatical forms have been created over a vast period of time by individual men and women, the underlying grammatical structure and interrelationships of language are mostly derived from an *unconscious rationality* which is discovered only after its emergence and development. The same is true of the Hegelian Idea.

The categories or relations of thought examined in *Logic* are nothing more than expressions of language freed from their sensuous and figurate material and brought into logical connection with one another. Moreover, the dialectical advance and transition of the categories spelled out in *Logic* represent the way these expressions are (unconsciously) employed by people in their social and political life.[53] By the same token, the *Philosophy of Right* lays bare the logical design forged by each individual's *instinct of reason* in the actual structure and institutions of society. The relationship between the unconscious rationality of individuals and the form taken by society and the state is outlined by Hegel in a noteworthy passage from the *Science of Logic*:

If an object, for example the state, *did not correspond at all* to its Idea, that is, if in fact it was not the Idea of the state at all, if its reality, which is the self-conscious individuals, did not correspond at all to the Notion, its soul and its body would have parted; the former would escape into the solitary regions of thought, the latter would have broken up into single individualities. But because the Notion of the state so essentially constitutes the nature of these individualities, it is present in them as an urge so powerful that they are impelled to translate it into reality, be it only in the form of external purposiveness, or to put up with it as it is, or else they must needs perish. The worst state, one whose reality least corresponds to the Notion, in so far as it still exists, is still Idea; the individuals still obey a dominant Notion.[54]

Hegel returns again and again to the *instinctive quality* of human rationality, observing that the task of science is precisely to throw light on the unconscious logic of thought and society. In the *Encyclopaedia Logic*, for example, he points out that 'concrete formations of consciousness, such as individual and social morality, art and religion' are the necessary result of the development of reason. Nevertheless, the evolution of these formations 'must, so to speak, go on behind consciousness, since those facts are the essential nucleus which is raised into consciousness' through dialectical inquiry.[55] Similarly, Hegel argues in the *Philosophy of Right* that while the state is a product of subjective human will, this expresses only one side of the matter. On the other side, as 'the nature of human beings *en masse*,' the state grows out of the instinct of reason which underlies struggle and progress in history. Referring to the state as the 'objective will,' Hegel warns,

We must remember the fundamental conception that the objective will is rationality implicit or in conception, whether it be recognized or not by individuals, whether their whims be deliberately for it or not. We must remember that its opposite, i.e. knowing and willing, or subjective freedom ... comprises only one moment, and therefore a one-sided moment, of the Idea of the rational will, i.e. of the will which is rational solely because what it is implicitly that it also is explicitly.[56]

Hegel contrasts the rational will embodied in the state with the notion of the general will put forward by Rousseau. The French theorist, notes Hegel, reduces the idea of the state to a contract based on the 'private self-will' of each of its members.[57] Rousseau is correct in showing the relationship between the state and human will; but he mistakenly supposes that this relationship is rooted in the *arbitrary will* of the individual. 'The universal will is not to be looked on as compounded of definitively individual wills, so that these remain absolute; otherwise the saying would be correct: "Where the minority must obey the majority, there is no freedom." '[58]

The identity of individual will and the state, of course, is a vital component of Hegel's concept of the social individual. But the arbitrary will constitutes only the second of what Hegel defines as the three levels of will.[59] These levels of subjective will have their objective social correlates respectively in the family, civil society, and the state. Feeling – the 'impulses, desires, inclinations, whereby the will finds itself determined in the course of nature'[60] – comprises the immediate form of the will. It is also the principle of the family, a social relation which fulfils the individual's need to give and receive love within a more or less stable framework, and which provides for the reproduction and socialization of children.[61] The utilitarian concerns of the individual occupy the second arbitrary level of the will. On one hand, the arbitrary will is rational because it hinges on thought and reflection. On the other hand, it is capricious and unpredictable since its content is given to it, either as impulses and inclinations which clamour for satisfaction, or as objects which remain external and alien to it. The arbitrary will is the source of the Understanding mode of thought which Hegel connects with bourgeois society; not surprisingly, therefore, something like the arbitrary will is used as a model for the ideal consumer and producer of classical economics. It is the basis – not of the state as Rousseau supposed – but of the contractual relationships between individuals which make up the economy or 'system of needs' in what Hegel calls 'civil society.'[62]

Hegel argues against Rousseau that the state has its source in the third and highest order of will which he identifies with the principle of reason. 'The universal will must really be the rational will, even if we are not conscious of the fact; the state is therefore not an association which is decreed by the arbitrary will of individuals.'[63] Brought to consciousness of itself by dialectical science, the rational will recognizes only itself as its 'object, content, and aim' and becomes 'free not only *in* itself but *for* itself also; it is the Idea in its truth.'[64] At this stage, individual will loses the aspect of dependency and alienation characteristic of the arbitrary will and fulfils itself in a world peculiarly its own. This world of realized freedom, in which the will gives play to all its potentialities and confronts no external barriers to its own self-expression, is the state. Thus for Hegel, the development of the state into 'a systemized whole,' is the ultimate object of the instinct of reason. 'The absolute goal,' he writes, 'or, if you like, the absolute impulse, of free mind ... is to make its freedom its object, i.e. to make freedom objective as much in the sense that freedom shall be the rational system of mind, as in the sense that this system shall be the world of immediate actuality ... In making freedom its object, mind's purpose is to be explicitly, as Idea, what the will is implicitly.'[65]

Like Marx, Hegel believes that the emerging bourgeois world reveals the outlines of a future rational order. It only remains for philosophy or dialectical science to make the world conscious of its own implicit rationality in order for that rationality to be fully actualized through social and political action.[66] In this sense, therefore, the organic union of family, civil society, and the state in modern bourgeois society represents for Hegel the Idea of freedom. But these forms of objective will not only prefigure a future order; they also appear together as stages in the historical development of society.[67] The patriarchal principle of the family, for example, shaped all three elements of the social structure of the Oriental world in the same way as the simplest categories of Being dominated Eastern philosophy and religion. In ancient China and India the head of the family is embodied in the state as a despotic ruler whose subjects 'are in the position of children or subordinates.'[68] Social relationships are guided by admonitions and punishments from higher authority, rather than by the inner reflection and morality of the individual. Similarly, economic relations are bounded almost entirely by the framework of family relations.

The principle of subjective freedom which underlies the arbitrary will originated in Greece and was subsequently adopted and deepened in Rome. As a result, these nations were the first to develop something approaching an autonomous civil society founded on independent trade and industry. Nevertheless, freedom in ancient society remained imperfect and partial. By restricting personal liberty and the right of ownership to a few, slavery everywhere stifled the inner dynamic of civil society. Limited in the secular realm, subjective freedom was fully manifested in the mature Roman state only as the arbitrary will of the ruler. The autocrat in turn confronted an empire increasingly fragmented into separate and diverse personalities and nations related to the state almost entirely through the abstraction of force.

Hegel contends that the growth of modern constitutional government based on the principle of the rational will had to await the appearance of the essence of rationality – the freedom of the individual. This supreme moment of rationality begins with Christianity and its teachings. By recognizing the equality before God of every human being, Christianity implicitly acknowledges the right of each individual to the free ownership of property (including in the concept of property the individual's right to sell for a limited time his or her capacity to work). Accordingly, Christianity – especially in the form of Protestantism – unleashes the dialectic of civil society and establishes the principle of individual liberty as the basis of the modern state.

The rational principle underlying the movement of history is carried forward precisely by those oppressed groups and classes (and their allies) who stand to benefit most from its realization. This is the lesson of Hegel's discussion in the *Phenomenology* of the relationship between master and slave, a discussion which is repeated in the *Encyclopaedia* and elsewhere.[69] Nevertheless, each stage of society has the Idea at its core – even if only in the immediate form of the family as in Oriental society. The contradiction between the Idea and the imperfection of its realization in society made manifest by the misery of the oppressed is the motive force of historical progress:

In actual existence, progress thus appears as an advance from the imperfect to the more perfect, although the former should not be understood in an abstract sense as merely imperfect, but as something which at the same time contains its own opposite, i.e. what is commonly called perfection, as a germ or impulse ... Thus the imperfect, in so far as it contains its own opposite within itself, is a contradiction; and although it certainly exists, it must surely be overcome and resolved.[70]

This account of the Hegelian Idea, which will be substantiated in detail throughout this book, is a long way from that offered by Marx in the opening pages of *Capital*. Hegel's emphasis on struggle and conflict in history and his identification of rationality with the social movements of underprivileged groups and classes are also, of course, chief elements in Marx's social theory. (In fact, these notions were original to neither Hegel nor Marx and were widely current in Hegel's day, especially among French historians of the Revolution of 1789 and the followers of Saint-Simon.[71]) Nor is there a significant difference between the two regarding their view of the role of economic factors in the unfolding of history.[72] For Hegel, work and industry are crucial to the growth of individual consciousness and will, as well as to the development of the objective manifestations of will in society. The ancient Greek state, for example, fails because it cannot withstand the penetration of subjective freedom into the realm of trade and industry. Moreover, one of the central themes of the *Philosophy of Right* is the relationship between advances in culture and politics on one hand and 'the moment of liberation intrinsic to work' on the other.[73]

Like Marx, Hegel sees the labour process as a fundamental mode of human activity. Accordingly, the Idea itself is actualized in society by the rational will of the individual through an interlocking movement which recreates at a higher level the three moments comprising the dialectics of labour.[74] At this level, the first phase of ideality – purpose – appears as a mixture of the conscious and implicit political and social objectives of the human subject. The means are the practical activity of the subject in co-operation with others which brings about the desired, along with the unconscious, end or goal. Referring to the realization of the Idea in history, Hegel observes:

Aims, principles, and the like are present at first in our thoughts and inner intentions, or even in books, but not yet in reality itself. In other words, that which exists only *in itself* is a possibility or potentiality which has not yet emerged into existence. A second moment is necessary before it can attain reality – that of actuation or realization; and its principle is the will, the activity of mankind in the world at large. It is only by means of this activity that the original concepts or implicit determinations are realised and actualised.[75]

4 COMMUNISM AND THE STATE

For Marx freedom or rationality is identical with communism and is ultimately reached through development of the consciousness of the proletariat and the overthrow of private property and social classes. Something like Marx's vision of communism also animates Hegel's social and political theory, with some crucial distinctions. The most important of these is that, unlike Marx, Hegel does not anticipate the withering away of the state. On the contrary, the state appears as the reality of the Idea in society and performs the same role as Marx's communism in the maximum development of individual freedom. Similarly, property and social classes do not vanish but remain as institutions which manifest and guarantee individual liberty. Convinced that the economic system of society is the fundamental social reality, Marx devotes little attention to political institutions. Hegel takes a different view and as a result he constructs a more powerful theory of modern capitalism than does Marx and at the same time offers a substantive glimpse into the future.

Hegel's concrete and withering critique of bourgeois society in the *Philosophy of Right* foreshadows at nearly every point the analysis of capitalism offered by Marx almost fifty years later. It is almost as though the spare paragraphs of Hegel's book served as broad sketches for the rich detail of *Capital*.[76] Both theorists argue that the capitalist economy is characterized by its capricious and desultory nature, by its extensive and steadily expanding scope, and above all, by the class inequalities it generates and reproduces. The basic tendency of bourgeois society, according to Hegel and Marx, is to disbar the mass of people from the ownership of property and to expropriate wealth from those who produce it.[77] Moreover, the secret source of the anarchy and inequality of capitalism lies in the peculiar quality of the commodity and the wrenching contradiction that lurks within the heart of bourgeois private property. This contradiction, as I will show, is insisted upon just as much by Hegel as by Marx.

Yet to concentrate only on the negative side of capitalist production, notes Hegel, is to forget that 'this social movement has in it the aspect of liberation.' As an expression of human will, civil society contains an implicit rationality manifested in the (unconscious) convergence of individual and social interests. The interdependence of individuals encouraged by bourgeois industry and exchange thus turns 'subjective self-seeking ... into a contribution to the satisfaction of the needs of everyone else. That is to say, by a dialectical advance, subjective self-seeking turns into the mediation of the particular through the universal, with the result that each man in earning, producing, and enjoying on his own account is *eo ipso* producing and earning for the enjoyment of everyone else.'[78] Marx also refers to the unifying, social aspect of capitalism, suggesting 'that this is precisely the beauty and the greatness of it: this spontaneous interconnection, this material and mental metabolism which is independent of the knowing and willing of individuals, and which presupposes their reciprocal independence and indifference.'[79]

The creation of a social bond between individuals is only part of the 'aspect of liberation' which Hegel feels is immanent within bourgeois society. The other part takes the form of education or *Bildung*, a term which for Hegel means both the process of education and the highly cultured form of mind which is its result. Hegel argues that the production and consumption of commodities in civil society, especially those which concern 'mental needs arising from ideas,'[80] performs a cultural and educational function, deepening the capacities, knowledge, and self-consciousness of the individual and stimulating his or her involvement in the general affairs of society. Marx, too, refers to 'the cultivation of all the qualities of the social human being, production of the same in a form as rich as possible in needs, because rich in qualities and relations – production of this being as the most total and universal possible social product [which] is ... a condition of production founded on capital.'[81]

For Marx, of course, education in capitalist society is much more than a gentle and linear process of learning; it also takes the harsh and discontinuous form of class struggle through which the proletariat advances from a class *in itself*, with only an implicit class consciousness and no political organization, to a class *for itself*, ready to impose its viewpoint on the governance of society. One of the deepest prejudices regarding Hegel's theory of the state concerns its supposed lack of the notions of class struggle and the political role of the working class.[82] As we have already seen, however, Hegel views the development of the social individual precisely within the framework of the social class to which he or she belongs. Thus when he speaks of the practical, cultural education of the individual in civil society he refers specifically to the situation of the 'skilled worker' who must adapt his or her 'activity according not only to the nature of the material worked on, but also, and especially, to the pleasure of other workers.' In addition, Hegel emphasizes the 'demand for equality of satisfaction with others' which is a necessary moment of civil society, and which becomes a 'fruitful source of the multiplication of needs and their expansion.' Demands for equality, as Hegel is well aware, must often involve conflict and bloody struggle. Moreover, the notion of struggle itself is built into Hegel's concept of education or *Bildung*. Education, he suggests, is a 'hard struggle' for 'liberation,'[83] and the terms of this struggle are precisely the class relations of force, domination, and servitude which operate between master and slave.[84]

For Hegel, the relation of master and slave is reproduced in civil society as the extreme division between 'the dependence and distress' of the industrial proletariat on one hand, and the 'concentration of disproportionate wealth' among the magnates of capital on the other.[85] Moreover, the roots of this bitter cleavage, as well as its political solution, are to be found in the relations of property and value that underlie the dialectics of civil society.

While Marx's analysis of the inner dynamic of bourgeois political economy begins with the nature of the commodity, Hegel's theory of civil society and the state starts with the notion of personality. Nevertheless, the point of these initial investigations is the same. *Both culminate in a theory of exploitation grounded in the notion of capitalist property rights.* Elaboration and proof of this argument, which challenges virtually all interpretations of Hegel's social theory, constitutes one of the main themes of this book, and cannot, of course, be thoroughly rehearsed in an introductory chapter.

Instead I shall concentrate on some essential differences between the views of Hegel and Marx and connect these differences to their conceptions of the nature of communism and the state.

Marx reduces all classes within bourgeois society to the fundamental contradiction between capitalists and workers, an antagonism based on their relationship to the means of production. The property relation, however, is only one moment or aspect of the Hegelian theory of social class. Class in Hegel's view also includes the related characteristics of *consciousness* and *function*. Moreover, the property relation itself is interpreted by Hegel in dialectical fashion to include both of its opposing terms. On this basis, Hegel delineates three major class groupings in civil society: the *business class* of capitalists and workers, the *agricultural class* consisting of nobles and peasants, and the *universal class* of civil servants.[86]

In his conception of the property relation itself, as in most of his concepts, Hegel includes a psychological dimension that is absent from Marx's categories. This dimension is extremely important since it provides the background for the struggle within and between class groupings which is central to Hegel's theory.[87] Ownership of property, Hegel suggests, is the means whereby an individual in civil society affirms his or her personality and gains recognition from others.[88] The worker, however, is defined precisely in his or her *lack of property*; hence the element of recognition vital for establishing the worker's personality is missing. In civil society, therefore, the education or *Bildung* of the worker takes the form of a *struggle for property rights*, a struggle aimed at providing the worker with a 'determinate existence of being something universally recognized, known, and willed, and having a validity and an objective actuality mediated by this known and willed character.'[89]

Both Hegel and Marx contend that the increasing poverty of the workers in civil society and the steady enrichment of a diminishing number of capitalists stems directly from the bourgeois property relationship. But in his discussion of property Hegel stresses a distinction unexplored by Marx between the *formal, abstract ownership* of the means of production by the capitalist, and the *concrete possession* of them by the worker. According to Hegel, ownership of a thing is implied in the *constant use* of it, the concept of property in the last analysis simply refers to the relation of use. Nevertheless, the 'empty Understanding' characteristic of the bourgeoisie awards the right to ownership of capital to the employer and ignores the flesh-and-blood design, manufacture, and utilization of the instruments of production by the worker. Thus the realization of the worker's personality in the thing he or she produces – that is, in his or her property – is blocked by what Hegel calls the capitalist's own 'insanity of personality.'[90] The competing property claims of the two sides of the business class demarcate the field of battle between worker and capitalist in civil society.

Hegel argues, however, that both the capitalist and the worker actually contribute to the labour process. The activity of the worker presupposes the authority and decision-making capacity of the capitalist. The bourgeoisie differs from earlier ruling groups because it directly intervenes in the process of production instead of merely accepting or enforcing tribute from subordinate strata. Accordingly, its ownership of the means of production is not entirely formal or abstract. As members of the business class, both worker and capitalist are *owners*: they stand in relation to one another as participants in the production and re-production of commodities. Resolution of the conflict between them, therefore, can go in only one direction: 'Although their relation is not that of being common owners of a property, still the transition from it to common ownership is very easy.'[91]

In a passage reminiscent of Marx's notion of the relationship between base and superstructure, Hegel observes that the property relation operative within a class, along with its consciousness and function, actually correspond to 'its own basis of subsistence.'[92] In the case of the business class, its function is to form and adapt raw materials in order to satisfy human needs, and it performs this function through the creation by each of its members of 'the universal permanent capital' from which each draws a share determined not only by the formal capitalist property relation itself, but also by his or her industry and skill.[93] Thus what characterizes the business class above all, Hegel suggests, is its absolute reliance only upon itself: 'For what this class produces and enjoys, it has mainly itself, its own industry, to thank.'[94] Its independence of means is reflected in the consciousness of the business class, in its 'aims and interests ... mental culture and habit,'[95] and places it in bitter opposition to the other two groups in civil society, the agricultural and universal classes.

Before considering the position of these latter two classes, it is worthy of note that in strong contrast with Marx, Hegel sees no essential distinction in *structure of consciousness* between workers and capitalists. Apart from differences in level of education (which are often slight) and ownership claims (which, in the first instance, remain largely *unconscious* for the worker), the minds of the employer and the worker are alike. The roots of this identity are suggested by Hegel in his discussion of the relationship between master and slave. 'This status, in the first place, implies *common* wants and common concern for their satisfaction – for the means of mastery, the slave, must likewise be kept in life. In place of rude destruction of the immediate object there ensues acquisition, preservation, and formation of it, as the instrumentality in which the two extremes of independence and non-independence are welded together.'[96] The educational struggle of the worker, it is true, provides him or her with the potential to transcend the viewpoint of the business class – a potential the capitalist lacks. But within the framework of this struggle, the thinking of both sides reaches no further than the Understanding, which is itself a product of the bourgeois economic system. Thus Hegel connects the consciousness of the business class with ideas about property, freedom, and law and order – ideas which originated with the development of the business class in the towns of medieval society and which are concomitant with its self-dependence and initiative.

The consciousness and function of the business class are the reverse of those of the agricultural class. This group has its economic basis 'in the natural products of the soil which it cultivates,' and includes the hereditary aristocracy and the peasantry. Dependent on the cycles and caprice of nature, the agricultural mode of life 'owes comparatively little to reflection and independence of will.'[97] Instead of relying on the power of rationality and freedom embedded in law, as does the business class, the agricultural class upholds the patriarchal principle of the family and the relation of 'faith and trust.'[98]

Precisely because of these features, the form of the agricultural class alters over time and its influence in society diminishes. First of all, the family as embodiment of the patriarchal principle and source of capital in land is an early victim of bourgeois production, as Hegel shows.[99] Secondly, the relation of faith and trust, upon which the nobility founded its hereditary rights and privileges, is eroded by the rule of law.[100] While insisting that the nature of work on the land remains quite different from industrial production, Hegel concedes that these changes gradually transform the agricultural class into something resembling the business class in civil society. 'In the course of time,' he writes of the agricultural class, 'the character of this class as "substantial" undergoes modifications through the working of the civil law, in particular the administration of justice, as well as through the working of education, instruction, and religion. These modifications ... do not affect the substantial content of the class but only its form and the development of its power of reflection.'[101]

Marx's concentration on property relations in his theory of class allows him to overlook the function and consciousness of the educated middle class (the class, by the way, to which he himself belonged) and its connection with the state. This group, however, which has come to such prominence in late twentieth-century capitalism, is a major element in Hegel's social theory. For Hegel, the educated and politically conscious middle class is largely a creature of the state since most of its members belong to a group intimately connected with government, the universal class, or the class of civil servants. Concerned largely with its own material interests, the business class serves the ends of society only indirectly; similarly, the agricultural class (which more and more appears as a sub-element within the business class) is absorbed in cultivating the soil and consuming its products. But the universal class is dedicated to the totality of the affairs of society – the maintenance of order and public welfare – and consequently must find its basis of subsistence in the state.

Appointment to, and promotion within, the universal class is in principle regulated by objective factors such as education and skill rather than the accident of birth or wealth; membership is accordingly open to every individual with the requisite training and talent. For Hegel, the universal class includes the liberal professions and academe; and the rich mixture of intelligentsia and bureaucracy serves as an antidote to the inevitable routine and boredom of government service.[102] Similarly, the corrosive influence of family and other personal ties on the performance of government workers is diminished by the size and complexity of the state. All these factors generate in the consciousness of civil servants 'the habit ... of adopting universal interests, points of view, and activities.'[103]

The young Marx was intrigued by Hegel's notion of a universal class capable of representing the interests of the whole community, but he dismissed the idea that 'universal intelligence' could possibly belong to government bureaucrats. 'Hegel,' he wrote scornfully, 'gives us an empirical description of the bureaucracy, partly as it actually is, and partly according to the opinion which it has of itself.'[104] Later, of course, Marx's proletariat took the place of Hegel's universal class.

The middle or universal class was not the only Hegelian element abandoned by Marx in his construction of a radical theory of bourgeois society. Marx, with his expectations of imminent revolution, jettisoned every element of the Hegelian system which promised to restore unity to the disintegrating fabric of industrial capitalism.[105] He ignored Hegel's suggestion that the consciousness of the proletariat is not all that different from the Understanding of the bourgeoisie, and as a result he underestimated the potential for reformism in the working class movement as well as the distance of his own (middle-class) thinking from the thought pattern of the workers. Even more fatefully for his understanding of modern capitalism, Marx did not take seriously two institutions fundamental to Hegel's political and social theory: the corporation and the public authority.

If social class forms the individual's entry point into civil society, the corporation and the public authority mediate between the social individual and the state. The corporation performs this function for members of the business class while the universal class is accommodated by the public authority. For Hegel, the corporations of bourgeois society comprise all public and private institutions outside the sphere of the state proper: even the various churches are corporations, as are municipal and professional organizations. Nevertheless the predominant corporation is the incorporated business.[106] Business corporations represent various branches of the organization of labour, and in Hegel's theory they bear striking resemblance to the giant firms which now dominate advanced capitalist economies. However, in dialectical fashion the Hegelian business corporation also includes its opposite: the *labour union*.

What the business corporation represents most of all for Hegel is the transformation of the capitalist firm into a *social institution*, with all the trappings of respect and influence in government that status implies. But this transformation is purchased at great cost to the capitalist: gradual recognition of the property rights of the worker and acceptance of a growing state role in private industry. Neither of these developments occur without struggle and setback, as Hegel recognizes, but his sketch of the rights won by the worker in the corporation dramatically anticipates (and goes well beyond) the fundamental advances achieved by modern corporation workers, such as health and safety plans, grievance appeals, educational and retirement packages, and so forth. The social character of the corporation emerges most clearly, therefore, as the site for the educational struggle of the worker, and for his or her entry into the higher realm of the state. In its dual character as representative both of business and labour, the corporation raises the great mass of atomized and poverty-stricken workers of civil society into 'organized members of the state ... possessed of legitimate power.'[107]

The corporation comprises one pole of relative stability arising from the excesses of wealth and poverty in civil society; the police or public authority constitutes the other.[108] The role of the public authority is to curb and control the more destructive aspects of the bourgeois economic system. Government takes a large and expanding role in assuring public health and safety, regulating the quality and price of consumer goods, and attempting to alleviate and find a solution for the misery of the poor and dispossessed. Moreover, as capitalist enterprises burst through national boundaries in search of profits and an expanded market, the public authority is increasingly obliged to facilitate these activities and ensure that they benefit the nation as a whole. As a result of this latter role, however, the public authority finds itself a partner in colonial adventures and imperialist war, and its relations with other nations become 'on the largest scale a maelstrom of external contingency and the inner particularity of passions, private interests and selfish ends, abilities and virtues, vices, force, and wrong. All these whirl together, and in their vortex the ethical whole itself, the autonomy of the state, is exposed to contingency.'[109]

Hegel's account of the public authority anticipates in many ways the broad direction of the state in advanced capitalist society. Economic dislocation, poverty, and imperialism are forces that have combined in the more than 150 years since his death to create the apparatus of the modern state along lines indicated in the *Philosophy of Right*. Nevertheless, the government or public authority of civil society is entirely inadequate to Hegel's Idea of the state; nor does today's democratic state conform to the Hegelian ideal, any more than it does to Marx's vision of communism.

For Hegel, the bourgeois state is merely 'the *state external*'[110] – government devoted primarily to the protection of private property and abstract freedom. The members of civil society perceive the state as a *mere means* to the attainment of their particular ends, a perception carried over into bourgeois political theory. Nor is this view of the state simply a result of mystification and error. Government within civil society, at least in its beginnings, indeed does little more than shore up and extend the relations of private property and formal personal freedom. The *externality* of the capitalist state, notes Hegel, involves 'a separation and a merely relative identity of controller and controlled.' In other words, the state is powerless before the dynamic of civil society, unable to overcome the 'blind necessity' of the economic system[111] and incapable of realizing the 'final end of the state,' i.e., 'that *all* human capacities and *all* individual powers be developed and given expression in every way and in every direction.'[112]

Despite its manifest inadequacy, Hegel insists that the external capitalist state conceals under 'a motley covering' the form and inner structure of a truly rational order. It is this covering, he writes in the famous preface to the *Philosophy of Right*, 'which the concept has first to penetrate before it can find the inward pulse and feel it beating in the outward appearances.'[113] Just as the human figure is flawed in any and all of its manifestations on earth, but remains a sublime necessity in anything human, so too the existing state reveals the necessity of the Idea, even if only 'in the abstract.' Moreover, unlike the merely empirical human individual, who is trapped in the eternal cycle of nature, the state as a product of mind reveals the foremost characteristics of consciousness – development and progress. The task of dia-lectical science is to demonstrate the necessity of the Idea of the state, to locate the forces within civil society which point to its ultimate realization.

For Hegel, the Idea of the state is to be found at the *political level*, in the integration of civil society and the state through the emerging constitutional structure of government. Convinced that the political *form* of the modern world is adequate to the Idea, Hegel envisions a state whose general or-ganization follows the familiar pattern of parliamentary democracy.[114] But the *content* of Hegel's state differs fundamentally from that of bourgeois government which is entangled in the irrationality and caprice of private interest. At the level of civil society, the state is distinguished by its *separation* from economic and social institutions, but also by its *subordination* to them. In the higher sphere of the state, however, these institutions are unified with the circles of government and at the same time they are transformed or sublated. According to Hegel, the state becomes the guiding power in society precisely because the institutions of bourgeois society are educated up to its level. In other words, the Hegelian state is founded upon a revolutionary transformation of civil society. 'The state,' he writes, 'is precisely this totality in which the moments of the concept have attained the actuality corre-spondent to their degree of truth.'[115]

Hegel argues that the *unconscious identity* of individual and universal interests promoted by the class divisions and conflicts of bourgeois society is forged into an active, self-conscious principle within what he terms, the 'rational' or 'social' state. In the rational state, 'individuals ... do not live as private persons for their own ends alone, but in the very act of willing these they will the universal in the light of the universal, and their activity is consciously aimed at none but the universal end.' As in Marx's com-munism, the radical division between the individual and society disappears along with the alienation and selfishness of bourgeois existence. The social individual and the state achieve a dialectical identity. 'Unification pure and simple,' writes Hegel, 'is the true content and aim of the individual, and the individual's destiny is the living of a universal life. His further particular satisfaction, activity, and mode of conduct have this substantive and uni-versally valid life as their starting point and their result.'[116]

Marx suggests that communism will guarantee the social and economic rights of each individual and ensure that 'the process of material production ... becomes production by freely associated men, and stands under their conscious and planned control.'[117] Similarly, the *'work'* of Hegel's social state consists in maintaining the rights and promoting the welfare of indi-viduals, and ensuring that the family and civil society are protected and guided in the interests of the whole community.[118] Moreover, if communism is achieved through development of the consciousness of the proletariat, Hegel's rational state is rooted in and identical with the self-consciousness of the social individual, who has experienced the forming process of educational struggle in bourgeois society.

The state is mind knowing and willing itself after passing through the forming process of education. The state, therefore, knows what it wills and knows it in its universality, i.e. as something thought. Hence it works and acts by reference to consciously adopted ends, known principles, and laws which are not merely implicit but are actually present to consciousness; and further, it acts with precise knowledge of existing conditions and circumstances, inasmuch as its actions have a bearing on these.[119]

In contrast with Marx's vision of communism, where differences between classes, distinctions of power and authority, and even specialization of talent and ability ultimately disappear, Hegel's rational state retains the exuberant prodigality of life in modern society. To be sure, inequality in the crude shape of wealth and poverty, exploitation and servitude, have no part in the rational state, but there are still class divisions and conflicts. Moreover, these antagonisms ensure the integrity of the state and secure the personal freedoms of the individual. According to Hegel, the *active nucleus* of the social state is the tension between the business class on one side and the state executive and civil service on the other. The opposition of the business class, organized in corporations which are slowly being transformed into institutions of workers' control and direct democracy, is the *living counterpoise* which (along with the head of state) effectively prevents the universal class 'from acquiring the isolated position of an aristocracy and using its education and skill as means to an arbitrary tyranny.' Similarly, if the corporations are needed to shatter the arbitrary power of state functionaries, the universal class itself must act as a countervailing power over against the organizations of the business class: 'Of course Corporations must fall under the higher surveillance of the state, because otherwise they would ossify, build themselves in, and decline into a miserable system of castes.'[120]

Class conflict in the social state works itself out within the structure of the state itself, as a form of resistance and struggle between the legislature (composed largely of elected representatives from the corporations) and the state executive and civil service. But it also reflects the organic division of the rational state into the personal sphere of the family (symbolized by the head of state), the particularized sphere of civil society (the legislature), and the 'strictly political state,' i.e., the constitution, government, and so forth[121] (the executive and civil service). In the rational state, therefore, civil society with its independent circles of culture and industry loses none of its strength and creative power, although its impulses of irrationality and destruction are curbed and redirected. Nor does the family wither away. It remains instead as the sphere of love and stability in which the unique character of the individual is nourished and protected.

The elements of Hegel's theory missing in Marx's – especially the role of the state, the corporation, and the universal class – accomplish a form of reconciliation Marx refused to accept. Nevertheless, reconciliation comes not as disguised reform of capitalism, but rather as transcendence of the bourgeois order and the emergence of a society which embraces the ideal of freedom projected by Marx. As I will argue in this book, the dynamic aspect of Hegel's vision makes him an even better guide than Marx to the complexities and developments of our own time.

2

Religion, Philosophy, and the Development of Individual Consciousness

1 PLATO, THE IDEA, AND THE SOCIAL INDIVIDUAL

In his *Marxism and Hegel*, Lucio Colletti argues that Hegel's philosophy concerns ' "the true infinite", the Christian *Logos*,' and that Hegel's notion of contradiction 'bears upon one precise topic: the problem of proving the existence of God.'[1] Colletti's argument is not new; one of the first British Hegelians, J.H. Stirling, contended in his *The Secret of Hegel*, written in 1865, that God is 'the secret origin and constitution of Hegel.'[2] The notion that Hegel is essentially a religious thinker is shared by Marxist and non-Marxist commentators alike. Marcuse, for example, observes that 'Hegel's philosophy was deeply rooted [in] the Christian tradition.'[3] Similarly, C.J. Friedrich states that 'Hegel was and wanted to be a Christian philosopher.'[4]

The conception of him as a theologian is connected with the notion that Hegel sees the development of society as the progress of what he calls the World Spirit toward freedom. 'This march of freedom is interpreted [by Hegel] as what the World Spirit wants, as it seeks to realize itself. And in its effort to realize itself it employs peoples, world-historical peoples to do its work.'[5] According to this view there is a place for God, but certainly not for the human individual, in Hegel's philosophy. Hegel's 'subject,' says Marcuse, 'does not designate any particular form of subjectivity (such as man) but a general structure that might best be characterized by the concept "mind". Subject denotes a universal that individualizes itself, and if we wish to think of a concrete example, we might point to the "spirit" of a historic epoch.'[6] The World Spirit embodies the Hegelian 'Absolute Idea' which Marcuse and other writers identify with the thought of God. 'God in [the Hegelian] formula means the totality of the pure forms of all being, or, the true essence of being ... [Thus] the absolute idea has to be conceived as the actual creator of the world.'[7]

Hegel's use of religious terms in his philosophy, and his notions of the World Spirit and the Absolute Idea, have led many commentators to compare him with Plato. Colletti, for instance, suggests that Hegel embraces the 'Platonic-Christian tradition' of the *negative* conception of the sensible world.'[8] In other words, Hegel, like Plato, views the universe as the manifestation of a divine Mind; the world has no true reality – it only reflects the thought of God.

Hegel is indeed in the Platonic tradition, but his interpretation of Plato's philosophy bears no resemblance to that of Colletti. For Hegel, Plato's philosophy concerns nature and society as they are conceived in theory, in the theoretical concepts of men and women. Plato's thought, writes Hegel, 'embraces in an absolute unity reality as well as thinking, the Notion and its reality in the movement of science, as the Idea of a scientific whole.' Hegel denies, for example, that Plato's *Republic* is merely the ancient philosopher's notion of what the world should look like; a dream toward which reality will be made to correspond. Plato's ideal state 'is reality, not a world above us or beyond, but the present world looked at in its truth.' Of course, Plato's state is not that of the moderns, the one in which contemporary individuals find themselves; rather it concerns the 'Greek morality according to its substantial mode, for it is the Greek state-life which constitutes the true content of the Platonic Republic.'[9]

Hegel's criticism of what he sees as common misinterpretations of Plato may be used just as well to controvert received but mistaken opinions about Hegel. The notion, for example, that according to Platonic dogma, 'God made the world, that higher beings of a spiritual kind exist, and, in the creation of the world, lent God a helping hand ... stands word for word in Plato, and yet it does not belong to his philosophy.' Hegel argues that Plato uses such notions as 'pictorial conceptions' to explicate his philosophy; nevertheless, 'all that is expressed in the manner of pictorial conception is taken by the moderns in sober earnest for philosophy.' As if to anticipate current misconceptions of his own theories, Hegel goes on to say that 'such a representation of Plato's philosophy can be supported by Plato's own words; but one who knows what Philosophy is, cares little for such expressions, and recognizes what was Plato's true meaning.'[10]

According to Hegel, the greatest achievement of Plato's philosophy is its recognition of the intellectual and social world of men and women. Plato goes beyond the ordinary world of sense perception and constructs theories about the 'idea world,' that is, the world of science and society. 'What is peculiar in the philosophy of Plato is its application to the intellectual and supersensuous world, and its elevation of consciousness into the realm of spirit. Thus the spiritual element which belongs to thought obtains in this form an importance for consciousness, and is brought into consciousness.'[11]

For Plato, as for Hegel, men and women interact with each other on the basis of their shared beliefs of what the world is like, rather than in response to the blunt realities of ordinary sense perception. On this view, human consciousness takes an active role in the determination of social relationships. For example, the commonly held ideas people have of marriage sets before them their privileges and taboos, prepares their moral pitfalls, and stimulates their joys and anguish, all in a manner the natural sexual relationship, if it were a simple reflection in consciousness, would be incapable of doing. Similarly, human thought is also the active force behind the construction of science and the entire social world. 'The State,' for instance, 'really rests on thought, and its existence depends on the sentiments of men, for it is a spiritual and not a physical kingdom.'[12]

No less than the state, natural science depends for its existence on the thinking activity of men and women. The findings of science are not a simple record of objects and relationships given to thought by the observation of external nature. If science were only that, its historical development would be incomprehensible; we would have to say that Newton did not formulate Einstein's relativity equation because he did not observe nature closely enough. To grasp the laws of nature, human thought must penetrate the superficial appearance of things and construct theories capable of making sense of contradictory phenomena. Scientific theories are themselves a product of the general progress of human thought, and they hinge on the development of consciousness and society. Scientific theory, or what Hegel calls 'the speculative,' certainly deals with external reality, with actuality: 'We are wrong in representing the speculative to be something existent only in thought or inwardly, which is no one knows where.' But it is equally incorrect to suggest that human thought and imagination take no independent role in the construction of science. The speculative 'is really present,' writes Hegel, 'but men of learning shut their eyes to it because of their limited point of view. If we listen to their account, they only observe and say what they see; but their observation is not true, for unconsciously they transform what is seen through their limited and stereotyped conception; the strife is not due to the opposition between observation and the absolute Notion, but between the one Notion and the other.'[13]

When Hegel writes of the 'Idea' or the 'Notion' in Plato, or when he uses these terms in other contexts, he is not referring, as many commentators believe, to a religious image or to a logical construct somehow outside the thoughts and reality of living human beings. The Idea – even the Absolute Idea – is neither a logical construct nor the thought of God, but the scientific expression of society and nature as it has been developed by the thinking activity of individual human beings. 'Philosophy in its ultimate essence is one and the same, every succeeding philosopher will and must take up into his own, all philosophies that went before, and what falls specially to him is their further development.' No less than that of any other philosopher, Plato's task was to take up, systematize, and develop the ideas of those who came before him. In the Idea of Plato, 'we see all manner of philosophic teaching from earlier times absorbed into a deeper principle, and therein united. It is in this way that Plato's philosophy shows itself to be a totality of ideas: therefore, as the result, the principles of others are comprehended in itself.'[14]

Hegel observes that the thinkers of his time, especially those concerned with religion, were returning to Plato in order to understand their own epoch. But this return was misguided. Both Plato's philosophy and religion 'have their due place and their own importance, but they are not the philosophy of our own time.' The social reality of Hegel's period, the new industrial society arising from the cataclysm of 1789, demanded a new philosophy and a new way of looking at the world. 'We must stand above Plato,' advises Hegel, 'i.e. we must acquaint ourselves with the needs of thoughtful minds in our time, or rather we must ourselves experience these needs.'[15]

Hegel is impatient with efforts to discover in Plato ideas which have a direct bearing on the constitution of modern states. Karl Popper, for example, identifies Plato as a precursor of the 'enemies' of what Popper calls the 'open society' or modern democracy.[16] For Hegel, however, this is to read into Plato 'the crude notions' of moderns who are 'unable to conceive the spiritual spiritually.' Anyway it 'is foolish' and 'a moral hypocrisy,' notes Hegel, 'to pretend to be better than others who are then called enemies.' Hegel suggests that to understand Plato we should attempt to consider his thought with respect to the needs and reality of Plato's time. 'Plato,' Hegel suggests, 'is not the man to dabble in abstract theories and principles; his truth-loving mind has recognized and represented the truth, and this could not be anything else than the truth of the world he lived in, the truth of the one spirit which lived in him as well as in Greece. No man can overleap his time, the spirit of his time is his spirit also; but the point at issue is, to recognize that spirit by its content.'[17]

Plato lived during a period when the original Greek democracy was crum-

bling and only 'preponderating individualities or ... masters in statesman-
ship' were able to hold it together. Not only Plato but the Greek people
themselves 'were then altogether dissatisfied with their democratic constitution, and the conditions resulting from it.' The disintegrating force was
the development of private property and the demand for individual rights
within the state. Plato denied both because he felt, rightly as it turned out,
that these would end up destroying Greece. It is pointless, therefore, to
attempt to consider modern democracy in terms of Plato's ideal state. 'In
modern states,' writes Hegel, 'we have freedom of conscience, according to
which every individual may demand the right of following out his own
interests; but this is excluded from the Platonic idea.'[18]

The greatest shortcoming of Plato's philosophy is neither its opposition
to private property nor its condemnation of democracy, since these may be
explained within the context of Plato's epoch. What tends to undermine
Plato's vision is his constant recourse to sensuous images and ordinary
conceptions, like that of 'God,' to express what Hegel calls 'the speculative
Notion.' The Notion refers to the cumulative product of the development
of human thought, the power of the theorist to separate out sensuous images
and conceptions, and work with theoretical constructs alone. 'The merit of
Philosophy consists alone in the fact that truth is expressed in the form of
the Notion.'[19] Plato lacks the ability to express ideas purely in theoretical
terms and as a result he frequently falls back on myths and allegories to
convey his ideas.

The Platonic myth is useful in that it helps elucidate his thought. Nevertheless, the value of Plato's philosophy does not rest in its employment of
mythology; myth is superfluous to speculative thinking and adds nothing
to its progress. Yet in the study of Plato's philosophy, 'men often lay hold
of nothing but these myths.' Misconceptions about Plato led thinkers in
Hegel's time to ignore the speculative aspects of his thought, and concentrate
on the merely 'pictorial' side of his philosophy. Accordingly, just as Colletti
and other modern thinkers claim to discover religion in his system, Hegel's
contemporaries evinced 'an obstinate determination to lead back the Platonic
philosophy to the forms of our former metaphysic, e.g. to the proof of the
existence of God.'[20]

The most damaging misinterpretation of Plato concerns the meaning of
the Platonic Ideas. In his account of these Ideas, Hegel indirectly furnishes
an explication of his own use of the term Idea. As pointed out above, many
commentators interpret Hegel's Idea as the product of a Cosmic Spirit, or
God, which realizes itself through the unintended consequences of the activities of large masses of people or nation-states. One of the most recent

examples of this approach appears in Charles Taylor's *Hegel*: 'History' for Hegel, 'is to be understood teleologically as directed in order to realize *Geist*. What happens in history has sense, justification, indeed, the highest justification. It is good, the plan of God.'[21] There is no doubt that Hegel often writes as though the Idea really is the thought of God or an independent logical construct. But as Hegel says regarding Plato's philosophy, these notions do not belong to his philosophy but rather to its method of presentation.[22]

Misapprehension of Plato's thought takes two directions. First, the Ideas such as the 'just' and the 'beautiful' are taken as intelligible objects in the mind of God. The 'Ideas ... are made into ... transcendent existences which lie somewhere far from us in an understanding outside this world.' On this interpretation the Ideas are 'liberated from the actuality of the individual consciousness' and the subject of these Ideas 'even comes to be represented only as something which is apart from consciousness.' The second misconception is to see the Ideas as ideals in people's minds 'which produce nothing that either has reality now or can ever attain to it.' In other words, the Ideas are mere fancies, very attractive in themselves, but impossible of attainment in the hard practical reality of society. 'They are defined as intellectual perceptions which must present themselves immediately, and belong either to a happy genius or else to a condition of ecstasy or enthusiasm. In such a case they would be mere creations of the imagination, but this is not Plato's nor the true sense.'[23] The received interpretation of Hegel's Idea resembles the first way in which Plato's Ideas are usually seen, i.e., as things liberated from individual consciousness and existing apart from ordinary human beings.

Hegel's Idea as well as the Ideas of Plato 'are not immediately in consciousness, but they are in the apprehending knowledge; and they are immediate perceptions only in so far as they are apprehending knowledge comprehended in its simplicity and in relation to the result; in other words, the immediate perception is only the moment of their simplicity.' What Hegel means is that the Idea, as he interprets it, is something that is manifested in concrete social reality through conscious human activity and struggle, and later given theoretical form by philosophy. 'The past [is] something which has taken shape. For the past is the preservation of the present as reality ... From out of ... formlessness the universal first comes into form in the present.'[24] Hegel identifies the Idea with the notion of freedom; this notion, as it is actualized in modern society, is the product of centuries of human striving and conflict, although it appears to contemporary men and women as 'immediate perception,' as the 'moment of its simplicity.' The philosopher, in turn, gives the Idea theoretical form and considers the history of human thought and society in terms of the development of this Idea.[25]

An easily accessible way to illustrate Hegel's method of approach to history is to compare the Idea with, say, the automobile. To construct a history of the automobile, the first concern would be to consider its development in the late nineteenth century and then trace back all the elements in human history which eventually came together in this development. Inventions like the wheel and the discovery of the spark as a means to release energy and so on would be treated as stages or moments in the development of the automobile. The approach to history, then, would be single-minded. The historian would not trouble to wonder whether the automobile should have been invented or whether something else might have been invented instead. As Hegel puts it, 'Philosophy indeed treats of nothing which is not and does not concern itself with what is so powerless as not even to have the energy to force itself into existence.'[26] Similarly, the historian would not be concerned with ages and peoples that added little or nothing to the advance of the automobile, even though they are worthy of study in other respects.

From the vantage point of the present the invention of the wheel may be seen as necessary to the invention of the motor car, but the historian would not suggest that the inventor of the wheel was seized by the Idea of the automobile, and was its unwilling creator, although the unreflecting observer might suppose that this was the historian's purpose. Certainly the invention of the wheel reflected its inventor's desire for freedom and the ability to roam about the world more freely than he or she could without it, but the notion of freedom in this respect probably did not lead the inventor to comprehend that some day whole continents would be traversed effortlessly by single individuals in their own automobile. For the historian, the wheel's invention would be seen in the context of the needs and desires of the people in whose society the inventor belonged. Because of these material aspects the inventor would put the wheel to other uses than those which might have assisted in the further development of the automobile. Nevertheless, his or her conscious activity was a necessary element behind its eventual emergence.

For the religiously-minded, as many people were in Hegel's day, the evolution of the motor car might be seen as the wonderful work of an all-knowing God who puts His subjects to the sublime task of creating advanced transport. Most of us do not see the development of the automobile in quite this manner; nor does Hegel imagine that this is the way the Idea originated. The progress of the notion of individual freedom in the consciousness of men and women and its actualization in history and society is no doubt a more worthy object of historical reflection than is the history of the automobile. But this is only because *the history of the development of machinery is only one aspect of the history of the development of human consciousness.* That the material and social conditions of human existence are the product of the rational activity of men and women is a central message of Hegel's philosophy. Ideology in its broad sense as human thinking activity is, in Hegel's terminology, the divine creator of all human reality. It marks the alienation of consciousness in our day that the thought of men and women is considered by Marxists and their bourgeois opponents alike as merely the reflection of things and structures which in fact are created by the rational activity of people themselves.

In his discussion of Plato's Ideas, Hegel says that the Idea of freedom is 'the absolute power'; as such it 'has certainly to realize itself; in other words, God rules in the world.'[27] When Hegel uses the term God or when he refers to religious conceptions, he almost always qualifies this use with phrases like 'in other words,' 'in religious language,' and so on.[28] But it is important to point out that God is not for Hegel a 'pictorial conception' only: God (and religious figures in general) formed a part of the consciousness of the societies and peoples with which Hegel deals. Accordingly, he often speaks as though God does exist, or did exist, in the thought and times he discusses. In that God was a present and real entity for people, their actions and desires are incomprehensible unless He is treated as such; to allow people their religion is at once to respect and understand their culture. 'A nation conceives of God in the same way as it conceives of itself and of its relationship to God, so that its religion is also its conception of itself.'[29] Hegel observes that 'history is the Idea working itself out in a natural way,' i.e., through the action of ordinary human beings, 'and not with the consciousness of the Idea.' The outcome of this action has certainly been 'what is right, moral and pleasing to God'; that is, it has contributed to the increased rationality and freedom in modern society, 'but we must recognize that action represents at the same time the endeavours of the subject as such for particular ends.'[30]

No less than Marx, Hegel recognizes that people must and do act in accordance with the material reality in which they exist. While in their activities people try to realize what for them appears to be the just and the moral, their activities are, nevertheless, mixed up with purely personal desires, expectations and goals. 'Men must have brought forth from themselves the rational along with their interests and their passions, just as it [the rational] must enter into reality through the necessities, opportunities, and motives that impel them.'[31] The thought and ideas of human beings are not mere illusions, even when these ideas are of a religious nature, and even though they are conditioned by material existence. The ideology of men and women, no matter at what stage of civilization, contains an inner rationality which survives its own time and takes root in the succeeding one. Lack of recognition of this kernel of rationality in the ideology of a people or group in society mars certain Marxist accounts of historical change and transformation. A lacuna is particularly apparent, as I will argue later in this and the following chapter, in Marxist notions about the role of religion in society.

According to Hegel, the Idea 'is only on the one side produced through thoughts, and on the other through circumstances, through human actions in their capacity as means.' As discussed in Chapter 1, Hegel's famous notion of 'the cunning of reason,' which most commentators associate with a divine agency that achieves its ends independently of the thought and will of men and women, has nothing to do with a power outside and above individual human consciousness. Reason, the most essential aspect of consciousness, is realized both consciously and unconsciously by individuals in society. The ends people pursue often seem opposed to the notion of freedom; and certainly the ruling powers of the world – what Marx calls the ruling classes – are most often in no way concerned with the realization of freedom. 'But that does not really matter; all those particular ends are really only means of bringing forth the Idea, because it is the absolute power. Hence the Idea comes to pass in the world, and no difficulty is caused, but it is not requisite that those who rule should have the Idea.'[32]

In his critique of Plato's notion of the ideal state, Hegel observes that the rulers of the world are saddled with human subjects. They use the minds and activity of people to produce the wealth and circumstance on which their power rests. But human rationality is an explosive material that must be handled delicately lest it overturn the world of those who make use of it. Regardless of the efforts of the ruling powers, the progress they foster by exploiting their subjects will eventually lead to their own destruction. 'Men,' Hegel points out, 'do not remain at a standstill, they alter, as likewise do their constitutions.'[33] Every nation or society is founded upon what its members consider to be right and just:[34] but as people develop their society, they also change their notions about how society should be governed. 'If a nation can no longer accept as implicitly true what its constitution expresses to it as the truth, if its consciousness or Notion and its actuality are not at one, then the nation's mind is torn asunder.' When this occurs two things are possible. First, the nation may either change its laws 'quietly and slowly,' or it may 'by a supreme internal effort dash into fragments this law which still claims authority.'[35]

The alternatives are obvious: reform or revolution. The second possibility is that the nation remains at a standstill or is absorbed by 'another nation [which] has reached its higher constitution.' If the time for revolution is ripe (a moment that can be determined 'by philosophy alone') the constitution may be changed without a shot being fired. 'Revolutions take place in a state without the slightest violence when the insight becomes universal; institutions, somehow or other, crumble and disappear, each man agrees to give up his right.' But for this to happen the government must recognize that its time has come; if it does not, 'that government will fall, along with its institutions, before the force of mind. The breaking up of its government breaks up the nation itself; a new government arises, – or it may be that the government and the unessential retain the upper hand.'[36]

In his youth, Hegel was a fervent supporter of the revolutionary principles of the Girondins; but he opposed the Terror believing that it jeopardized the achievements of the Revolution.[37] In the account of revolution and reform he provides in his discussion of Plato, Hegel makes clear that he never lost his faith in the principles espoused by the revolutionaries in France; nor did he transfer his allegiance to reaction – the 'unessential.' His philosophy remains on the side of revolution.

Since the Ideas of Plato concern the social and intellectual world, they are 'the True, that which is worthy to be known – indeed, the Eternal, the implicitly and explicitly divine.'[38] Throughout his writings, Hegel uses terms with religious connotations like 'divine,' 'eternal,' 'soul,' 'spirit,' and so forth, to refer to the products, not of an omniscient creator, but of conscious human activity or 'ideality.' By using religious expressions to illustrate his argument, Hegel relates these intellectual productions to a social reality which exists apart from any one person, and which predates and will survive any particular individual. An instructive example of Hegel's use of religious imagery to refer to the rational activity of men and women appears in the *Philosophy of Right*. After describing the agricultural mode of life as a form of rationality, in that it provides 'security' and 'lasting satisfaction of needs,' Hegel refers approvingly to an explanation of ancient agrarian festivals and images: 'It was because the ancients themselves had become conscious of the divine origin of agriculture and other institutions associated with it that they held them in such religious veneration.'[39]

For Plato, as for Hegel, human consciousness is immanent and self-determining. Therefore, the development of thought appears to be closer to the recollection of a content already in the mind than to the ordinary conception of learning for which mind is a mere *tabula rasa* on which external reality is imprinted. Hegel observes that in one sense Plato's 'recollection ... is certainly an unfortunate expression, in the sense, namely, that an idea is reproduced which has already existed at another time.' But he contends there is another sense of the term that brings out the actual nature of the development of individual consciousness, 'namely that of making oneself inward, going inward, and this is the profound meaning of the word in thought.'[40] What Hegel means is that in the process of learning the individual becomes familiar with external nature as it is comprehended by human thought, and with society, which is itself the product of the rational activity of men and women, as well as the object of their theoretical or speculative efforts.[41] Moreover, the individual makes these thoughts his or her possession and develops them further. 'In this sense, it may undoubtedly be said that knowledge of the universal is nothing but a recollection, a going within self, and that we make that which at first shows itself in external form and determined as a manifold, into an inward, a universal, because we go into ourselves and thus bring what is inward in us into consciousness.' There is no doubt, however, that Plato himself interpreted recollection in the first sense of the term. Nevertheless, he was attempting to express what is in essence the genuine quality of human consciousness: his error lay in employing myth and sensuous images to propound 'the true Notion that consciousness in itself is the content of knowledge.'[42]

Plato connects the notion of subjective or individual consciousness as recollection with the religious conception or picture image of the eternal nature of the human soul. However, 'immortality has not ... the interest to Plato which it has to us [moderns] from a religious point of view.'[43] The idea of immortality, of course, is an essential element in Christianity. As a result, Colletti among others ascribes belief in immortality to Hegel 'precisely in the same sense that for the Christian death is the beginning of the true life, which commences when one passes from the here and now over to the beyond.'[44] Neither Plato nor Hegel, however, entertain a belief in immortality. Plato confused the universal nature of human thought, its conceptual and active power, with the concept of recollection as mere memory, the dredging up of a previously given content. He then added to the confusion by suggesting that each individual soul is preformed and belongs to a period before the birth of the determinate individual. In modern times, something resembling Plato's notion is retained in the theory of genetic inheritance. But genetic theory was unavailable to Plato, and so he illustrated the idea of preformation by comparing it to the doctrine of immortality. Historians of philosophy, observes Hegel, have seized upon Plato's allusion 'to what really is an [early] Egyptian idea, and a sensuous conception merely, and say that Plato has laid down that such and such was the case.' But the notion of immortality was not put forward by Plato at all; nor does it have anything to do with his philosophy, 'any more than what afterwards is said regarding God.'[45]

The doctrine of immortality expresses 'in the simple language of the religious mind' the real relationship between the individual and society; a relationship Hegel calls the 'passage from subjectivity to objectivity' or 'the genuine Infinity.'[46] The individual comes into a social world constructed independently of his or her effort and will; but the growth of the individual and the actualization of the person's thought and ideas in society through work prepares the ground for immortality: long after the individual has disappeared from the earth, his or her activity will be reflected in the development and continuity of social existence. As Hegel puts it, 'work is just this moment of activity concentrating itself on the particular, which nevertheless goes back into the universal, and is for it.' The social bond which holds society together is found nowhere else but in the consciousness and activity of each individual within it, and in the striving of the social individual to carve out a personal identity in the universal or society. ('What is concrete and true (and everything true is concrete) is the universality which has the particular as its opposite, but the particular which by its reflection into itself has been equalized with the universal. This unity is individuality ... in accordance with its concept; indeed, individuality in this sense is just precisely the concept itself.') 'The bond,' says Hegel, 'is the subjective and individual, the power which dominates the other, which makes itself identical with it.'[47]

Society can exist only so long as it satisfies the conscious needs and desires, the rationality, of the individuals who make it up. 'The universal is living spirit only in so far as the individual consciousness finds itself as such within it.' Society is not a mere assembly of individuals externally held together like cogs in a wheel or a mob of mindless automatons bounced back and forth by alien causal laws. 'The universal is not constituted of the immediate life and being of the individual, the mere substance, but formed of conscious life.' Just as society is constituted of rational individuals with their own interests and goals, each individual is also dependent on society, and can find a place only within it. 'Individuality which separates itself from the universal is powerless and falls to the ground, the one-sided universal, the morality of individuality cannot stand firm.'[48]

In a paragraph in the *Encyclopedia Logic*, Hegel sums up the relationship between the individual and society. 'Something [the individual: D.M.] in its passage into the other [society: D.M.] only joins with itself. To be thus self-related in the passage, and in the other, is the genuine Infinity.'[49] What Hegel expresses here in the abstract language of Logic is phrased in more concrete terms in the *Philosophy of Right*: 'The state exists immediately in custom, mediately in individual self-consciousness, knowledge, and activity, while self-consciousness in virtue of its sentiment toward the state finds in the state, as its essence and the end and product of its activity, its substantive freedom.'[50]

Hegel denies that his own and Plato's idealism has anything to do with the 'false idealism' according to which 'the individual produces from himself all his ideas, even the most immediate.' But the notion that 'knowledge comes entirely from without' is just as incorrect as the one which holds that all knowledge comes from within. The conception that knowledge comes from education and learning only is 'found in empirical philosophies of a quite abstract and rude kind ... Carried to an extreme, this is the doctrine of revelation' where God reveals all to the virgin minds of believers.[51]

What Plato and Hegel oppose, of course, is the same materialist doctrine criticized by Marx in the third of his *Theses on Feuerbach*: 'The materialist doctrine that men are products of circumstances and upbringing, and that, therefore, changed men are products of other circumstances and changed upbringing, forgets that it is men that change circumstances and that the educator himself needs educating.' And Marx adds, in a passage which, as I will show, captures the inner meaning of Hegel's philosophy: 'The coincidence of the changing of circumstances and of human activity can be conceived and rationally understood only as *revolutionising practice*.'[52]

According to Hegel, Plato tries wherever possible within the limitations of his time to separate myth from reality; he uses myth and religious imagery to explicate his philosophy and never descends to the grave speculations of modern theologians about such topics as the immortality of the soul and the fall of man and woman. Since Hegel went to great lengths to extract the rational dimension of Plato's thought, he would doubtless be appalled at the hash made of his own philosophy by many commentators. In a passage on Plato, Hegel exposes the dynamic element behind his and Marx's notion of 'revolutionising practice': 'What Plato expressed as the truth is that consciousness in the individual is in reason the divine reality and life; that man perceives and recognizes it in pure thought, and that this knowledge is itself the heavenly abode and movement.'[53] Truth lies neither in Cosmic Mind nor, as contemporary Marxists suggest it does, in the reified consciousness of a social class: it can only be found in the consciousness of the social individual.

2 HEGEL'S ATHEISM

There is no mode of intelligent being
higher than life in which existence
would be possible.[54]

As John Plamenatz observes, 'it has been both asserted and denied that Hegel was an atheist.'[55] The question of atheism, of course, is important for the consideration of Hegel's work in a way it is not for that of most other writers. Hegel's use of religious imagery has led, as I have indicated, to interpretations of his thought based largely on the notion that he is a religious thinker.[56] After his death in 1831, the Hegelian school itself split over the question of Hegel's attitude to religion.[57] Right-wing Hegelians felt that 'Hegel's philosophy justified Christianity,'[58] while the Young Hegelians of the left argued that Hegel opposed religion. Even among the Young Hegelians themselves there was dissension about Hegel's religious beliefs. In 1841, Marx and Bruno Bauer 'began to write a book with the intriguing title *The Last Trump over Hegel the Antichrist.*'[59] Marx's contribution to the work never appeared, but in this and other publications Bauer tried 'to prove that Hegel was an atheist and ... that his own atheism ... could be traced to Hegel.'[60]

Two works published by Feuerbach in 1843 established his 'intellectual leadership of the [Young Hegelians]'[61] and 'admitted validity to the claim of the Hegelians of the right that they could use Hegel's philosophy to justify Christianity as the absolute religion.'[62] Deeply influenced by Feuerbach, Marx attacked Bauer and accepted Feuerbach's proclamation that '*The Hegelian Philosophy is the last refuge and the last rational mainstay of theology.*'[63] Marx, however, soon returned to the view that Hegel's philosophy is atheistic and not Christian. He came to see Feuerbach's own attack on religion as a continuation of 'certain points ... which Hegel had left in mystic semi-obscurity.' For the mature Marx, Hegel along with Leibnitz, 'laboured to dethrone God,' and his philosophy 'reduced ... all things' including 'religion and law ... to a logical category.'[64]

Sidney Hook remarks that the relationship between Hegel and Marx 'is ... one of the most challenging problems in the history of thought.'[65] It is certainly a central problem for contemporary Western Marxism. But the evolution of Marx's attitude to Hegelian philosophy, particularly with respect to its religious (or atheistic) character, has not been satisfactorily elucidated by most Marxists. After 1845, Marx no longer refers to Hegel as a theologian: just as he turns against Feuerbach's epistemology in the

Theses on Feuerbach, he also rejects Feuerbach's reading of Hegel. In the *Manuscripts of 1844*, Marx lends qualified support to Feuerbach's notion of Hegel as a theologian: 'Hegel's ... merely *apparent* criticism' is based on 'what Feuerbach designated as the positing, negating and re-establishment of religion or theology – but it has to be grasped in more general terms.'[66]

The 'more general terms' are worked out by Marx and Engels in *The Holy Family*; this book – which was written after the *Manuscripts* – furnishes a secular interpretation of Hegel, an interpretation to which Marx and Engels will adhere in all their subsequent writings. Hegel, they observe,

thinks [he] has overcome the *objective world*, the sensuously perceptible real world, by transforming it into a 'Thing of Thought', a mere *determinateness of self-consciousness* ... Hegel makes man the *man of self-consciousness* instead of making self-consciousness the *self-consciousness of man*, of real man, i.e., of man living also in a real, objective world and determined by that world. He stands the world *on its head* and can therefore *in his head* also dissolve all limitations, which nevertheless remain in existence for *bad sensuous consciousness*, for *real* man.[67]

For Engels and the mature Marx, Hegel is not a theologian but simply an idealist who believes that 'eternal truth is nothing but the logical, or, the historical, process itself.' He asserts 'the primacy of spirit to nature' and assumes 'world creation in some form or other,' but his notion of creation is not a religious one and 'becomes still more intricate and impossible than in Christianity.'[68]

The nature of Hegel's absolute idealism will be dealt with in the following chapters, where I will argue that Marx and Engels are incorrect in their assessment of it. But if Marx and Engels deny that Hegel is a Christian thinker, the approach of twentieth-century Marxists is either to contend – as do Hook, Marcuse, and Colletti – that Hegel is a theologian, or, alternatively, to ignore altogether – as do Lenin[69] and Althusser[70] – the religious aspects of his thought. Both these approaches tend to underestimate the impact of Hegel on Marx, and overlook the contribution Hegel's thought could make to the further development of contemporary Marxism. As I will demonstrate in this and later chapters, Hegel's absolute idealism, which culminates in the absolute Idea or freedom, is concerned with the unity of theory and practice later urged by Marx in the *Theses on Feuerbach*: 'The philosophers have only *interpreted* the world, in various ways; the point, however, is to *change* it.'[71] Far from being original to Marx, this statement paraphrases a similar aphorism in Hegel's *Encyclopedia Logic*: 'While

Intelligence merely proposes to take the world as it is, Will takes steps to make the world what it ought to be.'[72]

Hegel's absolute idealism emerged from his critique of Christianity and Kant's subjective idealism; Marx's historical materialism is its direct descendant. Nevertheless, its meaning has not been an object of study for Western Marxism. Thus Marcuse, on approaching what he considers to be Hegel's religiously minded notion of absolute idealism, throws up his hands and admits, 'we cannot follow the Doctrine of the Notion beyond the point we have reached,' since it 'is ... overwhelmed by the ontological conceptions of absolute idealism.'[73] Lenin's estimate of Hegel's philosophy is close to the one I will outline below; in spite of this, however, Lenin confuses the speculative and revolutionary content of Hegel's thought with religion. 'I cast aside for the most part,' Lenin explains, 'God, the Absolute, the Pure Idea, etc.'[74] The standpoint of Western Marxism with regard to absolute idealism may be traced back to Marx and Engels themselves: 'The absolute idea,' mocks Engels, 'is only absolute in so far as [Hegel] has absolutely nothing to say about it.'[75]

The mistaken notions about Hegel fostered by Marx and Engels caused Lenin, for example, to dismiss the Introduction to Hegel's *Lectures on the History of Philosophy*. The Introduction, claims Lenin, is 'extremely lengthy, empty and tedious on the relation of philosophy to religion in general, an introduction of almost 200 pages – impossible!!'[76] But the Introduction is crucial to an understanding of Hegel; moreover, had Lenin carefully followed it, he would have come across the following remark:

Philosophy has thus placed itself in opposition to Religion ... Of their relations ... we must not hesitate, as if such a discussion were too delicate, nor try to help ourselves by beating about the bush; nor must we seek to find evasions or shifts, so that in the end no one can tell what we mean. This is nothing else than to appear to wish to conceal the fact that Philosophy has directed its efforts against Religion.

Instead of considering himself a Christian philosopher, Hegel reckons Christianity to be inferior to all modern philosophy, including, of course, his own. While philosophy has a rich history of continual development and progress, 'The content of Christianity, which is the Truth ... remained unaltered as such, and has therefore little history or as good as none.' What Hegel regards as 'the Truth' of Christianity will be considered in detail in the next section; but this truth, for Hegel, is lower than that attained by philosophy:

It was in the Christian religion that the doctrine was advanced that all men are equal before God, because Christ has set them free with the freedom of Christianity. These principles make freedom independent of any such things as birth, standing or culture. The progress made through them is enormous, but they still come short of this, that to be free constitutes the very idea of man.[77]

Hegel argues that through the centuries Christianity has been 'an impelling power which has brought about the most tremendous revolutions; but the conception and knowledge of the natural freedom of man is a knowledge of himself which is not old.' For Hegel, the modern notion of freedom is derived not from Christianity, but from principles developed by Rousseau and later given theoretical form by Kant. The doctrine of Rousseau informed the ideals of the great Revolution of 1789; ideals then incorporated into philosophy by German idealism.[78] Hegel saw his own philosophy as a continuation in theory of the French Revolution: philosophy owes no debt to religion. In fact, Hegel's formulation of the relationship of German philosophy with the French Revolution corresponds to that of Marx, who is also no Christian. 'In politics the Germans have thought what other nations have done. Germany was their theoretical conscience.'[79] Hook makes a grave error when he suggests in his influential *From Hegel to Marx* that 'Marx was probably the first thinker to characterise the philosophy of Kant as "the German theory of the French revolution".'[80] But his error is symptomatic of the view of Hegel as either as a religious mystic or as a hopeless idealist.

There is little question that a great deal of Hegel's philosophy appears to substantiate the thesis that he is a theologian, just as there are passages in Plato which may be interpreted in this manner. One problem, as I have suggested above, is that Hegel often does not separate religious thinking from philosophy. Human thought for Hegel is a unity and should be treated as such; religion merely expresses in picture-thought ideas which are fully conceptualized only in science and philosophy. But there is an additional problem which dogs especially the writings he published in his lifetime, and – though to a lesser extent – his lectures and the notes he prepared for them. Anticipations of censorship by the Prussian authorities were never far from Hegel's mind.[81] Doubts about his theological orthodoxy already lost him a place in the Royal Prussian Academy of Sciences. An outright declaration of atheism would have placed his career as a professor in considerable jeopardy; a similar avowal of unorthodoxy had earlier cost Fichte his academic chair.[82] The result of these pressures on Hegel is recalled by Heine, who was one of Hegel's students:

I stood behind the maestro as he composed it [the music of atheism: G.L.] of course he did so in very obscure and abstruse signs so that not everyone could decipher them – I sometimes saw him anxiously looking over his shoulder, for fear that he had been understood ... It was not until much later that I understood why he had argued in the *Philosophy of History* that Christianity was an advance if only because it taught of a God who had died, while pagan gods were immortal. What progress it would be, then, if we could say that God had never existed at all![85]

Lukács observes that the authenticity of Heine's account 'has often been questioned by bourgeois scholarship.'[84] This interpretation of Hegel, however, need not rest on Heine's testimony alone. The assumption that God and religion have no place in Hegel's philosophy is the only one consistent with Hegel's direct statements on the matter. Further, if – as I have shown above – Hegel denies the existence of religious conceptions in Plato, there is no reason to suppose that he would then import these conceptions into his own philosophy. His depiction of Plato's attitude toward God and philosophy indirectly corroborates Heine's testimony about his own feelings toward religion. According to Hegel, Plato

expresses the most exalted ideas regarding the value of Philosophy, as also the deepest and strongest sense of the inferiority of all else ... in a manner such as nowadays we should not venture to adopt. There is in him none of the so-called modest attitude of this science towards other spheres of knowledge, nor of man towards God. Plato has a full consciousness of how near human reason is to God, and indeed of its unity with Him.

As though looking over his shoulder in just the way Heine describes, Hegel goes on:

Men do not mind reading this in Plato, an ancient, because it is no longer a present thing, but were it coming from a modern philosopher [i.e., Hegel himself: D.M.] it would be taken much amiss. Philosophy to Plato is man's highest possible possession and true reality; it alone [not God: D.M.] has to be sought of man.[85]

In his discussion of the philosophy of Plato and of Aristotle, Hegel alludes

to the division between exoteric and esoteric philosophy traditionally supposed to apply to their writings. Exoteric philosophy deals with non-con-
troversial and conventional issues, but esoteric philosophy explores dangerous and subversive ideas and, therefore, the philosopher must be careful
how much and to whom he or she reveals any esoteric thoughts. Hegel
rejects this division and observes that thinkers are driven by the desire to
communicate their ideas to others: 'they cannot keep them in their pockets.'[86] But in his discussion of the relationship between religion and philosophy in the *Philosophy of Mind*, Hegel falls back on the distinction between
esoteric and exoteric philosophy. He cautions that this discussion, which
attempts to refute the charges of pantheism and atheism levelled against his
philosophy, is 'exoteric,' since 'exoteric discussion is the only method available in dealing with the external apprehension of notions as mere facts –
by which notions are perverted into their opposite.' Hegel's meaning is clear:
the accusations of atheism and pantheism concern pictorial conceptions
only; accordingly they are dealt with on the exoteric level to keep the
Philistines happy. But 'the esoteric study of God and identity, as of cogni-
tions, and notions, is philosophy itself'[87] – and if this esoteric study, Hegel
implies, indicates the non-existence of God, then so much the better. For
Hegel, freedom of thought is the first condition of philosophy, and means
that neither theology nor God are philosophy's proper object: 'the Philosophy which we find within Religion does not concern us,' and further, 'the
simple existence which is not sensuous and which the Jews thought of as
God (for all Religion is thinking), is ... not a subject to be treated of by
Philosophy.'[88]

According to Hegel, the exoteric notion of God is the simple image that
belongs to religious faith; but the esoteric notion, the philosophical conception of God, does not concern a Supreme Being, rather *the real object
of this esoteric conception is the human individual*. The various definitions
of God found in religion and philosophy represent attempts by human
thought to grasp its own nature: 'Without the world,' i.e., the natural and
social world of men and women, 'God is not God.'[89] The notion of freedom
and the conception of the individual which Hegel finds in the doctrine of
Christianity is the subject of the next section. Before turning to this discussion, however, it is necessary to touch on a final point concerning Hegel's
personal religious belief or lack of it. 'I am a Lutheran,' Hegel declares in
the Introduction to the *History of Philosophy*, "and will remain the same.'
Although this admission need not affect anyone's ability to construct a
secular theory of history and society, it throws considerable doubt on the
conjecture that Hegel is an atheist. As I will show in the next chapter,

however, Luther is not so much a religious figure for Hegel as he is the admittedly limited proponent of a new and revolutionary conception of the social individual: 'It was with Luther first of all that freedom of spirit began to exist in embryo, and its form indicated,' continues Hegel ironically, 'that it would remain in embryo.'[90]

Hegel's estimate of Luther is taken up by the young Marx: 'Germany's *revolutionary* past is theoretical – it is the *Reformation*. In that period,' continues Marx, 'the revolution originated in the brain of a monk [Luther], today in the brain of a philosopher ... Luther, without question, overcame servitude through devotion but only by substituting servitude through *conviction* ... He liberated the body from its chains because he fettered the heart with chains.'[91] Hegel's understanding of the 'Lutheran faith without any other accessories' reveals his own (atheistic) standpoint: 'God is ... in spirit alone, He is not a beyond but the truest reality of the individual.'[92] The subversive content of Hegel's depiction of God is seized by Marx:

To be radical is to grasp things by the root. But for man the root of man is himself. What proves beyond doubt the radicalism of German theory, and thus its practical energy, is that it begins from the resolute *positive* abolition of religion. The criticism of religion ends with the doctrine that *man is the supreme being for man*. It ends, therefore, with the *categorical imperative to overthrow all those conditions* in which man is an abased, enslaved, abandoned, contemptible being.[93]

Marx, it is true, wrote this passage while still an ardent disciple of Feuerbach.[94] But both he and Feuerbach were then engaged in battering down a door already thrown open by Hegel, a point subsequently recognized by the mature Marx. 'Compared with Hegel,' he admits, 'Feuerbach is extremely poor.'[95]

3 THE IDEA OF CHRISTIANITY

Hegel's attitude towards religion is complex and antithetical to the modern notion of religion as a quaint if beautiful expression of myth and fantasy. The contemporary standpoint is an inheritance from the Enlightenment which sought to banish faith entirely from its new-found realm of science and technology. For Feuerbach and the young Marx, as for the Enlightenment thinkers, religion is merely the alienated expression of the human desire to escape an imperfect world. On this view, religion is merely ideology or false consciousness: 'It is the *opium* of the people.'[96] In their approach to religion, both Feuerbach and the young Marx make use of Feuerbach's ' "genetic-critical" method. This consists simply in tracing conceptions and beliefs back to their origin in the experience and attitudes of men.'[97] The genetic-critical method reduces religion to the 'natural experiential phenomenon or set of phenomena which it takes over and transports into what is allegedly another world.' This method, Kamenka observes, 'has become one of the standard ways of dealing with "ideologies" as opposed to theories – we show how they arose and what needs they satisfy or what longings they appeal to.'[98]

Treating human thought as ideology, where ideology is seen as false consciousness, and reducing it to its 'material base' is easy; it is more difficult, however, to discover the positive or rational elements in thought through study of the reality from which it originates. 'We get to know the affirmative side later on both in life and in science,' Hegel remarks; 'thus we find it easier to refute than to justify.'[99] The genetic-critical approach to religion conceals, even from itself, the elements of human rationality in religion; accordingly, it finds little in religious notions that might appeal to modern men and women. This sort of history of ideas, notes Hegel, 'occupies itself with truths which *were* truths – namely, for others, not with such as would come to be the possession of those who are occupied with them.' To understand religion, the investigator should 'enter ... into an inner relation' with it and attempt to absorb the truths faith expresses. 'For here it is with the value of his *own* spirit that man is concerned, and he is not at liberty humbly to remain outside and to wander about at a distance.' The point in the investigation of religions is 'to recognise the meaning, the truth, and the connection with truth; in short, to get to know what is *rational* in them. They are human beings who have hit upon such religions, therefore there must be *reason* in them, and amidst all that is accidental in them a higher necessity.'[100]

Hegel argues that religions must be justified by research; that is, the rational elements in religions should be brought out even if they represent a fairly elementary form of truth. 'We must do them this justice, for what is human, rational in them, is *our own* too, although it exists in our higher consciousness as a moment only. To get a grasp of the history of religions in this sense, means to reconcile ourselves even with what is horrible, dreadful, or absurd in them, and to justify it.' The justification of religion, however, does not imply our acquiescence to it. 'We are on no account,' Hegel emphasizes, 'to regard it as right or true, as it presents itself in its purely immediate form – there is no question of doing this – but we are at least to recognise its beginning, the source from which it has originated as being in human nature.'[101]

In his treatment of religion, then, Hegel is not occupied, as are Feuerbach and the young Marx, with a search only for its negative aspects. In his *Early Theological Writings* which contain 'what must be one of the harshest accusations ever to have been levelled against the Church,'[102] Hegel had already dealt with this side of religion. Nor did he lose his awareness of the negative aspect of Christianity. In the *History of Philosophy*, for example, he writes: 'All the passions [the Church] has within itself – arrogance, avarice, violence, deceit, rapacity, murder, envy, hatred – all these sins of barbarism are present in it, and indeed they belong to its scheme of government.'[103]

Hegel recognizes the role of religion as what Marx calls 'the opium of the people,' and observes in the *Philosophy of Right* that 'it may seem suspicious that religion is principally sought and recommended for times of public calamity, disorder, and oppression, and that people are referred to it as a solace in face of wrong or as a hope in compensation for loss.' Since religion is often used to justify tyranny, Hegel continues, 'we ought not to speak of religion at all in general terms and ... we really need a power to protect us from it in some of its forms and to espouse against them the rights of reason and self-consciousness.' For Hegel, as for Marx, religion of any kind has absolutely no place in the constitution of a rational society. Nevertheless, 'it is of course also open to it to remain something inward, to accommodate itself to government and law, and to acquiesce in these with sneers and idle longings, or with a sigh of resignation.'[104]

Hegel's approach to religion is identical to that recommended by the mature Marx in a passage where he rejects the genetic-critical method applied earlier by Feuerbach and himself: 'A history of religion that is written in abstraction from [the] material basis [of society] is uncritical. It is, in reality, much easier to discover by analysis the earthly kernel of the misty creations of religion than to do the opposite, i.e. to develop from the actual, given relations of life the forms in which these have been apotheosized.'[105] This passage comes from *Capital*, but Marx had previously rejected Feuerbach's method in his *Theses on Feuerbach*: 'Feuerbach starts out from the fact of religious self-alienation, the duplication of the world into a religious, imaginary world and a real one. His work consists in the dissolution of the religious world into its secular basis. He overlooks the fact that after completing this work, the chief thing still remains to be done.'[106] Marx's early critique of religion was written when he still thought Hegel's emphasis on economics and civil society was misguided. 'The "one-sidedness" and "limit" of Hegel consist ... in the fact that his "standpoint is that of modern political economy." '[107] Later Marx ruefully admits that his study of Hegel 'led me to the conclusion that ... legal relations ... political forms [and even religion: D.M.] originate in the material conditions of life, the totality of which Hegel ... embraces with the term "civil society"; that the anatomy of this civil society, however, has to be sought in political economy.'[108]

The method Hegel applies to the study of religion is the same as that he employs in the investigation of Plato's philosophy. As I have outlined above, Hegel separates the rational and 'eternal' aspects of Plato's thought from its mythological expression. Further, he demonstrates that the elements in Plato which are alien to modern conceptions, such as the attack on democracy, are rooted in the material and political realities of Plato's time, i.e., the development of private property and the 'subversive' notion of individual rights. 'It is thus,' writes Hegel, 'a substantial position on which Plato takes his stand, seeing that the substantial of his time forms his basis, but this standpoint is at the same time relative only, in so far as it is but a Greek standpoint, and the later principle [of individual freedom] is consciously banished.' Similarly, in his examination of the Christian religion, Hegel shows that Christianity has its beginnings within a certain material framework, namely slave society, and that it incorporates the rational elements of Greek philosophy. In fact, Christianity is the existential or social form which carried the thought of the ancient Greek philosophers 'into actuality.'[109]

Because modern philosophy and science arose in opposition to its teachings, Christianity is the central object of Hegel's critique of religion: the most rational of all world religions is also the chief opponent of reason and philosophy. The rational character of Christianity accounts for its survival in the modern age; but the limits of its rationality foretell its eventual collapse. Despite these limits, 'philosophy indeed can recognize its own forms in the categories of the religious consciousness, and even its own teachings in the doctrines of religion – which therefore it does not disparage.' Religion, however, fails to extend the same courtesy to science and philosophy; ignorance of its own nature leads it to oppose philosophy: 'the religious consciousness does not apply the criticism of thought to itself, does not comprehend itself, and is therefore, as it stands, exclusive.'[110] Since Hegel's time, of course, Christianity has learned to adapt itself to science; the outburst in the 1920s against Darwinism and the opposition of the Roman Catholic Church to effective forms of birth control may prove the last gasps of Christian opposition to science. However, the compromising attitude of the modern Church stems less from the nature of Christianity than from its loss of support in the consciousness of men and women. As Hegel's student Heine puts it: 'Religion, when it can no longer burn us alive, comes to us begging.'[111]

A negative critique, such as that of Feuerbach and the young Marx, can furnish no answer for the continued existence of religion. Nor can it penetrate the illusions of religion and grasp its rational core. 'Though philosophy must not allow herself to be overawed by religion, or accept the position of [God's] existence on sufferance, she cannot afford to neglect these popular conceptions. The tales and allegories of religion, which have enjoyed for thousands of years the veneration of nations, are not to be set aside as antiquated even now.'[112] The inner rationality of the Christian religion is a product of its historical development. Christianity incorporates the discoveries of neo-Platonist philosophy and these in turn 'are ... not only moments in the development of reason, but also in that of humanity; they are forms in which the whole condition of the world expresses itself through thought.' Neo-Platonism in the Roman world reflected 'the development of private rights relating to the property of individual persons.'[113] The evolution of merchant and trading fortunes, which threw into question the Greek polity and influenced the thought of Socrates and Plato, continued apace in Rome and found expression in its philosophy.

Roman power crushed all national feelings and showed 'itself as the withdrawal into the aims and interests of private life.' Just as 'abstract Christians only care for their own salvation,' the people of Rome lost the feeling of unity with society that had existed in Greece, and attended only to their own personal interests.

In this condition of disunion in the world, when man is driven within his inmost self, he has to seek the unity and satisfaction, no longer to be found in the world, in an abstract way. The Roman world is thus the world of abstraction, where one cold rule was extended over all the civilized world. The living individualities of national spirit in the nations have been stifled and killed; a foreign power, as an abstract universal, has pressed hard upon individuals. In such a condition of dismemberment it was necessary to fly to this abstraction ... to this inward freedom of the subject as such.

Along with the renewed, if abstract, interest in the individual, the industrial achievements of Rome brought with them 'contempt for nature ... inasmuch as nature is no longer anything for itself, seeing that her powers are merely the servants of man, who, like a magician, can make them yield obedience, and be subservient to his wishes.'[114] These aspects of Roman thought – 'the pure egotism of the will in opposition to others'[115] and the nullity of external nature – were annexed by Christianity. But where neo-Platonism failed to discover concrete truth in the consciousness of the individual, i.e., the unity of the free individual with society, with the divine, this hurdle was overcome by Christianity:

within Christianity the basis of Philosophy is that in man has sprung up the consciousness of the truth ... and then that man requires to participate in this truth. Man must be qualified to have this truth present to him; he must further be convinced of this possibility ... The first point of interest in the Christian religion thus is that the content of the Idea should be revealed to man; more particularly that the unity of the divine and human nature should come to the consciousness of man.[116]

Christian identification of the human with the divine emerges from the principle of a victim of Roman power – the Jewish people and their religion. Where the Romans worship a multitude of alien gods who reflect the chaotic particularity of subjective interest – the Jews turn to their 'invisible and non-sensuous God ... whom they also make an object of conception as a person.'[117] This single, abstract Deity compensates the Jews in their terrible sorrow and loss under foreign rule, and, combined with the concrete particularity of Roman thought, effects the reconciliation of the individual with the divine later fully realized in Christianity. 'It was the Jewish nation which preserved the idea of God as representing the ancient sorrow of the world. For here we have the religion of abstract sorrow, of the one Lord, and because of this the reality of life appears relatively to this abstraction and in this abstraction, as the infinite wilfulness of self-consciousness, and is at the same time bound up with the abstraction.'[118]

Absolute unity between the individual and society is posited by Christianity with its notion of the relationship between the individual and God. 'Man himself ... is comprehended in the Idea of God, and this comprehension may be thus expressed – that the unity of man with God is posited in the Christian religion.'[119] Because Christianity teaches the oneness of women and men with God, He 'ceases to be for them mere object, and, in that way, an object of fear and terror.' The notion of Christ, who 'revealed ... himself to men as a man among men, and thereby redeemed them ... is only another way of saying that the antithesis of subjective and objective is implicitly overcome.'[120] But because Christianity finds the truth of individual consciousness only in the existence of God and Jesus Christ, it fails to recognize the real, concrete human individual and puts Christ in the place of man and woman. 'Christianity ... revealed to man what absolute reality is; it is a man, but not yet Man or self-consciousness in general.'[121]

Abstracting from the neo-Platonist doctrine of the nullity of the external world, and neglecting to notice that nature is an objective reality which may be shaped by human will, Christianity fostered the 'bad idealism' for which everything, including nature, is merely a creation of thought. The stage was set for its opposition to and supersession by science and philosophy:

> In Christianity the root of truth ... was not only the truth as against the heathen gods, but as against Philosophy also, against nature, against the immediate consciousness of man. Nature is there no longer good, but merely a negative; self-consciousness, the thought of man, his pure self, all this receives a negative position in Christianity. Nature has no validity, and affords no interest; its universal laws, as the reality under which the individual existences of nature are collected, have likewise no authority; the heavens, the sun, the whole of nature is a corpse.[122]

Another aspect of the historical development of Christianity is of supreme importance. The Christian religion was above all a cosmopolitan religion; it united 'the free universality of the East and the determinateness of Europe,' because 'its origin happens to be the country where East and West have met in conflict.'[123] Further, it reflected the imperial power of Rome over all other nations; nationality lost its importance for religion as it had for Rome. As Rome was a world power, Christianity became a world religion. Rome enslaved the world and, as the antagonist of Roman slavery, Christianity united all races and nations against its power. Sixty years after Hegel's death, Engels called attention to the parallels between Christianity and socialism:

> The history of early Christianity has notable points of resemblance with the modern working-class movement. Like the latter, Christianity was originally a movement of oppressed people: it first appeared as the religion of slaves and emancipated slaves, of poor people deprived of all rights, of peoples subjected or dispersed by Rome. Both Christianity and the workers' socialism preach forthcoming salvation from bondage and misery; Christianity places this salvation in a life beyond, after death, in heaven; socialism places it in this world, in a transformation of society ... Three hundred years after its appearance Christianity was the recognized state religion in the Roman world empire, and in barely sixty years socialism has won itself a position which makes its victory absolutely certain.[124]

The parallels between Christianity and socialism however, are closer than

Engels imagines. Hegel, for example, speaks of the 'perfect democracy' of the early Christian Church, and also of the radical implications of its doctrine. 'We may say that nowhere are to be found such revolutionary utterances as in the Gospels; for everything that had been respected is treated as a matter of indifference – as worthy of no regard.'[125] Christ's teaching has 'the character of negation against everything that exists at hand. In so far as it affirms the universal ... it is a revolutionary doctrine, which partially sets aside all that is established and in part nullifies and overthrows it.' Nor is the Christian revolution merely one of abstract consciousness; it also manifests itself in the real world through bloody conflict and struggle. 'This new religion ... has its vitality ... in that energy which constitutes the sole, eternal interest of the man who has to fight and struggle in order to obtain it because it is not yet associated with world consciousness and does not exist in harmony with the state of the world.'[126]

Christianity forms the basis of Hegel's absolute idealism; and this philosophy, as I will show, constitutes the foundation of Marx's historical materialism. Through Christianity men and women 'attain to the consciousness of heaven upon earth, the elevation of man to God'; absolute idealism, in turn, recognizes that the social and natural world as comprehended by science and philosophy, 'has its root in God, but only the root.'[127] Before human beings can understand their own relation to nature and society, they must conceptualize this relation in picture-thought as the relation of God to the world; later they will recognize that God is no one else but themselves. The notion of God represents a necessary stage in the historical development of human consciousness: just as many children in modern society are at first attracted by the idea of a Supreme Being, but then abandon it when they achieve a mature consciousness of themselves, so too did earlier men and women form an image of God. 'The idea which a man has of God,' notes Hegel, 'corresponds with that which he has of himself, of his freedom ... when a man knows truly about God, he knows truly about himself too: the two sides correspond with each other. At first God is something quite undetermined; but in the course of the development of the human mind, the consciousness of that which God is gradually forms and matures itself, losing more and more of its initial indefiniteness, and with this the development of true *self*-consciousness advances also.'[128]

Hegel argues that Christianity 'brings about the whole revolution that has taken place in the world's history'; the truth of Christianity is its recognition of the supremacy of individual human consciousness and activity as expressed in the life of the mortal Christ. No less than Christianity, of course, other religions have adopted an anthropomorphic concept of God.

The Greeks, for example, imagined gods who were like men and women, but 'they were not anthropomorphic enough.'[129] On one hand, the Greek gods retained the trivial aspects of the human character as well as its divine or creative qualities. But mere identity of the individual with God is inadequate to the principle of self-consciousness, which involves a prodigious development of self-dependence and social morality. 'This unity must not be superficially conceived, as if God were only Man, and Man, without further condition, were God. Man, on the contrary, is God only in so far as he annuls the merely Natural and Limited in his Spirit and elevates himself to God ... for the Natural is the Unspiritual.'[130] On the other hand, the anthropomorphism of the Greeks (as well as that of other non-Christian religions) only went so far as the *form* of the human being: the gods remained something separate from the real, concrete individual. For the Greeks, 'man is not divine as man, but only as a far-away form and not as "this," and subjective man.' Christianity conceives of God as He has become in the flesh, in Christ; and Christ bears this resemblance to man and woman: He is mortal. Paraphrasing Hegel and without distorting his meaning, we can say: 'that God himself is dead ... constitutes the great leading Idea of Christianity.'[131]

Another fundamental truth of Christianity is that men and women 'become free, that is to say, upright and moral ... by the way of education' in society. The individual can prove him- or herself to God only through responsible social interaction with others: 'the evil element is the aspect of separation and estrangement, and this estrangement is to be negated.' The purely natural individual never reaches the level of self-consciousness because he or she lacks the social framework within which to develop a rich individuality. Through worship and the repentance of sin, Christianity teaches the individual the absolute desirability of proving his or her worth in society:

the natural will is not the will as it ought to be, for it ought to be free, and the will of passion is not free. By nature Spirit is not as it ought to be; by means of freedom only does it become such. That the will is by nature evil is the form under which this truth is presented [in Christianity]. But man is only guilty if he adhere to this his natural character. Justice, morality, are not the natural will, for in it a man is selfish, his desire is only toward his individual life as such. It is by means of worship, accordingly, that this evil element is to be annulled.

For Hegel, then, the principle of Rousseau according to which man was born free, but is everywhere in chains is incorrect, and had already been confuted by Christianity. In Christianity 'the natural man is represented as evil.'[132] It is only in and through society that freedom and morality are attained. Thus Marx's notion that human nature is 'the ensemble of the social relations,'[133] simply expresses a basic truth of Christianity.

Hegel denies that the truths of the Christian religion 'were so to speak ready made in the mind of God': Christianity is nothing other than a stage in the autonomous development of human consciousness. But Christianity can be grasped in this way only from the perspective of modern times. In the same way as the wheel's inventor could not see it as a moment in the development of the motor car, the early Christian was unaware that the Christian Idea represents a step in the progress of individual human consciousness. 'History,' Hegel remarks, 'is the process of mind itself, the revelation of itself from its first superficial, enshrouded consciousness, and the attainment of this standpoint of its free self-consciousness.' The notion that society is a platform on which human players fulfil and realize themselves belongs to Christianity, and informs the development of the child through the stages of maturity, no less than it does the progress of humanity. *It is the basis of Marx's and Hegel's notion of revolutionizing practice*: 'Mind,' says Hegel, 'is the living moment, proceeding from its immediate existence to beget revolutions in the world, as well as in individuals.'[134]

Hegel argues that Christianity 'has made the intelligible world of Philosophy the world of common consciousness.'[135] Through the teachings of the Church the ordinary person arrives at a knowledge of the nature of God (and therefore of the human individual) previously known only by the greatest thinkers of antiquity. This, Hegel writes, 'is the very grandeur of the Christian religion that, with all this profundity, it is easy of comprehension by our consciousness in its outward aspect, while, at the same time, it summons us to penetrate deeper.'[136] In the doctrine of original sin, for example, 'what is said of him as such, what every member of the human race really is in himself, is represented here in the form of the first man, Adam.' The individual learns about good and evil, and comes to realize that evil is natural and can be eradicated only through knowledge of God and self-development in society. This concept of the benefit of education seems elementary to us moderns, but it was not an idea easily arrived at by humankind as a whole. 'The abrogation of mere naturalness is known to us simply as education, and arises of itself; through education subjection is brought about, and with that a capacity for becoming good is developed. Now if this appears to come to pass very easily, we must recollect that it is of infinite importance that the reconciliation of the world with itself, the making good, is brought about through the simple method of education.'[137] Paradoxically, the notion of sin and repentance encourages independent and rational thought in the popular mind. The individual is from the beginning involved in a contradiction: the believer is reputed sinful by nature, and can reach the divine only by proving him- or herself worthy before God; 'yet I am at the same time referred *into myself*, for thought, knowledge, reason are *in me*, and in the feeling of sinfulness, and in reflection upon this, my freedom [to overcome evil and sin] is plainly revealed to me ... Rational knowledge, therefore, is an essential element in the Christian religion itself [because] this subjectivity, this *selfness* (not selfishness) is just the principle of rational knowledge itself.'[138]

Two principal consequences naturally follow the propagation of Christianity. The first is recognition of the infinite rights and worth of the ordinary individual. Each person, regardless of birth, sex, or class, is made in God's image; every human soul is divine and of equal importance for God. Thus to take up the principle of Christianity is to deny forever the right of someone to take another into slavery. Christianity teaches that the human being 'is *actually* free,' and, writes Hegel in a remarkable passage,

When individuals and nations have once got in their heads the abstract concept of full-blown liberty, there is nothing like it in its uncontrollable strength, just because it is the very essence of mind, and that as its very actuality. Whole continents, Africa and the East, have never had this Idea, and are without it still. The Greeks and Romans, even the Stoics, did not have it ... It was through Christianity that this Idea came into the world. According to Christianity, the individual *as such* has an infinite value as the object and aim of divine love, destined as mind to live in absolute relationship with God himself, and have God's mind dwelling in him: i.e. man is implicitly destined to supreme freedom.[139]

Sidney Hook, who suggests that both Marx and Hegel assert 'the priority of the group over the individual,' and deny 'natural rights, or conscience,' also criticizes as 'mere abstractions'[140] Hegel's argument that Christianity was instrumental in making freedom an essential and active principle in the formation of individual consciousness and society. But Christianity is itself a product of the material framework of ancient society, and once installed in the consciousness of men and women it had irrevocable consequences for the secular as well as the religious realm. 'If, in religion as such,' writes Hegel,

man is aware of this [free] relationship to the absolute mind as his true being, he has also, even when he steps into the sphere of secular existence, the divine mind present with him, as the substance of the state, of the family, etc. These institutions are due to the guidance of that spirit [of freedom], and are constituted after its measure; whilst by their existence the moral temper comes to be indwelling in the individual, so that in this sphere of particular existence, of present sensation and volition, he is *actually* free.

As Hegel writes in *The Philosophy of History*, 'the inner shrine of man ... is the *point du depart* for determining secular relations.'[141]

Christianity is merely a vanishing stage or moment in the historical development of humanity.[142] It, and religion generally, are only necessary so long as people do not realize that both nature and society can be made subject to their conscious and rational will. 'Because thinking consciousness is not the outward universal form for all mankind, the consciousness of the true, the spiritual and the rational, must have the form of Religion, and this is the universal justification of this form.'[143] The same position is held by Marx, who observes in *Capital*:

The religious reflections of the real world can, in any case, vanish only when the practical relations of everyday life between man and man, and man and nature, generally present themselves to him in a transparent and rational form. The veil is not removed from the countenance of the social life-process, i.e. the process of material production, until it becomes production by freely associated men, and stands under their conscious and planned control. This, however, requires ... a long and tormented historical development.[144]

To recognize the limits of Christianity, however, is not to deny its role in making the notion of freedom a kind of second nature for men and women. 'Christianity in its adherents,' writes Hegel, 'has realized an ever-present sense that they are not and cannot be slaves; if they are made slaves, if the decision as regards their property rests with an arbitrary will, not with laws or courts of justice, they would find the very substance of their life outraged. This will to liberty is no longer an *impulse* which demands its satisfaction, but the permanent character – the spiritual consciousness grown into a non-impulsive nature.'[145]

The second great result of the spread of Christianity concerns the development of the independent '*secular State*.'[146] Christianity, it is true, guarantees heaven in the beyond, and therefore relegates freedom to another world instead of making it a principle of state and government. But from the teachings of Christianity it occurred to men and women that heaven should be constructed on earth, in a rational state which would protect the rights of the individual. 'On the appearance of Christianity it is first of all said: "My kingdom is not of this world"; but the realization has and ought to be in the present world. In other words the laws, customs, constitutions, and all that belongs to the actuality of the spiritual consciousness should be made rational.'[147] And further, 'Freedom in the State is preserved and established by Religion, since moral rectitude in the State is only the carrying out of that which constitutes the fundamental principle of Religion. The process displayed in History is only the manifestation of Religion as Human Reason – the production of the religious principle which dwells in the heart of man, under the form of Secular Freedom.'[148]

The growth of the modern state during the Middle Ages was neither the unintended consequence of mindless human action guided by 'the cunning of reason,' nor was it the result, as some Marxists would have it, of the endless shuffle of modes and relations of production across the stage of history. The modern state 'cannot be in the beginning, but must come forth after being worked upon by mind and thought'; and it was 'in Christianity [that] these absolute claims of the intellectual world and of spirit had become the universal consciousness.' Accordingly, 'even under the feudal system ... justice, civil order, legal freedom gradually emerged. In Italy and Germany cities obtained their rights as citizen republics, and caused these to be recognized by the temporal and ecclesiastical power; wealth displayed itself in the Netherlands, Florence and the free cities on the Rhine. In this way men gradually began to emerge from the feudal system ...'[149]

3

From Theology to Absolute Idealism

1 THEOLOGY, ENLIGHTENMENT, AND ABSOLUTE IDEALISM

According to Feuerbach, religious speculation or theology is *'belief in ghosts'*[1]; it is worse than dreaming, for 'where dreams can illuminate reality, once they are properly interpreted, theology obscures reality by resisting such interpretation, by treating the fantasies that constitute religion as direct representations of (another) reality.'[2] 'I have only betrayed the secret of the Christian religion,' writes Feuerbach in *The Essence of Christianity*, 'only extricated it from theology's *web of lies and delusions*.'[3] Somewhat the same view of theology is put forward by Engels, although he extends it to include philosophy as a whole. 'As to the realms of ideology which soar still higher in the air – religion, philosophy, etc. – ' writes Engels in one of his letters on historical materialism, 'these have a prehistoric stock ... of what we should today call bunk.'[4]

The conjecture that theology, or at least early Christian theology, is 'bunk' has become part of received wisdom. For Hegel, however, this view is utterly mistaken. It is true that theology is merely exegesis – it must work on a given form, i.e., the Bible – but nevertheless each person brings to the Bible his or her own notions and opinions. These, in turn, derive from, or concern, reality, 'what is given by the senses.' No one can expound a doctrine without slipping into it his or her personal conceptions. 'We find what we look for, and just because I make it clear to myself, I make my conception, my thought, a factor in it; otherwise it is a dead and external thing, which is not present for me at all.' To make something clear to ourselves is simply to recognize ourselves in it. Just as different people in modern times can make diverse readings, say of Marx, earlier thinkers found a myriad of opposed ideas and notions in the Bible. 'Thus have men made of the Bible what may be called a nose of wax.'[5] Hegel's problem is to find in speculative theology the elements of reality that the theologians put into it. 'Commentaries on the Bible do not so much make us acquainted with the content of the Scriptures, as rather with the manner in which these things were conceived in the age in which they were written.'[6] Hegel's method in regard to theology, therefore, like his approach to religion generally, is precisely the 'materialist ... and scientific one' recommended by the mature Marx.[7]

Arguments about the nature and existence of God are in reality arguments about the nature of the individual and his or her relation to society: they represent an attempt by earlier generations to come to grips with the social reality in which they found themselves.[8] This is Hegel's meaning when he writes, 'a reason-derived knowledge of God is the highest problem of philosophy,' and 'God,' in turn, is 'our true and essential self.'[9] The theological arguments of the Fathers of the Church, and those of medieval schoolmen such as Duns Scotus and Thomas Aquinas, were alienated and external to their real content – the life activity of the human individual – simply because of the undeveloped and alienated nature of their own society. In the world of the schoolmen, for example,

life as a whole fell into two parts, two kingdoms. Directly opposite the spiritual worldly kingdom there stands the independent worldly kingdom, emperor against pope, papacy and Church ... there the world beyond, here the world beside us ... The culture which now begins to show itself is confronted by this incomplete reality, as an actual world in opposition to the world of thought; and it does not recognize the one as present in the other. It possesses two establishments, two standards of measure and weight, and these it does not bring together but leaves mutually estranged.[10]

The estranged and irrational character of feudalism found political expression in the Crusades which exhibited all the 'frenzy, foolishness and grossness' of the system that spawned them. The Crusaders, with 'utter lack of judgement and forethought, and with the loss of thousands on the way,' reached Jerusalem, it is true; but why did they go there? The Christians clearly 'did not understand themselves'; they went in search of holy spots which had absolutely no relevance to their immediate needs. 'Barbarians all the time, they did not seek the universal, the world-controlling position of Syria and Egypt, this central point of the earth, the free connection of commerce.' 'Bonaparte,' Hegel wryly continues, 'did this when man became rational.' The Crusaders were forced 'by the Saracens and by their own violence and repulsiveness' to admit that they had 'deceived themselves.

This experience taught them that they must hold to the actual reality which they despised, and seek in this the realization of their intelligible world.'[11] Like the Crusaders, the schoolmen were reluctant to consider anything in the world of experience worthy of real interest. The arts and sciences were banished from universities; and 'law and right, the recognition of actual man, were not esteemed as pertaining to the social relationships of life, but to some other sphere.' The rationality of ordinary existence yielded to the 'utter barbarism of thought' which 'keeps to another world, and does not have the Notion of reason – the Notion that the certainty of self is all truth.'[12]

Its alienated form did not prevent theology from expressing some fundamental truths – truths that Hegel incorporates into absolute idealism. Before considering these ideas, however, an alternative conception of Hegel's notions about religion and theology, as put forward in Charles Taylor's *Hegel*, deserves a brief discussion. Taylor rejects arguments, such as the one I have made above, that Hegel is an atheist for whom 'man as a natural being is at the spiritual summit of things.' Instead, he sees Hegel as an (unorthodox) Lutheran Christian who is somehow unable to recognize his own heresy. Hegel's 'is a genuine third position' between orthodoxy and Enlightenment atheism, 'which is why it is so easy to misinterpret.' For Taylor, this third position means that 'God comes to knowledge of himself through man's knowledge of him.'[13] This is correct as far as it goes, except that Taylor does not draw what seems to be the obvious conclusion: if God is only human self-knowledge, then God himself must be human. For what kind of God is He if He cannot even get to know Himself? As Hegel puts it, 'God's becoming man is, in fact, an essential moment of religion'; and: 'in religion as in the presentation of truth, what is essentially represented is the unfolding of the history of what humanity is.'[14] Pressed to its conclusion, Taylor's understanding of what he calls Hegel's 'bizarre' doctrine is bizarre indeed: 'This process of self-knowledge,' writes Taylor, 'is one which is slowly and painfully realized through history; for it is part of the self-realization of *Geist*. And in the early stages, God's self-consciousness will be very rudimentary and inadequate, very distorted one might even say. But even in this primitive form, it is recognizably a consciousness of God.'[15] It may be 'recognizably a consciousness of God,' but is it recognizable to anyone as God's consciousness?

Taylor's interpretation of Hegel's philosophy of religion has many adherents. Its justification is found in the following passage from the *Encyclopaedia*: 'God is God only so far as he knows himself, his self-knowledge is, further, a self-consciousness in man and man's knowledge *of* God, which proceeds to man's self-knowledge *in* God.'[16] Andrew Seth, in a work published in 1892, comments on a similar passage in Hegel, and arrives at an entirely different conclusion from that of Taylor – one which corresponds with Marx's opinion on the subject. ' "God is not a Spirit beyond the stars," says Hegel, "He is Spirit in all spirits." – a true thought finely expressed. But if the system leaves us without any self-conscious existence in the universe beyond that realized in the self-consciousness of individual philosophers, the saying means that God, in any ordinary acceptation of the word, is eliminated from our philosophy altogether.' For Seth (as for Marx) the conclusion is unavoidable: the Hegelian system 'sacrifices ... the best interests of humanity ... to a logical abstraction styled the Idea, in which both God and man disappear.'[17]

Although Taylor is wrong in his depiction of Hegel's philosophy of religion, he is right in saying that Hegel takes up a genuine third position between Enlightenment atheism (and deism) and religious orthodoxy. I shall sketch out the main elements of this position and show their connection to what Hegel calls the truths of religious speculation or theology. Hegel defines consciousness as 'the essential *relation* of knowledge and its object.'[18] Arising from the 'severance or division of consciousness,' religion is by definition an alienated consciousness. 'The believing consciousness weighs and measures by a twofold standard; it has two sorts of eyes, two sorts of ears, speaks with two voices, has duplicated all ideas without comparing the twofold meanings. In other words, faith lives in two sorts of non-*notional* perceptions, the one the perceptions of the *slumbering* consciousness which lives purely in non-notional thoughts, the other those of the *waking* consciousness which lives solely in the world of sense; and in each of them it has its own separate housekeeping.'[19] All religion is symptomatic of a divided or alienated consciousness because faith separates the mundane activities of men and women from the higher realm of divine existence and thought. 'In their simple relation,' religion and everyday life

already constitute two kinds of pursuits, two different regions of consciousness, and we pass to and fro from one to the other *alternately* only. Thus man has in his actual worldly life a number of working days during which he occupies himself with his own special interests, with worldly aims in general, and with the satisfaction of his needs; and then he has a Sunday, when he lays all this aside, collects his thoughts, and, released from absorption in finite occupations, lives to himself and to the higher nature which is in him, to his true essential being.[20]

When people raise their thoughts to God they are actually reflecting on the infinite relations of the intellectual and social world. 'In religion man places himself in a relation to this centre, in which all other relations concentrate themselves, and in so doing he rises up to the highest level of consciousness and to the region which is free from relation to what is other than itself, to something which is absolutely self-sufficient, the unconditioned, what is free, and is its own object and end.'[21] Thought about the intellectual and social realm is free thought; for it is thought which has only itself for an object. The intellectual and social world is the creation of men and women; to conceive this world in all its infinite relations is to engage in absolutely free endeavour. 'Thinking means that, in the other, one meets with one's self. It means a liberation, which is not the flight of abstraction, but consists in that which is actual having itself not as something else, but as its own being and creation, in the other actuality with which it is bound up by the force of necessity.'[22]

Enlightenment thinkers deny the existence of a higher (social) realm posited by religion; and oppose alike the Church's 'superstition and its truth.'[23] Rousseau, for example, sees reality in terms of 'the arbitrary choice of the individual';[24] he has no notion of the unity of the individual with society, what Hegel calls the unity of the finite and the infinite. Similarly, Kant's philosophy lacks a social basis; the morality of the individual is conceived in terms of an abstract moral law, the postulate of practical reason.[25] Religion at least retains this concept even if in an alienated form: 'A present and actual church is an actuality of the kingdom of God upon earth, in such a way that this last is present for every man – every individual lives and must live in the kingdom of God. In this disposition we have the reconciliation of every individual; thereby each becomes a citizen of this kingdom, and participates in the enjoyment of this certainty.'[26]

Absolute idealism aims at uniting the social dimensions of religion with the abstract individualism of Enlightenment: 'Philosophy demands the unity and intermingling of these two points of view; it unites the Sunday of life when man in humility renounces himself, and the working-day when he stands up independently, is master of himself and considers his own interests.'[27] It was Luther who first expressed the absolute unity of the individual's life activity with worship of the divine; Hegel's philosophy had only to conceive this unity in rational (non-religious) terms. 'It is science alone that can comprehend the kingdom of God and the socially Moral world as one Idea, and that recognizes the fact that the course of Time has witnessed a process ever tending to the realization of this unity.'[28]

'The highest concrete content' of absolute idealism is the unity of the individual with society. 'It is the power which unites in itself what appears to consciousness infinitely removed from one another – the mortal and the absolute. This absolute is itself "this" first of all as this concrete, not as abstraction, but as the unity of universal and individual; this concrete consciousness is for the first time truth.'[29]

Theology obscures the identity of the individual with society by dividing the mind of the believer from its object, from God. 'The Spirit which bears witness is further itself distinguished from me as an individual; my testifying spirit is another, and there only remains to me the empty shell of passivity.' Hence, when Anselm declared he had proved the existence of God by showing that He must be something greater than what can merely be thought, he forgot that thought itself is a human property. Thus the unity of thought and being is found not in God, but in the individual and his or her relation with society. 'Though I see the truth of [Anselm's] proposition, I have not attained to the final point, the object of my desire; for there is lacking the I, the inner bond, as inwardness of thought. This lies only in the Notion, in the unity of the particular and the universal, of Being and thought.'[30]

Enlightenment thought, which Hegel also refers to as 'finite thought' or the 'understanding consciousness,' develops out of and in relation to religious consciousness and theology. Although faith is alienated or divided within itself, there is at first no realization of this division in the mind of the believer. The religious person in the Middle Ages, for example, accepts religion along with the personal conditions of life 'as a lot or destiny which he does not understand. *It is so.*' The individual subordinates his or her life to the higher region of God and heaven. But with the development of society and social relations, the individual becomes ever more acutely aware of a social and intellectual world of his or her own creation. 'Although he sets out from what *is*, from what he finds, yet he *is* no longer merely one who knows, who *has* these rights; but what he *makes* out of that which is given in knowledge and in will is *his* affair, *his* work, and he has the consciousness that he has produced it. Therefore these productions constitute his glory and his pride, and provide for him an immense, an infinite wealth – that world of his intelligence, of his knowledge, of his external possession, of his rights and deeds.'[31]

Without being conscious of the process, the individual is building a realm which begins to threaten the domain of religion and God. 'In the World, secular business cannot be ... repudiated; it demands accomplishment, and ultimately the discovery is made, that Spirit finds the goal of its struggle and its harmonization, in that very sphere which it made the object of its resistance – it finds that *secular pursuits are a spiritual occupation*.'[32] The universe takes on a more and more divided aspect: on one side the individual is free and self-determining; on the other, he or she must submit to what seems now to be an alien power. Gradually the individual comes to differentiate between the human world of knowledge and society, and the other, alien, realm of God. 'Its religion is accordingly distinguished from what we have in that region of independence by this, that it restricts knowledge, science, to the *worldly side*, and leaves for the sphere of religion, feeling and faith.'[33]

Despite the illusion of independence, however, life in a developing bourgeois society is subject to chance and arbitrariness; furthermore, the individual is keenly aware of being conditioned and determined by external forces. This feeling also runs through science and knowledge generally. 'Man demands his right; whether or not he actually gets it, is something independent of his efforts, and he is referred in the matter to an Other. In the act of knowledge he sets out from the organisation and order of nature, and this is something *given*. The content of his sciences is a matter outside of him.'[34] The feeling of outward determination, of an order alien to individual will, led the thinkers of early bourgeois society, like Descartes, Malebranche, and Spinoza,[35] to suggest that everything is the creation of God, hoping thereby to get on with the pursuit of science and knowledge. 'The matter,' writes Hegel, 'is settled with the *one* admission, that God has made everything, and this religious side is thereby satisfied *once for all*, and then in the progress of knowledge and the pursuit of aims nothing further is thought of the matter.'[36]

At this point there is no adequate theory about the relation between God and the social and natural universe: 'the relation of God to the other side of consciousness is undetermined and general' and is expressed simply as 'God has created all things.' But this cold and lifeless attitude does not recognize that everything of real interest to the individual is inevitably an object or product of his or her self-conscious activity. Moreover, if everything is created by God for certain divine ends, how is it that there is so much evil and conflict in the world? 'The idea of God and of His manner of operation as universal and necessary is contradicted by this inconsistency, which is even destructive of that universal character.' As a result God is abandoned and nothing accepted beyond what can be externally demonstrated to human consciousness. Everything is looked at in terms of cause and effect, and these categories are applied to the universe of things, and their relations with one another.

It is no longer sufficient to speak of God as the cause of lightning, or of the downfall of the Republican system of government in Rome, or of the French Revolution; here it is perceived that this cause is only an entirely general one, and does not yield the desired explanation. What we wish to know ... is ... not the reason which applies to all things, but only and exclusively to this definite thing ... Therefore this knowledge does not go above or beyond the sphere of the finite, nor does it desire to do so, since it is able to apprehend all in its finite sphere, is conversant with everything, and knows its course of action. In this manner science forms a universe of knowledge, to which God is not necessary, which lies outside of religion, and has absolutely nothing to do with it ... of the infinite and eternal, nothing whatever is left.[37]

For this type of thought – the origins of which Marx suggests are to be found in 'the men and women of the court of Charles II, Bolingbroke, the Walpoles, Hume, Gibbon, and Charles Fox'[38] – the world has lost its absolute connection in the mind of the individual. God and religion have shrivelled up into an empty kingdom of the Eternal. Everything is seen to be connected one to another, but a unified theory of the universe has died along with God. The opposition between Enlightenment and theology is complete.

Where Enlightenment thinkers retain a religious consciousness it is only to conceive God as a remote Supreme Being, 'as the Infinite, with regard to which all predicates are inadequate, and are unwarranted anthropomorphisms. In reality, however, it has, in conceiving God as the supreme Being, made Him hollow, empty, and poor.' Following the example of the Enlightenment, modern theology pushed knowledge of God to the background. 'It no longer gives our age any concern that it knows nothing of God; on the contrary, it is regarded as the mark of the highest intelligence to hold that such knowledge is not even possible.' Ignorance of the nature of God 'must ... be considered as the last stage in the degradation of man.'[39] Degeneration has reached a point where anyone trying to investigate the nature of religion and God will be either opposed or ignored. It is the philosopher's duty to rescue the dogmas of the Church from the awkward hands of the theologians and oppose them to the finite consciousness of the Enlightenment.

For Hegel, there are three fundamental truths in Christian theology: the notions of incarnation and of resurrection, and the concept of the Holy Trinity. The first two were treated in detail in the last chapter, and are involved, as we shall see, in the conception of the Trinity itself. Incarnation was discussed in the section on the Idea of Christianity which shows that the doctrine expresses the unity of the individual with society and the absolute importance of education (*Bildung*) and self-development. The doctrine of resurrection and immortality is dealt with in the section on Plato:

the idea of everlasting life concerns the eternal nature of human knowledge and social activity.

Only the 'childlike relation' represented by the concept of the Triune God, Hegel declares, could adequately express the identity of, and distinction between, the individual and God or Spirit, because it includes the element of mediation between these two extremes. Christ, the Son of God, is identical with Him, with the Creator of heaven and earth, but Christ is also a unique individual who lives a phenomenal, mundane existence and dies in torment. In death His unity with ordinary mortals is manifest, as is the divine element in every sinner: 'Precisely the portrayal of the process is what man, what Spirit is – namely, both God and dead implicitly.'[40] Resurrection completes the moment of mediation in which the spirit returns purified to itself, to the right hand of God. United in the Holy Spirit of love, the Three become One.

As interpreted by Hegel the Trinity becomes a pictorial representation of the self-realization of the social individual and constitutes 'the one syllogism of the absolute self-mediation of spirit,' a truth which later emerges as 'the object of *philosophy*.'[41] The first, or universal, moment of the Trinity – the concept of God the Father – expresses the infinite potential, the creative drive of the individual, his or her capacity for self-development in and through labour in society. Accordingly, the essence of God is also that of the individual. 'God's essence as Spirit is to be for another, to reveal himself; he does not create the world once and for all, but rather is the eternal Creator, the one who reveals himself eternally. He is this *actus*: this is his concept, his determination.'[42]

The pure thought of God the Father, however, is not only eternal content but also infinite abstraction. In order to exist as real, God must have an object, an Other; the moment of *universality* must pass over into that of *particularity*. In this second phase God creates the world and gives up to it His only begotten Son. Here is the world of nature and society into which the individual is born and with which he or she must struggle in order to survive. 'On one hand is heaven and earth, the elemental and the concrete nature – on the other hand, standing in action and reaction with such nature, the spirit, which therefore is finite.' The particular is the world of appearance, of alienation, a realm of inversion and evil, a slaughterhouse and self-betrayal of the individual's infinite nature. 'That spirit as the extreme of inherent negativity, completes its independence till it becomes wickedness, and is that extreme through its connection with a confronting nature and through its own naturalness thereby investing it.'[43]

The final phase is that of individuality, the sphere of developed culture and society where the alienated self accomplishes a return to unity with the Holy Spirit, pictorially represented as the Church, the community of believers.[44] The moment of individuality, accordingly, is also the *social* moment, the eternal moment of *love* and of *knowledge*. For Hegel, love implies a relationship between two individuals in so far as these individuals form a unity with one another by finding their respective selves in the other person. Realized on a much larger scale in society, where each person comes to recognize what he or she is through relations with others, love is what Hegel calls 'universal self-consciousness.' This form of consciousness, he writes, 'is the affirmative awareness of self in an other self: each self as a free individuality has his own "absolute" independence, yet in virtue of the negation of its immediacy or appetite without distinguishing itself from that other. Each is thus universal self-consciousness and objective; each has "real" universality in the shape of reciprocity, so far as each knows itself recognized in the other freeman, and is aware of this in so far as it recognizes the other and knows him to be free.' Universal self-consciousness becomes possible only within the Christian community where equality of the individual before God makes slavery a blasphemy against Christ. 'The master confronted by his slave was not yet truly free, for he was still far from seeing in the former himself. Consequently, it is only when the slave becomes free that the master, too, becomes completely free.'[45] Moreover, within the unity of the Holy Spirit the principle of love becomes 'moral love for the neighbour in [the] particular circumstances in which one is related to him.'[46]

In addition to love, the moment of individuality in the concept of the Trinity also represents *knowledge*. Christ is the second Adam sent to earth to teach men and women the Divine Truth: the knowledge of good and evil. Knowledge bequeaths a gift of eternity, for the Truth is eternal. 'We call something that can die "mortal," while that which can reach a state in which death does not enter is "immortal".' Knowledge is eternity in precisely this sense, for to share in the pure resource of knowledge and truth is to commune with the infinite. Immortality does not come later, after death; 'rather it is a present quality.' The notion of eternity, although distorted by the pictorial aspect of Christianity, is its greatest message. 'Spirit is eternal, therefore for this reason already present; Spirit in its freedom does not exist within the sphere of limitation. As thinking and purely cognitive, it has for its object the universal – this is eternity.'[47]

For the savage, consciousness of knowledge as the eternal element in human existence is not nearly compelling enough to forego the forbidden fruit of lust and selfish desire. Much more urgent is the threat of eternal damnation endured amongst the tortures of Hell. This threat, intrinsic to the concept of the Trinity, is used to good effect by the medieval Church to grind down the rough surfaces of the barbarian mind. 'The Church fought the battle' against barbarism and evil 'with the violence of rude sensuality in a temper equally wild and terroristic with that of its antagonist: it prostrated the latter by dint of the terrors of hell, and held it in perpetual subjugation, in order to break down the spirit of barbarism and tame it into repose.'[48]

In the moment of individuality all three aspects of the Trinity are represented. Christ, as love and knowledge, is also God and human. Through his life and torment on earth 'wickedness is implicitly overcome,' and even in death 'he, as infinite subjectivity, keeps himself unchanged, and thus, as absolute return from that negativity and as universal unity of universal and individual essentiality, has realized his being as the Idea of the spirit, eternal, but alive and present in the world.' Christ's earthly agony stands for the moment of particularity, but so does the rise of the individual from the depths of barbarism to the standpoint of civilized society. The alive and present 'divine man who is the Idea of spirit' is also the ideal of perfection for the finite individual who sheds his or her natural character in order 'to close ... in unity with that example (who is his implicit life) in the pain of negativity, and thus to know himself made one with the essential Being.' The unity of the individual with the Holy Spirit, the third moment of the Trinity, thus takes place through the travail of education in society, a mediation through which 'the Being of Beings ... brings about its own indwelling in self-consciousness, and is the actual presence of the essential and self-subsisting spirit who is all in all.'[49]

The history of religion is the story of the struggle of men and women to overcome external authority and alienation, a struggle pictorially anticipated by the concept of the Trinity. With victory over external power finally won by Christianity, which teaches that 'man and God – are one,' theology cleared the way for science and philosophy. The stages of religion reflect the stages of society, and the notion of God reflects the position of the individual. 'In the East only one individual is free, the despot; in Greece the few are free; in the Teutonic world ... all are free, that is, man is free as man.' In Eastern society the subjection of the individual is almost complete: 'In the brightness of the East the individual disappears.' Consequently, the oriental God is only an abstract spirit in the beyond who inspires the individual with fear in the same way as society itself is based on fear. 'The man who lives in fear, and he who rules over men through fear, both stand upon the same platform; the difference between them is only in the greater power of will which can go forth to sacrifice all that is finite for some particular end.'[50] The relation between the subjugation of men and women in oriental society and Eastern religion is also noted by Marx:

Oriental despotism ... restrained the human mind within the smallest possible compass, making it the unresisting tool of superstition, enslaving it beneath traditional rules, depriving it of all grandeur and historical energies ... These little communities [which made up Indian society] were contaminated by distinctions of caste, and by slavery, ... they subjugated man to external circumstances instead of elevating man into the sovereign of circumstances ... they transformed a self-developing social state into never changing natural destiny, and thus brought about a brutalizing worship of nature, exhibiting its degradation in the fact that man, the sovereign of nature, fell down on his knees in adoration of Hanuman, the monkey, and Sabbala, the cow.[51]

By contrast, the Greeks grasped as human consciousness 'what they opposed to themselves as the Divine.' But, enmeshed in the relations of slave society, the ancients were unable to recognize the absolute creativity and worth of the individual, and urged subordination of the individual to the state and society. The Greek gods are not apprehended in thought; they are given content through sensuous images and are subject to the limits of this medium itself. The gods are jealous, war among themselves, and are prey to the natural forces that influence men and women. 'The medium of sense,' Hegel observes, 'can only exhibit the totality of mind ... as a circle of independent, mental or spiritual shapes; the unity embracing all these shapes remains, therefore, a wholly indeterminate, alien power over against the gods.'[52] In a famous passage undoubtedly influenced by Hegel, Marx connects Greek mythological art to the undeveloped character of ancient society.

Is the view of nature and social relations on which the Greek imagination and hence Greek [mythology] is based possible with self-acting mule spindles and railways and locomotives and electrical telegraphs? What chance has Vulcan against Roberts & Co., Jupiter against the lightning rod and Hermes against Credit Mobilier? All mythology overcomes and dominates and shapes the forces of nature in the imagination and by the imagination; it therefore vanishes with the advent of real mastery over them.[53]

Unlike the deities of the Orientals and the Greeks, 'the Christian God,' says Hegel, 'is God not known merely, but also self-knowing; he is a personality not merely figured in our minds, but rather absolutely actual.' When theologians began to consider the character of God they found that certain categories like 'substance,' 'necessary essence,' 'cause which regulates and directs ... according to design,' and so on were appropriate enough for things in the material world like stones, wheelbarrows, and watches, but 'inadequate to express what is or ought to be understood by God.' These concepts refer to 'a subordinate level of facts,' i.e., inorganic nature and its 'merely contingent' qualities. Even the properties of organic nature – 'the organic structures, and the evidence they afford of mutual adaptation' – even these properties are 'incapable of supplying the material for a truthful expression to the idea [of] God.'[54] Religious thinkers were forced to go beyond these categories and adopt ones approximating the concepts Hegel applies to the nature of the human mind. 'The highest definition of the Absolute is that it is not merely mind in general but that it is mind which is absolutely manifest to itself, self-conscious, infinitely creative mind ... Just as in philosophy we progress from the imperfect forms of mind's manifestation .. to the highest forms of its manifestation, so, too, world-history exhibits a series of conceptions of the Eternal, the last of which shows forth the Notion of absolute mind.'[55]

The Christian notion of the Triune God, 'the highest definition of the Absolute,' embraces 'the distinctive determinateness of the Notion of mind, *ideality*.'[56] Ideality, in turn, is the fundamental category of absolute idealism, for what it expresses is that 'Mind ... should not merely be pure thought, but that it should be thought which makes itself objective, and therein maintains itself and is at home with itself.' Ideality concerns the active and creative nature of human thought, what Marx will later call revolutionizing practice: 'the fundamental idea,' remarks Hegel, is 'Thought which is its own object, and which is therefore identical with its object, with what is thought; so that,' as in the Trinity formula, 'we have the one and the other, and the unity of both.' It is through ideality, through the practical activity of men and women in society, that 'liberty and happiness are attained for the subject.'[57] The concept of ideality expresses the absolute identity of the individual with society; but this identity is creative and transforming – it 'is *absolute negativity*.'[58]

In Christian theology 'God is conceived of as making himself an object to Himself, and further, the object remains in this distinction in identity with God; in it God loves Himself.' The abstract, differentiating consciousness of the Enlightenment abandons entirely this theological notion of an identity which posits difference and settles for pure, lifeless identity, I = I. Absolute idealism, on the other hand, 'which is no longer abstract, but which sets out from the faith of man in the dignity of his spirit, and is actuated by the courage of truth and freedom, grasps the truth as something *concrete*, as fulness of content, as Ideality, in which determinateness – the finite – is contained as a moment.'[59] Transforming, creative human practice remains a mystery for the Enlightenment consciousness or to what Hegel also calls the 'understanding,' or 'materialized conception.' 'To materialized conception existence stands in the character of something solely positive, and quietly abiding within its own limits: though we also know ... that everything finite (such as existence) is subject to change.' The very nature of human individuals – their consciousness and the contradictions contained within it – forces them out of themselves and spurs them on to change and improve their environment. 'Such changeableness in existence,' Hegel declares, 'is to the superficial eye a mere possibility, the realization of which is not a consequence of its own nature. But the fact is, mutability lies in the notion of existence, and change is only the manifestation of what implicitly is. The living die, simply because they bear within themselves the germ of death.'[60]

2 IDEALITY, WORK, AND ABSOLUTE IDEALISM

Hegel's notion of ideality has been entirely overlooked by Marxist and non-Marxist commentators alike. Ideality appears in the *Phenomenology* variously as alienation, estrangement, or externalization; but it is the same concept Hegel uses in his later works. 'The world,' writes Hegel in the *Phenomenology*, 'is the *existent* Spirit, which is the individual Self, which has consciousness and distinguishes itself as "other", or as world, from itself.'[61] Similarly, the concept of human work or externalization developed in the *Phenomenology* is simply an aspect of the wider concept of ideality. The poverty of current Marxist commentary on Hegel is illustrated by the work of Colletti. According to this writer, absolute idealism stands for nothing but the union of God with human beings and the world: 'The meaning of [Hegel's] argument could not be clearer: God becomes real in the world ... the civil and political institutions of modern bourgeois society ... which to us seem to be historical institutions ... to Hegel appear ... as the presence itself of God in the world – not profane realities but "mystical objects", not historical institutions but sacraments.'[62]

Like Marx, Colletti is indebted to Feuerbach for the basic assumptions of his critique of Hegel. 'Pantheism,' remarks Feuerbach, 'makes God into a present, real, and material being' and therefore, Hegel's philosophy embodies 'pantheistic idealism.'[63] Marx's failure to question many of the aspects of Feuerbach's critique of Hegel which he absorbed as a young man has left an unfortunate legacy in the writings of Western Marxism. Nevertheless, as I have argued above, Marx – unlike Colletti and others – came to reject Feuerbach's assumption that Hegel is a religious thinker. Marx's reason for doing so, especially regarding Hegel's 'pantheism,' is a good one; while Hegel never responded directly to the accusation of atheism, except to observe that what is regarded as atheism and what is not is culturally relative,[64] he denies in the strongest terms that his philosophy is a form of pantheism. 'To impute Pantheism instead of Atheism to Philosophy,' Hegel declares, 'is part of the modern habit of mind – of the new piety and new theology. For them philosophy has too much of God: – so much so, that, if we believe them, it asserts that God is everything and everything is God.'[65]

According to Hegel, pantheism – this 'all-one doctrine ... this stale gossip of oneness or identity' – is much more invidious than the charge of atheism which at least 'presupposes a definite idea of a full and real God, and arises because the popular idea does not detect in the philosophical notion the peculiar form to which it is attached.' For the naive critic of absolute idealism, 'each and every secular thing is God. It is only his own stupidity, and the falsifications due to such misconception, which generates the imagination and allegation of such pantheism.'[66] Charles Taylor observes that Hegel's system 'breaks asunder' and yields 'an impossible conclusion' because Hegel cannot decide between 'Romantic pantheism' and 'orthodox theism.'[67] In contrast with Colletti, Taylor at least recognizes the existence of this contradiction, but the fault lies in Taylor's interpretation, not in Hegel's philosophy. Hegel writes:

If any difficulty emerge in comprehending God's relation to the world, [the critics of absolute idealism] at once and very easily escape it by admitting that this relation contains for them an inexplicable contradiction; and that hence, they must stop at the vague conception of such relation, perhaps under the familiar names of e.g. omnipresence, providence, etc. Faith in their use of the term means no more than a refusal to define the conception, or to enter on a closer discussion of the problem. That men and classes of untrained intellect are satisfied with such indefiniteness, is what one expects; but when a trained intellect and an interest for reflective study is satisfied, in matters admitted to be of ... supreme interest, with indefinite ideas, it is hard to decide whether the thinker is really in earnest with the subject.[68]

Colletti observes that the problem of Hegel's philosophy is to get past abstract notions of finite and infinite which impair the ordinary conception of God's relations with the world. For this conception, God is at once an object, a finite thing, and also a spirit who resides in the beyond, an infinite being. 'The terms of the problem to be solved by idealism,' says Colletti, 'are all here ... In order to comprehend the infinite in a coherent fashion, the finite must be destroyed, the world annihilated ... [But] once the finite is expunged ... the infinite can pass over from the beyond to the *here* and *now*, that is, become flesh and take on earthly attire.' This is how Colletti arrives at the conclusion that absolute idealism is actually pantheism. 'The "principle" of idealism has been actualized. In place of the world now annihilated, one has substituted the "true" reality. It is not, however, the Revolution that has taken place but only the Transubstantiation.'[69] The problem of absolute idealism – once it is recognized that for Hegel God is the fully developed social individual – is here correctly posed: to posit a unity between God and the world left open by Enlightenment thinkers and by a theology which makes God at once finite and infinite – a unity, as Hegel observes, 'to be called incomprehensible by the agnostic.' 'Though philosophy,' he writes, 'certainly has to do with unity in general, it is not, however, with abstract unity, mere identity, and the empty absolute, but with concrete unity (the notion).' In other words, Hegel's philosophy is concerned with unity as contradiction, as the unity which posits difference: 'Each step in [the] advance [of philosophy] is a particular term or phase of this concrete unity, and ... the deepest and last expression of unity is the unity of absolute mind itself.'[70]

The unity of absolute mind or reason is precisely the unity of theory and practice urged by Marx in his *Theses on Feuerbach*. 'Theoretical and practical mind,' states Hegel, 'reciprocally integrate themselves ... Both modes of mind are forms of Reason, for both in theoretical and in practical mind what is produced – though in different ways – is that which constitutes Reason, a unity of subjectivity and objectivity.'[71] Ideality – the key term in absolute idealism and the basis of the unity of theory and practice – 'can be called,' he writes, 'the *quality* of infinity; but it is essentially the process of *becoming*.'[72] It makes its first appearance in the 'Doctrine of Being' in the *Encyclopaedia Logic* where Hegel indirectly explains why he calls his philosophy absolute idealism. There is no distinction, he argues, between the finite and the infinite, or at least the distinction between them as comprehended by the Understanding is incorrect. 'The truth of the finite is rather its ideality ... This ideality of the finite is the chief maxim of philosophy; and for that reason every genuine philosophy is idealism.'[73] 'It is the very nature of the finite,' writes Hegel,

to transcend itself, to negate its negation, and to become infinite. Thus the infinite does not stand ... as if the finite had an enduring being *apart from* or *subordinate* to the infinite ... But the finite itself in being raised into the infinite is in no sense acted on by an alien force; on the contrary, it is its nature to be related to itself as limitation, – both limitation as such and as an ought – and to transcend the same, or rather, as self-relation to have negated the limitation and to be beyond it. It is not in the sublating of finitude in general that infinity in general comes to be; the truth is rather that the finite is only this, through its own nature to become itself the infinite.[74]

Thus, according to Hegel, the finite – the social individual – is at once determined by and creates through his or her work the developing actuality of society. 'The concrete is the universal which makes itself particular, and in this making of itself particular and finite yet remains eternally at home with itself.'[75]

Earlier in the *Encyclopaedia Logic*, Hegel declares that 'the tendency of all man's endeavours is to understand the world, to appropriate and subdue it to himself: and to this end the positive reality of the world must be as it were crushed and pounded, in other words, idealized.'[76] Here is the true meaning for 'idealize' and 'ideality' which Colletti mistakes for the notion that 'the world has disappeared. That which *seemed* finite, in reality is infinite. An independent material world no longer exists.'[77] Ideality for Hegel is the unity of theory and practice achieved by sensuous human activity. (This meaning is most clearly expressed in the *Philosophy of Right* (§44, 41-2) where ideality refers to the individual's appropriation and use of natural objects in the labour process.)

'Hence,' Hegel observes, 'ideality has not received its proper estimation, when you allow that reality is not all in all, but that an ideality must be recognized outside it. Such an ideality [i.e., God: D.M.] external to it or it may be even beyond reality, would be no better than an empty name.' Ideality – active human consciousness and practice – exists not outside the world but in it; its presence is felt everywhere in nature as well as society. But ideality without human sensuous activity, as expressed in the 'bad idealism' which sees everything in terms of non-materialized thought, is abstract and void – a nullity. 'Ideality,' Hegel declares, 'only has a meaning when it is the ideality of something: but this something is not a mere indefinite this or that, but existence characterized as reality, which, if retained in isolation, possesses no truth.'[78]

As the basic category of mind, ideality is what separates human beings from the rest of nature. 'The distinction between Nature and Mind is not improperly conceived, when the former is traced back to reality, and the latter to ideality as a fundamental category.' Ideality is the expression of human self-consciousness or being-for-self: 'Being-for-self may be described as ideality, just as Being there-and-then was described as reality.' The 'I' of the human being is, according to Hegel, 'the reference-to-self which is infinite, and at the same time negative'; in other words, the 'I' stands for a particular person and also his or her active relationship with other individuals, nature, and society. 'Man,' says Hegel, 'is distinguished from the animal world, and in that way from nature altogether, by knowing himself as 'I': which amounts to saying that natural beings never attain a free Being-for-self, but as limited to Being-there-and-then, are always and only Being-for-another.' Hegel's notion of Being-for-self and ideality is related to 'Being Determinate' which he calls 'the truth of ... Alteration.' Alteration, in turn, refers to work, to the transforming power of human practice. 'Alteration ... exhibits the inherent contradiction which originally attaches to determinate being, and which forces it out of its own bounds.'[79]

Ideality is the truth of identity, a truth, as we have seen, first arrived at by theology which sees God not only as the One God (the individual), but also as an infinitely creative and transforming power. 'Identity in its truth, as an ideality of what immediately is, is a high category for our religious modes of mind as well as all other forms of thought and mental activity.' The notion of God as ideality 'is to see that all the power and the glory of the world sinks into nothing in God's presence, and subsists only as the reflection of his power and glory.'[80] To view 'the ego, therefore spirit as such, or God'[81] as ideality is to grasp the true nature of human revolutionizing practice: 'In the same way, Identity, as self-consciousness, is what distinguishes man from nature, particularly from the brutes which never reach the point of comprehending themselves as 'I', that is, pure self-contained unity.'[82] The revolutionizing potential of human self-conscious activity is captured in the phrase of the Church, 'sic transit gloria mundi,' no less than it is by Shelley:

> I met a traveller from an antique land
> Who said: Two vast and trunkless legs of stone
> Stand in the desert ...
> And on the pedestal these words appear:
> 'My name is Ozymandias, king of kings:
> Look on my works, ye Mighty, and despair!'
> Nothing beside remains. Round the decay
> Of that colossal wreck, boundless and bare
> The lone and level sands stretch far away.

For Hegel, the activity of the 'I', the self-identical human being, is what stands in the way of absolute authority, as well as the abstract identity of the Enlightenment or the understanding. Identity and the other so-called laws of formal logic, such as that of the excluded middle, are important and indeed vital for the finite, non-human, sciences and other branches of knowledge.[83] But they are unable to account for the creative movement, the inner dialectic, of human thought and activity.

Hegel's Logic is aimed precisely at constructing a methodology and a theory of human social activity. Lenin makes this point in his commentary on Hegel: 'When Hegel endeavours – sometimes even huffs and puffs – to bring man's purposive activity under the categories of logic, saying that this activity is the "syllogism" ... that the subject (man) plays the role of a "member" in the logical "figure" of that "syllogism", and so on, – THEN THAT IS NOT MERELY STRETCHING A POINT, A MERE GAME. THIS HAS A VERY PROFOUND, PURELY MATERIALISTIC CONTENT.'[84]

Aristotle developed the ordinary logic of the understanding, but Hegel attributes to him also the discovery of the significance of ideality. In his discussion of what he sees as Aristotle's development of the notion of ideality, Hegel emphasizes the element of human labour-power – a concept later made the foundation of Marx's *Capital*. For Aristotle, 'the energy of thinking and the object of thought are the same'; but this identity 'is ... no dry identity of the abstract understanding.'[85] According to Aristotle, thought alone is the 'unmoved mover'; thought is the ultimate source of activity. But thought also constitutes the unity between the activity itself and the content and object of activity.[86] Aristotle lived in the bustling trade and manufacturing city-state of Athens. His problem in searching for an umoved mover, as he called it, was to explain the nature and characteristics of human activity in connection with the simple tools and machinery employed in the beautiful products of Greek artistry and design.

Aristotle argues that activity is imperfect if it does not contain its end in itself. That is, activity as true or perfect activity is the action of human beings guided by their own rational consciousness. Men and women use tools to change and transform their external environment – tools are employed to serve the particular ends of those who invent and use them. But tools themselves lack in their inner nature what makes them tools: they cannot act of themselves, but require a human master and designer. Hegel quotes Aristotle as follows: ' "Suppose that an instrument, such as an axe, were a natural body, this form, this axehood, would be its substance, and this its form would be its soul, for if this [its soul: D.M.] were to be taken away from it, it would no longer be an axe, the name only would remain.

But soul is not the substantial form and Notion of such a body as an axe, but of a body which has within itself the principle of movement and of rest." ' What is true of the tool or instrument of production is equally true of the raw material on which it is employed. ' "Brass is in capacity a statue; yet the motion to become a statue is not a motion of the brass so far as it is brass, but a motion of itself, as the capacity to become a statue. Hence this activity is an imperfect one ..." i.e. it has not its end within itself, "for mere capacity whose activity is movement is imperfect." '87

Human thought and purposive activity – ideality – constitute the energy which links subject and object of labour into the unity of the product. Hegel observes that, for Aristotle, 'thought, as being the unmoved which causes motion, has an object, which, however, becomes transformed into activity, because its content is itself something thought, i.e. a product of thought, and thus altogether identical with the activity of thinking. The object of thought is first produced in the activity of thinking, which in this way separates the thought as an object.'88 What this means is that thought as the design or purpose of the human subject is brought into reality as a product of labour through the machine- or tool-assisted activity of the worker on the object of that activity. *Hegel makes this concept of human thinking activity the programmatic basis of his whole philosophy*: 'The act,' writes Hegel, 'thus is really one, and it is just this unity of differences which is the concrete. Not only is the act concrete, but also the implicit [i.e., the inner plan or design: D.M.] which stands to action in the relation of subject which begins, and finally the product is just as concrete as the action or as the subject which begins.' The absolute Idea, the notion of freedom, is 'concrete' because it is this 'unity of differences': it is the ideal that men and women carry around in their heads, and also the reality they construct and strive to realize in society through their concrete, sensuous activity, their ideality. 'Thus the Idea,' notes Hegel, 'is in its content concrete within itself, and this in two ways: first it is concrete potentially, and then it is its interest that what is in itself should be there for it.'89

Echoes of Hegel's notion of ideality and his discussion of Aristotle reverberate throughout the whole of *Capital*. Consider, for example, the following passage in Chapter VII of Volume I, 'The Labour Process and the Valorization Process':

In the labour process ... man's activity *via* the instruments of labour, effects an alteration in the object of labour which was intended from the outset. The process is extinguished in the product. The product of the process is a use value, a piece of natural material adapted to human needs by means of a change in its form.

Labour has become bound up in its object: labour has been objectified, the object has been worked on. What on the side of the worker appeared in the form of unrest ... now appears, on the side of the product, in the form of being ... as a fixed, immobile characteristic. The worker has spun, and the product is a spinning.[90]

Aristotle taught that machinery and tools, no less than raw materials as they are transposed into the finished product of labour, are nothing but the result of human practice or ideality. Men and women have the power and ability to create the tools and machinery which then operate directly on the object of labour. For Hegel, the modern factory, with its complex machinery which operates directly on the raw material of production under the guidance of a human operator, is the historical culmination of Aristotle's ruminations on the unmoved mover. Marx shares this view, but he also points out the less desirable features of the employment of machinery under capitalism (features with which Hegel too is well acquainted, as will be discussed below).

'If', dreamed Aristotle, the greatest thinker of antiquity, 'if every tool, when summoned, or even by intelligent anticipation, could do the work that befits it, just as the creations of Daedalus moved of themselves, or the tripods of Hephaestus went of their own accord to their sacred work, if the weavers' shuttles were to weave of themselves, then there would be no need either of apprentices for the master craftsmen, or of slaves for the lords.' And Antipater, a Greek poet of the time of Cicero, hailed the waterwheel for grinding corn, that most basic form of all productive machinery, as the liberator of female slaves and the restorer of the golden age. Oh those heathens! They understood nothing of political economy and Christianity ... They did not, for example, comprehend that machinery is the surest means of lengthening the working day. They may perhaps have excused the slavery of one person as a means to the full human development of another. But they lacked the specifically Christian qualities which would have enabled them to preach the slavery of the masses in order that a few crude and half-educated parvenus might become 'eminent spinners', 'extensive sausage-makers' and 'influential shoe-black dealers'.[91]

Hegel's discussion of the concept of ideality in Aristotle illuminates an extremely important (and little understood) section of *Logic* which Hegel calls 'Teleology.' This section was discussed above in Chapter 1 where I argued that it concerns the dialectics of labour and involves three aspects or moments – subjective end or purpose, the means (of production), and the realized or objective end. 'The teleological relation,' writes Hegel, 'is a syllogism in which the subjective end coalesces with the objectivity external to it, through a middle term which is the unity of both. This unity is on one hand the *purposive* action, on the other the *Means*, i.e. objectivity made directly subservient to purpose.' Hegel distinguishes the means (of production) from 'the material or objectivity which is pre-supposed,' i.e., the raw material or object to be worked on.[92] Accordingly, we have what Marx later calls 'the simple elements of the labour process ... (1) purposeful activity, that is work itself, (2) the object on which that work is performed, and (3) the instruments of that work.'[93]

Hegel notes that the dialectical moment of means in the labour process 'is broken up into two elements external to each other, (*a*) the action and (*b*) the object which serves as Means.'[94] The means 'is accordingly a merely *mechanical object*' which relates to the object of labour through a 'mechanical or chemical' process which is manipulated and controlled by the worker ('the Notion' or self-conscious individual in Hegel's terminology). The subordination of the means, object, and process of labour to the purposeful will of the worker is for Hegel an example of the 'cunning of reason': 'That the end posits itself in a *mediate* relation with the object,' he writes in the *Science of Logic*, 'and *interposes* another object *between* itself and it, may be regarded as the *cunning* of reason. The finitude of rationality has ... this side, that the end enters into relationship with the presupposition, that is, with the externality of the object. In the *immediate relation* to the object, it would itself enter into the sphere of mechanism or chemism and thereby be subject to contingency and the loss of its determination as the Notion that is in and for itself. But as it is, it puts forward an object as means, allows it to wear itself out in its stead, exposes it to attrition and shields itself behind it from mechanical violence.'[95] In other words, by means of tools and instruments the worker impresses a form on the object of labour without becoming directly involved in the process and thereby endangering life and limb. Thus the history of technology may be seen as an attempt (however uneven and prone to reversals) to distance the worker from the hazards of labour while at the same time increasing production.

Greek society was viewed by Hegel as the first to begin to realize the potential of industry and trade, and tear itself away from dependence on agriculture; the Greek achievement is evident in Aristotle's concept of labour no less than in the concrete products of Greek civilization. Accordingly, Hegel begins his account of Greek art and politics in the *Philosophy of History* with a discussion of the relationship between men and women and nature which points back to the notion of means in Logic: 'Man with his necessities sustains a practical relation to external Nature, and in making it satisfy his desires, and thus using it up, has recourse to a system of *means*. For natural objects are powerful, and offer resistance in various ways. In order to subdue them, man introduces other natural agents; thus turns Nature against itself, and invents *instruments* for this purpose. These human inventions belong to Spirit, and such an instrument is to be respected more than a mere natural object.'[96]

Hegel, like Marx, views the development of the means of production as the paramount factor in the rise of society out of the externality of nature. Thus, in a passage marked by Lenin in his Conspectus on Hegel's *Science of Logic* with the comments 'the germs of historical materialism in Hegel,' 'Hegel and historical materialism,'[97] Hegel writes, 'The *means* is *superior* to the *finite* ends of *external* purposiveness: the *plough* is more honourable than are immediately the enjoyments procured by it and which are ends. The *tool* lasts, while the immediate enjoyments pass away and are forgotten. In his tools man possesses power over external nature, even though in respect of his ends he is, on the contrary, subject to it.'[98]

Hegel argues that 'self-existent ideality'[99] in the form of the dialectics of labour is the medium through which the individual in society develops his or her special capacity, talent, character, and so forth. The notion of work as a form of self-actualization appears most prominently in the *Phenomenology's* discussion of the relationship between master and slave. Hegel suggests that the slave develops and realizes his or her self-consciousness through work for the master, while the master loses altogether the feeling of independent self-certainty by growing dependent on the slave.

Through work ... the bondsman becomes conscious of what he truly is ... Work ... is desire held in check, fleetingness staved off; in other words, work forms and shapes the thing. The negative relation to the object becomes its *form* and something *permanent*, because it is precisely for the worker that the object has independence. This negative middle term or the formative *activity* is at the same time the individuality or pure being-for-self of consciousness which now, in the work outside of it, acquires an element of permanence. It is in this way, therefore, that consciousness, *qua* worker, comes to see in the independent being [of the object] its *own* independence.[100]

Marx employs the master-slave dialectic in his notion of the growth of proletarian class consciousness in capitalist society, and, as I have noted in Chapter 1, the concept (understood as *Bildung* or education) plays a similar role in Hegel's theory of bourgeois society in the *Philosophy of Right*. Both writers emphasize the fundamental role of work in the realization of self-consciousness. 'An individual,' says Hegel in the *Phenomenology*, 'cannot know what he [really] is until he has made himself a reality through action.'[101] Marx suggests the same notion in *Capital*: through the process of labour the individual 'acts upon external nature and changes it, and in this way he simultaneously changes his own nature. He develops the potentialities slumbering within nature, and subjects the play of its forces to his own sovereign power.'[102]

The notion of labour as self-development is utilized by Hegel to express the essence of the Greek Spirit which, he suggests, 'is the plastic artist, forming the stone into a work of art.' The artist begins work on a block of stone with an end or purpose in mind, an ideal which can be realized only through the means and activity of labour. 'In this formative process the stone does not remain mere stone – the form being only superinduced from without; but it is made an expression of the Spiritual, even contrary to its nature, and thus *transformed*. Conversely, the artist *needs* for his spiritual conceptions, stone, colors, sensuous forms to express his idea. Without such an element he can no more be conscious of the idea himself, than give it an objective form for the contemplation of others; since it cannot in Thought alone become an object to him.' The Greek Spirit comes to know itself through its own productions which contrast strongly with the half-human, half-animal forms of the early Egyptians. Self-consciousness, the awareness and independence of the human spirit, is accordingly translated from mere potentiality or purpose to the realm of actuality through the dialectics of labour. 'The Egyptian Spirit also was a similar laborer in Matter, but the Natural had not yet been subjected to the Spiritual. No advance was made beyond a struggle and a contest with it; the Natural still took an independent position, and formed one side of the image, as in the body of the Sphinx. In Greek Beauty the Sensuous is only a sign, an expression, an envelope, in which Spirit manifests itself.'[103]

It is an expression of the state of Hegelian scholarship, and especially that of western Marxism, that Marx's use in *Capital* of the following quotation from Hegel on the 'cunning of reason' to refer to the labour process has gone unexplained. 'Reason is as cunning as it is powerful. Cunning may be said to lie in the intermediative action which, while it permits the objects to follow their own bent and act upon one another till they waste away, and does not itself directly interfere in the process, is nevertheless only working out its own aims.'[104] Marx uses the quotation as a reference for a passage directly influenced by Hegel's account of the labour process in *Logic*. 'An instrument of labour,' observes Marx, 'is a thing, or a complex of things, which the worker interposes between himself and the object of his labour and which serves as a conductor, directing his activity onto that object. He makes use of the mechanical, physical and chemical properties of some substances in order to set them to work on other substances as instruments of his power, and in accordance with his purposes.'[105]

Although this citation is of utmost importance, Marcuse and Colletti[106] do not even refer to it, and Hook in *From Hegel to Marx* only observes that it is 'in an interesting connection'[107] – which connection, however, Hook neglects to discuss. Charles Taylor fails to notice that the passage from Hegel has to do with the labour process and provides an abstruse interpretation of its meaning. Hegel, says Taylor,

invokes here ... his famous image of the 'cunning of Reason,' by which the higher purpose makes use of lower level principles in encompassing its end. Rather than working directly on the object, the higher purpose slips another object between itself and what it wants to transform. If it were to enter directly into the interaction of things, it would be a particular thing itself and would go under like all such things. But it cunningly saves itself from this fate by having its work done for it by the mechanical interaction of things in the world.[108]

In his reference to Hegel, Marx omits the last few sentences of the passage which refer to the meaning commonly associated with Hegel's use of the term: 'With this explanation, Divine Providence may be said to stand to the world and its process in the capacity of absolute cunning. God lets men do as they please with their particular passions and interests; but the result is the accomplishment of – not their plans, but his, and these differ decidedly from the ends primarily sought by those whom he employs.'[109] But Hegel is no more suggesting that God is the reason behind history than He is the moving force behind the labour process. As I mentioned in Chapter 1, the cunning of reason, in this meaning of the term, refers to the historical process through which the ideality of women and men eventually creates the possibility and actuality of freedom in modern society. It is useful to recall again the analogy of the Idea of the automobile used in Chapter 2. The automobile was not the actuating force behind the invention of the wheel; but seen from the standpoint of the present, the wheel was a necessary element in the 'divine plan' of the automobile.

For Hegel, the means of production and the raw material on which they are employed are only 'ideal' – that is, the object and result of human ideality, or labour-power.[110] Through the development of industry men and women exercise their dominion over chemical and mechanical processes:

science is employed rationally in the productive effort. As Hegel puts it, 'mechanical and chemical technique, through its character of being externally determined, offers itself spontaneously to the end relation.'[111] The tremendous productive forces developed under the bourgeois mode of production, which march in step with the achievements of science and technology, make possible for the first time in history the reconciliation of nature and human design. 'Through this process,' states Hegel, 'there is made explicitly manifest what was the notion of design: viz. the implicit unity of subjective and objective is now realized. And this,' he continues, 'is the Idea.'[112]

In following chapters I will discuss more fully what Hegel means by the Idea or truth, but his notion of truth connotes more than correspondence between a thing and our image of it. Truth means the unity of thought and being as obtained through human will or ideality. 'The will's activity consists in annulling the contradiction between subjectivity and objectivity and giving its aims an objective instead of a subjective character, while at the same time remaining by itself even in objectivity ... [T]his activity is in essence the development of the substantive content of the Idea ... a development through which the concept determines the Idea, itself at first abstract, until it becomes a systematized whole.'[113] The Idea of absolute idealism is *dialectical*, that is, it is the dynamic self-creation of human self-consciousness: 'it is the free notion giving character to itself, and that character, reality.'[114]

Like the categories of human thought, the stages of social development and the modes of production belonging to them are creations of human ideality. This is why Hegel's *Logic* connects the emergence of the absolute Idea with the appearance of the bourgeois mode of production. But as manifestations of ideality, the forms of society are subject to unrest and progressive change in the same manner as the human consciousness which gives rise to them. 'The stages ... are not, when so distinguished, something permanent, resting upon themselves. They have proved to be dialectical; and their only truth is that they are dynamic elements of the idea.' The Idea is the formative element of society, but only because it is also the possession of every living individual. 'When we hear the Idea spoken of, we need not imagine something far away beyond this mortal sphere. The idea is rather what is completely present: and it is found, however confused and degenerated, in every consciousness.'[115] Somewhat the same notion is expressed by Marx in the *German Ideology*, although Marx seems unaware of this similarity: 'The ideas and thoughts of people were, of course, ideas and thoughts about themselves and their relationships, their consciousness of *themselves* and of people in *general* – for it was the consciousness not merely of a single individual but of the individual in his interconnection with the whole of society and about the whole of the society in which they lived.'[116]

For Hegel, and – as I will argue – for Marx as well, *the social individual is the identical subject-object of history; he or she is both determined by and the creator of society and its ojective forms.* 'Only the notion itself,' writes Hegel, referring to the human individual,

[is free and the genuine universal: in the Idea, therefore, the specific character of the notion is only the notion itself – an objectivity [i.e., nature and society: D.M.] into which it, being the universal, continues itself, and in which it, being the universal, continues itself, and in which it has only its own character, the total character. The Idea is the infinite judgement, of which the terms are severally the independent totality; and in which, as each grows to the fullness of its own nature, it has thereby at the same time passed into the other.[117]

3 PROTESTANTISM, ABSOLUTE IDEALISM, AND REVOLUTIONIZING PRACTICE

According to Hegel, knowledge of the human mind is 'the highest and hardest, just because it is the most "concrete" of sciences.' The goal of this science explains its difficulty: 'the aim of all genuine science is just this, that mind shall recognize itself in everything in heaven and on earth. An out-and-out Other simply does not exist for mind.'[118] The forms of religion are also forms of human ideality; they are created by men and women in their endeavour to comprehend the absolute. The aim of religion, like all forms of human knowledge, 'is to divest the objective world that stands opposed to us of its strangeness, and, as the phrase is, to find ourselves at home in it: which means no more than to trace the objective world back to the notion – to our innermost self.'[119]

The Protestant religion is the highest form of religious consciousness; through it, philosophy as well as industry and commerce were given freedom and added impetus in the modern world. With the defeat of the Roman Catholic Church in northern Europe and the advent of secular government, writes Hegel, in a passage which anticipates Max Weber's argument in the *Protestant Ethic and the Spirit of Capitalism*[120] by almost a century,

With this commerce and the arts are associated. It is implied in the arts that man brings what is divine out of himself; as artists were at one time so pious that as individuals they had self-abnegation as their principle, it was they from whose subjective abilities these representations [of the nascent bourgeoisie] were produced. With this is connected the circumstance that the secular knew that it had in itself the right to such determinations as are founded on subjective freedom. In his handicraft the individual is taken in reference to his work, and is himself the producer. Thus men came to the point of knowing that they were free, and insisting on the recognition of that freedom, and having the power of exercising their activity for their own objects and interests ... The man who was moved to seek what was moral and right ... looked round about him ... The place which was pointed out to him is himself, his inner life, and external Nature.[121]

The Christian doctrine in its original form, with its emphasis on the individual's unity with Christ, 'first gave to human consciousness a perfectly free relationship to the infinite and thereby made possible the comprehensive knowledge of mind in its absolute infinitude.'[122] But in the Roman Catholic Church as it was constituted in the Middle Ages this 'perfectly free relationship' was impossible; Christian doctrines were interpreted for the individual by the priests in the name of the Church. The Bible, written in Latin and available only to the initiated, was unknown to the common people except from on high. Individual conscience itself was consigned to the Church in the form of *confession* and faith became a matter of external observance prompted by the command of the priest. In the midst of its own 'lust of power, riotous debauchery ... barbarous and vulgar corruption, hypocrisy and deception,' the Roman Church taught 'slavish deference to *Authority*' and betrayed the fundamental principles of Christianity by underwriting 'serfdom, which made a man's body not his own, but the property of another' and which 'dragged humanity through all the barbarism of slavery and unbridled desire.'[123] The revolution effected by Protestantism concerned precisely the presentation of religion to the ordinary individual. The principle of Protestantism 'is simply this, that it led man back to himself, and removed what was alien to him, in language especially.'[124]

Protestantism everywhere cleared away the barriers which separate the individual from God; the saints and the priesthood were alike overthrown; the Virgin was pushed from her place as the mediator between the believer and God. But Protestantism's most profound advance was to make available the teachings of Christianity in the language of the faithful. For Luther 'to have translated for German Christians the book on which their faith is grounded ... is one of the greatest revolutions which could have happened.'[125] With this signal act 'Luther repudiated' the Church's 'authority and set up in its stead the *Bible* and the testimony of the Human Spirit.'[126] It is interesting to observe that Marxism – the most influential and revolutionary doctrine in human history – itself owes a great debt to Luther's translation of the Bible (which Hegel calls 'the People's Book'), since – as S.S. Prawer informs us – 'the vocabulary, phrasing, rhythm, and characters of Luther's Bible are recalled again and again in Marx's own prose.'[127]

Nor was this revolutionary transformation – reflected and encouraged as it was by Luther's Bible – limited to religion alone. 'Italy,' writes Hegel, 'in the same way obtained grand poetic works when the vernacular came to be employed by such writers as Dante, Boccaccio and Petrarch.' But, Hegel adds significantly, 'Petrarch's political works were however written in Latin.' The abolition of the believer's estrangement from God meant also that servitude in religion disappeared. Men and women no longer prostrated themselves before God or fell upon their knees. Mumbling unknown prayers in a foreign tongue disappeared from religious worship at the same time as men and women ceased 'to study the sciences in such.'[128] Consciousness of their oneness with God led people to question the authority of rulers who claimed that they were responsible to God alone. The overthrow of the priests led to the overthrow of kings. As Hegel observes with regard to the seventeenth-century English Revolution,

the distinction between priests and laymen does not exist among Protestants, and priests are not privileged to be the sole possessors of divine revelation, and still less does there exist any such privilege which can belong exclusively to a layman. To the principle of the divine authorisation of the ruler there is accordingly opposed the principle of this same authorisation which is held to be inherent in the laity in general. Thus there arose a Protestant sect in England, the members of which asserted that it had been imparted to them by revelation how the people ought to be governed, and in accordance with the directions thus received from the Lord, they raised the standard of revolt, and beheaded their king.[129]

The birth of Protestantism, which in turn reflects the development of individual consciousness, finds its basis for Hegel in the growth of private property and social relations in the Middle Ages. 'Possession, personal property, is ... a part of what pertains to man; it is by his own will'; as such, it is connected with the evolution of 'Freedom, conscience [which] belong also to man.'[130] Accordingly, the Reformation occurred in those countries where handicrafts and trade had attained a superior development in the towns of the medieval period. By contrast Protestantism was stifled in the predominantly agricultural and feudal Slavonic nations since 'in agriculture the agency of nature predominates; human industry and subjective activity are on the whole less brought into play in this department of labor than elsewhere. The Slavonians therefore did not attain so quickly or readily as other

nations the fundamental sense of pure individuality ... that which we designated above as "political power", and could not share the benefits of
dawning freedom.'[131] The dialectical relationship of political freedom with
the emergence of capitalism and free enterprise is also emphasized by Marx:

Greek society was founded on the labour of slaves, hence had as its natural basis
the inequality of men and of their labour powers. The secret of the expression
of value, namely the equality and equivalence of all kinds of labour because and
in so far as they are human labour in general, could not be deciphered until the
concept of human equality had already acquired the permanence of a fixed popular opinion. This however becomes possible only in a society where the commodity-form is the universal form of the product of labour, hence the dominant
social relation is the relation between men as possessors of commodities.[132].

Hegel argues, as we have seen, that the revolution in language was one
of the major achievements of the Reformation. Language is the vehicle of
consciousness, the means for its manifestation. 'Manifestation,' Hegel explains, 'is Being for Other ... What is for an "Other", exists for this very
reason in a sensuous form ... thought ... is only capable of being communicated by the one to the other through the sensuous medium of sign or
speech, in fact, by bodily means.'[133] By liberating the Bible for all men and
women, Protestantism liberated the whole world of literature, politics, science, and philosophy for the individual. 'In speech,' notes Hegel,

man is productive; it is the first externality that he gives himself, the simplest
form of existence that he reaches in consciousness. What man represents to himself, he inwardly places before himself as spoken. This first form is broken up and
rendered foreign if man is in an alien tongue to express or conceive to himself
what concerns his highest interest. This breach with the first entrance into consciousness is accordingly removed; to have one's own right to speak and think in
one's own language really belongs to liberty. This is of infinite importance, and
without this form of being-at-home-with-self subjective freedom could not have
existed.[134]

Hegel's observations on the importance of language are taken up by Marx
in The German Ideology. 'Language,' says Marx, 'is as old as consciousness,
language is practical consciousness that exists also for other men, and for
that reason alone it really exists for me personally as well; language, like
consciousness, only arises from the need, the necessity, of intercourse with
other men.' After this passage, Marx crosses out the following words, prob-

ably to avoid any truck with 'idealism': 'My relationship to my surroundings is my consciousness.' But Hegel's influence crops up again further on: 'neither thoughts nor language in themselves form a realm of their own ... they are only *manifestations* of actual life.'[135]

The revolutionary significance Hegel finds in the Reformation has become an object of modern historical science. Engels, in his classic *Peasant War in Germany*, was among the first after Hegel to grasp this significance,[136] although he presents Protestantism and Christianity as external forms that almost by coincidence express real concepts like liberty and freedom. According to Engels, for example, Thomas Muenzer preached his radical doctrines 'mostly in a covert fashion, under the cloak of Christian phraseology.'[137] Engels' interpretation of the relationship between religion and reality is embraced by Christopher Hill, who contrasts the 'materialist' with the 'theological' aspects of Winstanley's writings, and describes Winstanley's 'astonishing,' because radical, interpretation of Biblical sources as 'a remarkable feat.'[138] For Hegel, however, Christianity, like other forms of popular conception, is not a 'cloak,' but an integral aspect of the believing consciousness: to see it as such requires insight as well as imagination. Greek mythology, for instance, 'is not a mere cloak ... it is not merely that the thoughts were there and were concealed. This may happen in our reflecting times; but the first poetry does not start from a separation of prose and poetry. If philosophers used myths, it was usually the case that they had the thoughts and then sought for images appropriate to them.'[139] If men and women use religious images to express thoughts, it is only because their consciousness has not developed to the point at which they can express themselves purely in the form of theoretical concepts.

Hegel's contention that Protestantism represents the highest point reached by religious consciousness in expressing the freedom and infinite rights of the individual has drawn criticism of his 'Protestant bias' from Plamenatz[140] and other scholars. Hegel, however, is referring to the world-historical role of Protestantism, not its current form. Marx, who has never been accused of bias toward Protestantism, echoes Hegel's analysis in a passage where he compares the Protestant critique of Catholicism with the struggle of the bourgeoisie against the feudal system. 'In so far as the bourgeois economy did not mythologically identify itself altogether with the past, its critique of the previous economies, notably of feudalism, with which it was still engaged in direct struggle, resembled the critique which Christianity levelled against paganism, and also that of Protestantism against Catholicism.'[141]

Rather than glorifying Protestantism, Hegel views its development 'partly, no doubt, as a separation from the Catholic Church, but partly as a reformation from within. There is a mistaken idea that the Reformation only effected a separation from the Catholic Church; Luther just as truly reformed the Catholic Church.' Protestant theology is much inferior to that of Catholicism because it emerged shorn of the rich Roman Catholic heritage of Greek philosophy and the principle of subjective freedom. 'Even to the present day we shall find in the Catholic Church and in her dogmas the echoes, and so to speak the heritage, of the philosophy of the Alexandrian school; in it there is much more that is philosophic and speculative than in the dogmatism of Protestantism.'[142]

The triumph of Protestantism in northern Europe and the separation of philosophy from theology meant at first the rejection of the speculative or theoretical content of religion. 'As for the enrichment of Christian conceptions through the treasures of the philosophy of the ancient world,' he observes, 'and through the profound ideas of all earlier oriental religions, and the like – all this is set aside.' While the theology of the medieval schoolmen shut itself up 'in the centre point of the individual,' i.e., God, 'man became conscious of his will and his achievements, took pleasure in the earth and its soil, as also in his occupations.'[143] The invention of gunpowder made the heroism of the feudal period more dangerous than sublime. Moreover, by depriving the nobility of the advantage it derived from armour, gunpowder 'was one of the chief instruments in freeing the world from the dominion of physical force, and placing the various orders of society on a level. With the distinction between the weapons they used, vanished also that between lords and serfs.'[144] Without the lure of chivalry and the tournament, enterprising individuals turned their thoughts to 'the exploration of the earth, or the discovery of the passage to the East Indies. America was discovered, its treasures and people – nature, man himself; navigation,' Hegel continues, 'was the higher romance of commerce.'[145] The same juncture is isolated by Marx: 'The circulation of commodities is the starting-point of capital. The production of commodities and their circulation in its developed form, namely trade, form the historic presuppositions under which capital arises. World trade and the world market date from the sixteenth century, and from then on the modern history of capital starts to unfold.'[146]

Hegel argues that religion reflected this new direction towards the external world, and as a result 'the Reformation of Luther had inevitably to come.' Lutheranism focused attention on the present, on experience, and goaded men and women 'to understand laws and forces, *i.e.* to transform the individual of perceptions into the form of universality.' The 'works' of ordinary people were now the object of faith and God was conceived 'in spirit alone, He is not a beyond but the truest reality of the individual.' Lutheranism encouraged the individual to be 'satisfied in his activity, to have joy in his work and to consider his work as something both permissible and justifiable ... Art and industry receive through this principle new activity, since now their activity is justified.' The search for profit and the inclination of men and women to improve themselves through work and labour 'receive ... highest confirmation, and that is ... sanctification through religion.'[147]

The new philosophy, freed by the Reformation from theology, turned its attention to the self-consciousness of the individual and the understanding of what was taken to be the 'pre-supposed object.' Theology's separation from philosophy spelt its death as a theory of the individual, nature, and society: its 'home and private metaphysics, are thus [now] frequently a quite uncultured, uncritical thought – the thought of the street.' True, Christianity retains its 'particular subjective conviction' – its historical truth – 'but these thoughts which constitute the criterion are merely the reflections and opinions which float about the surface of the time.' Thus, the Reformation brought about the utter dissolution of theology: 'When thought comes forth on its own account,' declares Hegel, referring to modern philosophy, 'we thereby separate ourselves from theology.'[148]

After the defeat of theology, the unity of thought and being constitutes the chief problem of the new philosophy. Like all successful movements, eighteenth-century Enlightenment itself breaks into two opposed sides.[149] Materialism supposes thought to be caused by the action of external objects on the mind, while idealism sees the categories of thought as independent of the external world. Materialism is concerned with experience or reality in nature and society as well as in the life activity of the human being. Its paramount concern is with what exists – the present. As the young Marx puts it, with regard to the French Enlightenment, 'the downfall of seventeenth-century metaphysics can be explained by the materialistic theory of the eighteenth century only as far as that theoretical movement itself is explained by the practical nature of French life at the time. That life was turned to the immediate present, worldly enjoyment and worldly interests, the *earthly* world. Its anti-theological, anti-metaphysical, and materialistic practice demanded corresponding anti-theoretical, anti-metaphysical and materialistic theories.'[150]

The method of materialism is that of 'finite' or natural science; the method of observation and deduction, the formation of universal laws, and so on. According to Hegel, the empirical sciences are 'finite, because their mode of thought, as a merely formal act, derives its content from without. Their content therefore is not known as moulded from within through the thoughts which lie at the ground of it, and form and content do not thoroughly interpenetrate each other.'[151] Materialism marked a great advance over scholastic or medieval philosophy which set aside the human power of observation and approached arguments respecting nature from the vantage point of abstract hypotheses. Moreover, the development of all science and philosophy depends on the findings of empirical science, 'for mind is essentially a working upon something different.'[152]

Materialism, however, fails to notice that the categories of thought are not only a result of the action of external objects on the mind, but rather, as Immanuel Kant explains, the categories are formed independently of experience or a priori: 'the highest legislation of Nature must lie in ourselves, that is in our understanding, and ... we must not seek the universal laws of nature in nature by means of experience; but conversely must seek Nature, as to its universal conformity to law, in the conditions of the possibility of experience which lie in our sensibility and in our understanding.'[153] Science, notes Hegel, deals with 'a variety of sensuous properties and matters; [however,] these matters (elements) also stand in relation to one another [and] the question is, Of what kind is this relation?'[154] The verification (or falsification) of theory depends on observation; but theory itself is a product of the active power of the human mind. Materialism, with its reliance on the method of the natural sciences, fails to appreciate the independent role of theory. The physicists, says Hegel,

devote their attention to what they call experience, for they think that here they come across genuine truth, unspoiled by thought, fresh from the hand of nature; it is in their hands and before their faces. They can certainly not dispense with the Notion [theory: D.M.], but through a kind of tacit agreement they allow certain conceptions, such as forces, subsistence in parts, &c., to be valid, and make use of these without in the least knowing whether they have truth and how they have truth. But in regard to the content they express no better the truth of things, but only the sensuous manifestation.[155]

Hegel's contention that the external appearance of things must be penetrated by theory appealed greatly to the mature Marx. 'The older he grew,' observes S.S. Prawer, 'the more he came to agree with Hegel and the German idealists that truth lay below the level of immediate empirical perception. It had to be dug for by well-informed men with a gift for theorizing and philosophic reflection.'[156] For Hegel, as for Marx, materialism (and natural science with it) deludes itself when it imagines that its categories deal only with things as they are directly perceived by the senses. Many 'facts' are actually theoretical constructs which, as Hegel suggests, 'cannot be verified by observation.' Even 'matter itself,' he notes, '– furthermore form which is separated from matter – whether that be the thing as consisting of matters, or the view that the thing itself subsists and only has proper ties, is all a product of the reflective understanding which, while it observes and professes to record only what it observes, is rather creating a metaphysic, bristling with contradictions of which it is unconscious.'[157]

The Hegelian critique of materialism is taken up by Marx in *Capital*, where he applies it to theories about the nature of laws of competition under the bourgeois mode of production: 'A scientific analysis of competition is possible only if we can grasp the inner nature of capital, just as the apparent motions of the heavenly bodies are intelligible only to someone who is acquainted with their real motions, which are not perceptible to the senses.' If theory or ideality is necessary to penetrate the mysteries of the natural realm, it is so much the more indispensable for comprehending what Marx, following Hegel, calls 'the supra-sensible or social' world.[158]

The human mind – like all natural organisms – is a product of self-development which proceeds independently of sources external to it. The external or finite methodology of materialism and natural science is thus incapable of grasping the immanent or 'necessary' character of human consciousness. Before Hegel, Kant had already elucidated the principle of living organisms that materialism fails to comprehend: '*an organized natural product is one in which every part is reciprocally both end and means.*'[159] For Kant, as for Hegel, freedom is both the end and means of human development, and 'the concept of freedom,' Kant declares, 'is the stumbling block of all empiricists.'[160] Under the influence of Feuerbach, the young Marx overlooks materialism's inability to comprehend organic processes and the active and transforming nature of human consciousness. As the young Marx points out, for materialism the human individual is something like a machine, and is subject to the forces of nature: 'Every human passion is a mechanical motion ending or beginning. The objects of impulses are what is called good. Man is subject to the same laws as nature; might and freedom are identical.'[161] In an important passage Kant emphasizes the contrast between the 'formative power' of natural organisms and the 'motive power' of mere machinery. 'In a watch,' he observes,

one part is the instrument by which the movement of the others is effected, but one wheel is not the efficient cause of the production of the other. One part is certainly present for the sake of another, but it does not owe its presence to the agency of that other. For this reason, also, the producing cause of the watch and its form is not contained in the nature of this material, but lies outside the watch in a being that can act according to ideas of a whole which its causality makes possible. Hence, one wheel in the watch does not produce the other, and, still less, does one watch produce other watches, by utilizing, or organizing, foreign material; hence it does not of itself replace parts of which it has been deprived, nor, if these are absent in the original construction, does it make good the deficiency by the subvention of the rest; nor does it, so to speak, repair its own causal disorders. But these are all things which we are justified in expecting from organized nature. – An organized being is, therefore, not a mere machine. For a machine has solely *motive power*, whereas an organized being possesses inherent *formative* power, and such, moreover, as it can impart to material devoid of it – material which it organizes. This, therefore, is a self-propagating formative power, which cannot be explained by the capacity of movement alone, that is to say, by mechanism.[162]

According to Hegel and the mature Marx, human consciousness is an infinitely creative, transforming power and manifests itself through practice in the external, social world. 'Work,' notes Hegel, 'is the result of the disunion [between human beings and nature], it is also the victory over it. The beasts have nothing more to do but to pick up the materials required to satisfy their wants: man on the contrary can only satisfy his wants by himself producing and transforming the necessary means. Thus even in these outside things man is dealing with himself.'[163] Materialism, on the other hand, holds that mind is *determined* by the outside world: that is, by the world of nature and society that human ideality itself transforms and creates. Despite its defects, materialism makes a genuine attempt to overcome the separation of thought and being, to provide a solution for what is, after all, the supreme problem of philosophy. 'We must recognize in materialism,' suggests Hegel, 'the enthusiastic effort to transcend the dualism which postulates two different worlds as equally substantial and true, to nullify this tearing asunder of what is originally One.'[164] This accomplishment of materialism is also recognized by the young Marx: 'If,' for materialism, 'man's senses are the source of all his knowledge ... then conception, thought, imagination, etc., are nothing but phantoms of the material world more or less divested of its sensuous form ... An *incorporeal substance* is just as much nonsense as an *incorporeal body*. *Body, being, substance*, are one and the same *real* idea. One cannot separate the thought from matter *which* thinks. Matter is the subject of all changes.'[165]

Idealism – the second approach to the problem of unity of thought and being – proceeds from thought and makes everything a product of mind. 'What Realism draws from experience is now derived from thought *à priori*.'

Nevertheless, Hegel argues, the two sides overlap – materialism must give experience the form of thought as laws and theories, while the abstract universality of idealism is in need of a determinate content derived from sensuous reality. 'The philosophic systems are therefore no more than modes of this absolute unity, and only the concrete unity of those opposites is the truth.'[166] The same unity is urged, of course, by Marx. 'The chief defect of all hitherto existing materialism ... is that the thing, ... reality, sensuousness, is conceived only in the form of the *object* ... or of *contemplation*, ... but not as human *sensuous activity, practice*, not subjectively. Hence it happened that the *active* side, in contradistinction to materialism, was developed by idealism – but only abstractly, since ... idealism does not know real, sensuous activity as such.'[167] For Hegel and for Marx, philosophy is now posed with the question which they both believe can only be answered by a philosophy which constitutes the unity of materialism and idealism: 'How is, and how can thought be identical with the objective?'[168]

The answer provided by Hegel's absolute idealism, which I will outline in more detail in the following chapters, is the one which excited Marx in 1845 and prompted him to set down the *Theses on Feuerbach*: 'The question whether objective ... truth can be attributed to human thinking is not a question of theory but is a *practical* question. In practice man must prove the truth, that is, the reality and power, the this-sidedness of his thinking. The dispute over the reality or non-reality of thinking which is isolated from practice is a purely scholastic question.'[169] The same excitement which infuses Marx's *Theses* also races through Lenin's 1914 commentary on Hegel's *Logic*. 'Remarkable,' Lenin exclaims, 'Remarkable: Hegel comes to the "Idea" as the coincidence of the Notion and the object, as *truth, through* the practical purposive activity of man ... Undoubtedly, in Hegel practice serves as a link in the analysis of the process of cognition, and indeed as the transition to objective ("absolute", according to Hegel) truth.' 'Marx,' Lenin continues, 'consequently, clearly sides with Hegel in introducing the criterion of practice into the theory of knowledge: see the Theses on Feuerbach.' The conclusion to be derived from Hegel is obvious: 'Man's consciousness,' says Lenin, 'not only reflects the objective world, but creates it.' Lenin's study of Hegel led him to a further conclusion. For Hegel, he writes, '*Practice is higher than (theoretical) knowledge*, for it has not only the dignity of universality, but also of immediate actuality.'[170]

A little less than three years after Marx's discovery of revolutionizing practice in Hegel, Marx wrote the *Communist Manifesto*; three years after writing the Conspectus, Lenin made a revolution.

The new relationship of men and women to philosophy and science exemplified by the revolutionizing practice of Marx and Lenin is anticipated by Hegel. The philosophers of the ancient world, he writes, were 'self-sufficing individualities ... they kept the external connection with the world all the further removed from themselves because they did not greatly approve of much therein present; or at least it [the world: D.M.] ever proceeds on its way, according to its own particular laws, on which the individual is dependent.' In the Middle Ages philosophers were chiefly clergy, theologians; and 'in the transition period' from medieval to modern times 'the philosophers showed themselves to be in an inward warfare with themselves and in an external warfare with their surroundings, and their lives were spent in a wild, unsettled fashion.'[171] Thus the Italians Bruno and Vanini were burnt at stake by the Inquisition; the Frenchman Cardanus was imprisoned and tortured; his compatriot Ramus was murdered.

It is different with modern thinkers. They no longer constitute a class or group by themselves: 'we find them generally in connection with the world, participating with others in some common work or calling ... They are involved in present conditions, in the world and its work and progress.' The new position of philosophy and science results from the rationality and universal connection of individuals with one another that sets bourgeois society apart from past epochs. 'This connection is of such power that every individuality is under its dominion, and yet at the same time can construct for itself an inward world.'

The external life of the individual may be set apart from his or her inward existence, while in past ages a person's inward life was dominated by his or her occupation: a priest was a priest; a peasant, a peasant.

Now, on the contrary, with the higher degree of strength attained by the inward side of the individual, he may hand the external over to chance; just as he leaves clothing to the contingencies of fashion, not considering it worth while to exert his understanding upon it. The external he leaves to be determined by the order which is present in the particular sphere in which his lot is cast. The circumstances of life are, in the true sense, private affairs, determined by outward conditions, and do not contain anything worthy of our notice.

Accordingly, Marx – a man whose outward personality and prejudices conformed in most ways to the respectable middle-class standards of his time – could go about his business in London, trudging daily to his seat in the British Museum, spinning the web of revolution. But Marx like all other individuals in capitalist society had to 'seek to act in connection with others'; he found in those dark days in London that 'The calling of philosophy is not, like that of the monks, an organized condition. Members of academies of learning are no doubt organized in part, but even a special calling like theirs sinks into the ordinary commonplace of state or class relationships, because admission thereinto is outwardly determined. The real matter is to remain faithful to one's aims.'[172]

4

Alienation and Ideology

'In the social production of their existence,' writes Marx in the preface to *A Contribution to the Critique of Political Economy,* 'men inevitably enter into definite relations, which are independent of their will, namely relations of production appropriate to a given stage in the development of their material forces of production.'[1] What Marx means by the phrase, 'independent of their will,' is elucidated in *The Eighteenth Brumaire of Louis Napoleon* where he writes: 'Men make their own history, but they do not make it just as they please; they do not make it under circumstances chosen by themselves, but under circumstances directly encountered, given and transmitted from the past. The tradition of all the dead generations weighs like a nightmare on the brain of the living.'[2] Nevertheless, Marx's observation in the preface is enthusiastically embraced by Louis Althusser and his followers, who deny that, for Marx, men and women are 'free' and 'constitutive' actors in the human drama. Individuals, Althusser declares, 'work in and through the determinations of the *forms of historical existence* of the social relations of production and reproduction.'[3]

For Althusser, history is 'a process without a Subject or Goal(s)' in which men and women may act only as agents determined by their social relations. Social relations, in turn, are a product of the class struggle – what Althusser calls the *'motor'* of history. Althusser unites his interpretation of Marx with a corresponding vision of Hegel. Both thinkers, he argues, deny the 'philosophical ideology of the Subject'; that is, they do not see the human individual as the subject of history, nor do they posit the liberation and freedom of men and women as history's goal.[4] Hegel substitutes the Idea for the human individual and Marx substitutes class struggle for the Hegelian Idea.

According to Althusser, history in Marx's view, 'is a terribly positive and active structured reality, just as cold, hunger and the night are for his poor worker.'[5] The basic assumptions of Althusser's structuralist Marxism are summed up by Nicos Poulantzas: '1. The distinction between real processes and processes of thought, between being and knowledge. 2. The primacy of being over thought; the primacy of the real over knowledge of the real.' Poulantzas (and Althusser) believe that 'in the strong sense of the term, only *real, concrete, singular* objects exist,' and therefore 'the final aim of the process of thought is knowledge of these objects.'[6] Both Poulantzas and Althusser forget, however, that a corpse is also a 'terribly positive and active structured reality,' even if the activity of its *'decentred'* structure[7] is only decomposition. A corpse most certainly has existence 'in the strong sense of the term' – it is a *'real, concrete, singular'* object; in fact, as Hegel notes, a corpse is the ultimate realization of the primacy of being over thought.[8] Because individual human consciousness and will cannot be seen, heard, smelled, or prodded with one's foot, it lacks reality 'in the strong sense' for the Althusserians, and cannot be an object of thought.[9] The case is different for Hegel and Marx.

According to Marx, the object of social science 'is always what is given, in the head as well as in reality'; economic categories, for example, 'express the forms of being, the characteristics of existence.'[10] Hegel also emphasizes that philosophy and science are concerned with 'the apprehension of the present and the actual,' and that truth in science 'means that concept and external reality correspond.'[11] For both thinkers, the present, in Marx's words, 'points beyond itself ... towards a past lying behind' it and towards the future as well.[12] 'The great thing,' Hegel writes, 'is to apprehend in the show of the temporal and the transient the substance which is immanent and the eternal which is present.'[13] This view of society as something with a past as well as a future is predicated on the notion that it 'is a kind of independent organism,'[14] a living unity which finds its life in the breath, pulse, and consciousness of the men and women who make it up. For Hegel and Marx, the concept of a living organism expresses the essence of the dialectic in history, the activity of living, conscious individuals in the process of the production, reproduction, and transformation of society. From the standpoint of both thinkers, the 'most basic final outcome' of human history is the full 'elaboration and development of the human personality and its freedom.'[15] History is not Althusser's lifeless 'process without a Subject or

Goal(s),' but the record and reality of the striving of individual men and women towards the multi-faceted expression of their character and personality, towards freedom.

One of Althusser's primary aims is to expunge the humanistic element in Marxism which, he believes, stems from the young Marx's assimilation of Feuerbach's materialist inversion of Hegelian philosophy. It is paradoxical, therefore, that Althusser's conception of Hegel's Idea as a process without a subject or goal is anticipated in the writings of the young Marx and Feuerbach. 'Hegelian philosophy,' writes Feuerbach, 'made thought, – namely, the subjective being conceived, however, without subject, that is, conceived as a being distinct from the subject – into a divine and absolute being.'[16] For Hegel, adds the young Marx, 'the divine process of man ... must have a bearer, a subject. But the subject first emerges as a result. This result ... is therefore *God – absolute Spirit – the self-knowing and self-manifesting Idea*. Real man and real nature become mere predicates – symbols of this esoteric, unreal man and of this unreal nature.' Thus Hegel's philosophy concerns 'the *absolute subject* as a *process* ... a pure, *restless*, revolving within self.'[17] According to Feuerbach and the young Marx, the truth of the historical process lies not in the Hegelian Idea but in man and woman as *species being*, as the generic essence of humankind. 'The new philosophy,' says Feuerbach, 'makes man – with the inclusion of nature as the foundation of man – the unique, universal and highest object of philosophy ... Truth does not exist in thought for itself or in knowledge for itself. Truth is only the totality of human life and of the human essence ... The essence of man is contained only in the community and unity of man with man.'[18]

Hegel, however, had already condemned the notion of *species being* or man as a hopeless abstraction. A person, he writes, 'is a specific existence; not man in general (a term to which no real existence corresponds) but a particular human being.' A particular human being, in turn, must be seen within the context of his or her sensuous activity in society. 'The first glance at History convinces us that the actions of men proceed from their needs, their passions, their characters and talents; and impresses us with the belief that such needs, passions and interests are the sole springs of action – the efficient agents in this scene of activity.' It is not the Idea that creates history, but the concrete action of individual men and women guided by their interests, passions and desires. 'Only by this activity [is the] Idea as well as abstract characteristics generally ... realized, actualized; for of themselves they are powerless. The motive power that puts them in operation and gives them their determinate existence, is the need, instinct, inclination, and passion of man.'[19]

At first attracted by Feuerbach's concept of *species being*, Marx later rejects it and turns to Hegel's view that the human individual is above all an active, social being: 'Feuerbach resolves the religious essence into the *human* essence. But the human essence is no abstraction inherent in each single individual. In its reality it is the ensemble of the social relations ... The human essence ... can with [Feuerbach] be comprehended only as a 'genus,' as an internal, dumb generality which merely *naturally* unites the many individuals.'[20] Along with Hegel's notion of the human individual as a social being, Marx also comes to accept his conception of the determinant role of men and women in the making of history. 'When,' writes Marx in his critique of Proudhon's 'quasi-Hegelian phrases' in the *Poverty of Philosophy*,

When ... we ask ourselves why a particular principle was manifested in the eleventh or in the eighteenth century rather than in any other, we are necessarily forced to examine minutely what men were like in the eleventh century, what they were like in the eighteenth, what were their respective needs, their productive forces, their mode of production, the raw materials of their production – in short, what were the relations between man and man which resulted from all these conditions of existence. To get to the bottom of all these questions – what is this but to draw up the real, profane history of men in every century and to present these men as both *the authors and the actors of their own drama.*[21]

Althusser's contention that Hegel's view of history concerns a 'process without a Subject or Goal(s)' is not the only, or the most important, of Feuerbach's and the young Marx's contributions to contemporary Marxism. The materialist assumptions of the Althusserians, which are shared by many Marxists, also have their roots in the writings of Feuerbach and the young Marx. As Vogel points out, 'in its final and distinct formulation, Feuerbach's philosophy is based on sense perception.' 'The real in its reality or taken as real,' Feuerbach explains, 'is the real as an object of the senses; it is the sensuous. Truth, reality, and sensation are identical. Only a sensuous being is a true and real being. Only through the senses, and not through thought for itself, is an object given in the true sense.'[22] The young Marx, who contrasts the '*sober philosophy*' of Feuerbach with the '*drunken speculation*' of Hegel, suggests that 'sense experience (*see* Feuerbach) must be the basis of all science. Science is only genuine science when it proceeds from sense experience, in the two forms of *sense perception* and *sensuous* need; i.e. only when it proceeds from nature.'[23]

The emphasis on sense perception, with its obvious distinction from and dependence on external objects, leads to the conclusion that the object, sensuous being, has priority over thought and mind: 'we make the real, that is, the sensuous,' Feuerbach points out, 'into its own subject and give it an absolutely independent, divine, and primary meaning which is not first derived from the idea,' i.e., from thought.[24] In his essay on Feuerbach, Engels approvingly summarizes the latter's materialist position: 'the material, sensuously perceptible world to which we ourselves belong is the only reality; and ... our consciousness and thinking, however supersensuous they may seem, are the product of a material, bodily organ, the brain. Matter is not a product of mind, but mind itself is merely the highest product of matter. This is, of course, pure materialism.'[25]

In Feuerbach's philosophy, the human mind and thought are essentially passive in relation to the independent, external object. 'Only that thought which is determined and rectified by sensuous perception is real and objective thought – the thought of objective truth ... Perception takes matters in a broad sense, whereas thought takes them in a narrow sense. Perception leaves matters in their unlimited freedom, whereas thought gives them laws, which, however, are only too often despotic. Perception enlightens the mind, but determines and decides nothing.' His conception of the passive nature of the mind is summed up in the phrases: 'Things must not be thought of otherwise than as they appear in reality ... The laws of reality are also the laws of thought.'[26] The young Marx was never comfortable with this aspect of Feuerbach's materialism, although it is accepted by some western Marxists. Timpanaro, for example, claims that 'we cannot ... deny or evade the element of passivity in experience: the external situation which we do not create but which imposes itself on us.'[27] Even in 1843-44, however, when Feuerbach's influence on him was at its height, Marx is aware of a tremendous discrepancy between reality and thought which, he feels, should be balanced in favour of the latter. 'Will the enormous gulf,' he asks, 'between the demands of German thought and the replies of German actuality match the same gulf that exists between civil society and the state, and within civil society itself? Will theoretical needs immediately become practical ones? It is not enough that thought should tend towards reality, reality must also tend towards thought.'[28] Marx, of course, utterly rejects the passive content of Feuerbach's materialism in the famous eleventh Thesis on Feuerbach.

According to Feuerbach, objectivity or truth is obtained only when the conception of an object is identical with the object itself, as corroborated by the testimony of an independent observer. 'The distinction between the object in itself and the object for us – namely, between the object in reality and the object in our thought and imagination – is ... necessarily and objectively grounded ... You think only because your ideas can themselves be thought, and they are true only when they pass the test of objectivity, that is, when they are acknowledged by another person apart from you for whom they are an object.'[29] Feuerbach's criterion of truth or objectivity is accepted by most modern Marxists. Lukács, for example, claims that true knowledge is 'a reflection of reality'[30] and Ted Benton, a British theorist, observes that 'adequacy to the object of knowledge is the ultimate standard by which the cognitive status of thought is to be assessed.'[31] Marx, as I have already pointed out, rejects this standard of truth in favour of the criterion of practice: 'The dispute over the reality or non-reality of thinking which is isolated from practice is a purely *scholastic* question.'[32] Sidney Hook observes that 'Marx did not live to develop the *implications* of his scientific theory of truth.'[33] But, as I will argue, the dialectical theory of truth associated with Marx is the ultimate concern of Hegel's absolute idealism. Significantly, Western Marxism has made no attempt to develop Marx's theory of objectivity or explore Hegel's. The Althusserian Decourt rightly observes that 'one hundred years after the Eleventh Thesis of Feuerbach [Marxism] remains in a state of theoretical non-elaboration such that the question of its (theoretical) existence can still be asked.'[34]

Feuerbach's materialist epistemology lends itself easily to an uncritical regard for the methods and achievements of natural science. 'The most perfect, and hence divine, sensuous knowledge,' notes Feuerbach,

is indeed nothing other than the most sensuous knowledge that knows the most minute objects and the least noticeable details, that knows the hair on man's head not by grasping it indiscriminately in one lock but by counting them, thus knowing them all, hair by hair ... this divine knowledge ... become[s] real knowledge in the knowledge of the natural science gained through the telescope and microscope ... it alone demonstrated anatomically in the grub of the butterfly 288 muscles in the head, 1,647 in the body, and 2,186 in the stomach and intestines. What more can one ask?[35]

The seeds of what Hook calls Feuerbach's ' "Degenerate" Sensationalism' – which consisted among other things in his contention in 1850 that 'man is what he eats'[36] – may already be found in this 1843 passage. But the young Marx at first fully accepts Feuerbach's worshipful attitude to the natural sciences and echoes his dictum that '*Philosophy must again unite itself with natural science, and natural science with philosophy.*'[37] 'The first object for man – man himself,' writes the young Marx, 'is nature, sense experience; and the particular sensuous human faculties, which can only find objective realization in *natural* objects, can only attain self-knowledge in the science of natural being ... Natural science will one day incorporate the science of man ... there will be a *single* science.'[38]

As he did with most other aspects of Feuerbach's philosophy – with the exception of its materialist inversion of Hegel – Marx also came to reject Feuerbach's unquestioning enthusiasm for natural science: 'Feuerbach speaks in particular of the perception of natural science; he mentions secrets which are disclosed only to the eye of the physicist and chemist: but where would natural science be without industry and commerce? Even this "pure" natural science is provided with an aim, as with its material, only through trade and industry, through the sensuous activity of men.'[39] Nevertheless, Feuerbach's respect for natural science is one of his most enduring legacies to modern Marxism, and his contention that the natural sciences are divine while philosophy (and its modern-day off-shoot, bourgeois social science) is simply a collection of errors and fantasies[40] has appealed to generations of Marxists.

Feuerbach glorifies the human senses at the expense of what Hegel calls ideality – the theoretical and practical activity of men and women. Human superiority over other animals lies neither in consciousness and will nor in reason, but rather in the development of the senses of feeling, hearing, seeing, and so on.

Man does not have the sense of smell of a hunting dog or of a raven, but only because his sense of smell is a sense embracing all kinds of smell; hence it is a freer sense which, however, is indifferent to particular smells. But, wherever a sense is elevated above the limits of particularity and its bondage to needs, it is elevated to an independent and theoretical significance and dignity ... Even the lowest senses, smell and taste, elevate themselves in man to intellectual and scientific acts. The smell and taste of things are objects of natural science. Indeed, even the stomach of man, which we view so contemptuously, is not animal but human because it is a universal being that is not limited to certain kinds of food ... He who concludes his view of man with the stomach, placing it in the class of animals, also consigns man, as far as eating is concerned, to bestiality.[41]

These observations are actually drawn from Hegel's *Philosophy of Mind*; but where Hegel relegates sensation to the lowest level of thought, Feuerbach never attains to a critical examination of the higher levels of consciousness which Hegel, following Kant, calls understanding and reason.[42]

The belief, which Feuerbach inherited from Kant, that nature is a sort of 'thing-in-itself' available only to the senses and ultimately beyond the grasp of human reason and sensuous activity, has influenced even those thinkers who are outside the mainstream of Marxist thought. Accordingly, Giddens in his *New Rules of Sociological Method*, suggests that, 'The difference between society and nature is that nature is not man-made, is not produced *by* man. Human beings, of course, transform nature ... But nature is not a human production; society is ... Theories men develop may, through their technological applications, affect nature, but they cannot come to constitute features *of* the natural world as they do in the case of the social world.'[43] But what exactly is 'the natural world'? As Marx points out, the natural world, as we know it, is nothing like the original nature which confronted the earliest human being. He mockingly observes that even the cherry tree – which Feuerbach uses to confute Hegel's Absolute Idea by demonstrating that it is not an ethereal idea but something that he can bump his own head on – even this cherry tree 'like almost all fruit trees, was, as is well known, only a few centuries ago transplanted by *commerce* into our zone, and therefore only *by* this action of a definite society in a definite age it has become "sensuous certainty" for Feuerbach.'[44] If the industrial revolution, for example, created modern British society, it also created an entirely new form of nature in the British countryside. That is, it not only transformed nature, but *created a new one*; a world of sheep and cattle breeds, varieties of vegetation, and so on, quite unknown before. Further, modern biology stands on the threshold of an era where life itself will no longer be God's or nature's prerogative, but one of the creations of human theory and practical activity.

There is no nature standing external to and outside of human consciousness and ideality. Men and women transform and create nature by taking advantage of natural laws as they are grasped in theory, in the same way as they transform and create society by developing and using their own natural human rationality. The individual, says Marx, must recognize 'nature (equally present as practical power over nature) as his own real body.'[45]

Of course, it may be countered that we can never transform the whole of nature, that some aspects of reality are and always will be unaffected by human endeavour; a part of nature will remain forever external to human beings. For Hegel, however, this objection begs the question. Human appropriation of natural objects necessarily involves the individualization of objects 'into single parts, into a breath of air or a drink of water.' If the unity of the individual with nature is perforce a unity of the individual with single objects, this does not negate the ultimate union of the individual with nature. 'In the fact that it is impossible to take possession of an external "kind" of thing as such, or of an element, it is not the external physical impossibility which must be looked on as ultimate, but the fact that a person, as will, is characterized as individual, while as person he is at the same time *immediate* individuality; hence as person he is related to the external world as to single things.'[46]

For Hegel, alienation – which since Engels has also been called false consciousness – is that type of human consciousness which persists in seeing things as external to, somehow outside of, human theory and sensuous practice. Consciousness is the relation of knowledge to its object; and knowledge in turn 'means such an acquaintance with the object as apprehends its distinct and special subject matter.'[47] False consciousness or alienation, on this definition, is the view that certain aspects of reality – whether social or natural – are beyond the reach of knowledge, of human rationality, and of practical activity. Recognition of the essential unity of mind with society and nature is the ultimate meaning, states Hegel, of the phrase '*Know thyself*': 'the summons to the Greeks of the Delphic Apollo, *Know thyself*, does not have the meaning of a law externally imposed on the human mind by an alien power; on the contrary, the god who impels to self-knowledge is none other than the absolute law of mind itself. Mind is, therefore, in its every act only apprehending itself, and the aim of all genuine science is just this, that mind shall recognize itself in everything in heaven and earth. An out-and-out Other simply does not exist for mind.'

Abolition of alienation, otherness, false consciousness, is the truth of ideality, human sensuous activity, revolutionizing practice: 'This triumph over externality which belongs to the Notion of mind, is what we have called the ideality of mind. Every activity of mind is nothing but a distinct mode of reducing what is external to the inwardness which mind itself is, and it is only by this reduction, by this idealization or assimilation, of what is external that it becomes and is mind.'[48] What distinguishes the individual from external nature is that a person may impose his or her will upon natural objects and transform them through labour according to a preconceived purpose. 'This,' says Hegel, 'is the absolute right of appropriation which man has over all "things".' The attitude towards things which the right of appropriation fosters directly contradicts 'The so-called "philosophy" which attributes reality in the sense of self-subsistence and genuine independent self-enclosed existence to unmediated single things, to the nonpersonal ... While so-called "external" things have a show of self-subsistence for consciousness, intuition, and representative thinking, the free will idealizes that type of actuality and so is its truth.'[49]

'Finite mind' – which Hegel also calls the 'understanding,' 'reflection,' the Enlightenment consciousness, and so on (and which Marx calls bourgeois thought) – considers the outside world, nature, to be an external reality that is only passively transformed by human ideality and remains outside of, or alienated from, ideality or human theory and practice. There is no doubt of the 'distinctive determinateness of external Nature and Mind as such,' says Hegel, but this distinction is overcome by revolutionizing practice. 'We have said that mind negates the externality of Nature, assimilates Nature to itself and thereby idealizes it. In finite mind which places Nature outside of it, this idealization has a one-sided shape: here the activity of our willing, as of our thinking, is confronted by an external material which is indifferent to the alteration which we impose on it and suffers quite passively the idealization which thus falls to its lot.' According to Hegel, 'absolute mind' – which Marx would call communist consciousness – recognizes the essential unity of mind with society and nature as achieved through ideality or revolutionizing practice: 'Only in ... absolute mind ... does the Idea apprehend itself in a form which is neither merely the one-sided form of Notion or subjectivity, nor merely the equally one-sided form of objectivity or actuality, but is the perfect unity of these its distinct moments, that is, in its absolute truth.'[50]

Feuerbach's materialism, its reliance and dependence on sensation and external reality, corresponds to what Hegel calls the first stage of human consciousness – that of 'finding a world presupposed before us.'[51] 'It is only to the external and immediate stage of consciousness,' writes Hegel in the *Philosophy of Nature*, 'that is, to *sensuous* consciousness, that Nature appears as the First, the immediate, as mere being.'[52] The second stage, that of 'generating a world of our own creation,' is reached by Kant's philosophy which will be considered in the next chapter. Both these ways of considering the world belong to 'finite mind' – to bourgeois (and western Marxist) consciousness. Finitude is itself the result of the activity of consciousness; *it is a false consciousness that creates itself.* 'It is a shadow cast by the mind's own light – a show or illusion which the mind implicitly imposes as a barrier to itself, in order, by its removal, actually to realize and become conscious of freedom as *its* very being, i.e. to be fully *manifested.*'[53]

Hegel's conception of finite consciousness is brilliantly explicated by Marx in the famous section of *Capital* called 'The Fetishism of Commodities and Its Secret.' Marx observes that a commodity embodies nothing more than human labour-power, and the value of a commodity is an expression of the human labour required to produce it. Commodities are equivalent to one another, that is, they may be exchanged for one another because they embody human labour-power considered in the abstract as universal labour or value. Money, as the universal equivalent, is the social mediator between commodities as values and facilitates their exchange. All this, however, is beyond the ken of the economist who insists on seeing value, not as abstract human labour manifested in the object, but rather as an *aspect of the external object itself.* 'The mysterious character of the commodity-form consists therefore simply in the fact that the commodity reflects the social characteristics of men's own labour as objective characteristics of the products of labour themselves, as the socio-natural properties of these things. Hence it also reflects the social relation of the producers to the sum total of labour as a social relation between objects, a relation which exists apart from and outside the producers.'[54]

In bourgeois society, production takes place as 'the labour of private individuals who work independently of each other.' The social character of labour is overlooked since everyone appears to be pursuing his or her private ends, independently of anyone else. The only *conscious* productive social relation between people is the private exchange of money and commodities on the market place.

In other words, the labour of the private individual manifests itself as an element of the total labour of society only through the relations which the act of exchange establishes between the products, and, through their mediation, between the producers. To the producers, therefore, the social relations between their private labours appear as what they are, i.e. they do not appear as direct social relations between persons in their work, but rather as material ... relations between persons and social relations between things.

In their market activities, what individuals are really doing is equating 'their different kinds of labour as human labour. *They do this without being aware of it.*'[55] In other words, the meaning of their interaction is obscured by 'a shadow cast by the mind's own light' – an illusory appearance brought about by bourgeois ideality itself.

The classical economists, such as Smith, James Mill, and Ricardo, had advanced as far as what Hegel calls the second stage of consciousness; 'generating a world as our own creation.' They recognized the wealth of bourgeois society as a creation of human labour, but could not go beyond this point because they took the commodity relation as an eternal and objectively valid aspect of all societies, not just of capitalism. *In a word, the classical economists thought they had discovered a relationship equivalent to one in the natural sciences.* They applied the external methodology of finite science, which has no knowledge of human consciousness and will, to a province in which ideality is the ultimate category.

The belated scientific discovery that the products of labour, in so far as they are values, are merely the material expressions of the human labour expended to produce them, marks an epoch in the history of mankind's development, but by no means banishes the semblance of objectivity possessed by the social characteristics of labour. Something which is only valid for this particular form of production, the production of commodities, namely the fact that the specific social character of private labours carried on independently of each other consists in their equality as human labour, and, in the product, assumes the form of the existence of value, appears to those caught up in the relations of commodity production (and this is true both before and after the above-mentioned scientific discovery) to be just as ultimately valid as the fact that the scientific dissection of the air into its component parts left the atmosphere itself unaltered in its physical configuration.[56]

The formulas of the classical economists, 'which bear the unmistakable stamp of belonging to a social formation in which the process of production has mastery over man, instead of the opposite, appear to the political economists' bourgeois consciousness to be as much a self-evident and nature-imposed necessity as productive labour itself.' The bourgeois economists could not foresee, nor could they comprehend, the transformation of capitalist society into a social form in which the rationality of freely associated individuals, rather than the abstract forces of the market, will rule and determine social relations.[57] Nevertheless, the alienation or false consciousness characteristic of the bourgeois epoch is a necessary phase or moment in the transformation to Hegel's third stage of human consciousness: 'gaining freedom from' the natural and social world 'and in it.'[58] Marx outlines the historical dimensions of these three stages in the *Grundrisse*:

Relations of personal dependence (entirely spontaneous at the outset) are the first social forms, in which human productive capacity develops only to a slight extent and at isolated points. Personal independence founded on *objective* ... dependence [i.e., capitalism] is the second great form, in which a system of general social metabolism, of universal relations, of all-round needs and universal capacities is formed for the first time. Free individuality, based on the universal development of individuals and on their subordination of their communal, social productivity as their social wealth, is the third stage. The second stage creates the conditions for the third.

Capitalism is a barrier to consciousness; the alienation it imposes – the subordination of individuals to the rule of capital – is only the necessary precondition for development of a freer and richer individuality. As it stands, bourgeois society is a 'mass of antithetical forms of the social unity, whose antithetical character can never be abolished through quiet metamorphosis.' Nevertheless, 'if we did not find concealed in society as it is the material conditions of production and the corresponding relations of exchange pre-requisite for a classless society, then all attempts to explode it would be quixotic.'[59]

2 ALIENATION AND NATURAL SCIENCE

'Feuerbach,' writes Vogel, 'is one of those thinkers who in the course of their philosophic careers radically changed their views.' Although he was for fifteen years a loyal disciple of Hegel, 'Feuerbach's distinct contribution is made as an empiricist, not as an idealist.'[60] As shown in the previous section, Feuerbach's empiricism linked him not only to materialism but also to natural science. Natural science lends itself most easily to the abstract quantitative relations of mathematics, and, remarks Hegel, 'this mere math-ematical view ... viz. quantity, is no other than the principle of Materialism.' Quantity or number is the thought-form closest to sensuous perception, to Feuerbach's sensationalism. 'Number is a thought, but thought in its com-plete self-externalization. Because it is a thought, it does not belong to perception: but it is a thought which is characterized by the externality of perception.'[61]

Number is a category of thought since it is not really a part of the external world; numbers are thoughts people independently attach to objects and do not constitute the objects themselves. Nevertheless, number expresses an essential aspect of objects, namely 'what is many, and in reciprocal exclu-sion.'[62] Number is an essential aspect of Feuerbach's ultimate standard of objectivity: the intersubjectively valid correspondence between thought and its object. We know a thing is singular, a 'one,' for example, because we can see it and touch it; other thought-forms tend to elude this certitude. 'The ordinary definition of truth, according to which it is "the harmony of the conception with the object," is certainly not borne out by the conception; for when I represent to myself a house, a beam, and so on, I am by no means this content, but something entirely different, and therefore very far from being in harmony with the object of my conception.'[63]

The exact sciences, such as physics, are so called because of their reliance on number as an absolute category. 'Strictly speaking,' notes Karl Mann-heim, 'from this point of view, only what is measurable should be regarded as scientific ... the ideal of science has been mathematically and geometrically demonstrable knowledge ... Modern positivism (which has always retained its affinity for the bourgeois-liberal outlook and which has developed in its spirit) has always adhered to this ideal of science and of truth.'[64] Just as the early bourgeois philosophers attempted to put their ideas in mathematical form and 'regarded with envy the systematic structure of mathematics,'[65] contemporary thinkers admire and try to imitate the method of natural science. For Marxists and their bourgeois opponents alike, 'science is a *neutral structure* containing *positive knowledge* that is independent of culture, ideology, prejudice.'[66] Of course, natural science *is* (to a degree) neutral and objective. But besides being neutral and objective it is also an alienated and severely limited system of thought – for it treats its object as something other to, and independent of, human ideality.

The limitation of natural science is also the limitation of bourgeois thought itself, where bourgeois thought means what Hegel calls 'reflection,' the 'understanding' and so on. Limitation is rooted in the bourgeois mode of production, in the production of commodities, of things produced for profitable sale in the market. It lies in a view of reality as a collection of things external to, and independent of, consciousness and will. It is a form of thought which sees objects created by human endeavour as *things* alienated or apart from consciousness. 'The empty abstraction of a matter without properties,' notes Hegel, 'which, when a thing is my property, is supposed to remain outside me and the property of a thing, is one which thought must master.'[67] It is worth recalling that the term alienation, which classical German philosophy took over from the English language, has as one of its primary meanings 'the action of transferring the ownership of anything to another.'[68]

A primary aspect of alienation, therefore, is that the worker sees the product of his or her conscious activity as a *thing belonging to the capitalist*. 'Capitalist production,' writes Marx, 'is the first to develop the conditions of the labour process ... on a large scale – it tears them from the hands of the individual independent worker, but develops them as powers that control the individual *worker* and are *alien* to him. In this way capital becomes a highly mysterious thing.' The labour process under capitalism, Marx continues, 'does not reproduce just capital, but also the product,' i.e., the commodity. At the beginning of the labour process, 'the conditions of production confronted the worker as capital only in the sense that he *found* them existing as *autonomous* beings opposed to himself. What,' at the end of the process, 'he now finds so opposed to him is the product of his own labour.'[69]

Not only the commodity and capital itself are considered to be independent, autonomous things, but also science, culture, and so on – all these are believed to be aspects of an independent, alien capitalism existing opposed to, and apart from, the individual. 'The transposition of the social productivity of labour into material attributes of capital,' Marx observes, 'is so firmly entrenched in people's minds that the advantages of machinery, the use of science, invention, etc. are *necessarily* conceived in this *alienated* form, so that all these things are deemed to be *attributes of capital.*'

A most alarming side of alienation of human consciousness and ideality *from itself* is the mystified view, propounded by all shades of the political spectrum, that the great progress achieved in production, consumption, education, and so on represents the achievement of the bourgeoisie, and not of individuals from all classes. Profit and the availability of consumer goods through increased production and reduced (real) prices under capitalism

appear to be the direct *act* and *achievement of the capitalist,* who functions here as the personification of the *social* character of labour, of the *workshop as a whole.* In the same way, *science,* which is in fact the general intellectual product of the social process, also appears to be the direct offshoot of capital (since its application to the material process of production takes place in isolation from the knowledge and abilities of the individual worker). And since society is marked by the exploitation of labour by capital, its development appears to be the productive force of capital as opposed to labour. It therefore appears to be the *development of capital,* and all the more so since, for the great majority, it is a product with which the *drawing off of labour-power* keeps pace.[71]

For Hegel and Marx, the labour process as it occurs under the bourgeois mode of production is a process of outward necessity. The production of commodities by the worker is accomplished according to a force and direction contrary to his or her inclination. In Marx's words, '[l]abour capacity relates to its labour as to an alien, and if capital were willing to pay it *without* making it labour it would enter the bargain with pleasure.'[71] Hegel's analysis of the labour process as it occurs *specifically* under capitalism appears in a subdivision of the *Encyclopedia Logic* entitled 'The Doctrine of Essence' which is concerned with the categories of the understanding or bourgeois consciousness. Here he discusses the production of 'the fact' or commodity, a process which is entirely external or alien to the individual worker. Everything in this process is pre-supposed or independent of the individual: the conditions of labour are 'prior, and so independent ... contingent and external.' The design and plan for the commodity to be produced 'is also ... something presupposed or ante-stated ... an independent content by itself.' The individual worker is free and independent, but his or her labour 'is possible only where the conditions are and the fact.'

Because the labour process is accomplished by elements which 'stand to each other in the shape of independent existences,' it 'has a limited content for its fact. For the fact is this whole, in phase of singleness. But since in its form this whole is external to itself, it is self-externalized even in its own self and in its content, and this externality, attaching to the fact, is a limit of its content.' Hegel's analysis is extremely abstract, but its meaning is clear: 'Whatever is necessary is through an other, which is broken up into the mediating ground (the Fact and the Activity) and an immediate actuality or accidental circumstance, which is at the same time a Condition. The necessary, being through an other, is not in and for itself: hypothetical, it is a mere result of assumption.'[72]

Hegel's abstract analysis is elucidated by Marx. All things under capitalism, he writes,

confront the individual workers as something *alien, objective, ready-made*, existing without their intervention, and frequently hostile to them ... As objects they are independent of the workers whom they *dominate*. Though the workshop is to a degree the product of the workers' combination, its entire intelligence and will seem to be incorporated in the capitalist or his under-strappers ... and the workers find themselves confronted by the *functions* of the capital that lives in the capitalist. The social forms of their own labour ... the forms of *their own* social labour, are utterly independent of the individual workers.

If the worker is alienated, so is the capitalist. Like the worker, the employer has no interest in the commodity: its production and sale is regulated and determined by autonomous market forces. Not the commodity, but profit, is the aim of the entrepreneur; the labour process itself appears as a necessary evil required for amassing profit. This 'highly impoverished and abstract content ... makes it plain that the capitalist is just as enslaved by the relations of capitalism as is his opposite pole, the worker, albeit in a quite different manner.'[73]

Given the alienated character of bourgeois consciousness and society, there is little difficulty in understanding why the development of natural science constitutes one of its most outstanding achievements. As Karl Korsch suggests, 'Bourgeois consciousness necessarily sees itself as apart from the world and independent of it, as pure critical philosophy and impartial science.'[74] Nor is it surprising that both natural science *and its object* are felt to be independent of the social activity of individual human beings. But the object of science, after all, is not just the thing being investigated but also and most important *the thing as it is placed and understood within a theoretical system*. And this system is, above everything else, a product of the development of consciousness, 'the accumulated knowledge of society.'[75] If under the bourgeois mode of production, 'capital comes to be thought of as a *thing*,' this same 'transformation may be observed in the forces of nature and science, the products of the general development of history in its abstract quintessence. They too confront the workers as the *powers* of capital.'[76]

The conception of capital, natural science, and nature as independent and autonomous powers existing apart from consciousness and ideality is paralleled, of course, by the materialist belief in matter as the ultimate and inviolable component of reality. 'The dominant *basic trend* in contemporary bourgeois philosophy, natural sciences and humanities,' writes Korsch, 'is inspired not by an idealist outlook but by a *materialist outlook that is coloured by the natural sciences*.'[77] And for the natural sciences matter is the fundamental category. In this field, notes Hegel, 'the universal, which is the final result of analysis, is only the indeterminate aggregate – of the external finite – in one word, Matter.'[78]

According to Vogel, Feuerbach's materialism 'takes matter as a real and independent being and therefore bases itself on sensation as the primary means of the authentic cognition of reality.' 'Being, apart from thought,' writes Feuerbach, 'is matter – the substratum of reality.'[79] The young Marx shares this view and observes that 'the first and most important of the inherent qualities of *matter* is *motion*.'[80] The idea that moving matter is, as Engels and Lenin suggest, 'the only reality,' the 'objective reality given to us in sensation,' and so forth, is the foundation of dialectical materialism as well as most other variants of Marxism. Nevertheless, the idea of an independent, autonomous, alien, moving matter is a myth, according to Hegel:

Materialism ... looks upon matter, *qua* matter, as the genuine objective world. But with matter we are at once introduced to an abstraction, which as such cannot be perceived, and it may be maintained that there is no matter, because, as it exists, it is always something definite and concrete. Yet the abstraction we term matter is supposed to lie at the basis of the whole world of sense, and expresses the sense-world in its simplest terms as out-and-out individualization, and hence a congeries of points in mutual exclusion.[81]

Writing from a neo-Kantian standpoint, Karl Popper echoes Hegel's observations on materialism and applies them to the program of modern science. Scientific thought, says Popper, started from the assumption that matter 'was ultimate; essential; substantial; an essence or substance neither capable of further explanation nor in need of it, and thus a principle in terms of which everything else had to be, or could be, explained.' But 'modern physics contains *explanatory theories* of matter, and of the properties of matter ... In thus *explaining matter* and its properties modern physics transcended the original programme of materialism.' The world now appears to be not a collection of independent things available as such to sensuous conception, but rather 'an interacting set of events or processes'[82] that can only be understood and grasped through theory, *through human ideality.*

Hegel observes that the main categories of natural science such as 'matter, force, those of one, many, generality, infinity, etc.' were among the earliest creations of philosophy and were first employed by medieval metaphysicians in their attempt to determine the existence and nature of God. They were taken over quite uncritically in the sixteenth century by the sciences and applied directly to nature. 'And all the while ... scientific empiricism ... is unaware that it contains metaphysics – in wielding which, it makes use of these categories and their combinations in a style utterly thoughtless and uncritical.'[83] Similarly, the sensuous conceptions of time and space, postulated by Kant as the bedrock of human thought, were mindlessly utilized by science right into the early twentieth century when they were suddenly exploded by Einstein. Their demise may have come earlier had scientists been sensitive to Hegel's critique of these 'absolute' categories.[84]

Feuerbach's philosophy (as well as that of empirical science) is the philosophy of sensuous perception. It thrives on the belief that 'reflection is the means of ascertaining the truth, and of bringing the objects before the mind as they really are. And in this belief it advances straight upon its objects, takes the materials furnished by sense and perception, and reproduces them from itself as facts of thought; and then, believing this result to be the truth, the method is content.'[85] This view was first systematically questioned by Kant, not from faith in the priority of mind over matter, but because he took very seriously Hume's scepticism about the ability of thought adequately to reflect reality.[86]

Both Kant and Hegel would agree with Feuerbach that sensuous perception is the only way an object can be received into the mind: consciousness is dependent for its content on the external world. As Hegel affirms, '*Everything is in sensation* (feeling): if you will, everything that emerges in conscious intelligence and in reason has its source and origin in sensation; for source and origin just means the first immediate manner in which a thing appears.'[87] Similarly Kant's *Critique of Pure Reason* is full of passages acknowledging the priority of the senses in the act of knowledge. 'Without the sensuous faculty,' writes Kant, 'no object would be given to us, and without the understanding no object would be thought.'[88] Furthermore both thinkers would accept Feuerbach's definition of objectivity: the intersubjectively valid correspondence between an object and the representation of it. Nor are they opposed to the empiricist notion of the objective fact: 'our consciousness is, in the matter of its contents,' writes Hegel, 'only in the fact and its characteristics ... thought is only true in proportion as it sinks itself in the facts [and] restricts itself to that universal action in which it is identical with all individuals.'[89] But Feuerbach's definition refers only to the lowest form of objectivity; there are other and higher forms of truth. The second of these forms is constructed by Kant and is discussed in the next chapter; the third, that of the union of theory and practice, is developed by Hegel and Marx.

As suggested above, Feuerbach's definition of objectivity flows from the empiricist doctrine that consciousness is essentially passive in relation to the external world. This doctrine, Hegel argues, represents 'a doctrine of bondage: for we become free, when we are confronted by no absolutely alien world, but depend upon a fact which we ourselves are.' According to empiricism, 'we must take what is given just as it is, and we have no right to ask whether and to what extent it is rational in its own nature.'[90] The parallel with Marx is obvious: for what he struggles to overcome is the situation in which the 'material conditions' of capital 'confront labour as *alien, autonomous powers*, as value – objectified labour – which treats living labour as a mere means whereby to increase and maintain itself.'[91] Marx, therefore, is concerned to discover whether capital 'is rational in its own nature'; his answer, of course, is that capitalism is far from rational – it is instead a minefield of contradictions: 'within bourgeois society, the society that rests on *exchange value*, there arise relations of circulation as well as of production which are so many mines to explode it.'[92] Truth, then, involves something more than Feuerbach's notion of validity: in recent times, says Hegel, 'it became urgent ... to justify thought, with reference to the results it had produced' (Hegel means the French Revolution), and this 'constituted one of the main problems of philosophy.'[93]

Natural or empirical science is everywhere distinguished by its reluctance to consider the categories it applies to reality. The essential anti-intellectualism of science must be obvious to anyone who has ever considered the political and theoretical backwardness evinced by many scientists whenever they wander outside their own realm,[94] not to mention the absolutely over-whelming attention paid by natural science in the modern world to novel methods and means of bringing about death and destruction to humanity and nature.[95]

The alienated character of natural science has been noted by modern philosophers of science. Popper, for example, refers to the *'instrumentalist view* ... which is accepted by our leading theorists of physics [and which] has become part of the current teachings of physics.' According to this dogma, *'The world is just what it appears to be. Only the scientific theories are not what they appear to be.* A scientific theory neither explains nor describes the world; it is nothing but an instrument.'[96] Similarly, as Giddens points out, 'Kuhn's formulation of "normal science" suggests that the de-velopment of science, outside of certain "revolutionary phases" of change, depends upon a suspension of critical reason.' Unlike Popper who urges the further progress of natural science through 'the immanent "permanent rev-olution" of critical reason,' Kuhn suggests that 'the suspension of critical reason ... is a necessary condition for the success of natural science.'[97]

The view that theories are instruments, while the real is only what is given in sensation, is a hangover from the ideas of Feuerbach and other materialists. For Hegel, such a conception is nonsense: 'Pure science ... contains *thought in so far as this is just as much the object in its own self, or the object in its own self in so far as it is equally pure thought.*'[98] If the categories of science reflect the nature of reality, this implies that they should be constantly criticized and subjected to the unrelenting tyranny of critical reason, to Popper's 'permanent revolution.' Emphasis on theory in science, in place of its current and crude reliance on sensuous perception, experiment, and so on, would be simply to recognize Hegel's dictum that 'Everything which is human, however it may appear, is so only because the thought contained in it works and has worked ... Thought is the essential, substantial and effectual ... We must, however, consider it best when Thought does not pursue anything else, but is occupied only with itself – with what is noblest – when it has sought and found itself.'[99]

Both Marxists and non-Marxists have railed against Hegel's 'denigration of science and common sense in favour of metaphysical speculation.'[100] But for Hegel, science and common sense *are* metaphysics; metaphysics, that is, of the lowest order.[101] Nevertheless, the categories of science are perfectly adequate to 'the household needs of knowledge' and should not be rejected out of hand. Categories like cause or force have a definite relation to reality, even if it is only the reality of sensuous perception. Everyone has felt or applied a 'force,' and 'causation' is immediately available to the least cultured mind: we see ourselves as the cause of certain things and recognize that a ball, for example, flies because we threw it.[102]

Much has been written recently about what separates science from mythology, and the curtain of bogus respectability that science has drawn around itself accounts for a lot of this speculation. Giddens, for example, asks, 'In what sense –, if any, is Western science able to lay any claim to an understanding of the world that is more grounded in 'truth' than that of the Azande, who perhaps simply operate with a different overall cosmology ... to that of science?' After considering various aspects of scientific method, Giddens concludes, 'There is *no way* of justifying a commitment to scientific rationality rather than, say, to Zande sorcery, apart from premises and values which science itself presupposes, and indeed has drawn from historically in its evolution within Western culture.'[103]

Hegel and Marx, however, would have no part in this hand-wringing relativism of the understanding consciousness. Science is, as Marx points out, one of 'the *general* products of human development.' As such, 'science' is 'realized *in the machine*' and 'becomes manifest to the workers in the form of capital.' Capital, in turn, is a *tremendous progressive force*: 'The tendency and the result of the capitalist mode of production is steadily to increase the productivity of labour.' Capital brings about a reduction in prices and cheapening of commodities, 'an increase in the *quantity of goods*, in the *number* of articles that must be sold. That is to say, a constant *expansion of the market* becomes a necessity for capitalist production.'[104] These achievements are possible because capital is linked to science; they would be impossible without science and would gain nothing from 'say, ... Zande sorcery.' Belief in science does not require what Giddens despairingly calls 'a Kierkegaardian "leap into faith." '[105]

Natural science represents 'the onward movement of a peaceful addition of new treasures to those already acquired.' Its achievements are recognizable everywhere in advanced industrial societies, and its impact (both positive and negative) is beginning to be felt in the impoverished countries of the Third World. Nevertheless, the principles, methodology, and technique of natural science represent the work of an *alienated* and *disjointed* consciousness. Natural science takes its objects, method, and logic as given, and then proceeds on this basis guided by a 'natural or educated sense of right and duty.'[106] Its principle is the principle of alienation, of bondage, of acceptance of the external world as it appears and is grasped by the categories of early metaphysics and common sense. Its greatest error lies in its uncritical reception of objects selected at random and as they are given by the senses. Its error is the fundamental error of materialism, an error that

Marx combats on every page of *Capital*. Reliance on materialist methodology, on Feuerbach's sensuous perception, is the foundation of all false consciousness, all of what Marx calls, following Kant and Hegel, '*illusory reflection*' or appearance. 'We shall see,' he writes, 'that this illusion is one that springs from the nature of capitalist production itself. But it is evident even now that this [illusion: D.M.] is a very convenient method by which to demonstrate the eternal validity of the capitalist mode of production and to regard *capital* as an *immutable natural element* in human production as such.'[107]

5

Kant and the Bourgeois World of Abstraction

Lukács suggests in *History and Class Consciousness* that Kant's philosophy, unlike that of Feuerbach, 'refuses to accept the world as something that has arisen ... independently of the knowing subject, and prefers to conceive of it as its own product.'[1] But, as Lukács recognizes, Kant is far from vulgar idealism, according to which the external world is merely the creation of consciousness. In fact, Kant is concerned to show the limits of reason in relation to reality; beyond these limits, he argues, reason becomes '*transcendent*' and dissolves into 'illusory appearance.'[2] Nevertheless, Kant emphasizes the active nature of consciousness in its representation of the external world, and shows that our knowledge of reality is predicated on categories, like cause and effect, that the mind develops *a priori* or independently of experience. 'Kant,' says Karl Popper, 'assumed ... that *the world as we know it is our interpretation of the observable facts in the light of theories that we ourselves invent.*'[3] As Hegel observes, 'according to Kant all knowledge, even experience, consists in thinking our impressions – in other words, in transforming into intellectual categories the attributes primarily belonging to sensation.'[4]

What Kant does in philosophy, then, is to make the same affirmation about the world as the classical political economists like Smith and Ricardo do in economics. In Hegel's words, they are engaged in 'generating a world as our own creation.'[5] If Kant sees experience itself as dependent on human consciousness, the political economists regard values and wealth as 'the material expressions of the human labour expended on them.'[6] Both discoveries are theoretical equivalents to the subjection of nature and the unleashing of human productivity made possible by the bourgeois mode of production.

Kant's philosophy, Popper argues, 'makes it possible to look upon science, whether theoretical or experimental, as a human creation, and to look upon its history as part of the history of ideas, on a level with the history of art or of literature.'[7] Kant might have been expected to influence greatly the methodology of natural science, for one of the questions he attempts to answer is, 'How is pure natural science possible?'[8] Yet in the same way as classical political economy did not banish 'the semblance of objectivity possessed by the social characteristics of labour,'[9] Kant's epistemology left the external and finite methodology of natural science untouched. Both political economy and natural science went on as before, convinced they were dealing only with *things* and not social relations or the categories of human thought. The reason for this failure is the same in both instances. Kant accepts the categories he employs in the *Critique of Pure Reason* just as they are developed in formal logic; instead of criticizing these categories he takes them to be the natural and eternal expressions of thought. As a result, 'the facts, and modes of observation' given currency by Kant 'continue quite the same as in' empirical science.[10] Similarly, because it accepts the bourgeois organization of industry 'as the eternal natural form of social production,' classical political economy fails to examine critically capitalism's defining characteristic – 'the value-form of the product of labour.'[11]

Like Kant, classical political economy remains imprisoned by the categories of the understanding consciousness. In fact, for both Hegel and Marx, political economy represents the ultimate expression of the understanding or bourgeois consciousness in the realm of empirical science. Political economy studies the system of social needs and production, but only from the point of view of the abstract individual who pursues his or her selfish interests. This pursuit, in turn, is shown to produce the interdependence of people in civil society. But the bourgeois mind sees no necessity for subjecting the economic sphere itself to control of individuals united in the state. As Marx observes, the call for a rational organization of society based on universal principles is absolute anathema for the understanding consciousness.

The same bourgeois consciousness which celebrates the division of labour in the workshop, the life-long annexation of the worker to a partial operation, and his complete subjection to capital, as an organization of labour that increases its productive power, denounces with equal vigour every conscious attempt to control and regulate the process of production socially, as an inroad upon such sacred things as the rights of property, freedom and the self-determining 'genius' of the individual capitalist. It is very characteristic that the enthusiastic apologists of the factory system have nothing more damning to urge against a general organization of labour in society than that it would turn the whole of society into a factory.[12]

In the *Philosophy of Right*, Hegel celebrates the achievements of classical political economy – 'a science which is a credit to thought because it finds laws for a mass of accidents.' Nevertheless, the method of political economy is severely limited because it takes its stand on the same soil as the bourgeoisie itself. The development of political economy, he writes

affords the interesting spectacle (as in Smith, Say and Ricardo) of thought working upon the endless mass of details which confront it at the outset and extracting therefrom the simple principles of the thing, the Understanding effective in the thing and directing it. It is to find reconciliation here to discover in the sphere of needs this show of rationality lying in the thing and effective there; but if we look at it from the opposite point of view, this is the field in which the Understanding with its subjective aims and moral fancies vents its discontent and moral frustration.[13]

Hegel has been represented as a bitter opponent of the Kantian philosophy; and recent Marxist commentators, like Colletti[14] and Benton,[15] attribute to him an absolute denial of Kant's thought, or at least his epistemology. Writes Colletti, 'One could say, indeed, that there are two main traditions in Western philosophy in this respect [i.e., epistemology]: one that descends from Spinoza and Hegel, and the other from Hume and Kant. These two lines of development are profoundly divergent. For any theory that takes science as the sole form of real knowledge – that is, falsifiable, as Popper would say – there can be no question that the tradition of Hume-Kant must be given priority and preference over that of Spinoza-Hegel.'[16] But Hegel's position with regard to Kant is the same as that of Marx to classical political economy. Marx and (as I will show) Hegel accept and go beyond the categories of political economy; in Hegel's phrase, they dialectically transcend or sublate the analyses of thinkers like Smith and Ricardo. Hegel explains this process with reference to the history of philosophy:

The relation ... of the earlier to the later systems of philosophy is much like the relation of the corresponding stages of the logical Idea: in other words, the earlier are preserved in the later; but subordinated and submerged. This is the true meaning of a much misunderstood phenomenon in the history of philosophy – the refutation of one system by another ... The refutation of a philosophy ... only means that its barriers are crossed, and its special principle reduced to a factor in the completer principle that follows.[17]

Rather than abandon Kant, Hegel accepts his thought as 'the base and the starting-point of recent German philosophy.'[18] The distinction made by Kant between 'thought and thing ... is the hinge on which modern philosophy turns.'[19] Kant rejects the materialist notion that thought passively reflects the true nature of reality. Instead, he holds that thought merely grasps phenomena as they are given to our sensations; we can never really know the thing-in-itself, but only its appearance as registered by our sensations.[20] If the categories of thought give the law of nature, as Kant suggests, this is because the nature we know is just our subjective conception of it. Objectivity does not lie in the correspondence between an external object and the way it appears in sensation, as Feuerbach (and common sense) would suggest. Categories or concepts that give meaning and coherence to the world like cause and effect, existence, contingency, and so on, are derived not from sensation, but from thought.[21] Accordingly, Kant applies the term objective only to things as they are grasped by the categories; things as they appear in sensation are merely subjective. Hegel observes that this classification, though confusing, is justified since 'the perceptions of sense are the properly dependent and secondary feature, while the thoughts are really independent and primary ... Our sensations ... are subjective; for sensations lack stability in their own nature, and are no less fleeting and evanescent than thought is permanent and self-subsisting.' Kant's distinction between the subjectivity of sensation and the objectivity of thought is now universally accepted in the sciences and humanities. Scientists try to resist the interference of merely subjective feelings in their work; and the criticism of art is based, not on 'the particular and accidental feeling or temper of the moment,' but rather 'on those general points of view which the laws of art establish.'[22]

According to Kant, we have knowledge of the objects of the external world only because we are able to unite the manifold content provided by sensation with and through the categories of thought. This unifying action of the ego or 'I' comprises 'the transcendental unity of self-consciousness.' However, the categories themselves are without any real content; while they furnish the conditions for the possibility of experience, they add nothing to experience. The notion that the unity of the external world belongs to an effort of thought rather than to the way things are immediately presented to sensation seems to threaten belief in the reality of that world. Kant's solution is to postulate the existence of an unknowable universe of things-in-themselves or 'noumena' alongside the phenomenal world of human consciousness. 'I can only say of a thing in itself,' writes Kant, 'that it exists without relation to the senses and experience ... To this transcendental object we may attribute the whole connection and extent of our possible perceptions, and say that it is given and exists in itself prior to all experience. But the phenomena, corresponding to it, are not given as things in themselves, but in experience alone.'[23] Thus, despite his emphasis on the objectivity of thought as opposed to sensation, Kant reimposes the externality or alienation of thought from its object – the characteristic of the understanding or bourgeois consciousness.[24]

Kant's conception of noumena or things-in-themselves is aimed at staking out the subject area of natural science. He is concerned once and for all to destroy the belief that abstract theorizing has a place in science. The field of science is objective knowledge; and such knowledge can only be obtained by a synthesis of the categories of thought with sense data. The function of the Kantian thing-in-itself is elaborated by Colletti:

When Kant declares that the thing-in-itself is unknowable, one (if not the only) sense of his argument is that the thing-in-itself is not a true object of cognition at all, but a fictitious object, that is nothing more than a substantification or hypostasization of logical functions, transformed into real essences. In other words, the thing-in-itself is unknowable because it represents the false knowledge of the old metaphysics. This is not the only meaning of the concept in Kant's work, but it is one of its principal senses.

According to Colletti, 'when Hegel announces that the thing-in-itself can be known, what he is in fact doing is to restore the old pre-kantian metaphysics.'[25] But Hegel is actually in sympathy with Kant's program for natural science in so far as it outlines the meaning and conditions for objectivity in the second sense of the term, i.e., knowledge obtained through the concrete union of the categories of thought with the data of sensation. Restricted to the first level of objectivity, Feuerbach and his predecessors among the early empiricist philosophers like David Hume are unable to distinguish theoretically between the data given by sense impressions in a sleeping or imaginative state as opposed to the conscious or waking state. 'An impression' for Hume, writes R.G. Collingwood, 'is distinguished from [a merely imaginative] idea only by its force or liveliness; but this force may be of two kinds. It may be the brute violence of crude sensation, as yet undominated by thought. Or it may be the solid strength of a sensum firmly placed in its context by the interpretive work of thought. Hume did not recognize the difference.'[26]

Recognition of this distinction is the strength of Kantian objectivity: with 'judgements of experience' based on the categories of thought, notes Kant, 'what experience teaches me under certain circumstances, it must always teach me and everybody; and its validity is not limited to the subject nor to its state at a particular time.'[27] Hegel outlines Kant's position as follows:

in the waking state man behaves essentially as concrete ego, an intelligence: and because of this intelligence his sense-perception stands before him as a concrete totality of features in which each member, each point, takes up its place as at the same time determined through and with all the rest. Thus the facts embodied in his sensation are authenticated, not by his mere subjective representation and distinction of the facts as something external from the person, but by virtue of the concrete interconnection in which each part stands with all parts of this complex ... In order to see the difference between dreaming and waking we need only keep in view the Kantian distinction between subjectivity and objectivity of mental representation (the latter depending upon determination through the categories).[28]

Colletti suggests that Marx subscribes to Kantian objectivity, evidenced by his discussion of the method of political economy in the *Grundrisse*.[29] Colletti is correct, of course, but only in so far as Hegel also accepts Kant's definition of validity. For Marx's discussion of method, as I will show, is based entirely on Hegel.

Hegel urges that facts shown to be objective in the Kantian sense should themselves be subjected to the scrutiny of thought. 'We are chiefly interested in knowing what a thing is: i.e. its content, which is no more subjective than it is objective.' The construction of the atomic bomb, for example, as well as its employment over Hiroshima and Nagasaki in 1945 certainly conformed to all the requirements of Kantian objectivity: but these events raised certain questions for which objectivity in the Kantian sense is irrelevant. 'If mere existence be enough to make objectivity,' Hegel remarks, 'even a crime is objective: but it is an existence which is nullity at the core, as is definitely made apparent when the day of punishment comes.'[30] Similarly, Marx never questions the objectivity of the capitalist mode of production as revealed by the categories of political economy. Nevertheless, capitalism is based on an exploitative system that necessarily dooms it to 'a historical and transitory' existence.[31]

Both Hegel and Marx point to a third and higher level of objectivity: a form of truth that recognizes the essential unity of human theory and sensuous practice. This critical form of objectivity involves employment of universal values and principles by the investigator, and rejects the bourgeois distinction between facts and values – between the intellect and the heart.[32] Rationality, as it appears in the objectivity of society, represents the manifestation of human thought and will, or ideality, which is itself an amalgam of emotions, desires, and so forth. To examine society as though it were an external thing, an object like that treated by natural science, is to overlook the most important aspect of its formation. Consequently, Ernest Mandel, for example, is wrong when he rejects the theory that Marx's 'Capital is essentially an instrument for the revolutionary overthrow of capitalism by the proletariat' and that therefore 'it is impossible to separate the "scientific" content of Capital from its "revolutionary" intention.' For Mandel, 'Marx strove ... to analyse capitalism in an objective and strictly scientific way;' he tried to build a 'rock-like foundation of scientific truth'; and 'sought to discover objective laws of motion.'[33] But Mandel limits objectivity to its Kantian form, and forgets that for Marx, capitalism is 'historical and transitory' because it fails to conform to the most elementary demands of human reason, demands which, as I shall argue, are themselves made possible by the progress fostered by capitalism.

Like Colletti, Marx is under the impression that Hegel retreats from the Kantian notion of the reality of the external world. 'Hegel,' he writes, 'fell into the illusion of conceiving the real as the product of thought concentrating itself, probing its own depths, and unfolding itself out of itself.'[34] Marx derives his interpretation from Feuerbach's materialist critique and inversion of Hegelian speculative philosophy. But, as I have argued above and as I hope to demonstrate conclusively in this study, Marx is fundamentally wrong in his estimation of Hegel's thought. In any case, his formulation of 'the concrete' or objective in the Grundrisse merely repeats Hegel's remarks on the subject. 'By concreteness of contents,' writes Hegel, 'it is meant that we must know the objects of consciousness as intrinsically determinate and as the unity of distinct characteristics.'[35] And further: 'The concrete is the unity of diverse determinations and principles; these, in order to be perfected, in order to come definitely before consciousness, must first of all be presented separately.'[36] Compare these passages from Hegel with the following one from the Grundrisse: 'The concrete is concrete because it is the concentration of many determinations, hence unity of the diverse. It appears in the process of thinking, therefore, as a process of concentration, as a result, not as a point of departure, even though it is the point of departure in reality and hence also the point of departure for observation ... and conception.'[37]

According to Hegel, while Kant made a great contribution to knowledge by demonstrating that thought, rather than sense perception, produces a unified and meaningful vision of the world, he nevertheless failed to realize the implications of his own argument. For it is not merely the action of our personal self-consciousness that introduces unity into the variety of sense perception; unity is a property of the real world which human consciousness discovers through the effort of thought. 'Though the categories, such as unity, or cause and effect, are strictly the property of thought, it by no means follows that they must be ours merely and not also characteristics of the objects. Kant however confines them to the subject-mind, and his philosophy may be styled subjective idealism: for he holds that both the form and the matter of knowledge are supplied by the Ego – or knowing subject – the form by our intellectual, the matter by our sentient ego.' The rationality or law-governed character of the external world as revealed by the action of thought, 'is itself the absolute. The absolute is, as it were, so kind as to leave individual things to their own enjoyment, and it again drives them back to the absolute unity.'[38] Far from being an abstract product of our personal self-consciousness, the laws of nature are objective and real; their reality is confirmed by human sensuous practice which takes advantage of these laws in the productions of science and industry. As Engels observes, 'If we are able to prove the correctness of our conception of a natural process by making it ourselves, bringing it into being out of its conditions and making it serve our own purposes into the bargain, then there is an end to the Kantian ungraspable thing-in-itself.'[39]

Lukács rightly alludes to the limitations of Engels' critique of Kant's thing-in-itself; industry and science under capitalism remain external and alienated activities that by no means overcome the division between thought and its object postulated by Kant.[40] Nevertheless, *in practice* alienation is in part transcended by the bourgeois mode of production, as Kant himself admits;[41] it only remains for alienation to be superseded *in theory* as well as *in practice* by – as Marx argues – the communist revolution. Hegel puts this (dialectical) idea very succinctly: The 'reason world' of society and culture is perceived by the individual in bourgeois society as a complex of 'unconditioned and likewise universal powers, to which he must subject his individual will ... Now, to turn these rational (of course positively rational) [i.e., flawed: D.M.] realities into speculative principles, the only thing needed is that they be *thought* ... By this,' Hegel explains, 'we only mean two things: first, that what is immediately at hand [i.e., bourgeois society: D.M.] 'has to be passed and left behind [in theory: D.M.] and secondly, that the subject-matter of such speculations, though in the first place only subjective, must not remain so, but be realized or translated into objectivity' – through ideality or revolutionizing practice.[42]

In his commentary on Hegel's *Logic*, Lenin describes the third, or Hegelian, form of objectivity: 'The unity of the theoretical idea (of knowledge) *and of practice* – this NB – and this unity *precisely in the theory of knowledge*, for the resulting sum is the "absolute, idea" (and the idea = "das objektive Wahre" [the objectively true].'[43] Hegel's third form of objectivity, the unity of theory and practice, is present in what he calls 'free mind,' reason or concrete will; Marx would call it 'communist consciousness.'

There are three phases of free mind: the first phase is theoretical. Theory seizes the external object so that 'the seemingly *alien* object receives, instead of the shape of something given, isolated and contingent, the form of something inwardized, subjective, universal, necessary, and rational.' The externality or *objectivity* of the object, of course, is unaffected by this activity of theory; but at the same time, in knowledge the object has become something *subjective*. 'Of the content of this knowledge I know that it *is*, that it has objectivity, and at the same time that it is in me and therefore subjective.' It is a mistake to see theory as passive in relation to its object, for mind is engaged in seeking the rational quality, the law-like form of the object. 'Intelligence strips the object of the form of contingency, grasps its rational nature and posits it as subjective: and conversely, it at the same time develops the subjectivity into the form of objective rationality.' But free theoretical mind does not stop at mere objectivity in the abstract Kantian sense – it aims at determining to what degree the object is rational in itself: in other words, theory is *critical*. 'Free mind does not content itself with a simple Knowing; it wants to *cognize* ... it wants to know not merely *that* an object *is*, and what it is *in general* and with respect to its contingent, external determinations, but it wants to know in what the object's *specific, substantial nature* consists.'[44]

Through the action of theoretical mind the externality of the object is annulled; the object becomes a part of the thinker, an aspect of his or her thinking activity. 'Consequently ... thinking has no other content than itself, than its own determinations which constitute the immanent content of the form; in the object, it seeks and finds only itself.' In this way, then, '*Thought is Being*.' But the materialists need not rejoice at the discovery of this so 'idealist' notion, since no one is questioning the external reality of the object itself. 'The object is distinguished from thought only by having the form of being, of subsisting on its own account.' Nevertheless, 'thinking stands here in a completely free relation to the object.' In its theoretical activity, mind takes *possession* of the object; the object has become the *property* of consciousness. This forms the transition from mere theory to a *thinking will.* 'But when intelligence is aware that it is determinative of the content, which is *its* mode no less than it is a mode of being, it is Will.'[45]

Will, or practical mind, is the second stage of Hegelian objectivity; through the action of will mind becomes objective to itself, distinguishing its theoretical activity from itself as objective reality. For Hegel, as Lenin observes, '*Practice is higher than (theoretical) knowledge*, for it has not only the dignity of universality, but also of immediate actuality.'[46] The sphere of will or practice is the universal reality, i.e., society, and the content of the will is freedom. 'True liberty, in the shape of moral life, consists in the will finding its purpose in a universal content, not in subjective or selfish interests.'

In the Hegelian conception, theory seeks the universal or rational aspects of its object; that is, it looks for those qualities of the object connected with concrete freedom. Similarly, Marx studies capitalist society in order to isolate those elements which will make possible the transition to communist society. In the second level of objectivity, practical mind is concerned with actualizing the rational elements in society, i.e., it attempts to bring forward and develop the inward rationality illuminated by theory. 'It belongs to the Idea of freedom that the will should make its Notion, which is *freedom itself*, its content and aim. When it does this it becomes *objective* mind, constructs for itself a world of its freedom, and thus gives to its true content a self-subsistent existence.' Free will, or objective mind, is the third stage of objectivity, i.e., 'the unity of theoretical and practical mind';[47] and objective mind in its full development is really only Hegel's term for what Marx later calls communist society.

According to Hegel, the speculative and dialectical content of absolute idealism rises above the abstract contrast between subjectivity and objectivity, characteristic not only of Kant's subjective idealism but also of the consciousness and ideology of bourgeois society as a whole. In place of the division between subjectivity and objectivity, dialectical thought 'evinces its own concrete and all-embracing nature.' Nevertheless, it must not be forgotten that 'subjective and objective are not merely identical but also distinct.' Human ideality is at once subjective – it is a property of the individual, as well as objective – it creates through its activity the concrete forms of the external world, like economy and culture. Kant, along with bourgeois (and Marxist) thinkers generally, cannot grasp this unity in difference, and therefore for them, 'the reason world may be styled ... mystical – not however because thought cannot both reach and comprehend it, but merely because it lies beyond the compass of understanding.'[48]

Emptying the categories of any real content except that given by sense experience, Kant forgot that nature and society, as they are theorized, produced, and reproduced by human conscious activity, are not only objective facts but are also the products of ideality. Sense experience is moulded by mind in so far as the categories reveal the inner pattern of reality and are actualized in the outside world by human practice. Far from being empty, as Kant supposes, logic or the system of categories constitutes the form of the real world. 'If nature as such,' writes Hegel, 'as the physical world, is contrasted with the spiritual sphere, then logic must certainly be said to be the supernatural element which permeates every relationship of man to nature, his sensation, intuition, desire, need, instinct, and simply by so doing transforms it into something human, even though only formally human, into ideas and purposes.'[49]

Economy, culture, religion, and so on are 'concrete formations of consciousness'; as such, their development is inseparable from the evolution of human consciousness itself.[50] But for individuals within the bourgeois mode of production, the creations of ideality appear as external and alien facts that exist apart from and dominate individuals.

Kant's subjective idealism mirrors the distrust of reason and thought characteristic of the bourgeois mind. 'It marks the diseased state of the age,' Hegel writes, 'when we see it adopt the despairing creed that our knowledge is only subjective, and that beyond this subjective we cannot go.' By asserting the essential unknowability of the thing-in-itself, Kant divided thought from its object 'by an impassable gulf.' Moreover, the authority on which Kant makes this distinction *represents the most extreme form of alienation*: 'Kant ... holds that what we think is false, because it is we who think it.'[51]

In a passage already quoted, Colletti suggests that for Hegel the 'thing-in-itself can be known' and that, therefore, he restores 'the old pre-kantian metaphysics.'[52] Hegel observes, however, that the thing-in-itself is simply devoid of all qualities which consciousness finds in its object, 'all its emotional aspects, and all specific thoughts of it.' Consequently, there is no great difficulty in seeing 'what is left – utter abstraction, total emptiness ... the negative of every image, feeling and definite thought.' Moreover, 'this *caput mortuum* is still only a product of thought, such as accrues when thought is carried on to abstraction unalloyed: that it is the work of the empty "Ego", which makes an object out of this empty self-identity of its own.' Hegel's dismissal of Kant's thing-in-itself must be among the most abrupt in the history of philosophy: 'one can only read with surprise the perpetual remark that we cannot know the Thing-in-itself. On the contrary there is nothing we can know so easily.' Instead of restoring the 'old pre-kantian metaphysics,' Hegel seeks only to reinstate 'the natural belief of men ... that thought coincides with things.' Notes Hegel, 'everything we know both of outward and inward nature, in one word, the objective world, is in its own self the same as it is in thought, and to think is to bring out the truth of our object, be it what it may. The business of philosophy is only to bring into explicit consciousness what the world in all ages has believed about thought. Philosophy therefore advances nothing new; and our present discussion has led us to a conclusion which agrees with the natural belief of mankind.'[53]

Although he rejects the Kantian thing-in-itself, the whole construction of Hegel's *Logic* is based on Kant's notion that the categories of thought are the actual building blocks of human experience. The categories are con-stituents of the logical Idea, and the Idea is simply the *a priori* basis through which individual consciousness is necessarily led 'onwards in due progress to the real departments of Nature and Mind.' What Kant fails to acknowl-edge, however, is the active power of thought; for him, the activity of consciousness is separated altogether from human practice and ideality. Kant's 'great error is to restrict our notions of the nature of thought to its form in the understanding alone. To think the phenomenal world rather means to recast its form, and transmute it into a universal. And thus the action of thought has also a *negative* effect upon its basis: and the matter of sensation, when it receives the stamp of universality, at once loses its first and phenomenal shape. By the removal and negation of the shell, the kernel within the sense-percept is brought to light.'[54]

Because the Idea is based on 'the material world perceived by the senses'[55] it does not 'come into possession of a content originally foreign to it: but by its own native action is specialized and developed to Nature and Mind.' In the case of nature, for example, the Idea begins as 'Perception or Intuition, and the percipient Idea is Nature': in other words, external nature is first given to consciousness by sense perception. Consciousness then works up this concrete content into categories and laws which are not external to nature, as Kant suggests, but rather express its essence and reality. This is Hegel's meaning when he writes on the final page of the *Encyclopedia Logic* that 'Enjoying ... an absolute liberty, the Idea does not merely pass over into life' as passive sense perception, or as Kantian 'finite cognition allow life to show in it: in its own absolute truth it resolves to let the "moment" of its particularity, or of the first characterization and other-being, the immediate idea, as its reflected image, go forth freely as Nature.'[56]

Like Marx's work in the *Grundrisse* and *Capital*, Hegel's logic studies 'thought in its actions and its productions.' Whereas the Kantian categories are simply taken over from formal logic, the categories in dialectical logic reflect the history of philosophy itself.[57] Similarly, Marx's *Capital*, as Korsch points out, 'is indeed precisely a theoretical comprehension of history.'[58]

The history of philosophy constitutes the development of the categories of thought which men and women use to comprehend, utilize, and transform the relations of the natural and social world. Consequently, the *Logic* is merely the exposition of that history in dialectical (i.e., logical and developmental) form. But it is also something else: it 'recognizes and adopts ... the empirical facts contained in the several sciences ... it appreciates and applies towards its own structure the universal element in these sciences, their laws and classifications ... it preserves the same forms of thought, the same laws and objects – while at the same time remodelling and expanding them with wider categories.'[59] In the same way, Marx employs the categories and laws of political economy in his concrete analyses and also invents new ones, like surplus value and the social individual. Read along with Hegel's other works, especially the *History of Philosophy* and the *Philosophy of Right*, the *Logic* is what would now be called an exposition in the sociology of knowledge. But with this difference: it is a sociology concerned not with ideology as false consciousness, but with human thought as an expression of the essence of the world. Seen in this way, Hegel's system is infinitely more powerful and more advanced than anything ever attempted in the field.

2 CONTRADICTION AND FREEDOM

Kant's epistemology, which guarantees only an illusory unity of consciousness with its object, and leaves the thing-in-itself outside of cognition, represents what Hegel calls 'abstract ideality.'[60] This is the form of ideality commonly thought to apply to his philosophy as well: an abstract essence or Idea, which leaves reality outside of consciousness, or, rather, refuses to recognize external reality at all, except in an abstract manner. Marxists and their opponents are unified in this vision of Hegel. Accordingly, Karl Popper observes that 'Hegel's philosophy ... permitted [him] to construct a theory of the world out of pure reasoning.'[61] And even the Hegelian Marxist Karl Korsch suggests that 'For Hegel, the practical task of the Concept in its "thinking activity" (in other words, philosophy) does not lie in the domain of ordinary "practical human and sensuous activity" (Marx). It is rather "to grasp what it is, for that which is, is Reason".'[62] But for Hegel, of course, ideality is precisely the relation between practical, sensuous activity and its object, which he refers to as 'an identity with itself in its difference.'[63]

Contrary to Kant's belief, the ego is at once *identical with* and *distinct from* the external reality it constructs through the categories. The world as it truly is cannot be known except through thought, but it also exists independently of thinking. The freedom of the ego consists in its ability to separate itself from the natural world and to recognize that world as an *external object* separate from consciousness. Kant's philosophy 'places every determinateness of things both as regards form and content, in consciousness ... This crude presentation ... is directly contradicted by the consciousness of freedom, according to which I know myself rather as the universal and undetermined, and separate off from myself those manifold and necessary determinations, recognizing them as something external for me and belonging only to things. In this consciousness of its freedom the ego is to itself that true identity reflected into itself, which the thing-in-itself was supposed to be.'[64]

Kant recognizes one side of ideality: the translation of the external world, as it is given in sensation, into the categories of mind. But he fails to emphasize the active side of consciousness: the theoretical and practical activity that transforms and creates the natural and social world. Nevertheless, he does admit the unity of theory and practice through what he calls pure practical reason. Practical reason concerns the faculty of will 'which is a faculty either of bringing forth objects corresponding to conceptions or of determining itself, i.e., its causality to effect such objects.' The precepts of will, says Kant, 'themselves produce the reality of that to which they refer (the intention of the will) – an achievement which is in no way the business of theoretical concepts.' Kant's notion of the freedom of the will has radical implications: 'For, in fact, the moral law ideally transfers us into a nature in which reason would bring forth the highest good were it accompanied by sufficient physical capacities; and it determines our will to impart to the sensuous world the form of a system of rational beings.'[65] With Kant, however, even the unity of theory and practice remains purely abstract. The will is determined by moral laws, but the content of these laws remains indeterminate in the extreme,[66] as evidenced by his *Funda-*

mental Law of Pure Practical Reason: 'So act that the maxim of your will could always hold at the same time as a principle establishing universal law.'[67]

In Kant's philosophy, the fundamental determinant of the will is simply 'abstract identity ... there must be no contradiction in the act of self-determination.'[68] In other words, the will is determined by moral laws it is bound to obey; it cannot contradict them without contravening morality itself. These laws, which are presented to the individual by his or her reasoning faculty, are absolute; acting according to them constitutes 'duty.' 'The relation of ... will to [moral] law is one of dependence under the name of "obligation". This term implies a constraint to an action, though this constraint is only that of reason and its objective law. Such an action is called *duty*.' Obligation or duty really represents the individual's freedom to conform to moral laws which themselves are the product of his or her thinking reason. 'The moral law expresses nothing else than the autonomy of the pure practical reason, i.e., freedom.'[69]

Hegel is impressed with Kant's 'Practical Reason [which] does not confine the universal principle of the Good to its own inward regulation: it first becomes *practical*, in the true sense of the word, when it insists on the Good being manifested in the world with an outward objectivity, and requires that the thought shall be objective throughout, and not merely subjective.' But Kantian free will is governed entirely by the abstract identity of the understanding: conformity of the will to moral law. Further, the laws of the will have in themselves no social content. 'To say that a man must make the Good the content of his will raises the question, what that content is, and what are the means of ascertaining what good is. Nor does one get over the difficulty by the principle that the will must be consistent with itself, or by the precept to do duty for the sake of duty.' Kant strips the concept of freedom of any content it had in metaphysics and fails to originate 'any special forms, whether cognitive principles or moral laws.' Nevertheless, by recognizing the absolute autonomy of human thought in social or moral practice, Kant 'absolutely refused to accept or indulge anything possessing the character of an externality. Henceforth the principle of the independence of Reason, or of its absolute self-subsistence, is made a general principle of philosophy, as well as a foregone conclusion of the time.'[70]

Hegel argues, 'The principle of free mind is to make the merely given element in consciousness [i.e., the external world as perceived by the senses: D.M.] into something mental [the categories of thought: D.M.] and conversely to make what is mental into an objectivity' through revolutionizing practice or ideality. In Kant's epistemology, however, the identity of subject and object 'is still *abstract*, the formal identity of subjectivity and objectivity. Only when this identity has developed into an actual difference and has made itself into the identity of itself and its difference, therefore, only when mind or spirit steps forth as an immanently developed totality, not till then has that certainty *established* itself as truth.'[71] Lenin outlines Hegel's argument as follows: 'The activity of man, who has constructed an objective picture of the world for himself, *changes* external actuality, abolishes its determinateness (= alters some sides or other, qualities, of it), and thus removes from it the features of Semblance, externality and nullity, and makes it as being in and for itself (= objectively true) ... The result of activity is the test of subjective cognition and the criterion of OBJECTIVITY WHICH TRULY IS.'[72]

For Kant, reality as perceived by the ego – the singular or simple 'identity of my Self'[73] – is characterized by *the absence of contradiction*; consequently, non-contradiction must be the foremost principle of thought. As Karl Popper observes, 'it can easily be shown that if one were to accept contradictions then one would have to give up any kind of scientific activity: it would mean a complete breakdown of science. This can be shown by proving that *if two contradictory statements are admitted, any statement whatever must be admitted*; for from a couple of contradictory statements any statement whatever can be validly inferred.'[74] Kant insists that if human reason operates without regard for the non-contradictory world of experience, it is bound to involve itself in arguments, which, although they contradict one another, can equally be shown logically valid. Kant explains that this 'natural and unavoidable dialectic of pure reason'[75] is one of the essential weaknesses of thought, against which it must constantly guard itself. Contradiction can only be eluded by constant reference to the non-contradictory facts given to us in external reality.

Mind is subject to a mass of internal contradictions; reality, however, is signally without contradiction. Kant's 'only motive,' Hegel writes, 'was an excess of tenderness for the things of the world. The blemish of contradiction, it seems, could not be allowed to mar the essence of the world; but there could be no objection to attaching it to the thinking Reason, to the essence of mind.'[76]

Most commentators believe that Hegel utterly rejects Kant's principle of non-contradiction; and this, suggests Karl Popper, 'makes his system secure against any sort of criticism or attack and thus it is dogmatic in a very peculiar sense, so that I should like to call it a "reinforced dogmatism." '[77] Hegel, however, is much influenced by Kant's discussion of contradiction and states that it is even 'more valuable' than his account of the nature and use of the categories. He agrees with Kant that non-contradiction is an essential element of formal logic and empirical science, where science deals with inorganic matter and sensuous conceptions like number and force. But the principle of non-contradiction has no application whatever to the world of living things, and especially to the intellectual and social universe. 'If in the end,' writes Hegel, 'Reason be reduced to mere identity without diversity ... it will in the end also win a happy release from contradiction at the slight sacrifice of all its facets and contents.'[78]

According to Hegel, when Kant shows that reason becomes 'transcendent' or prey to illusion and contradiction in its effort to comprehend the infinite, what he actually proves is the inability of the categories of the understanding or bourgeois mind to grasp the social and intellectual world. The sphere of social relations is certainly available to experience, but Kant's view of experience is limited to what immediately can be perceived by the senses: 'experience and observation of the world mean nothing else for Kant than a candle stick standing here, and a snuff-box standing there.'[79] Kantian freedom is simply an 'ought to be,' something to be striven for but never realized in the world of experience; it is an ideal conception that can only be approximated by political constitutions which are 'always nearer and nearer to the greatest possible perfection.'[80] But Hegel argues that freedom can be studied with reference to the empirical world; it takes a concrete form at each stage of development of society, a form which can be elucidated by science and connected with other social phenomena – law, religion, class structure, mode of production, and so on. In this (theoretical) reconstruction of society, however, something more than sense perception is involved. 'No one wishes to demand a sensuous proof or verification of the infinite; spirit is for spirit alone.'[81]

Marx accepts Hegel's view and applies it to 'vulgar economy' – the science which 'actually does no more than interpret, systematize and defend in doctrinaire fashion the conceptions of the agents of bourgeois production who are entrapped in bourgeois production relations.' The limitation of this science lies in its abstract and uncritical faith in the external world of sense experience. 'It should not astonish us ... that vulgar economy feels particularly at home in the estranged outward appearances of economic relations ... and that these relations seem the more self-evident the more their internal relationships are concealed from it ... But all science would be superfluous if the outward appearance and the essence of things directly coincided.'[82] Marx believes that freedom can be studied as it presents itself in concrete form in society; further, this study can reveal what Hegel calls 'the actually present Idea of the universal, of a total and perfect.'[83] That is, science can illuminate the eternal aspects of reality; elements which display the actual shape of the future. Capitalism, for example, 'gives rise to a stage, on the one hand, in which coercion and monopolisation of social development (including its material and intellectual advantages) by one portion of society at the expense of the other are eliminated; on the other hand, it creates the material means and embryonic conditions, making it possible in a higher form of society to combine this surplus-labour with a greater reduction of time devoted to material labour in general.'[84]

Marx's conception of history as well as his concrete analysis of the categories of bourgeois political economy are grounded on the principle of contradiction constructed by Hegel. Contradiction for Hegel is the essential principle of all living things;[85] thus appetite itself, the desire of a human being to overcome hunger and thirst, is simply an aspect of contradiction: for in the condition of hunger both of the following (contradictory) statements are possible: 'I am a self-sufficient unity'; 'I am not a self-sufficient unity.' Writes Hegel, 'Where a self-identical something bears within it a contradiction and is charged with the feeling of its intrinsic self-identity as well as the opposite feeling of its internal contradiction, there necessarily emerges the impulse to remove this contradiction.' Satisfaction of appetite itself represents the unity of the self-identical human being with the object that relieves hunger; he or she becomes 'an identity of itself and its difference': 'In the object, the subject beholds its own lack, its own one-sidedness, sees in it something which belongs to its own essential nature and yet is lacking in it. Self-consciousness is able to remove this contradiction since it is not [merely] being, but absolute activity; and it removes it by taking possession of the object whose independence is, so to speak, only pretended, satisfies itself by consuming it and, since it is self-end ... maintains itself in this process.'[86]

The absolute activity of the individual, however, involves more than the satisfaction of appetite, which, anyway, 'is always destructive, and in its content selfish: and as the satisfaction has only happened in the individual (and that is transient) the appetite is again generated in the very act of satisfaction.' A much more important aspect of contradiction involves the struggle of the individual to assert his or her freedom and independence over and against other individuals who deny them. This struggle, which Hegel calls, 'the process of *recognition*' forms an essential aspect of human history.[87] The struggle for freedom reflects a contradiction between what certain individuals and groups *know* to be their essential nature and what they actually *are* in society. Thus in the US slave states, two contradictory statements were equally valid: 'Blacks are inferior and have no claim to equal rights'; 'blacks are equal to others and are entitled to equal rights.'

The possibility and even *necessity* of *contradiction* in society lies in the inherent characteristics of the individual. 'Living beings as such,' notes Hegel, 'possess within them a universal vitality, which overpasses and includes the single mode; and thus, as they maintain themselves in the negative of themselves, they feel the contradiction to *exist* within them. But the contradiction is within them only in so far as one and the same subject includes both the universality of their sense of life, and the individual mode which is in negation with it.'[88] The young Marx applies this concept to the degraded situation of the proletariat in the mid-nineteenth century. 'The class of the proletariat,' he writes, 'feels annihilated in its self-alienation; it sees in it its own powerlessness and the reality of an inhuman existence. In the words of Hegel, the class of the proletariat is in *indignation* at that abasement, an indignation to which it is necessarily driven by the contradiction between its human *nature* and its conditions of life, which is the outright, decisive and comprehensive negation of that nature.'[89]

The limitation an individual may feel in his or her social position represents the consciousness of another unlimited and universal mode of existence – one that would make fulfilment and self-realization possible. 'A very little consideration might show that to call a thing finite or limited proves by implication the very presence of the infinite and unlimited, and that our knowledge of a limit can only be when the unlimited is *on this side* in consciousness.'[90]

The modern notion of freedom and equality for all men and women is nothing but a result and reflection of the principle of struggle and contradiction. Moreover, freedom and equality require not only their achievement for the particular individual, but also his or her recognition of these rights for others – *in itself a contradiction*. Notes Hegel, 'I am only truly free when the other is also free and recognized by me as free ... Freedom demands, therefore, that the self-conscious subject should not heed his own natural existence or tolerate the natural existence of others; on the contrary ... he should in his individual, immediate actions stake his own life and the lives of others to win freedom. Only through struggle, therefore, can freedom be won; the assertion that one is free does not suffice to make one so.'[91] The necessity for freedom to be universal in order to be real for the individual is emphasized by Marx: 'In the United States of America, every independent workers' movement was paralysed as long as slavery disfigured a part of the republic. Labour in a white skin cannot emancipate itself where it is branded in a black skin.'[92]

In the course of history the fight for independence and freedom 'ends in the first instance as a one-sided negation with inequality ... Thus arises the status of *master and slave*.' This relationship results in the formation of a state: 'the emergence of man's social life and the commencement of political union.'[93] 'The family is the first precondition of the state,' declares Hegel, 'but class divisions are the second.'[94] Class distinctions indicate the organic differentiation of society and the beginnings of a division of labour. These in turn – as shown by Hegel's account of the relationship between class struggle and the development of the Greek and Roman states – are necessary for the development of a constitution and political life. '[A] real state and a real Government,' says Hegel, 'arise only after a distinction of classes has arisen, when wealth and poverty become extreme, and when such a condition of things presents itself that a large proportion of the people can no longer satisfy its necessities in the way in which it has been accustomed so to do.'[95] Although founded on class antagonisms, the state facilitates economic and cultural development; it 'creates a *permanent* means and a provision which takes care for and secures the future.'[96] The relationship between contradiction, struggle, and human freedom is, of course, a basic element in Marx's materialist conception of history. 'The history of all hitherto existing society,' Marx declares in the *Communist Manifesto*, 'is the history of class struggles.'[97]

The notion of abstract identity and equality treasured by the understanding consciousness, with its naive faith in the principle of non-contradiction, leaves it completely unable to grasp the discordant reality of modern civil or bourgeois society. The capitalist mode of production is founded on what Hegel calls the rights of particularity; that is, what Marx calls the 'concept [of] bourgeois society'[98] is the principle of self-seeking aggrandizement and the pursuit of private wealth. Given this particularity, inequality is inevitable. 'The objective right of the particularity of mind is contained in the Idea. Men are made unequal by nature, where inequality is in its element, and in civil society the right of particularity is so far from annulling this natural inequality that it produces it out of mind and raises it to an inequality of skill and resources, and even to one of moral and intellectual attainment. To oppose to this right a demand for equality is a folly of the Understanding which takes as real and rational its abstract equality and its "ought to be".'[99] For the bourgeois mind, however, even the 'existence of "classes" generally' is in question, and the denial of the reality of classes is 'drawn from the consideration of the State in its "aspect" of abstract equity.' But equality in bourgeois society 'is something absolutely impossible; for individual distinctions of sex and age will always assert themselves; and even if an equal share in government is accorded to all citizens, women and children are immediately passed by, and remain excluded. The distinction between poverty and riches, the influence of skill and talent, can be as little ignored – utterly refuting those abstract assertions.'[100]

The evolution of animate nature is a peaceful and gradual process which nevertheless eludes the abstract categories of the understanding like 'quality, cause and effect, composition, constituents, and so on.' The animal, notes Hegel, is an end in itself, and 'in the living organism ... the final cause is a moulding principle and an energy immanent in the matter, and every member is in its turn a means as well as an end.' The notion that animate nature develops according to a teleological principle, to inner design, was first suggested by Kant. But it was abandoned by empirical science in Hegel's time, only to be taken up once again by Darwin in the middle of the nineteenth century. 'The principle of inward adaptation or design, had it been kept to and carried out in scientific application would have led to a different and a higher method of observing nature.' In contrast with nature, the evolution of society is based on splits, antagonisms, and contradiction. 'The spiritual is distinguished from the natural, and more especially from the animal, life, in the circumstance that it does not continue a mere stream of tendency, but sunders itself to self-realization.'[101]

For the understanding consciousness, the state of nature which characterized early man and woman was a blissful life of equality. But this notion, on which the understanding bases its abstract demand for equality, is completely mistaken. The arbitrariness and inequality of bourgeois society exemplify relations of a state of nature that are still in force and have not yet been suppressed by the rational impulse of men and women. 'The sphere of particularity, which fancies itself the universal, is still only relatively identical with the universal, and consequently it still retains in itself the particularity of nature, i.e. arbitrariness, or in other words the relics of the state of nature.'[102] Bourgeois society like 'nature in every part is in the bonds of individualism'; it is a 'state of inward breach' in which 'man pursues ends of his own and draws from himself the material of his conduct. While he pursues these aims to the uttermost, while his knowledge and his will seek himself, his own narrow self apart from the universal, he is evil; and his evil is to be subjective.' There are, of course, natural qualities in the individual such as 'social or benevolent inclinations, love, sympathy, and others, reaching beyond his selfish isolation.' But under capitalism, these qualities are subservient and restricted: 'so long as these tendencies are instinctive, their virtual universality of scope and purport is vitiated by the subjective form which always allows free play to self-seeking and random action.'[103]

Far from the harmonious development pictured by the understanding consciousness in accordance with Kant's sacred principle of non-contradiction, the progress of bourgeois society is founded on *alienation* of human labour-power, skill, and talent – their sale and transformation into commodities external to and independent of the individual who possesses them. Perhaps recognizing the massive social threat of this form of alienation to the principle of non-contradiction, Kant himself denies that labour-power as opposed to the product of labour may be considered a commodity. *Things* such as the product of an artisan or the wares of a merchant are certainly commodities. 'But guaranteeing one's labour (*praestatio operae*) is not the same as selling a commodity.' Significantly, he employs this distinction to justify the exclusion of certain social groups and classes – women, servants, and wage-labourers, among others – from membership and voting rights in the bourgeois state. The principle of non-contradiction, therefore, is maintained by denying rights of citizenship to anyone, as Kant puts it, who allows 'others to make use of him.'[104]

Hegel rejects Kant's distinction between the sale of labour power and the production and sale of other commodities (a rejection, as I will show in later chapters, which has profound consequences for his own theory of the state). 'The field of vision [of] the Understanding,' Hegel writes, 'is ... limited ... to the dilemma ... "either a thing or not a thing," ' where a ' "thing" is contrasted with "person" as such [and] means ... that whose determinate character lies in its pure externality.' In bourgeois society, however, 'attainments, erudition, talents, and so forth, are, of course, owned by free mind,' i.e., the individual, 'and are something internal and not external to it, but even so, by expressing them it may embody them in something external and alienate them ... and in this way they are put into the category of "things".' The category of things, then, becomes very large indeed: 'Mental aptitudes, erudition, artistic skill, even things ecclesiastical (like sermons, masses, prayers, consecration of votive objects), inventions, and so forth, become subjects of a contract, brought on to a parity, through being bought and sold, with things recognized as things.'[105] Accordingly, *the absolute principle of bourgeois society is the principle of contradiction*: 'My labour or ideality is a part of me' : 'My labour or ideality is a thing.' The result is pointed out by Marx: 'The bourgeoisie has stripped of its halo every occupation hitherto honoured and looked up to with reverent awe. It has converted the physician, the lawyer, the priest, the poet, the man of science, into its paid wage-labourers.'[106]

Where the understanding sees only harmony and non-contradiction, capitalism proceeds by tearing apart and crushing the very basis of social harmony, the family. Once the means of education and training for the individual, and a source of comfort and subsistence for those unable to earn a living in society, the family as a functioning economic unit is virtually dissolved by industrialization. The family holdings and inheritance, however meagre, which formerly provided a stable foundation for family members is replaced by an economic order which 'subjects the permanent existence of even the entire family to dependence on itself and to contingency.'[107] Again, Marx: 'The bourgeoisie has torn away from the family its sentimental veil, and has reduced the family relation to a mere money relation.'[108]

Capitalism creates the conditions in which the traditional educative role of the family is usurped by society, by what Hegel calls 'the universal family.' Both he and Marx urge that society take on this role, even over the protests of parents who for religious or personal reasons feel they can do a better job. 'The chief opposition to any form of public education usually comes from parents and it is they who talk and make an outcry about teachers and schools because they have a faddish dislike to them. None the less, society has a right to act on principles tested by its experience and to compel parents to send their children to school, to have them vaccinated, and so forth.'[109] Hegel's observations are taken up by Marx in the *Manifesto*: 'But you will say,' he writes, referring to the opponents of communism, 'we destroy the most hallowed of relations, when we replace home education by social ... The bourgeois claptrap about the family and education, about the hallowed co-relation of parent and child, becomes all the more disgusting, the more, by the action of Modern Industry, all family ties among the proletarians are torn asunder, and their children transformed into simple articles of commerce and instruments of labour.'[110] Hegel is also keenly aware of the exploitation and degradation of children under the bourgeois mode of production. 'Children are potentially free,' he writes, 'and their life directly embodies nothing save potential freedom. Consequently they are not things and cannot be the property either of their parents or others.' In a society where indentured service by working-class children was the rule rather than the exception, Hegel's (and Marx's) insistence on public education is much more radical than it sounds today. 'The services which may be demanded from children should ... have education as their sole end and be relevant thereto; they must not be ends in themselves, since a child in slavery is in the most unethical of all situations whatever.'[111]

Kant seeks to reduce capitalism's negative impact on bourgeois domesticity by legislating the principle of non-contradiction into the structure of the patriarchal family itself. Accordingly, he invents a form of property ('Personal Right of a Real Kind') which makes a man's wife (as well as his children and domestic servants) his thing-like possession.[112] For Hegel, however, the contradictions of bourgeois society that inevitably dissolve the family also undermine the foundations of women's domestic servitude. In marriage, Hegel observes, 'the wife is without the moment of knowing herself as *this* particular self in the other partner.'[113] While the husband may carve a place for himself in society, the social universe of the wife is limited and restricted to the family alone: 'man has his actual substantive life in the state, in learning, and so forth, as well as in labour and struggle with the external world and with himself so that it is only out of his diremption that he fights his way to self-subsistent unity with himself. In the family he has a tranquil intuition of this unity, and there he lives a subjective ethical life on the plane of feeling. Woman, on the other hand, has her substantive destiny in the family, and to be imbued with family piety is her ethical frame of mind.' Identification of the husband with society or the universal, and restriction of the wife to the family alone results in the sexual double standard. 'It must be noticed in connection with sex-relations that a girl in surrendering her body loses her honour. With a man, however, the case is otherwise, because he has a field for ethical activity outside the family. A girl is destined in essence for the marriage tie and for that only; it is therefore demanded of her that her love shall take the form of marriage and that the different moments in love shall attain their true rational relation to each other.'[114]

Comfortable assumptions about women and their place in society are destroyed by the contradictions of bourgeois society. The life of a woman confined to the family is 'a life which has not yet attained its full actualization.'[115] Her self-actualization only becomes possible with the dissolution of the patriarchal family by industrial capitalism. For Hegel, the distinction between the sexes within the family is natural rather than rational; and civil society absolutely destroys this immediate and natural relationship. The family is splintered into its independent members and distinctions between individuals on the basis of their role in the family disappears. 'Civil society tears the individual from his family ties, estranges the members of the family from one another, and recognizes them as self-subsistent persons.'[115] Even the eternal nature of marriage falls victim to the contradictions and vicissitudes of life in bourgeois society, and the possibility of divorce combined with economic uncertainty compel women to enter civil society as independent, self-subsistent persons rather than wives or family members. 'Marriage is of course broken up by the *natural* element contained in it, the death of husband and wife: but even their union of hearts, as it is a mere 'substantiality' of feeling, contains the germ of liability to chance and decay. In virtue of such fortuitousness, the members of the family take up to each other the status of persons; and it is thus that the family finds introduced into it for the first time the element, originally foreign to it, of *legal* regulation.'[116]

Supportive family relations are transformed into purely economic and self-seeking relations which paradoxically increase the dependence of individuals on one another. As Marx puts it, 'The general interest is precisely the generality of self-seeking interest.'[117] 'Subjective self-seeking,' Hegel observes, 'turns into a contribution to the satisfaction of the needs of everyone else. That is to say, by a dialectical advance, subjective self-seeking turns into the mediation of the particular through the universal, with the result that each man in earning, producing, and enjoying on his own account is *eo ipso* producing and earning for the enjoyment of everyone else.'[118]

Here, in other words, is the trinity relation discussed in Chapter 3: the unity of the extremes of finite and infinite, particular and universal – a unity thought impossible by the understanding consciousness with its abstract principle of non-contradiction. For revealed in this relation is simply another aspect of the chief contradiction that permeates bourgeois society – the contradiction that resides in the commodity relation and the alienation of human productive powers it entails. The individual in bourgeois society is supremely *independent*; but also utterly *dependent*. Recognition of this contradiction had, of course, a great impact on Marx:

The very necessity of first transforming individual products or activities into *exchange value*, into *money*, so that they obtain and demonstrate their social *power* in this *objective* ... form, proves two things: (1) That individuals now produce only for society and in society; (2) that production is not *directly* social, is not 'the offspring of association', which distributes labour internally. Individuals are subsumed under social production; social production exists outside them as their fate; but social production is not ... manageable by them as their common wealth.[119]

Kant's adherence to abstract identity trapped him in the proposition I = I; the individual is simple and self-same. The individual, however, is not simple and self-same, but rather the identity which posits difference, the absolute activity of ideality or revolutionizing practice. This activity unites the individual with society, while at the same time making him or her appear to be independent of it. 'Life is that inner existence which does not remain *abstractly* inner but enters wholly into its manifestation.'[120] The individual is above all the embodiment of productive and creative activity, the absolute force which changes external reality according to his or her needs and desires, and therefore creates a living unity between the object of activity and consciousness. 'A person,' says Hegel, 'must translate his freedom into an external sphere in order to exist as Idea.' Possession is the first manifestation of the activity of the individual, and 'To impose a form on a thing [i.e., to work on something: D.M.] is the mode of taking possession most in conformity with the Idea to this extent, that it implies a union of subject and object.'[121]

Through his or her conscious activity in society – ideality or revolutionizing practice – the individual posits a relation which Hegel calls, Reason or Idea. But in civil society – where people are 'independent, absolutely impenetrable, resistant, and yet at the same time identical with one another, hence not independent, not impenetrable, but, as it were, fused with one another' – this relation appears as a social reality independent of and opposed to the individual: 'Reason, as the *Idea* ... as it here appears, is to be taken as meaning that the distinction between notion and reality which it unifies has the special aspect of a distinction between the self-concentrated notion or consciousness, and the object subsisting external and opposed to it.'[122] Under capitalism, as Marx points out, 'the objective conditions of labour assume an ever more colossal independence, represented by its very extent, opposite living labour, and ... social wealth confronts labour in more powerful portions as an alien and dominant power. The emphasis comes to be placed not on the state of being *objectified*, but on the state of being *alienated*, dispossessed, sold.'[123]

The apparent externality to individuals of the very objects which they create leads precisely to the Kantian definition of objectivity: 'My idea is correct merely if it agrees with the object, even when the latter only remotely corresponds to its Notion and hence has hardly any truth at all.'[124] But the third, Hegelian form of objectivity – the union of consciousness with its object as achieved through practice or ideality[125] – has to be transferred to society as a whole. Society must be made subject to reason in the same manner as reason transforms and creates in its own image the objects of the external world. 'It belongs to the Idea of freedom that the will should make its Notion, which is *freedom itself*, its content or aim. When it does this it becomes *objective* mind, constructs for itself a world of its freedom, and thus gives to its true content a self-subsistent existence.'[126] What Hegel has in mind here is similar in many respects to that form of society which Marx calls communist society: 'In place of the old bourgeois society, with its classes and class antagonisms, we shall have an association, in which the free development of each is the condition for the free development of all.'[127]

The understanding consciousness is utterly repelled by, and incapable of grasping, the absolute union of the very extremes, individual and society, that the bourgeois mode of production actually does unite if only in an abstract and accidental manner. Its feelings of repulsion are due to the most far-reaching illusion of all within capitalism: the mystique of equality and free exchange which governs the relations of commodities. As Marx suggests, equality of exchange in the market is the basis of freedom and equality in bourgeois society as a whole.

> [W]hen the economic form, exchange, posits the all-sided equality of its subjects, then the content, the individual as well as the objective material which drives towards exchange, is *freedom*. Equality and freedom are thus not only respected in exchange based on exchange values but, also, the exchange of exchange values is the productive, real basis of all *equality* and *freedom*. As pure ideas they are merely the idealized expressions of this basis; as developed in juridical, political, social relations, they are merely this basis to a higher power.

Free exchange is so far from inequality and privilege that it is their very opposite: 'A worker who buys commodities for 3s. appears to the seller in the same function, in the same equality – in the form of 3s. – as the king who does the same. All distinction between them is extinguished.'[128] Accordingly, *in the realm of simple exchange the principle of non-contradiction reaches its highest expression.*

For the abstract understanding, the fundamental law of thought is that of identity, I = I; but the fundamental law of capitalist production eludes this equation. Instead of identity, there is an identity which posits difference. The capitalist invests his or her money (M) into commodities (C), not in order to satisfy the fundamental law of identity, $M = M$, but rather to achieve an altogether different result, where $M = M + m$. 'The capitalist knows,' writes Marx, 'that all commodities ... are in faith and in truth money ... and, what is more, a wonderful means for making still more money out of money.' Money becomes capital only on condition that it creates more money. '*In itself* ... money may only be defined as capital if it is employed, spent, with the aim of *increasing* it, if it is spent expressly in order to *increase* it. In the case of the sum of value or money this phenomenon is its *destiny*, its inner law, its tendency, while to the *capitalist*, i.e.

the owner of the sum of money, in whose hands it shall acquire its function, it appears as *intention, purpose.*' Although it supplies the vital energy to capitalist development, the transformation of money into more money seems to involve neither its transformation into commodities nor the production process itself.

In fact the relation of money with money is every bit as mysterious as the relation of the Holy Trinity itself. Notes Marx,

> in the circulation *M-C-M*, value suddenly presents itself as a self-moving substance which passes through a process of its own, and for which commodities and money are both mere forms. But there is more to come: instead of simply representing the relations of commodities, it now enters into a private relationship with itself, as it were. It differentiates itself as original value from itself as surplus-value, just as God the Father differentiates himself from God the Son, although both are of the same age and form, in fact one single person; for only by the surplus-value of [e.g.] £10 does the £100 originally advanced become capital, and as soon as this has happened, as soon as the son has been created and, through the son, the father, their difference vanishes again, and both become one, £110.[129]

What Hegel calls, 'the general capital' of society[130] – and what Marx terms, social capital – is actually the product of the labour of all individuals. Nevertheless, it appears as 'the means of production monopolized by a certain section of society, confronting living labour-power as products and working conditions rendered independent of this very labour power, [and which are] personified through this antithesis in capital.'[131]

The process by which capital accumulates magnificently and yet remains the property of an ever-diminishing group of private individuals is another of the great mysteries encountered by the exponents of the principle of non-contradiction. For the bourgeois mind, the exchange of commodities is based – as pointed out above – on the principle of identity. The individual sells his or her labour-power to the capitalist, who employs labour-power, and is given wages or a salary in exchange. Yet at the end of the labour process, the capitalist possesses commodities of a larger value than he or she originally advanced. In Marx's formula, we have (where C represents capital) $C = C'$.[132] Where now is Kant's and Popper's absolute law of non-contradiction? And what, moreover, has happened to liberty and equality?

According to Marx, the free and equal exchange of commodities in capitalist society 'appears as the surface process, beneath which, however, in the depths, entirely different processes go on, in which this apparent individual equality and liberty disappear.' The surface appearance is the quintessence of the bourgeois world of abstraction; below this realm of shades, mysterious forces are at work that turn an identity around into its opposite. 'Exchange value or, more precisely, the money system is in fact the system of equality and freedom, and ... the disturbances ... [encountered] in the further development of the system are disturbances inherent in it, are merely the realization of *equality and freedom*, which prove to be inequality and unfreedom.' For the vulgar economist, the sycophant of the bourgeoisie, there is no qualitative difference between capital as it is advanced by the capitalist, and capital plus profit as it emerges from the production process. Profit is the natural reward of the capitalist who, after all, risked his or her capital, employed his or her ingenuity, used his or her initiative, and so on. For the socialist opponents of the system, who are as imprisoned by abstractions as their opponents, 'there is, unfortunately, a difference, but, by rights, there ought not to be.'[133]

Marx's analysis follows the organic process of capitalist production; it is aimed at uncovering the inner dialectic of capital, the contradiction, $C = C'$: the identity which in exchange posits a difference between it and itself. As Hegel points out, however, the identity which posits difference can only be the human individual; things lack the ability to withstand contradiction, and cannot advance out of negativity or opposition. Moreover, things have no creative capacity or energy: as discussed in Chapter 3, a thing does not have its end in itself – it can achieve only imperfect activity, activity the subject of which lies outside it. Production is human only in so far as it accords with human ends and design: 'The purposive form of the product is the only trace left behind by the purposive labour.' Marx's investigation, therefore, leads him to the nature of individual human ideality, or – as it appears predominantly under capitalism – individual human labour-power.

He starts with the commodity, the ultimate being or identity of capitalism: 'Capitalist production is the first to make the commodity into the general form of all produce.'[134] His examination of the commodity follows guidelines suggested by Hegel in his dialectical analysis of the categories of thought in *Logic*. There Hegel observes that an identity, an object, should be studied only in so far as it includes difference. To look at a thing in its character as an identity and ignore other (contradictory) categories, such as difference and diversity, is the method of the abstract understanding. This abstract method 'may neglect a part of the multiple features which are found in the concrete thing (by what is called analysis) and select only one of them; or, neglecting their variety [it] may concentrate the multiple characters into one.'[135] Hegel is echoed by Marx, who notes that, for bourgeois commentators on the nature of capital, '*identity* is proved by holding fast to the features common to all processes of production, while neglecting their *specific differentiae*. The identity is demonstrated by abstracting from the differences.'[136]

A commodity for Marx is certainly a self-identical thing; it 'is, first of all, an external object, a thing which through its qualities satisfies human needs of whatever kind.' But a commodity is not only a self-identical thing; it also includes difference. 'Every useful thing is a whole composed of many properties; it can therefore be useful in various ways. The discovery of these ways and hence of the manifold uses of things is the work of history.'[137] Hegel remarks that philosophy 'lays bare the nothingness of the abstract, undifferentiated identity, known to the understanding'; nevertheless, 'it also undoubtedly urges its disciples not to rest at mere diversity, but to ascertain the inner unity of all existence.'[138] Thus Marx points out that a commodity is self-identical in that it represents a unity, i.e., value. But value itself is a unity which breaks down into difference: use-value (the commodity's intrinsic usefulness for the consumer), 'the material content of wealth' and exchange-value: 'the quantitative relation, the proportion, in which use-values of one kind exchange for use-values of another kind.'[139]

Here begins a journey into what must be among the great mysteries of intellectual history. For Marx's analysis of the commodity, and, as I will show, his theory of surplus value and even of the transition from capitalism into communism is, or seems to be, taken over directly from similar discussions in Hegel. Whether Marx is aware of the similarity between his views and those of Hegel may never be known. Perhaps it is safe to say that, since Marx adopts Hegel's dialectic method, he is led to the same discoveries made by Hegel a generation before him. Marx himself admits that in *Capital* 'I ... openly avowed myself the pupil of that mighty thinker, and even, here and there in the chapter on the theory of value, coquetted with the mode of expression peculiar to him.'[140] But Marx is less than honest either with his readers or with himself. The 'chapter on value' he refers to is Chapter 1. 'The Commodity'; this chapter, or at least that part of it devoted to the analysis of the commodity, simply reproduces similar discussions in the *Philosophy of Right*[141] and the *Philosophy of Mind*.[142] These discussions, in turn, are found, though in a much more abstract form, in the *Phenomenology*.[143]

In the *Philosophy of Mind*, Hegel observes that in contract – the act of buying and selling, or exchange – 'there is put into the thing or performance [i.e., the object of exchange: D.M.] a distinction between its specific *quality* [or what Marx calls use-value: D.M.] and its substantial being or *value*, meaning by value the quantitative terms into which that qualitative feature has been translated [i.e., its exchange-value: D.M.]. One piece of property is thus made comparable with another, and may be made equivalent to a thing which is (in quality) wholly heterogeneous. It is thus treated in general as an abstract, universal thing or commodity.'[144] Similarly, in the *Philosophy of Right*, he contrasts the value of a 'thing in use' with its 'universality' or the property which makes it possible to exchange the thing for other objects of utility. 'This, the thing's universality, whose simple determinate character arises from the particularity of the thing, so that it is *eo ipso* abstracted from the thing's specific quality, is the thing's *value*, wherein its genuine substantiality becomes determinate and an object of consciousness. As full owner of the thing, I am *eo ipso* owner of its value as well as of its use.' In fact, for Hegel as for Marx, the commodity – a thing with use-value and also exchange-value – is the vital element which separates the capitalist mode of production from the economy of the feudal period: 'The distinctive character of the property of a feudal tenant is that he is supposed to be the owner of the use only, not of the value of a thing.'[145]

One thing separates Marx's discussion of the commodity from that of Hegel: Hegel does not employ the term 'value' to refer to the usefulness of things, but only to their value in exchange. What Marx calls a thing's use-value is called simply its 'use' by Hegel and described as 'the specific need which it satisfies,' a need which 'is at the same time need in general [i.e., social need: D.M.] and thus is comparable on its particular side with other needs, while the thing in virtue of the same considerations is comparable with things meeting other needs.'[146] Given this difference, it is instructive to consider Althusser's argument that Marx's discussion of the commodity 'derives from ... Hegelian prejudice'; and that the most obvious result of this prejudice is Marx's use of the term, use-value. 'The fact is,' declares Althusser, 'that Marx had not taken the precaution of eliminating the word *value* from the expression "use-value" and of speaking as he should have done simply of the *social usefulness* of the *products*.'[147] Of course, had Marx done what Althusser suggests, then Marx would indeed have been a victim of 'Hegelian prejudice'!

For Hegel, 'the true Identity ... contains Being and its characteristics ideally transfigured in it.' What Hegel means is that identity refers, among other things, to the commodity – that is, an object produced for the purpose of exchange in the market; an object containing the result, or consisting of human labour-power or ideality. 'Identity is undoubtedly a negative – not however an abstract empty Nought, but the negation of Being and its characteristics. Being so, Identity is at the same time self-relation, and, what is more, negative self-relation; in other words, it draws a distinction between it and itself.'[148] A commodity may be sold or alienated by its owner because it retains the negative universality of human labour. 'This, the thing's universality, whose simple determinate character arises from the particularity of the thing, so that it is *eo ipso* abstracted from the thing's specific quality, is the thing's *value*, wherein its genuine substantiality becomes determinate and an object of consciousness.'[149] Hegel's observation is repeated by Marx: 'if we ... discard the use-value of commodities, only one property remains, that of being products of labour. But even the product of labour has already been transformed in our hands. If we make abstraction from its use-value, we abstract also from the material constituents and forms which make it a use-value. It is no longer a table, a house, a piece of yarn or any other useful thing. All its sensuous characteristics are extinguished.' In other words, abstracting from its use-value, a commodity represents only exchange-value or 'human labour in the abstract'[150] and therefore, in the production of exchange-value, human ideality or labour 'draws a distinction between it and itself.'

According to Marx, the exchange value of a commodity represents 'the amount of labour socially necessary, or the labour-time socially necessary for its production ... Commodities which contain equal quantities of labour, or which can be produced in the same time, have therefore the same value.' The labour-time socially necessary to produce a commodity varies according to a multitude of factors including 'the workers' average degree of skill, the level of development of science and its technological application, the social organization of the process of production, the extent and effectiveness of the means of production, and the conditions found in the natural environment.'[151]

Under capitalism, human labour-power is a commodity like any other; it may be bought and sold on the market according to the principle of identity or non-contradiction. Thus labour-power is purchased on the market at its full price: i.e., the wages or salary paid by the capitalist to the individual who alienates his or her labour-power equals the exchange-value of labour-power. Equivalent is matched by equivalent; I = I. Moreover, both the capitalist and the worker are self-subsistent individuals, and meet on the market in a spirit of freedom and equality. 'Labour-power,' writes Marx in a passage where he refers directly to Hegel's similar discussion in the *Philosophy of Right*:[152]

can appear on the market as a commodity only if, and in so far as, its possessor, the individual whose labour-power it is, offers it for sale or sells it as a commodity. In order that its possessor may sell it as a commodity, he must have it at his disposal, he must be the free proprietor of his own labour-capacity, hence of his person. He and the owner of money meet in the market, and enter into relations with each other on a footing of equality as owners of commodities, with the sole difference that one is a buyer, the other is a seller; both are therefore equal in the eyes of the law. For this relation to continue, the proprietor of labour-power must always sell it for a limited period only, for if he were to sell it in a lump, once and for all, he would be selling himself, converting himself from a free man into a slave, from an owner of a commodity into a commodity.[153]

Marx distinguishes a person's labour from his or her labour-power, since the capitalist merely purchases a person's ability to labour for a particular period; only a slave-owner purchases labour, i.e., the entire substance of a slave. Referring to the contract between the buyer of labour-power and its seller, Hegel writes, 'It is only when use is restricted that a distinction between use and substance arises. So here, the use of my powers differs from my powers and therefore from myself, only in so far as it is quantitatively restricted.'[154]
    The worker differs from the capitalist in that 'this worker must be free in the double sense that as a free individual he can dispose of his labour-power as his own commodity, and that, on the other hand, he has no other commodity for sale, i.e. he is rid of them, he is free of all the objects needed for the realization ... of his labour-power.'[155] Referring to the production process in bourgeois society, Hegel makes the same point: 'In this ... process ... dependence and want increase *ad infinitum*, and the material to meet these is permanently barred to the needy man because it consists of external objects with the special character of being property, the embodiment of the free will of others, and hence from his point of view its recalcitrance is absolute.'[156] Even freedom, then, is a contradiction in capitalist society; and the ultimate realization of freedom is ... *alienation*: 'Work can only be wage-labour when its *own* material conditions confront it as autonomous powers, alien property, value existing for itself and maintaining itself, in short as capital.' Moreover, as Hegel emphasizes, this type of freedom is the result of a historical process: the absolute dependence of the worker or needy person on the owner of private property is a feature of the evolution of the capitalist mode of production. Marx notes, 'Nature does not produce on the one hand owners of money or commodities, and on the other hand men possessing nothing but their own labour-power. This relation has no basis in natural history, nor does it have a social basis common to all periods of human history. It is clearly the result of a past historical development, the

product of many economic revolutions, of the extinction of a whole series of older formations of social production.'[157]

Like any commodity, the exchange-value of labour is determined by the labour-time socially necessary for its production; and this labour-time, writes Marx, 'is the same as that necessary for the production of those means of subsistence; in other words, the value of labour-power is the value of the means of subsistence necessary for the maintenance of its owner.' The means of subsistence, however, usually include more than the bare requirements of life, rather they, 'are themselves products of history, and depend therefore to a great extent on the level of civilization attained by a country ... In contrast, therefore, with the case of other commodities, the determination of the value of labour-power contains a historical and moral element. Nevertheless, in a given country at a given period, the average amount of the means of subsistence necessary for a worker is a known *datum*.'[158] Marx's definition of the value of labour closely follows that given by Hegel for the 'subsistence level ... necessary for a member of the society.' This level, he writes, is 'regulated automatically' and is based on 'the sense of right and wrong ... honesty and self-respect which makes a man insist on maintaining himself by his own work and effort.' Below this minimum is 'the lowest subsistence level, that of a rabble of paupers,' which is also 'fixed automatically, but the minimum varies considerably in different countries. In England, even the very poorest believe that they have rights; this is different from what satisfies the poor in other countries.'[159]

According to Marx, the price of labour-power is in addition determined by the time and energy spent by an individual to acquire his or her particular skills and training. 'In order to modify the general nature of the human organism in such a way that it acquires skill and dexterity in a given branch of industry, and becomes labour-power of a developed and specific kind, a special education or training is needed, and this in turn costs an equivalent in commodities of a greater or lesser amount.' The value of labour-power is subject to two countervailing or contradictory pressures. The first is what Marx calls, 'the reserve army of unemployed,' a 'relatively redundant working population' created by the increasing productivity of labour, trade cycles, and so on. 'The working population ... produces both the accumulation of capital and the means by which it is made relatively superfluous; and it does this to an extent which is always increasing.'[160] The surplus population offers two advantages to capital – it helps put pressure on wages by creating a group of workers ready to work for less than those already employed; and it offers a readily available supply of workers for periods of expansion.

Hegel also insists on the direct relationship between poverty and unemployment and 'the concentration of disproportionate wealth in a few hands,'[161] a relationship ignored by bourgeois economists.

The second force in determining wages, Marx argues, is the trade unions: 'The *trade unions* aim at nothing less than to prevent the *reduction of wages* below the level that is traditionally maintained in the various branches of industry.'[162] By maintaining and even raising wage levels however, trade unions also encourage development of machinery to increase the productivity of labour and ultimately the reserve army of unemployed. By a dialectical advance, therefore, demands for higher wages assure the increasing productivity and growth of the capitalist mode of production.

Human labour power is distinguished from other commodities in that its 'use-value possesses the peculiar property of being a source of value, whose actual consumption is therefore itself an objectification ... of labour, hence a creation of value.'[163] But at point of sale, labour-power is simply a capacity on the part of the worker; labour-power is not manifested or consumed except in the production process. Consequently, as Marx points out, 'In every country where the capitalist mode of production prevails, it is the custom not to pay for labour-power until it has been exercised for the period fixed by the contract, for example, at the end of each week. In all cases, therefore, the worker advances the use-value of his labour-power to the capitalist. He lets the buyer consume it before he receives payment of the price. Everywhere the worker allows credit to the capitalist.' That bourgeois society is one in which the less fortunate constantly lend to the rich is only another aspect of the 'non-contradictory' reality which escapes the notice of the understanding consciousness. But the fundamental contradiction within the bourgeois world of abstraction has yet to be explored. So far the analysis has lingered on appearances, on the luminous world of exchange, identity, and non-contradiction which Marx suggests,

is in fact a very Eden of the innate rights of man. It is the exclusive realm of Freedom, Equality, Property and Bentham. Freedom, because both buyer and seller of a commodity, let us say of labour-power, are determined only by their own free will ... Equality, because each enters into relation with the other, as with a simple owner of commodities, and they exchange equivalent for equivalent. Property, because each disposes only of what is his own. And Bentham, because each looks only to his own advantage. The only force bringing them together, and putting them into relation with each other, is the selfishness, the gain and the private interest of each.[164]

6

Capitalism, Class, and Profit

1 CAPITALISM AND ABSTRACT FREEDOM

Under capitalism, writes Marx, 'individuals are ... ruled by *abstractions*, whereas earlier they depended on one another. The abstraction, or idea, however, is nothing more than the theoretical expression of those material relations which are their lord and master.'[1] Bourgeois society is the kingdom of abstraction – of commodities expressed as abstract values, and of value itself expressed by that supreme abstraction, money. 'If we consider the concept of value,' notes Hegel,

we must look on the thing itself only as a symbol; it counts not as itself but as what it is worth. A bill of exchange, for instance, does not represent what it really is – paper; it is only a symbol of another universal – value. The value of a thing may be very heterogeneous; it depends on need. But if you want to express the value of a thing not in a specific case but in the abstract, then it is money which expresses this. Money represents any and every thing, though since it does not portray the need itself but is only a symbol of it, it is itself controlled by the specific value [of the commodity]. Money as an abstraction, merely expresses this value.

Since abstraction is the ruling principle of capitalist society, relations between individuals themselves take on a mystified cloak of abstraction. In civil or bourgeois society, notes Hegel, 'Needs and means [of production: D.M.] ... become something which has being for others by whose needs and work satisfaction for all is alike conditioned. When needs and means become abstract in quality ... abstraction is also a character of the reciprocal relations of individuals to one another. This abstract character, universality, is the character of being recognized and is the moment which makes concrete, i.e., social, the isolated and abstract needs and their ways and means of satisfaction.' The abstract or universal character of exchange and production relations in bourgeois society involves a civilizing force, because it simply expresses the universal dependence of individuals on one another:

> The fact that I must direct my conduct by reference to others introduces here the form of universality. It is from others that I acquire the means of satisfaction and I must accordingly accept their views. At the same time, however, I am compelled to produce means for the satisfaction of others. We play into each other's hands and so hang together. To this extent everything private becomes social.
> In dress fashions and hours of meals, there are certain conventions which we have to accept because in these things it is not worth the trouble to insist on displaying one's own discernment. The wisest thing here is to do as others do.[2]

Given the universal and abstract character of bourgeois society, freedom itself becomes an abstraction – free exchange, free competition, and free choice. The relation expressed by this abstract, contentless freedom is 'only ... the *illusory* reflection of the *capitalist* relation underlying it.'[3] It reflects 'nothing more than free development on a limited basis – the basis of the rule of capital. This kind of individual freedom is therefore at the same time the most complete suspension of all individual freedom, and the most complete subjugation of individuality under social conditions which assume the form of objective powers, even of overpowering objects – of things independent of the relations among individuals themselves.' The buying and selling of labour power presents the illusion of an exchange between two equal and independent individuals. In this exchange, the worker appears to confront 'an independent *individual*. It is clear that this is not his relation to the existence of capital as capital, i.e. to the capitalist class. Nevertheless, in this way everything touching on the individual, real person leaves him a wide field of choice, of arbitrary will, and hence of formal freedom.'[4]

For Kant, and the bourgeois mind in general, free choice is the essence of freedom. 'The categories of freedom,' he writes, 'are elementary practical concepts which determine the free faculty of choice.'[5] This conception of freedom remains dominant, as Plamenatz suggests, 'in England and other English-speaking countries [where] the philosopher has turned his mind chiefly to two closely connected though not identical ideas of freedom: freedom as absence of constraint by others, and freedom of choice.'[6] But Kant's notion of freedom, the freedom of bourgeois society, is a formal freedom only. It abstracts from any determinate content and therefore depends entirely 'on a content and material given either from within or from without.' Even if an individual can choose his or her job, or select from among a variety of consumer goods, or vote for the candidate of his or her choice, the item of choice and selection itself is external to and independent of the individual. The choice, in other words, 'is something other than the form of the will' of the individual 'and therefore something finite.'[7] By leaving the will of the individual outside the actual functioning of capitalist society, by making him or her subject to a despotic economic system, the freedom of bourgeois society is merely formal and external: a freedom of choice.

Freedom of choice is arbitrary, since the content of choice is not dependent on the individual, but rather *the individual is dependent on it.* 'The man in the street thinks he is free if it is open to him to act as he pleases but his very arbitrariness implies that he is not free.'[8] Nevertheless, this formal freedom, 'the capacity for determining ourselves towards one thing or another, is undoubtedly a vital element of the will.'[9] However flawed it may be, it is a necessary and essential element of human freedom. Consequently, in Hegel's 1831 essay on the English reform bill, he criticizes the lack in Britain of 'the modern principle in accordance with which only the abstract will of the individual as such is to be represented.' The absence of universal suffrage along with 'the purely formal principle of equality' leaves the country open to rule by a 'privileged class': 'the crass ignorance of fox-hunters and landed gentry' and the other 'great interests of the realm.' 'Nowhere more than in England,' notes Hegel in a passage still apposite today, 'is the prejudice so fixed and so naive that if birth and wealth give a man office they also give him brains.' The bribery and corruption endemic to the British political system in the nineteenth century are characteristic of a nation 'dominated by ... dexterity of reasoning in terms of [its] prejudices and by ... shallowness of principle,' and where 'the contrast between prodigious wealth and utterly embarrassed penury is enormous.'[10]

Avineri observes that 'Hegel is ... among the first political theorists to recognize that direct suffrage in a modern society would create a system very different from that envisaged by the advocates of such a system of direct representation.'[11] Hegel's critique, however, does not centre on direct suffrage itself, but on the nature of voting in the abstract context of bourgeois society. His criticisms of bourgeois democracy contrast strongly with the optimism expressed by Marx and Engels regarding extension of the franchise to the working class. 'Thus in 1852 [Marx] could write that: "Universal suffrage is the equivalent of political power for the working class of England ... Its inevitable result, here, is the political supremacy of the working class." ' It is symptomatic of the almost endearingly naive approach of western Marxism to the relation between Hegel and the founders of historical materialism that the optimism Marx and Engels entertain for the franchise is attributed by a leading Marxist writer to the pernicious influence of ... Hegel![12] His view, however, is diametrically opposed here to that of Marx and Engels.

'Experience proves,' notes Hegel, 'that the exercise of the right to vote is not so attractive as to provoke strong claims or the movements to which they give rise. On the contrary, what seems to prevail in the electorate is great indifference.' The ordinary citizens in British society 'see in their right a property which accrues to the benefit of those alone who wish to be elected to Parliament and on the altar of whose personal opinion, whim, and interest everything implicit in this right of participating in government and legislation is to be sacrificed.'[13] The result of popular suffrage, 'especially in large states,' writes Hegel, 'is more likely to be the opposite of what was intended: election actually falls into the power of a few, of a caucus, and so of the particular and contingent interest which is precisely what was to have been neutralized.'[14] As Marx put it in 1871, under capitalism the vote comes down to 'deciding once in three or six years which member of the ruling class [is] to misrepresent the people in Parliament.'[15] More even than Marx and Engels, however, Hegel anticipates the contemporary situation where 'under conditions of relative but nevertheless considerable political freedom, the parties of the working classes, the parties explicitly pledged to the defence and the liberation of the subordinate classes, have generally done much less well politically than their more or less conservative rivals, whose own purpose has preeminently included the maintenance of the capitalist system.'[16]

Hegel observes that apathy towards the vote is clearly out of tune 'with the fact that it is in this right that there lies the right of the people to participate in public affairs and in the higher interests of state and government.' Nevertheless voter indifference is understandable given the extremely limited effectiveness of a single ballot in a highly atomized and fractionated electorate. In France, for instance, notes Hegel, 'the number of voters to be on the roll under the new French electoral law is assessed at 200,000; the number of members to be elected is given in round figures as 450. It follows that one vote is a two-hundred-thousandth part of the total voting power and the ninety-millionth part of one of the three branches of the legislative power.'[17] The result of the atomistic principle concealed in the heart of universal suffrage is aptly outlined by Hegel:

'*Liberalism*' ... sets up ... this the atomistic principle, that which insists upon the sway of individual wills ... Asserting this formal side of Freedom – this abstraction – the party in question allows no political organization to be firmly established. The particular arrangements of the government are forthwith opposed by the advocates of Liberty as the mandates of a particular will, and branded as displays of arbitrary power. The will of the Many expels the Ministry from power, and those who had formed the Opposition fill the vacant places; but the latter having now become the Government, meet with hostility from the Many, and share the same fate. This agitation and unrest are perpetuated. This collision, this nodus, this problem is that with which history is now occupied, and whose solution it has to work out in the future.[18]

Given the futility and irrelevance of the vote, the call for individuals to step out of indifference and apathy and to vote, no matter for whom, is likely to fall on deaf ears:

If the individual has brought before him the usual story that, if *everyone* thought so indolently, the state's existence and, above all, freedom itself would be jeopardized, he is bound to remind himself just as much of the principle on which his duty and his whole right to freedom is built, namely that he should let himself be guided not by considering what others do but solely by his own will, and that what is finally decisive for him, what is even duly as his sovereign, is his own personal volition.

Even if the individual surmounts the cynicism fostered by the game of political musical chairs in government and the sense of insignificance connected with the limited power of a single vote, he or she must still merely vote for an individual or a party. The actual content of legislation – the law of the land – is expressly excluded from voting rights. 'Only,' writes Hegel, 'in the French democratic constitution of the year III under Robespierre – a constitution adopted by the whole people but of course all the less ... carried into effect – was it prescribed that *laws* on public affairs were to be brought before individual citizens for confirmation.'[19]

If freedom is interpreted by the understanding consciousness as freedom of choice, it is also connected, as Plamenatz suggests in the quotation given above, with absence of constraint. From this viewpoint, duty appears as the negation of freedom. This, of course, is precisely the definition of freedom adduced by that bourgeois thinker *par excellence*, Kant. The Kantian individual is a 'thing-in-itself,' a '*causa noumenon*,' 'the determination of which no physical explanation can be given.' As noted in the preceding chapter, he or she is guided by moral laws 'which are independent of all empirical conditions and which therefore belong to the autonomy of pure reason.' Individuals are able to act outside 'the natural law of appearances [phenomena] in their mutual relations, i.e. the law of causality. Such independence is called *freedom* in the strictest, i.e. transcendental sense.' We have seen, however, that Kant never gives any content to his notion of the moral laws and even his famous categorical imperative is simply an abstraction: 'So act that the maxim of your will could always hold at the same time as a principle establishing universal law.'[20] Hegel adopts a variation of this principle in the *Philosophy of Right*: 'Be a person and respect others as persons.'[21]

Hegel, however, makes this maxim only the beginning of his concrete analysis of the modern state, while Kant employs it as the basis of his moral philosophy and gives it no social content whatever. His principle 'would be admirable if we already had determinate principles of conduct. That is to say, to demand of a principle that it shall be able to serve in addition as a determinate of universal legislation is to presuppose that it already possesses a content. Given the content, then of course the application of the principle would be a simple matter.'[22] In Kant's philosophy, duty, understood as conformity to moral law, is simply a restriction on the freedom of the individual. And 'chill duty,' as Hegel puts it, 'is the final undigested lump left within the stomach, the revelation given to Reason.'[23] Accordingly, even duty and free will become *externalities* and *abstractions* opposed to the interests of the individual: 'The stage of morality on which man ... stands is respect for the moral law. The disposition which obliges him to obey it is: to obey it from duty and not from a spontaneous inclination or from an endeavour unbidden but gladly undertaken.'[24] The notion of duty as a restriction on individual freedom is a natural consequence of the external and alienated character of capitalist society: where objective reality is seen as independent of and *other* to the isolated individual, then any kind of duty must appear as a burden and a fetter.

Duty of the type outlined by Kant, Hegel argues, can only be dispensed with when the individual perceives him- or herself as achieving a concrete personal identity *with* and *through* society. 'The consummation of the realization of the Notion of objective mind, is achieved only in the State, in which mind develops its freedom into a world posited by mind itself, into the ethical [social: D.M.] world.'[25] As I will show, the state Hegel refers to resembles what Marx calls communist society. This state, says Hegel, 'exists when individuals, instead of being moved to action by respect and reverence

for the institutions of the state and of the fatherland, from their own con-
victions, and after moral deliberation, come of themselves to a decision,
and determine their actions accordingly.'[26] This conforms, of course, to the
moral principle embodied in Marx's vision of socialist society. Here, writes
Giddens, 'the character of moral authority will not demand the maintenance
of the Kantian element of obligation or duty, insofar as this is linked with
the necessity of adhering to moral norms which the individual finds anti-
pathetic.'[27]

As shown in Chapter 5, freedom of choice and the other cherished freedoms of bourgeois society rest on the relation between commodity owners –
the objective relation of contract, where one commodity owner, the worker,
exchanges his or her labour power for commodities in the form of wages
or money provided by the capitalist. Hegel observes, however, that even
the free and equal relation of contract involves an element of contradiction.
Contract concerns not only the commodity exchanged but also the will of
the persons who make the exchange; and exchange is possible only on
condition that ownership of a thing *means the potential not to own it.*
'Contract is the process in which there is revealed and mediated the contradiction that I am and remain the independent owner of something from
which I exclude the will of another only in so far as in identifying my will
with the will of another I cease to be an owner.' To put it another way,
alienation itself may be seen as 'a true mode of taking possession.'[28]

But the contradiction in the relation between buyer and seller of labour-
power goes further than its appearance in the form of a contract between
equals. First of all in the exchange between worker and capitalist, the capitalist provides commodities in the universal form of money while the worker
provides labour-power. Labour-power, in turn, produces commodities so
that the worker transforms the capital of the employer into commodities.
The commodities produced, therefore, are not produced by the capitalist
but rather by the worker. At the end of the labour process, the employer
is presented with an increased amount of capital while the worker has only
wages to spend on consumer goods. Kalecki sums up this situation very
simply: workers spend what they get; capitalists get what they spend.[29]
Instead of a relation between free and independent individuals, the buying
and selling of labour power produces a relation of dependence of the worker
on the capitalist, a *class relation.* 'The constant renewal of the relationship
of *sale and purchase* merely ensures the perpetuation of the specific relationship of dependency, endowing it with the deceptive *illusion* of a trans-
action, of a contract between equally free and equally matched *commodity
owners.* This *initial* relationship itself now appears as an integral feature of

the rule of objectified labour over living labour that is created in capitalist production.'[30]

2 CLASS AND THE INDIVIDUAL

For Marx as for Hegel, society 'is no solid crystal, but an organism capable of change, and constantly engaged in a process of change.' Both writers are fascinated with the conception of a living cell and its relationship with the organic body. For bourgeois society, notes Marx, 'the commodity-form of the product of labour, or the value-form of the commodity, is the economic cell-form.'[31] Hegel uses the notion of a living cell to explain the production and reproduction of class and other social relations:

Much the same thing as this ideality of the moments in the state occurs with life in the physical organism. Life is present in every cell. There is only one life in all the cells and nothing withstands it. Separated from that life, every cell dies. This is the same as the ideality of every single class, power, and Corporation as soon as they have the impulse to subsist and be independent. It is with them as it is with the belly of an organism. It too, asserts its independence, but at the same time its independence is set aside and it is sacrificed and absorbed within the whole.[32]

The organic imagery is not simply a play with metaphor; it expresses rather the identity between the consciousness and will of individuals – who, after all, are organic beings – and the manifestation of their rational activity, their ideality, in the living totality of society. Thus for the Russian reviewer of *Capital*, approvingly quoted by Marx, economic life is said to 'offer us a phenomenon analogous to the history of evolution in other branches of biology.' The reviewer goes on to observe: 'The old economists misunderstood the nature of economic laws when they likened them to the laws of physics and chemistry [because] social organisms differ among themselves as fundamentally as plants or animals ... one and the same phenomenon falls under quite different laws in consequence of the different general structure of these organisms, the variations of their individual organs, and the different conditions in which those organs function.'[33]

Marx's conception of capitalism as a living system, an organic unity, is an essential element of the dialectic method he took from Hegel. The Russian reviewer, states Marx, 'pictures what he takes to be my own actual method, in a striking and, as far as concerns my own application of it, generous way. But what else is he depicting but the dialectic method?' The Russian commentator also observes that 'Marx treats the social movement as a process of natural history, governed by laws not only independent of human will, consciousness and intelligence, but rather, on the contrary, determining that will, consciousness and intelligence.' This remark is inspired by the preface to the first edition of *Capital* where Marx writes that 'individuals are dealt with here only in so far as they are the personification of economic categories, the bearers ... of particular class-relations and interests. My standpoint, from which the development of the economic formation of society is viewed as a process of natural history, can less than any other make the individual responsible for relations whose creature he remains, socially speaking, however much he may subjectively raise himself above them.'[34] But even in the abstract realm of the capitalist mode of production individual consciousness and will is the substantial basis of social relations. If the individual is a living cell within the social organism, his or her influence on society cannot be reduced to a mechanical and determinate relation.

Whereas Marx begins *Capital* with the commodity, Hegel begins the *Philosophy of Right* with the free will of the individual. Nevertheless, the initial focus of both works is what Hegel calls 'abstract right' or the property relation. Moreover, throughout *Capital* Marx never loses sight of the consciousness and will — the ideality — of the individual. Perhaps because he himself drew attention away from it, this aspect of his work is ignored by most commentators. For them, Marx's explanation of social change lies in the evolution of the forces of production. Sidney Hook provides a convenient example of this interpretation. 'The gradual changes in human nature,' he writes, 'which are the result of the evolution of the forces of production produce sudden changes in the social relations of production. Sudden changes in the social relations of production can be effected only by political revolution. In class societies social evolution is impossible without political revolution at some point in the process.'[35]

This engineer's model of social change finds its definitive basis in the machinery, technology, and expertise of a particular social formation; it culminates in the Althusserian fantasy of society as a multi-layered monolith, a system of structures and superstructures, determined or over-determined in the last instance by the economic foundation. The warrant for this incredible vision is provided by Marx himself. 'My view,' he observes, 'is that each particular mode of production, and the relations of production corresponding to it at each given moment, in short "the economic structure of society", is "the real foundation, on which arises a legal and political superstructure and to which correspond definite forms of social consciousness", and that "the mode of production of material life conditions the general process of social, political and intellectual life".'[36] There is plenty of evidence, however, that Marx recognizes that the forces of production themselves may be reduced to the consciousness and will of the individuals who design, manufacture, and utilize them. 'Real wealth,' he writes, 'is the developed productive power of all individuals.' 'The productive power of labour [is] itself the greatest productive power.'[37] 'The mystification implicit in the relations of capital as a whole' prevents people from seeing that capital itself is the 'productive power either of the individual worker or of the workers joined together in the process of production.'[38] Etc., etc.

No less than Marx, Hegel is aware that human consciousness is conditioned by its social environment. 'Consciousness knows and comprehends only what falls within its experience; for what is contained in this is nothing but spiritual substance [society: D.M.], and this, too, as *object* of the self.'[39] But the social environment itself is the result of practical human activity, revolutionizing practice, and changes in society may be traced in the last instance only to the rational activity of individual human beings. For Hegel, 'the Dialectical principle constitutes the life and soul of scientific progress'; and the purpose of dialectic method 'is to study things in their own being and movement.' The essence of dialectic, in turn, is 'the universal and irresistible power before which nothing can stay, however stable and secure it may deem itself.' This essence is nothing other than individual consciousness or ideality which exhibits the character of the rational principle, i.e., it alone, and not the forces of production, is 'unconditioned, self-contained, and thus ... self-determining.'[40] To admit the individual as the principle of dialectic is *not* to abandon the notion that consciousness is a function of social environment. A person is *identical* with as well as *distinct* from society; neither can be explained without the other. For example, the cynical mode of life adopted by the ancient Greek philosopher Diogenes, writes Hegel, 'was nothing more or less than a product of Athenian social life, and what determined it was the way of thinking against which his whole manner protested. Hence it was not independent of social conditions but simply their result; it was itself a rude product of luxury. When luxury is at its height, distress and depravity are equally extreme, and in such circumstances Cynicism is the outcome of opposition to refinement.'[41]

S.S. Prawer perceptively observes that 'in face of that German idealist tradition which culminated in Hegel, a tradition in which "spirit" and "idea" were seen as fundamental, ultimate reality, Marx may well have felt compelled to over-emphasize the "conditioning" power exerted by relations of production and the "determining" power of man's social being.'[42] But if modern bourgeois society betrayed the ideal of the great French Revolution of 1789, it also betrayed the culmination of that ideal in the philosophy of German idealism. After Hegel, the understanding consciousness reigned supreme; only Marx managed to seize a part of the tradition which ended with Hegel.

The triumph of bourgeois consciousness was already an established fact when Marx began his scientific work. Indeed, Hegel and the idealist tradition generally were entirely dismissed by Marx's contemporaries; and Marx himself was under great pressure from the ruling positivism of the age. Although he refers in 1873 to the 'ill-humoured, arrogant and mediocre epigones who now talk large in educated German circles' and who 'take pleasure in treating Hegel ... as a "dead dog",' he is careful to distance himself from 'that mighty thinker.' The German reviewers of *Capital*, Marx informs us, 'cry out against my "Hegelian sophistry",' and even the sympathetic Russian reviewer finds it necessary to defend him from the charge that 'Marx is the most idealist of philosophers, and indeed in the German, i.e. the bad sense of the word.'[43] Today, Hegel and not Marx is seen 'as the most idealist of philosophers, and indeed in the German, i.e. the bad sense of the word.' Marx dodged the tar-brush of idealism, but since his teacher stood directly behind him, the result of his manoeuvre was inevitable: the more 'materialist' Marx's theory of history and society is felt to be, the more 'idealist' Hegel's philosophy is made to appear. But to see that the fundamental Hegelian categories of ideality and individual will are also the primary categories employed by Marx one has only to consult the pages of *Capital*.

For Marx, the individual capitalist is the 'conscious bearer' of the movement of capital. 'His person, or rather his pocket, is the point from which the money starts, and to which it returns.' Profit is the 'subjective purpose' of the capitalist: 'it is only in so far as the appropriation of ever more wealth in the abstract is the sole driving force behind his operations that he functions as a capitalist, i.e. as capital personified and endowed with consciousness and a will.' The capitalist is no mere pawn of the economic system; rather, the driving force of capital lies in the rational avarice – the consciousness and will – of individuals who personify capital. 'This boundless drive for enrichment, this passionate chase after value, is common to the capitalist and the miser; but while the miser is merely a capitalist gone mad, the capitalist is a rational miser. The ceaseless augmentation of value, which the miser seeks to attain by saving his money from circulation, is achieved by the more acute capitalist by means of throwing his money again and again into circulation.' The capitalist, in other words, has a rational ethic, a driving spirit, which finds expression in, and helps produce and reproduce, the capitalist mode of production. Thus, the proportion of profit the capitalist decides to reinvest is not altogether determined by external forces: 'it is the owner of the surplus-value, the capitalist, who makes this division. It is an act of his will.'[44]

Nor did the spirit and the rationality of the capitalist arise from the routine, mechanical functioning of the capitalist system, for these qualities existed prior to the establishment of capitalism, and were a cause rather than a result of its emergence. Capitalism's beginnings may be found in the feudal mode of production; but the rapid transformation of the forces of production under capitalism occurred long after, rather than with, its emergence as a system. 'It by no means suffices,' notes Marx, 'for capital to take over the labour process in its given or historically transmitted shape, and then simply to prolong its duration' in order to produce profit. 'The technical and social conditions of the process and consequently the mode of production itself must be revolutionized before the productivity of labour can be increased.' Initially, capitalist production differed from the handicraft trade of the guilds only 'by the greater number of workmen simultaneously employed by the same individual capital. It is merely an enlargement of the workshop of the master craftsmen of the guilds.'[45] Thus the changes which characterized the dissolution of the feudal system were first brought about by the rational and organizing activity of individuals within it.

A theory of social change based on the struggle between classes may certainly explain (to a degree) transformations from one political system to another: the revolutions of 1789 and 1917 are classic instances. But the origin and development of classes themselves remain to be accounted for. Marx suggests that the genesis of the industrial capitalist class by no means corresponded 'with the snail's pace of advance' connected with the dissolution of the feudal system. Feudalism nevertheless allowed for the creation of two forms of capital, 'usurer's capital and merchant's capital,' which were able to take advantage 'of the new world market, which had been created by the great discoveries of the end of the fifteenth century.'[46] In other words, we are back with Hegel's theory, outlined in Chapter 3, that the development of bourgeois society may be attributed to the new spirit of adventure and rationality which, among other things, replaced chivalry with 'the higher romance of commerce.'[47] Writes Marx: 'The discovery of gold and silver in America, the extirpation, enslavement and entombment in mines of the indigenous population of that continent, the beginnings of the conquest and plunder of India, and the conversion of Africa into a preserve for the commercial hunting of blackskins, are all things which characterize the dawn of the era of capitalist production. These idyllic proceedings are the chief moments of primitive accumulation.'[48]

Even after the establishment of the capitalist mode of production, the role of the consciousness and will of individuals remains paramount. Thus the theories of bourgeois economists, which were accepted and acted upon by individual capitalists, had a direct bearing on the further development of capitalism:

It was of decisive importance for the bourgeois economists, when confronted with the habitual mode of life of the old nobility, which, as Hegel rightly says, 'consists in consuming what is available', and is displayed in particular in the luxury of personal retainers, to promulgate the doctrine that the accumulation of capital is the first duty of every citizen, and to preach unceasingly that accumulation is impossible if a man eats up all his revenue, instead of spending a good part of it on the acquisition of additional productive workers, who bring in more than they cost.

Throughout *Capital* Marx emphasizes the managerial and supervisory activity of the capitalist, the vital part he or she plays in organizing and rationalizing the production process: 'the capitalist's ability to *supervise* and enforce *discipline* is vital.' The activity of the employer is nowhere presented as a mindless and mechanical function; instead the capitalist is active and rational – he or she carries out specific programs on the basis of rational calculation. 'That a capitalist should command in the field of production is now as indispensable as that a general should command on the field of battle.' The entire activity of the employer is aimed at avoiding objective social laws that are 'independent of [his or her] will';[49] yet it is precisely through the capitalist's consciousness and will that these laws are realized. As Hegel puts it, 'the law is no agent; it is only the actual human being who acts.'[50] Under capitalism, for example, economies of scale dictate that mass-produced commodities become cheaper, and this law 'becomes manifest as the desire of the individual capitalist who, in his wish to render this law ineffectual, or to *outwit it* and turn it to his own advantage, reduces the *individual* value of his product to a point where it falls *below* the socially determined value.'[51] Successful capitalists consciously strive to lower the cost of their commodities *for the purchaser*, a secret of the modern consumer economy definitively revealed by Henry Ford in the early twentieth century.

Consciousness and will are not just the property of the capitalist; they are equally an aspect of the individual worker. The modern worker, writes Marx, 'is ... a person who is something for himself *apart from his* labour, and who alienates his life expression only as a means towards his own life.'[52] The consciousness and will of the worker confront the capitalist *first*, as the labour power which the employer purchases on the market and utilizes in the labour process, and *second*, as active resistance to the exploitative power of capital. The worker and the capitalist form an essential, if antagonistic, unity: the capitalist cannot be a capitalist without the worker, and the wage or salary worker cannot be such without the capitalist. Their unity is what Hegel calls, a unity of opposites: 'Both are in essential relation to one another; and the one of the two is, only in so far as it excludes the other from it, and thus relates itself thereto.'

The notion of the unity of the capitalist with the worker is an essential element in the theory of class in both Hegel and Marx. In Hegel's terminology, their relation is one of opposition; but 'in opposition, the different is not confronted by any other, but by its other.' This relation is outlined in the *Encyclopedia Logic* as follows: 'the essential difference, as a difference, is only the difference of it from itself, and thus contains the identical: so that to essential and actual difference there belongs itself as well as identity. As self-relating difference it is likewise virtually enunciated as the self-identical. And the opposite is in general that which includes the one and its other, itself and its opposite.' For Hegel, ideality or revolutionizing practice, is an 'existence [which] agrees with its notion.'[53] The ideality of the capitalist, therefore, includes the worker; and the ideality of the worker includes the capitalist. Together they form an organic unity. 'Capital and wage-labour (it is thus we designate the labour of the worker who sells his own labour power),' writes Marx, 'only express two aspects of the self-same relationship.'[54]

Most commentators on Hegel do not understand his conception of social class because they fail to relate the dialectical analysis of the categories in speculative logic to his concrete discussion of society in the *Philosophy of Right*. But the *Philosophy of Right* must be seen as a concrete application of dialectic method; read outside this context, the work simply cannot be comprehended. 'In this book,' states Hegel in the preface to the *Philosophy of Right*, 'I am presupposing that philosophy's mode of progression from one topic to another and its mode of scientific proof – this whole speculative way of knowing – is essentially distinct from any other way of knowing ... It will be obvious from the work itself,' he continues, 'that the whole, like the formation of its parts, rests on the logical spirit. It is also from this point of view above all that I should like my book to be taken and judged. What we have to do with here is philosophical *science*, and in such science content is essentially bound up with form.'[55]

With regard to social class, writes Avineri, 'Hegel's point of departure is the exact opposite of Marx's.' As a result, 'one looks in vain for [the working] class in Hegel's system of estates. Obviously the worker is not part of the peasantry nor does he belong to the civil service. But neither does the commercial estate, the class of businessmen, include him.'[56] Another recent commentator, Raymond Plant, agrees with Avineri's verdict: 'Hegel did not define classes in terms of the relationship to the means of production.'[57] In fact, however, the worker is certainly included in what Hegel calls 'the business class'; this class is a unity which includes the opposites, capitalist and worker, just as the 'agricultural class' includes both great landowners and peasants.[58] The business class is concerned with the sphere of contract, and an *essential moment* of contract is: 'Contract for wages (*locatio operae*) – alienation of my productive capacity or services so far, that is, as these are alienable, the alienation being restricted in time or in some other way.'

The failure of commentators to see that the worker is actually a part of Hegel's business class derives from their unspoken assumption (perhaps prejudice) that the worker is a simple pawn in a system of production dominated and controlled by the capitalist, an assumption not shared by Hegel. His definition of the business class is worth quoting in full:

The business class has for its task the adoption of raw materials, and for its means of livelihood it is thrown back on its work, on reflection and intelligence, and essentially on the mediation of one man's needs and work with those of others. For what this class produces and enjoys, it has mainly itself, its own industry, to thank. The task of this class is subdivided into

(α) work to satisfy single needs in a comparatively concrete way and to supply single orders – craftsmanship;

(β) work of a more abstract kind, mass-production to satisfy single needs, but needs in more universal demand – manufacture;

(γ) the business of exchange, whereby separate utilities are exchanged the one for the other, principally through the use of the universal medium of exchange, money, which actualizes the abstract value of all commodities – trade.[59]

Hegel's definition of the business class, therefore, would include modern categories of workers – blue-collar, white-collar, service – as well as the class of owners of the means of production and exchange, the capitalists. But for Hegel as well as for Marx, the dialectical movement of modern society will eventually result in a real unity of the business class where the opposition and distinction between capitalist and worker disappear. Like all contradictory relations, the one between the capitalist and the worker 'is ... a contradiction, which, so far from persisting quietly in itself, is rather the expulsion of it from itself.' To grasp this process it is necessary to explore the dialectic of labour under capitalism as it is elucidated by both Hegel and Marx. This dialectic, as Hegel suggests, is 'objectively and intrinsically determined, and hence self-acting,' and, moreover, includes 'the universal or notion of the will.'[60] Accordingly, Marx defines human labour-power as 'a *self-acting capacity*, a *labour-power that expresses itself* purposively by converting the means of production into the material object of its activity, *transforming* them from their original form into the new form of the product.'[61] For Hegel, the work performed by the individual in the labour process is *ideal*, it demonstrates the 'unity of the notion and objectivity ... its "real" content is only the exhibition which the notion gives itself in the form of external existence, while yet, by enclosing this shape in its ideality, it keeps it in its power, and so keeps itself in it.'[62] Marx expresses the same notion in *Capital*. 'At the end of every labour process,' he writes, 'a result emerges which had already been conceived by the worker at the beginning, hence already existed ideally. Man not only effects a change of form in the materials of nature; he also realizes ... his own purpose in those materials.'[63]

Employing the means of production provided by the capitalist, the worker transforms raw material into the finished product, the commodity. In doing so, the worker abolishes in practice the distinction between him/herself and the object of labour. 'What virtually happens in the realizing of the End,' notes Hegel, 'is that the one-sided subjectivity and the show of objective independence confronting it are both cancelled. In laying hold of the means, the notion [i.e., the ideality of the worker: D.M.] constitutes itself the very implicit essence of the object.'[64] The relation theoretically expressed by Hegel is given concrete form by Marx. The worker, he writes, 'takes possession of the means of production and handles them simply as the means and materials of his work. The autonomous nature of these means of production, the way they hold fast to their independence and display a mind of their own, their separation from labour – all this is now *abolished* ... in practice. The material conditions of labour now enter into a normal unity with labour itself; they form the material, the organs requisite for its creative activity.'[65]

The commodity is the worker's product; it contains the result of his or her ideality, which has now become 'the very implicit essense of the object.' *It is the concrete result of the creative activity of the worker.* 'Real labour is what the worker really gives to the capitalist in exchange for the purchase price of labour, that part of capital that is translated into the wage. It is the expenditure of his life's energy, the realization of his productive faculties; it is his movement and not the capitalists'.' To the bourgeois mind, however, the product – the commodity– appears as the property of the entrepreneur. Accordingly, under capitalism 'the means of production appear not just as the means for accomplishing work, but as the means for *exploiting the labour of others*.' The result of this exploitation is that the product of the labour of the worker appears as an *alien object*, a *power set over against the individual*: 'Since the labour has ceased to belong to the worker even before he starts to work, what objectified itself for him is *alien labour* and hence a value, *capital*, independent of his labour-power. The *product* belongs to the capitalist and in the eyes of the worker it is as much a part of capital as the *elements of production*.'[66]

In the labour process the worker creates commodities, objectified labour, part of which appears as consumption goods for the worker, but the other part of which takes the form of consumption goods for the capitalist and investment goods, i.e., means of production that will be used to re-employ the worker. 'When we consider the individual commodity we find that a certain proportion of it represents *unpaid* labour, and when we take the *mass of commodities as a whole* we find similarly that a certain proportion of that also represents unpaid labour. In short, it turns out to be a product that costs the capitalist nothing.' The worker produces not only his or her subsistence goods, but also surplus-value, profit plus the replacement of the means of production used up in the labour process, for the capitalist. The worker, then, has created '*alien, autonomous powers* ... value – objectified labour – which treats living labour as a mere means whereby to maintain and increase itself.'[67] Here is the solution to the mystery C = C' – the identity which posits difference.

'The product of capitalist production,' writes Marx, 'is neither a mere *product* (a use-value), nor just a *commodity*, i.e. a product with an exchange-value, but a *product specific to itself*, namely *surplus-value*. Its product is *commodities* that possess more exchange-value, i.e. represent more labour than was invested for their production in the shape of money or commodities.' And the only element in the labour process capable of creating value, of expanding the value represented in the means of production and raw material, is what Marx calls 'variable capital,' i.e., living labour-power: 'The only real component of capital to enter the process of production is the living factor, labour-power itself.' Labour-power is 'the value-creating activity, the activity of the living factor embodied in the valorization process.' Without human ideality, without labour-power, machinery – which is itself simply objectified, past, dead labour – is incapable of producing value: 'A machine which is not active in the labour process is useless. In addition, it falls prey to the destructive power of natural processes. Iron rusts; wood rots. Yarn with which we neither weave nor knit is cotton wasted. Living labour must seize on these things, awaken them from the dead, change them from merely possible into real and effective use-values.'[68]

As Hegel puts it, 'the means of acquiring and preparing the particularized means appropriate to our similarly particularized needs is work. Through work the raw material directly supplied by nature is specifically adapted to these numerous ends by all sorts of different processes. *Now this formative change confers value on means and gives them their utility*, and hence man in what he consumes is mainly concerned with the products of men. It is the products of human effort which man consumes.'[69]

3 PROFIT, PRIVATE PROPERTY, AND FREEDOM

It is one of the great ironies of intellectual history that Marx – whose entire mode of approach to the study of the capitalist system is taken over from Hegel – did not himself realize that the exploitative relationship of the capitalist towards the worker he analyses in such detail in *Capital* had been worked out before him by Hegel. In fact, Marx misunderstands Hegel so thoroughly that he describes Hegel's approach to the labour process as 'comical.' 'According to this,' says Marx, 'man as an individual must endow his will with reality as the soul of external nature, and must therefore take possession of this nature and make it his private property.'[70] In *Reason and Revolution*, the Hegelian Marxist, Marcuse, follows Marx's lead: 'The notion of freedom in the *Philosophy of Right* ... loses its critical content and comes to serve as a metaphysical justification of private property.'[71] For Hegel, however, the most important aspect of private property is that, with its emergence, the individual was set free to the extent that his or her labour-power or ideality could be his or her own private property. This is the world-historical significance of private property: that the individual's labour can no longer be the property of another, either in the shape of slavery or feudal serfdom. The importance of this development is emphasized by Marx: 'The totality of the free worker's labour capacity appears to him as his property, as one of his moments, over which he, as subject, exercises domination, and which he maintains by expending it.'[72]

As discussed in the preceding chapter, the worker does not sell or alienate labour, i.e., the worker's whole being and life, but merely labour-power. Both Hegel and Marx emphasize the importance of this distinction, but while Marx credits Hegel with its discovery, he does not go on to examine Hegel's definition of private property in the context of the notion of free labour-power. Marx's failure to appreciate Hegel's theoretical analysis of private property turns on his inability to recognize in Hegel's mature works the fundamental concept of dialectic: ideality. Private property, Hegel argues, is possession; and possession or commodity ownership is obtained by *conscious human practice.* 'We take possession of a thing,' says Hegel, '(α) by directly grasping it physically, (β) by forming it, and (γ) by merely marking it as ours.' To form a thing is to *work* on it, to *expend labour* on an object. 'When I impose a form on something,' explains Hegel, 'the thing's determinate character as mine acquires an independent externality and ceases to be restricted to my presence here and now and to the direct presence of my awareness and will.' Hegel makes it clear he is referring to the labour process when he adds that included in the category of forming a thing 'falls the formation of the organic. What I do to the organic does not remain external to it but is assimilated by it. Examples are the tilling of the soil, the cultivation of plants, the taming and feeding of animals, the preservation of game, as well as contrivances for utilizing raw materials or the forces of nature and processes for making one material produce effects on another, and so forth.'[73]

Not only is the process of labour one aspect of property, of possession, it is also *the most significant aspect.* The labour process itself, the creative activity of labour, is the means through which the individual realizes his or her human capacities. To work is to establish and possess one's own personality and sense of self. 'This taking possession of one's self ... is the translation into actuality of what one is according to one's concept, i.e. a potentiality, capacity, potency. In that translation one's self-consciousness for the first time becomes established as one's own, as one's object also and distinct from self-consciousness pure and simple, and thereby capable of taking the form of a "thing".'

The right of property indicates a *social relation* that goes well beyond the mere satisfaction of human needs. This could be obtained under earlier modes of production that involved no private property; but private property represents a *value* that could not be achieved under earlier forms of society, the value of human personality. 'The rationale of property is to be found not in the satisfaction of needs but in the supersession of the pure subjectivity of personality. In his property a person exists for the first time as reason.'[74] In a society where private property is the norm, the significance of this social relation loses its impact and is ultimately taken for granted (although its importance is being rediscovered by feminist writers who connect women's subjection by men to their lack of property in this Hegelian sense of the term). But private property is the external manifestation of a person's freedom, the embodiment of his or her own consciousness and will. It represents an extension of the person's individuality and personality – an extension that is inviolable.

For Hegel, the notion that the private property of individuals should be held and shared in common is merely an abstraction of the understanding consciousness. Each individual is entitled to, and has the right of, private property; if people set about to share their goods in common, instead of keeping them under their own control, this simply indicates they distrust one another. A perfect trust and a sharing attitude would require no prior agreement between individuals to share their property. Private property is a determination of individual freedom; lack of private property negates that freedom. Notes Hegel,

The general principle that underlies Plato's ideal state violates the right of personality by forbidding the holding of private property. The idea of a pious or friendly and even compulsory brotherhood of men holding their goods in common and rejecting the principle of private property may readily present itself to the disposition which mistakes the true nature of the freedom of mind and right and fails to apprehend it in its determinate moments. As for the moral or religious view behind this idea, when Epicurus's friends proposed to form such an association holding goods in common, he forbade them, precisely on the ground that their proposal betrayed distrust and that those who distrusted each other were not friends.

Private property is a low form of human freedom or personality, since it is characterized by *externality* to the owner of property. But it is a necessary and essential aspect of human freedom, the only form of concrete and real freedom possible in the abstract context of bourgeois society: 'Even if my freedom is here realized first of all in an external thing, and so falsely realized, nevertheless abstract personality in its immediacy can have no other embodiment save one characterized by immediacy.'[75]

By embodying his or her will in an object which becomes private property, the individual translates his or her ideality into an external form. And the pre-eminent external manifestation of property is one's ability to alienate or sell for a limited time one's own labour-power or ideality. Thus in the property relation, reason or rationality – the purposeful activity of the individual – takes on the essential aspect of existence or *being*. In this relation, freedom becomes 'concrete, i.e. social'; that is, the individual's freedom in property is recognized and respected by other individuals. 'A person must translate his freedom into an external sphere in order to exist as Idea. Personality is the first, still wholly abstract, determination of the absolute and infinite will, and therefore this sphere distinct from the person, the sphere capable of embodying his freedom, is likewise determined as what is immediately different and separable from him.'[76]

Possession is essentially an aspect of will; a person possesses something only in so far as his or her will is embodied in the object. Even the body of a person remains that individual's possession just so far as his or her will is shown in it: 'I possess the members of my body, my life, only so long as I will to possess them. An animal cannot maim or destroy itself, but a man can.' Freedom is not an abstract quality that can be embodied in will alone; for a person to be truly free, he or she must be recognized as such by others. 'To be free from the point of view of others is identical with being free in my determinate existence.' Freedom as expressed in the possession of an external object is distinct from freedom in the person of the individual, because the will is intrinsic to the body and personality of the individual, but external to the object. 'If my body is touched or suffers violence, then, because I feel, I am touched myself actually, here and now. This creates the distinction between personal injury and damage to my external property, for in such property my will is not actually present in this direct fashion.' To steal a person's property is to violate an external embodiment of that person's free will; but 'murder, slavery, enforced religious observance, etc.' absolutely negate the victim's freedom.[77] As Marx suggests, 'the presupposition of the master-servant relation is the appropriation of an alien *will*.'[78]

The decline of slavery and serfdom in the modern world is a direct result of the apprehension by men and women that their body, as well as their ideality or labour-power, is *their own private property*, and not the possession of someone else. This awareness was not easily achieved, but once established it is impossible to take away. To argue against slavery on the basis of the natural rights of the individual is correct, says Hegel, in so far as this argument recognizes 'the absolute starting-point' that freedom is the essence of the individual. But it is incorrect in that it postulates that freedom is a *natural* characteristic. The basis of this view 'is the fashionable idea of a state of nature and a natural origin for rights, and the lack of the concept of rationality and freedom.'[79] Freedom is not a natural, but a social, relation; it has nothing to do with nature. Nature is in the chains of accident and caprice, and a natural existence is far from being one of freedom. In their natural state men and women were capable of being enslaved and did not regard slavery as an absolute negation of their own person. Had they done so, slavery would have been inconceivable. A truly free people would die rather than be enslaved: Hitler's attempt to crush Europe and Russia, no less than the US effort to impose an alien order in south-east Asia, were doomed from the start precisely because they failed to recognize this fundamental principle. 'Were the mere arbitrary will of the prince a law, and should he wish slavery to be introduced, we would have the knowledge that this could not be. To sleep, to live, to have a certain office, is not our real Being, and certainly to be no slave is such, for that has come to mean the being in nature. Thus in the West we are upon the soil of a veritable Philosophy.'[80] In human history, slavery was relatively justified because the peoples who were enslaved had not reached the point where they recognized themselves as free and independent individuals. It was the event of slavery itself that brought about the consciousness in people that they should and must be free.

To adhere to man's absolute freedom – one aspect of the matter – is *eo ipso* to condemn slavery. Yet if a man is a slave, his own will is responsible for his slavery, just as it is its will which is responsible if a people is subjugated. Hence the wrong of slavery lies at the door not simply of enslavers or conquerors but of the slaves and of the conquered themselves. Slavery occurs in man's transition from the state of nature to genuinely ethical conditions; it occurs in a world where a wrong is still right. At that stage wrong has validity and so is necessarily in place.[81]

Hegel's view is echoed by Marx: 'the *master-servant relation* ... forms a necessary ferment for the development and the decline and fall of all original relations of property and of production, just as it also expresses their limited nature.'[82]

In the sphere of private property so far discussed – the ownership by an individual of his or her own body and the products of his or her ideality – *equality* is meaningless. The natural ideality of different persons is far from equal: everyone has different talents, abilities, desires, and so on. In this sphere, freedom simply demands that 'everyone must have property'; but the concept of abstract ideality itself means that 'particularity is just the sphere where there is room for inequality and where equality would be wrong.' If everyone has diverse capacities by nature, 'we may not speak of the injustice of nature in the unequal distribution of possessions and resources, since nature is not free and therefore is neither just nor unjust.'[83] Those who demand equality in the abstract sphere of private property 'call to mind,' as Marx suggests, though in a different context, 'the advice given by the good Dogberry to the night-watchman Seacoal ... "To be a well-favoured man is the gift of fortune; but reading and writing comes by nature." '84

In common with many commentators, Marcuse interprets Hegel's dictum that 'Right is unconcerned about differences in individuals' as one of the 'regressive features of his *Philosophy of Right*.' Hegel's attitude, Marcuse assures his readers, 'typifies a social practice wherein the preservation of the whole is reached only by disregarding the human essence of the individual.'85 But Hegel's concern is to uphold 'the human essence of the individual' since difference rather than equality is what distinguishes one individual from another.

Use of a thing, Hegel suggests, 'implies a ... universal relation to the thing, because, when it is used, the thing in its particularity is not recognized but is negated by the user.' The constant use of a thing, prompted by human needs and desires, is the most universal aspect of possession. Moreover, if the use of a thing is restricted and controlled in order to assure its reproduction with the proceeds of its use, then possession reaches its highest pinnacle:

To use a thing by grasping it directly is in itself to take possession of a *single* thing here and now. But if my use of it is grounded on a persistent need, and if I make repeated use of a product which continually renews itself, restricting my use if necessary to safeguard that renewal, then these and other circumstances transform the direct single grasp of a thing into a mark, intended to signify that I am taking it into my possession in a universal way, and thereby taking possession of the elemental or organic basis of such products, or of anything else that conditions them.'86

What Hegel is referring to here, of course, is *capital*, means of production, a thing which 'continually renews itself.'87

Ownership of a thing, according to Hegel, entails nothing more than *constant use* of it; the concept of property in the final analysis means only the relation of use. To own a thing, where a thing includes a means of production, is simply to use it. 'My full use or employment of a thing is the thing in its entirety, so that if I have the full use of the thing I am its owner. Over and above the entirety of its use, there is nothing left of the thing which could be the property of another.' *It is at this point that Hegel embarks on a devastating critique of capitalist private property – the property relation thought to be absolute by the understanding or bourgeois consciousness.* 'If the whole and entire use of a thing were mine,' Hegel declares, 'while the abstract ownership was supposed to be someone else's, then the thing as mine would be penetrated through and through by my will ... and at the same time there would remain in the thing something impenetrable by me, namely the will, the empty will of another. As a positive will, I would be at one and the same time objective and not objective to myself in the thing – an absolute contradiction. Ownership therefore is in essence free and complete.'[88]

The modern worker in 'laying hold of the means' of production, as Hegel expresses it in the *Encyclopedia Logic*, is in effect laying claim to the ownership of the means of production. The commodities he or she produces embody the will of the producer and not the abstract will of the capitalist. They are therefore the private property of the worker. For Hegel, the relation between the worker and the means of production in capitalist society is totally *alienated* and *contradictory*. It is a relation of *necessity*: a product of a society ruled and governed by *abstractions*. Here the creative impulse and ideality of the individual represent unrealized 'inner capacity, mere possibilities'; this is the realm of 'external, inorganic nature, the knowledge of a third person, alien force and the like.'[89] The distinction posited by the bourgeois mind between the *abstract ownership of capital* and the concrete ideality of the means of production by the worker is nothing less than an 'insanity of personality.' Hegel's corrosive critique of capitalist private property should be quoted in full: 'To distinguish between the right to the whole and entire use of a thing and ownership in the abstract is the work of the empty Understanding for which the Idea – i.e. in this instance the unity of (a) ownership (or even the person's will as such) and (b) its realization – is not the truth, but for which these two moments in their separation from one another pass as something which is true.' What Hegel means is that the bourgeois mind distinguishes between ownership as possession and ideality, i.e., the labour of the worker, and ownership of the product of this relation, i.e., the ownership by the capitalist of the commodities produced by the worker. 'This distinction, then,' he continues, 'as a relation in the world of fact,' i.e. in the bourgeois world of commodity production, 'is that of an overlord to nothing, and this might be called an "insanity of personality" (if we may mean by "insanity" not merely the presence of a direct contradiction between a man's purely subjective ideas and the actual facts of his life), because "mine" as applied to a single object would have to mean the direct presence in it of both my single exclusive will and also the single exclusive will of someone else.'[90]

In Hegel's view, the modern capitalist is an 'overlord to nothing,' infected by an 'insanity of personality,' and the distinction between the property of the capitalist and that of the worker is completely hollow – a mystified creation of the bourgeois mind. This empty distinction is criticized by Marx almost a half century after Hegel: 'the transformation of money into capital,' he notes, 'breaks down into two wholly distinct, autonomous spheres, two entirely separate processes. The first belongs to the realm of the *circulation of commodities* and is acted out in the *market place*. It is the *sale and purchase* of *labour power*.'[91] This sphere concerns the relation Hegel calls 'contract,' or the exchange of a property right. 'A right arising from a contract,' says Hegel, 'is never a right over a person, but only a right over something external to a person or something which he can alienate [e.g., labour power: D.M.], always a right over a thing.'[92] The second sphere involved in the transformation of money into capital 'is the *consumption of the labour power that has been acquired*, i.e. the process of production itself.' This is the sphere which Hegel calls ownership through use. The bourgeois economists entirely ignore this second sphere, Marx observes, and treat 'the relationship between capitalist and worker [as] nothing but a relationship between commodity owners who exchange money and commodities with a free contract and to their mutual advantage ... This simple device is no sorcery, but it contains the entire wisdom of the vulgar economist.'[93]

Disease for Hegel is any kind of *alienation* of a part of an organic system from the whole; the result of disease is 'impotence and dependence on an *alien* power.' The bourgeois mind is diseased in exactly this sense: it is an alienated and divided consciousness which constantly reproduces *alienation* and *division* in the objects of consciousness. In its attitude to private property the alienation of bourgeois consciousness reaches its fullest height: it becomes an 'insanity of personality.' The mind of an insane person, observes Hegel, 'is shifted out from the centre of its actual world and, since it also still retains a consciousness of this world, has two centres, one in the remainder of its *rational* consciousness and the other in its *deranged* idea.'[94] The apotheosis of the *deranged idea* of the bourgeois mind is the notion of *abstract capitalist private property*. The 'insanity of personality' which results from what Marx describes as the empty and formal character of bourgeois private property means that 'all *material wealth confronts* the worker as the property of *commodity possessors*. What is proposed here is that he works as a *non-proprietor* and that the *conditions of his labour confront* him as *alien property*.' The contradictory character of bourgeois property relations means that 'the objective conditions essential to the realization of labour are *alienated* from the worker and become manifest as *fetishes* endowed with a will and a soul of their own ... It is not the worker who buys the means of production and subsistence, but the means of production that buy the worker to incorporate him into the means of production.'[95]

Hegel argues that the contract between the worker and the capitalist is a formal contract only, since the exchange between them is not the same as that between two equal commodity owners. In the capitalist exchange relation only one of the contractors receives property – the capitalist; the worker receives only wages which, instead of being property in the sense of a self-renewable resource, are only adequate to keep the worker alive and fill his or her immediate consumption requirements. 'Subsistence,' as Hegel points out, 'is not the same as possession.' While the worker surrenders property in the form of energy, talent, and skill, he or she receives no property in return. 'Contract implies two consenting parties and two things. That is to say, in a contract my purpose is both to acquire property and to surrender it. Contract is real when the action of both parties is complete, i.e. when both surrender and both acquire property, and when both remain property owners even in the act of surrender. Contract is formal where only one of the parties acquires property or surrenders it.' The worker, by possessing and employing the means of production, becomes their real owner, and the value created therefore belongs to the worker. 'As a full owner of the thing, I am *eo ipso* owner of its value as well as its use.' But the worker gets only a part of the value he or she creates; the capitalist pockets the rest. This formal relation Hegel refers to as '*laesio enormis*,' a relation which 'annuls the obligation arising out of the making of a contract.' The only *real* contract, says Hegel, is one where 'each party retains the same property with which he enters the contract and which at the same time he surrenders, what thus remains identical throughout as the property implicit in the contract is distinct from the external things whose owners alter when the exchange is made. What remains identical is the value, in respect of which the subjects of the contract are equal to one another whatever the qualitative external differences of the things exchanged. Value is the universal in which the subjects of the contract participate.'[96]

Marx – without recognizing that Hegel had already theorized the exploitative relation between capitalist and worker (although Hegel's theory may have operated as an unconscious subtext in his mind) calls the excess value created by the worker in the labour process and pocketed by the capitalist surplus-value. 'The fact,' he writes, 'that half a day's labour is necessary to keep the worker alive during 24 hours does not in any way prevent him from working a whole day. Therefore the value of labour-power, and the value which that labour-power valorizes ... in the labour-process, are two entirely different magnitudes.' The process of valorization is the creation of value in the labour process beyond the amount necessary to pay the worker's wages. 'If the process is not carried beyond the point where the value paid by the capitalist for the labour-power is replaced by an exact equivalent, it is simply a process of creating value; but if it is continued beyond that point it becomes a process of valorization.' Under the capitalist mode of production, then, 'the labour process is only the means whereby the valorization is implemented and the valorization process is essentially the *production of surplus-value*, i.e. the *objectification of unpaid labour*.'[97]

Marx's solution to the dilemma posed by the exploitation of the worker by the capitalist is well known: the workers must seize the means of production and replace capitalism with communist society. Although his critique of capitalist private property has gone virtually unrecognized by all commentators, not least Marx himself, Hegel's radical analysis of bourgeois society, which will be outlined in the following chapter, is familiar to most contemporary writers on Hegel. But Hegel, in contrast with Marx, is supposed to be without a solution. 'At the height of his critical awareness of the horrors of industrial society,' claims Avineri, 'Hegel ultimately remains quietistic ... his failure to find a solution to it within his system seems to justify a gnawing doubt.'[98] Avineri's influential account of Hegel's theory of the state evinces little appreciation of dialectic method and speculative logic.[99] The same ignorance pulses through the work of Marcuse: 'the tone [of] the entire *Philosophy of Right*,' he declares, marks 'the resignation of a man who knows that the truth he represents has drawn to its close and that it can no longer invigorate the world.'[100] Another writer on Hegel, Raymond Plant, suggests that Hegel's 'self-acknowledged failure to explain ... the problem of poverty ... demonstrated very clearly the limitations, even on its own terms, of the Hegelian enterprise in social and political philosophy.'[101] It is not only in Marx's time that Hegel is treated as a 'dead dog'!

Hegel's answer to the dilemma of bourgeois society is identical to that of Marx with this difference: he offers a much more concrete solution than Marx ever manages to achieve, a solution which will be outlined in the concluding chapters of this study. For now, however, it is necessary to return to Hegel's analysis of bourgeois private property. He suggests that in so far as the capitalist plays a direct role in the production process, in terms of the rational and decision-making activity described, for example, by Marx, his or her relation to the means of production is not entirely abstract. 'Were there nothing,' writes Hegel, 'in these two relationships' to the means of production 'except that rigid distinction' between the real ownership of the worker and the merely formal ownership of the capitalist, 'in its rigid abstraction, then in them we would not have two overlords (*domini*) in the strict sense, but an owner on the one hand [i.e., the worker: D.M.] and the overlord who was the overlord of nothing [i.e., the capitalist: D.M.] on the other. But on the score of the burdens imposed there are two owners standing in relation to each other.'

The resolution of the contradiction between the worker and the capitalist, therefore, can only go in one direction. 'Although their relation is not that of being common owners of a property, still the transition from it to common ownership is very easy.' This transition had already begun in Hegel's time with the remnants of feudal property, where the actual proceeds of the use of property were recognized as the property of the working tenant, while the landowner retained only the abstract ownership of the land: 'the yield of the property is calculated and looked upon as the essential thing, while that incalculable factor in the overlordship of a property, the factor which has perhaps been regarded as the honourable thing about property, is subordinated to the *utile* which here is the rational factor.'[102]

Far from being 'quiescent,' Hegel completes his discussion of capitalist private property and its necessary, because rational, transition to common ownership of the means of production, by pointing out the difficulties and the length of time involved. 'It is about a millennium and a half,' he writes, 'since the freedom of personality began through the spread of Christianity to blossom and gain recognition as a universal principle from a part, though still a small part, of the human race. But it was only yesterday, we might say, that the principle of the freedom of property became recognized in some places,' i.e., in France, where the Revolution swept away all feudal encumbrances and privilege. 'This example from history may serve to rebuke the impatience of opinion and to show the length of time that mind requires for progress in its self-consciousness.'[103] The reason the transition from capitalist to common ownership of the means of production will, nevertheless, be 'very easy' is cogently and convincingly presented by Marx:

The transformation of scattered private property resting on the personal labour of the individuals themselves into capitalist private property is naturally an incomparably more protracted, violent and difficult process than the transformation of capitalist private property, which in fact already rests on the carrying on of production by society, into social property. In the former case, it was a matter of the expropriation of the mass of the people by a few usurpers; but in this case, we have the expropriation of a few usurpers by the mass of the people.[104]

7

The External Capitalist State

1 THE CORPORATION AND THE EXTERNAL STATE

It is usually supposed by commentators that Hegel's discussion of the state in the *Philosophy of Right* refers to the Prussian state of his time. 'To a considerable extent,' writes Marcuse, 'Hegel's *Philosophy of Right* expresses the official theory of the [Restoration].'[1] For Hegel, however, Prussia in common with the other states of continental Western Europe and Britain, was an 'external state' – the state of the bourgeoisie and its fading partner, the landed aristocracy. Civil society, notes Hegel, 'may be prima facie regarded as the external state, the state based on need, the state as the Understanding envisages it.'[2] The bourgeois state is the '*state external*', according to Hegel, because it is almost entirely dedicated to protection of individual rights and capitalist private property.[3] The connection between the external state and civil society is so intimate that conventional political theorists tend to confound the principle of the state with civil society itself.[4] Kant, for instance, views the state as an 'external Power' intended to protect private property and formal personal freedom; the state's character as a collective unity and ethical universe is ignored.[5]

The external state, which for Hegel includes the capitalist economic system along with its institutions of law and public authority, is precisely 'the modern representative State' described by Marx as 'a committee for managing the common affairs of the whole bourgeoisie.'[6] For both thinkers, the capitalist state incorporates 'the right of subjective freedom' – i.e., the individual's property in his or her personality and labour-power – a right which 'has become the universal effective principle of a new form of civilization.' Nevertheless, the 'new form of civilization' heralded by both Hegel and Marx is definitely not bourgeois society. The external capitalist state is simply a 'stage of division', a point of transition to a much different social order.[7] The alienation and inversion of property rights characteristic of capitalism, writes Marx, is only an unavoidable and 'antagonistic stage' in the development of 'a free human society.'[8] In Hegel's terminology, the external capitalist state is merely a show, an appearance through which the theorist may perceive the glimmerings of a new civilization. Civil or bourgeois society, for Hegel, is a manifestly evil system governed by 'the law of nature ... the predominance of the strong and the reign of force, and a state of nature a state of violence and wrong, of which nothing truer can be said than that one ought to depart from it.'[9] Civil society is the 'abstract moment ... [the] moment of reality' in the development of individual human freedom, and as such it is a form which will only later coalesce into a rational, free state. 'The development we are studying is that whereby the abstract forms reveal themselves not as self-subsistent but as false.'[10]

Hegel argues that 'it is the separation between one man and another which makes civil society what it is.' In bourgeois society natural inequalities between individuals are allowed to take root, develop, and attain absolutely free scope; the result is vast wealth at one end of the social scale and absolute penury at the other. 'In these contrasts and their complexity, civil society affords a spectacle of extravagance and want as well as the physical and ethical degeneration common to them both.' For the capitalist, civil society is simply the arena of 'abstract need' or profit. Everything is subordinated to the pursuit of profit-making; and since the key to profit is production, production for profit becomes an end in itself. 'When civil society is in a state of unimpeded activity, it is engaged in expanding internally in population and industry. The amassing of wealth is intensified by generalizing (a) the linkage of men by their needs, and (b) the methods of preparing and distributing the means to satisfy these needs, because it is from this double process of generalization that the largest profits are derived.'[11]

To the capitalist, nothing could matter less than how his or her products are consumed provided they are sold at a profit. 'A large part of the annual product ... consists of the most tawdry products ... designed to gratify the most impoverished appetites and fancies.' And commodities are produced and sold precisely ... to produce and sell more commodities. 'Accumulate, accumulate!' writes Marx in an extraordinary passage in *Capital*. 'That is Moses and the prophets! "Industry furnishes the material which saving accumulates." Therefore save, save, i.e. re-convert the greatest possible portion of surplus-value or surplus product into capital! Accumulation for the sake of accumulation, production for the sake of production: this was the formula in which classical economics expressed the historical mission of the bourgeoisie.'[12] The same idea is expressed, though in more prosaic and theoretical terms, by Hegel. He observes that the external, alienated character of capitalist production is based on finite or limited designs and ends, i.e., profit. And 'in finite design ... even the executed End,' the commodity, 'has the same radical rift or flaw as had the Means and the initial End,' the design or plan of the commodity. 'We have got therefore only a form extraneously impressed on a pre-existing material: and this form, by reason of the limited content of the End, is also a contingent characteristic. The End achieved consequently is only an object, which again becomes a Means or material for other Ends, and so on for ever.'[13]

The drive for profit turns the capitalist into 'a machine for the transformation of surplus-value into surplus capital.'[14] The profit-seeker plunges into 'the unmitigated extreme of barbarism ... and the bestiality of contempt for all higher things ... . The mass of wealth, the pure universal, the absence of wisdom, is the heart of the matter.'[15] If the worker at least protests against the alienation he or she experiences under capitalism, the capitalist 'has his roots in the process of alienation and finds absolute satisfaction in it.' As a result, states Marx, 'the worker stands on a higher plane than the capitalist from the outset.' Profit, he observes, 'is therefore the determining, dominating and over-riding purpose of the capitalist; it is the absolute motive and content of his activity. And in fact it is no more than the rationalized motive and aim of the hoarder – a highly impoverished and abstract content which makes it plain that the capitalist is just as enslaved by the relationships of capitalism as is his opposite pole, the worker, albeit in a quite different manner.'[16]

According to Hegel, the alienation involved in the abstract pursuit of profit, as well as the desire to establish a secure source of capital, ultimately gives rise to the large corporation in modern society. The corporation has its material basis in the increased division of labour in civil society which splits the economy into different branches of industry within which various manufacturing and trade associations arise.

These organizations have a universal purpose which is 'wholly concrete and no wider in scope than the purpose involved in business,' i.e., profit. Operating 'under the surveillance of the public authority,' they offer the owning class not only a 'stable capital' but also a form of respectability unavailable to the grasping entrepreneur who tries 'to gain recognition for himself by giving external proofs of success in his business, and to these proofs no limits can be set.' Entrepreneurial wealth is based on 'a whole which is itself an organ of the entire society' and also on such elements as the 'increasing mechanization of labour.' These facts, argues Hegel, lend weight to 'complaints ... made about the luxury of the business classes and their passion for extravagance – which have as their concomitant the creation of a rabble of paupers.' Social pressure, therefore, plays a part in the desire of the capitalist to have his or her business incorporated by the state. 'Unless he is a member of an authorized Corporation ... an individual is without rank or dignity, his isolation reduces his business to mere self-seeking, and his livelihood and satisfaction become insecure.' Heading a corporation provides the entrepreneur with social prestige; it shows that 'he is actively concerned in promoting the comparatively disinterested end of this whole. Thus he commands the respect due to one in his social position.'[17]

Given the perverse dialectic of bourgeois society, the metamorphosis of isolated capitalists into corporate managers (a transformation also discussed by Marx[18]) has ominous results. What precisely distinguishes the early employer is that 'no class really exists for him, since in civil society it is something common to particular persons which really exists, i.e. something legally constituted and recognized.'[19] Formerly a loose collection of powerful entrepreneurs and their families, the propertied class has undergone its own managerial revolution. 'Wealthy families hold shares in a large number of companies and they form a pool from which corporate managers are recruited, though these managers may not come from families having a large stake in the companies which they run.'[20] In modern capitalism a tiny, interlocking group of corporate bosses leads a few dozen enormous firms which dominate the economy; this corporate élite exerts its considerable economic leverage and upper-class influence to enforce what Michael Useem calls 'classwide rationality': 'The classwide principle of organization is the product of inclusive and diffusely structured networks of intercorporate ownership and directorship linking ever concentrating units of capital. These networks define a segment of the corporate elite whose strategic location and internal coherence propel it into a political leadership role on behalf of the entire corporate community.'[21]

The giant corporation's stranglehold over the economic system produces in reaction a whole series of government agencies intended to control and regulate its activity. As Marx suggests, the corporation 'establishes a monopoly in certain spheres and thereby requires state interference.'[22] Subjective and contingent actions may be tolerated when they occur within individual small firms, but they cannot be allowed in large corporations where a single decision is likely to affect large numbers of people. Writes Hegel, 'This universal aspect makes private actions a matter of contingency which escapes the agent's control and which either does or may injure others and wrong them.' The extent and scope of the activities of public agencies vis-à-vis business is a focus for controversy and struggle; in wartime, however, the authority of the external state over business is likely to be very great, since 'many a thing, harmless at other times, has to be regarded as harmful.' Even in peacetime, however, the proliferation of government agencies to regulate and control industry – a development especially remarkable in the battered and polluted North American heartland of the multinational corporation, where working conditions and consumer products are gradually being placed under health and safety controls almost unknown in many countries – is inevitable. 'When reflective [i.e., bourgeois: D.M.] thinking is very highly developed, the public authority may tend to draw into its orbit everything it possibly can, for in everything some factor may be found which might make it dangerous in one of its bearings.'[23]

Hegel is keenly aware of the factors in bourgeois society which are likely to increase the rational control of the public authority over corporations. Much of this development is not foreseen by Marx and is underemphasized even by contemporary Marxists. The reason for Hegel's superiority over Marx in this regard is that his chief concern is with the growth of rational consciousness in the mind of the individual, even within the external capitalist state. In the writings published during his lifetime at least, Marx gives the impression that he did not expect capitalism to survive for long, and he therefore left off considering many developments, perhaps supposing them to be impossible in bourgeois society. This tendency, of course, is far from absolute, and the *Grundrisse* and the planned Part Seven of Volume I of *Capital* contain some remarkable anticipations of novel developments within modern capitalism. In this respect, Marx is more imaginative than his present-day followers.

In the *Philosophy of Right*, Hegel adumbrates a whole range of developments that are only now coming to fruition, such as the modern consumer movement, which has achieved a strong and extending grip especially in North America. 'The differing interests of producers and consumers,' he observes, 'may come into collision with each other; and although a fair balance between them on the whole may be brought about automatically, still their adjustment also requires a control which stands above both and is consciously undertaken.' Until recently the principle, 'let the buyer beware,' guided the relations of business and consumers. But the great shift in the outlook of consumers which occurred in the early 1960s in North America and which focused initially on automobile safety and food prices, realized an advance in consciousness urged by Hegel:

The right to the exercise of [public] control in a single case (e.g. in the fixing of the prices of the commonest necessaries of life) depends on the fact that, by being publicly exposed for sale, goods in absolutely universal daily demand are offered not so much to an individual as such but rather to a universal purchaser, the public; and thus both the defence of the public's right not to be defrauded, and also the management of goods inspection, may lie, as a common concern, with a public authority.

In addition to these activities, the external state also expands to include a range of services that facilitate the scope, expansion and efficiency of industry, as well as economic direction *per se*, which will be discussed below. The state also takes a much greater role in such areas as public health, social administration, and so on. 'These universal activities and organizations of general utility call for the oversight and care of the public authority.' In Hegel's time, as in our own, a debate raged as to the extent to which government should be allowed to interfere in civil society. For Hegel, however, the public responsibility of the state always takes precedence over the accidental and capricious sphere of business and commerce. 'The individual must have a right to work for his bread as he pleases, but the public also has a right to insist that essential tasks shall be properly done. Both points of view must be satisfied, and freedom of trade should not be such as to jeopardize the general good.'[24]

2 CLASS, CONSUMPTION, AND FREEDOM

Hegel disagrees with arguments, like that of Marx in the *Communist Manifesto*, that the rule of law in bourgeois society is 'but the will of [the capitalist] class made into a law for all, a will, whose essential character and direction are determined by the economical conditions of existence of [the bourgeoisie]'.[25] Hegel is concerned with the rational aspects of the external state; he is well aware that bad states exist, but what merely exists also in due time ceases to do so. His 1831 critique of British parliamentary government, for example, rivals in vehemence Marx's own dissection of the French regime in *The Civil War in France*. Consider, for instance, his account of the English occupation of Ireland:

It is well known that the majority of the Irish population adheres to the Catholic Church. The property that once belonged to it, the churches themselves, tithes, the obligation of parishioners to keep the church buildings in good repair and to provide furnishings for worship and wages for sextons, etc., all this has been taken away from it by right of conquest and made the property of the Anglican

Church ... Even the Turks have generally left alone the churches of their Christian, Armenian, and Jewish subjects; even where these subjects have been forbidden to repair their churches when dilapidated, they were still allowed leave to buy permission to do so. But the English have taken all the churches away from their conquered Catholic population ... The Irish, whose poverty and misery and consequential degradation and demoralization is a standing theme in Parliament, acknowledged by every Ministry, are compelled, out of the few pence they may have, to pay their own priest and construct a place for their services.

Throughout the Irish countryside, a people everywhere reduced to penury without parallel on the continent were stripped of the last vestiges of their dignity by absentee landowners. 'Those who already own nothing are deprived of their birthplace and their hereditary means of livelihood – in the name of justice. All this too is justice, that the landowners have the huts burnt so as to make sure of getting the peasants off the ground and cut off their chance of delaying their departure or creeping in under shelter again.' Nor was it likely that the English will improve conditions in Ireland by altering property laws in favour of the peasantry. Even 'under the Reform Bill, parliamentary legislation remains in the hands of that class which has its interest, and still more its fixed habits, in the hitherto existing law of property.'[26]

Criticism of the state, however, does not amount to a theory of the state; while Marx's writings are replete with devastating analyses of particular regimes, he offers no general political theory. Ultimately a critique of the state can only be convincing if it is carried out within the framework of some notion of what a state *is*, and this demands study of the positive or affirmative aspects of the state rather than its external or transitory appearance. 'The state is no ideal work of art; it stands on earth and so in the sphere of caprice, chance, and error, and bad behaviour may disfigure it in many respects ... The affirmative, life, subsists despite ... defects, and it is this affirmative factor which is our theme here.'[27]

Marx's view of the capitalist state as expressed in the *Communist Manifesto* is embraced by contemporary Marxists who argue that the state and law under capitalism constitute a repressive apparatus designed mainly to serve the interests of the ruling capitalist class.[28] For the strictly external bourgeois state, of course, the Marxist analysis is correct. As I argued in Chapter 1, the external state finds its basis in the *arbitrary will* of individuals, their freedom to choose from among various alternatives and to find outlets for purely personal desires and interests which inevitably have an exploitative class character. Nevertheless, even the bourgeois state reflects the *rational will* of individuals that transcends mere particular interests and unites men and women in a political community. It is upon the rational will that Marx bases his expectations for communist society, and it is this form of will which Hegel takes as the foundation for the rational state. The rational will is responsible for the emergence of the corporation and the public authority in civil society, institutions which also take a role at the higher level of the state. Moreover, it is the rational will which extracts a sense of order out of the competitive disorder of bourgeois life. 'Habit,' Hegel remarks, 'blinds us to that on which our whole existence depends. When we walk the streets at night in safety, it does not strike us that this might be otherwise. This habit of feeling safe has become second nature, and we do not reflect on just how this is due solely to the working of special institutions. Commonplace thinking often has the impression that force holds the state together, but in fact its only bond is the fundamental sense of order which everybody possesses.'[29]

The notion that force holds the capitalist state together is, of course, Lenin's position. For him, the state is an instrument for the exploitation of the oppressed class.[30] Consequently, he advocates destruction of the bourgeois state and its replacement by the dictatorship of the proletariat. Yet one of the incontestable results of the Russian Revolution was falsification of the Leninist theory of the state. 'Lenin,' writes Trotsky, 'did not succeed ... either in his chief work dedicated to this question (*State and Revolution*), or in the program of the party, in drawing all the necessary conclusions as to the character of the state from the economic backwardness and isolatedness of [Russia].'[31] The state is not simply the instrument of the ruling class – a superstructure standing above society – so much as it is an organism which expresses the degree of development of the rational will – i.e., the needs and consciousness of all its members. Lenin's failure to smash the Russian state follows from this fact. 'Russia,' observes Hegel, 'has a mass of serfs on the one hand and a mass of rulers on the other.'[32] The Soviet state which emerged from the Revolution of 1917 simply recreated, though on a much higher level, this subservient relation between the people and their rulers. It created, as admitted at the Twentieth Congress of the CPSU, 'a bureaucratic and police autocracy,' a regime in which people continued 'the habit of never thinking for themselves.'[33]

As Fernando Claudin points out, the Russian Revolution took place 'in a backward country where the overwhelming majority of the people were peasants and where there were no democratic traditions or institutions.'[34] In the *Eighteenth Brumaire of Louis Napoleon*, Marx observes that a nation of peasants is unlikely to develop an independent class- or self-consciousness among its members, a fact which makes it vulnerable to autocratic rule. 'In so far,' writes Marx of the French peasantry, 'as millions of families live under economic conditions of existence that separate their mode of life, their interests and their culture from those of the other classes, and put them in hostile opposition to the latter, they form a class. In so far as there is merely a local interconnection among these small-holding peasants, and the identity of their interests begets no community, no national bond and no political organization among them, they do not form a class.'[35] For Marx, class consciousness is an indispensable requirement for the development of what he calls a class in and for itself, an active class with the will and capability to put its interests into action on the political stage. The peasantry remains a class in itself, and fails to create an independent political consciousness among its individual members. A state based predominantly on this class, as was Russia in 1917 and China in 1949, will inevitably reflect the consciousness of individuals who, politically at least, are unable to think for themselves.

For Hegel and Marx, classes in modern society are based on the relationship of groups of people to the 'system of needs' or the means of production. 'The infinitely complex, criss-cross, movements of reciprocal production and exchange, and the equally infinite multiplicity of means therein employed,' notes Hegel, 'become crystallized, owing to the universality inherent in their content, and distinguished into general groups. As a result, the entire complex is built up into particular systems of needs, means, and types of work relative to these needs, modes of satisfaction and of theoretical and practical education, i.e. into systems, to one or other of which individuals are assigned – in other words, into class divisions.'[36] The agricultural class within civil society, the class of landowners and peasants, is dependent on nature and the soil, as well as on demands for its produce which are generated outside its circle of life. As a result, no independent or reflective consciousness is created among its members. 'The *agricultural* ... conditions of life,' says Hegel, 'brings with it the relation of lord and serf.'[37] Unlike the other classes in civil society the agricultural class is incapable of developing a 'particularity become objective to itself' – it stays, as Marx puts it, a class in itself. 'The agricultural mode of subsistence,' writes Hegel, 'remains one which owes comparatively little to reflection and independence of will, and this mode of life is in general such that this class has the substantial disposition of an ethical life which is immediate, resting on family relationship and trust.'[38]

When the Bolsheviks came to power in Russia they found themselves in control of a nation of peasants. Even the Russian working class itself was at a low level of development: 'side by side with the dreamer and the hero,' writes Deutscher, 'there lived in the Russian worker the slave; the lazy, cursing, squalid slave, bearing the stigmata of his past.'[39] The peasants, of course, were even more backward than the working class. One Bolshevik leader, Pyatakov, exclaimed about Russian peasants newly recruited as miners: 'Idiots! Barbarians! Illiterates! Even we did not know what a savage nation we had made the revolution with.' The suspicious temperament of the peasant pervaded the entire ruling stratum of the Russian Communist party, so that, even in 1921 when the Revolution was still young, incidents occurred that make the paranoid Nixon presidency look like a paragon of rationality. 'Brandler', writes Isaac Deutscher, referring to the leader of the German Communist party in 1921-23, 'recalls a telephone conversation he had with Lenin in 1921. There were crackling noises on the line all the time, and Lenin said: "Again some idiot is trying to listen in." Brandler adds that everybody was eavesdropping on everybody – even [the head of the secret police] Dzerzhinsky's phone was tapped.'[40]

According to Hegel, every individual within civil society must belong to a social class, for only through such membership does a person become 'something definite, i.e. something specifically particularized.' As a result, everyone must restrict 'himself exclusively to one of the particular spheres of need.' Class membership defines the manner in which an individual's personality is actualized in the world of work and becomes a vital part of his or her life and personality. It represents, Hegel observes, 'the disposition to make oneself a member of one of the moments of civil society by one's own act, through one's energy, industry, and skill, to maintain oneself in this position, and to fend for oneself only through this process of mediating oneself with the universal, while in this way gaining recognition both in one's own eyes and the eyes of others.' Social class, in other words, is the mediating institution between the individual and society; it is the link – the particular – which develops individual self-consciousness and assures the essential identity of a person with society.[41]

Bourgeois society eventually extinguishes divisions within the agricultural class, and reduces the differences in temperament between it and the business class. The bitter struggle between serfs and nobles which contributed to the decay of feudalism and the rise of monarchy culminated in the destruction of aristocratic privilege during the French Revolution.[42] At the same time capitalist industry and commodity relations eroded the family holdings upon which feudal rights and privileges were based, scattered the peasantry, and depressed aristocratic pretensions and position.[43] The activity of the agricultural class, i.e., farming, remains the same, but the consciousness and the social relations of this class, 'its form and ... its power of reflection' are raised to the level of the business class.[44]

This class, which I argued in Chapter 6 includes both the capitalist and the worker, has an entirely different ideology or consciousness from the agricultural class. Its relation to the system of needs is rational and self-determining, and rationality developed through work is reflected in the political sphere as well. According to Hegel, the self-directed activity of the business class and its political involvement have deep roots in the development of the free towns of the Middle Ages. As they organized in guild societies, 'artisans necessarily soon attained a superior position to that of the tillers of the ground, for the latter were forcibly driven to work; the former displayed activity really their own, and a corresponding diligence and interest in the result of their labours.'[45] Membership in the business class is conditioned 'partly by ... unearned principal (... capital) and partly by ... skill.' Wealth and capital, of course, are restricted to an ever diminishing group, but nevertheless, in contrast with the agricultural class, a wide section of the business class is characterized by social mobility and job changes from one sphere to another. 'What happens here by inner necessity occurs at the same time by the mediation of an arbitrary will, and to the conscious subject it has the shape of being the work of his own will.'[46] Civil society differs from Indian caste society as well as from feudalism in that men and women 'can maintain their individuality' by reaching beyond their parents' occupation and class. In India, however, 'we are met ... by the peculiar circumstance that the individual belongs to such a class essentially by *birth*, and is bound to it for life.' 'The individual,' notes Hegel, 'ought properly to be empowered to choose his occupation';[47] however limited this choice may be in bourgeois society, it is nevertheless real.

Emphasis on the importance of social mobility and versatility of skill among members of the business class is also found in Marx. Under capitalism, he observes, 'there is scope for variation (within narrow limits) to allow for the worker's *individuality*, so that partly as between *different* trades, partly in the *same* one, we find that wages vary depending on the diligence, skill or strength of the worker, and to some extent on his actual personal achievement.' The achievements of individual workers, of course, 'do not affect the general relationship between capital and labour,' but while opportunity may be highly restricted, 'it nevertheless remains open to individuals to raise themselves to higher spheres by exhibiting a particular talent or energy. In the same way there is an abstract possibility that this or that worker might conceivably become a capitalist and the exploiter of the labour of others.'[48] For Hegel as for Marx, the mediation of the arbitrary will of the individual with civil society and the state, as achieved through social mobility and the versatility of skill of the individual, 'is the more precise definition of what is primarily meant by freedom in common parlance.'[49]

Marx never fully worked out his theory of social class, and his only comprehensive attempt to do so remains a fragment at the conclusion of Volume III of *Capital*. There he discusses the 'three big classes of modern society based upon the capitalist mode of production,' namely, 'wage-labourers, capitalists and landowners.' Like Hegel, he suggests that 'landed property' will be transformed 'into the form of landed property corresponding to the capitalist mode of production.' But he offers no sustained discussion of class beyond some very general remarks regarding the source of income of the three great classes, and the significant difficulty of fitting 'physicians and officials' into these categories.[50] By contrast, Hegel's discussion of class in the *Philosophy of Right* is thorough and comprehensive. Thus along with the business and agricultural classes, he discusses the 'universal class' – that of the liberal professions and civil servants – and also the poor, a group Marx refers to in *Capital* as the 'lumpenproletariat.'[51] Both these groups are, for Hegel, a growing and progressively more predominant section within civil or bourgeois society.

As pointed out in the last chapter, Hegel treats the worker and the capitalist as an identity within a contradictory or polar unity. Consequently, he makes no distinction between the class consciousness of the bourgeoisie and that of the proletariat as, of course, is done in virtually all Marxist accounts of class and class consciousness. For Hegel the consciousness of the two groups is, or will eventually become, virtually identical. Civil society is the arena in which the consciousness of the worker and the capitalist are educated through conflict and struggle into the rational – or communist – state.[52] It is part of the dialectic movement, says Hegel, 'that the limitations of the finite do not merely come from without: that its own nature is the cause of its abrogation, and that by its own act it passes into its counterpart.'[53] This idea is also implicit in Marx's discussion, especially in the *Grundrisse* and the planned Part Seven of *Capital*, Volume I, entitled 'Results of the Immediate Process of Production.' According to Marx, the worker and the capitalist, as well as the political economist, share the same distorted vision of capital and the labour process. They 'all think of the *physical* elements of the labour process as *capital* just because of their physical characteristics.'[54] Similarly, the worker entertains an illusory view of the state that is more or less identical to that of the bourgeoisie and its apologists; a view which 'is of course consolidated, nourished and inculcated by the ruling classes by all means available.' If for the capitalist 'money becomes an end rather than a means,'[55] it is also an end for the worker. 'The more production becomes the production of commodities,' writes Marx, 'the more each person has to, and wishes to, become a *dealer in commodities*, then the more everyone wants to make money, either from a product, or from his *services*, if his product only exists naturally in the form of a service, and this *money-making* appears as the ultimate purpose of activity of every kind.'[56] The organic relation between the worker and the capitalist is re-created in the state, since 'every form of production creates its own legal relations, form of government, etc.' Thus, if the worker is subordinated to the capitalist in the production process, this relation reappears in the bourgeois state itself: 'the right of the stronger prevails in ... "constitutional republics" as well' as in other types of government, 'only in another form.'[57]

The essential question, however, is not whether the state is an instrument for the oppression of the worker, since oppression is pre-supposed in the economic system. The essential question is, rather, what are the elements in the state through which the worker, no less than the capitalist, finds expression and meaning for his or her individuality. The answer provides not only justification for the external capitalist state, but also the reason for its merely transitory and phenomenal existence. 'The state,' says Hegel, 'is actual, and its actuality consists in this, that the interest of the whole is realized in and through particular ends. Actuality is always the unity of universal and particular, the universal dismembered in the particulars which seem to be self-subsistent, although they really are upheld and contained only in the whole.'[58] The rationality and freedom achieved in Western capitalist democracies, however limited they may be and however flawed their application, are a result of the educational process experienced by individuals through their labour and activity in the bourgeois production system. This liberating and educational effect of labour under capitalism is, for both Hegel and Marx, the key factor in the transition to a new and higher form of civilization. 'The severe discipline of capital, acting on succeeding generations,' writes Marx, develops 'general industriousness as the general property of the new species.' The 'ceaseless striving [of capital] towards the general form of wealth,' he continues, 'drives labour beyond the limits of its natural paltriness ... and thus creates the material elements for the development of the rich individuality which is as all-sided in its production as in its consumption, and whose labour also therefore appears no longer as labour, but as the development of activity itself ... This is why *capital is productive; i.e. an essential relation for the development of the social productive forces.*'[59]

Marx's emphasis on the liberating effects of capitalism follows a similar formulation in the *Philosophy of Right*. For Hegel, civil or bourgeois society is devoted to satisfying the particular needs of individuals; nevertheless the universal relationships formed there give it a rational or social character which is reflected in the bourgeois mind itself. The aim of capitalist production, he writes, 'is the satisfaction of subjective particularity, but the universal asserts itself in the bearing which this satisfaction has on the needs of others and their free arbitrary wills. The show of rationality thus produced in this sphere of finitude is the Understanding, and this is the aspect which is of most importance in considering this sphere and which itself constitutes the reconciling element within it.'[60] Marx repeats Hegel's observation in a similar passage in the *Grundrisse*: 'capital creates the bourgeois society, and the universal appropriation of nature as well as of the social bond itself by the members of society. Hence the great civilizing influence of capital; its production of a stage of society in comparison to which all earlier ones appear as mere *local developments* of humanity.'

The most dramatic feature of capitalism is, in Marx's words, its 'constantly expanding and more comprehensive system of different kinds of labour, different kinds of production, to which a constantly expanding and constantly enriched system of needs corresponds.'[61] Richness in production and consumption leads to a corresponding richness in the individuality of persons within capitalism. The identity between production and consumption leads Hegel to suggest that only in civil society does the 'concrete, i.e. social' individual – the 'universal person' – become a reality. 'Here at the standpoint of needs,' writes Hegel, 'what we have before us is the composite idea which we call *man*. This is the first time, and indeed properly the only time, to speak of *man* in this sense.'[62]

For Hegel, the multi-faceted development of production and consumption, the creation of new branches of industry, and so on produce in the individual a sense of 'refinement, i.e. a discrimination between these multiplied needs, and judgement on the suitability of means to their ends.' The universality of social needs, their dependence on the *ideas* and *opinions* of individuals rather than on *external necessity*, have in them 'the aspect of liberation.'[63] This aspect of capitalism is also pointed out by Marx, who observes that the bourgeois mode of production leads to 'the discovery, creation and satisfaction of new needs arising from society itself, the cultivation of all the qualities of the social human being, production of the same in a form as rich as possible in needs, because rich in qualities and relations – production of this being as the most total and universal possible social product, for, in order to take gratification in a many-sided way, he must be capable of many pleasures ... hence cultured to a high degree.' Accordingly, for Marx, creation of the 'social human being' need not await the coming of communism; rather it is 'a condition of production founded on capital.'[64]

Critics of the capitalist state have all but ignored its humanizing moment and lament self-satisfied materialism and consumerism among the masses. Baran and Sweezy, for example, believe that 'advertising, product differentiation, artificial obsolescence, model changing, and all the other devices of the sales effort' are superfluous creations of a monopoly capitalism driven to any means to preserve itself and prevent stagnation.[65] While this approach correctly expresses one side of the matter, it ignores the positive aspect stressed not only by Hegel and Marx, but also by classical Marxism. Trotsky, for example, writes that freedom of consumption is exactly what differentiates Western capitalist society from Soviet authoritarianism. 'The very scope of human demands,' he writes, 'changes fundamentally with the growth of world technique. The contemporaries of Marx knew nothing of automobiles, radios, moving pictures, aeroplanes. A socialist society, however, is unthinkable without the free enjoyment of these goods.' Trotsky argues that bourgeois society in the 1930s was approaching 'the lowest stage of Communism,' and he bitterly contrasts the privileged consumption of the Russian bureaucracy with the generalized consumption then appearing in Western capitalist society:

How many years are needed in order to make it possible for every Soviet citizen to use an automobile in any direction he chooses, refilling his gas tank without difficulty en route? In barbarian society the rider and the pedestrian constituted two classes. The automobile differentiates society no less than the saddle horse. So long as even a modest 'Ford' remains the privilege of a minority, there survive all the relations and customs proper to a bourgeois society. And together with them there remains the guardian of inequality, the state.[66]

The critique of consumerism suggests that working-class individuals are somehow different from their bourgeois counterparts; but the worker and the capitalist are not really so different – both are driven by ambition and great expectations. The race to 'keep up with the Jones's' is merely bourgeois striving as it appears in working-class and middle-class individuals, and represents, as Trotsky suggests, the demand for equality among individuals within civil society. Development of the social relations of the individual stimulated by production and consumption under capitalism, writes Hegel, 'directly involves the demand for equality of satisfaction with others. The need for this equality and for emulation, which is the equalizing of oneself with others, as well as the other need also present here, the need of the particular to assert itself in some distinctive way, become themselves a fruitful source of the multiplication of needs and their satisfaction.'[67]

Projecting the view of Hegel and classical Marxism, widening consumer choice in contemporary civil society, greater flexibility in purchases, and increased access to production and goods made possible by rising incomes and extension of consumer credit to the working class, are not portents of capitalism's decline, but rather necessary and predictable moments of bourgeois production itself. These developments may also anticipate a future 'free goods' society, where consumption will be disciplined and controlled by the cultured and civilized consciousness of the social individual.[68] 'Free exchange among individuals,' states Marx referring to communist society, 'presupposes the development of material and cultural conditions' within the capitalist mode of production.[69] One of these conditions is the transcendence of need itself. 'The very multiplication of needs in civil society,' observes Hegel, 'involves a check on desire, because when many things are in use, the urge to obtain any one thing which might be needed is less strong, and this is a sign that want altogether is not so imperious.'[70] As Marx suggests, it is through the consumption and expenditure habits of the free worker that '*he learns to control himself, in contrast to the slave*, who needs a master.'[71]

Along with many other critics, Mandel complains that the sovereignty of the consumer much touted by bourgeois apologists is actually a myth since 'these "sovereign consumers" first have to be persuaded of their new needs' through advertising.[72] Both Marx and Hegel, however, observe that the essence of universal as opposed to merely necessary human needs is that they must be stimulated and goaded by advertising and example; otherwise they would not exist. 'What the English call "comfort",' writes Hegel, 'is something inexhaustible and illimitable. [Others can discover to you that what you take to be] comfort at any stage is discomfort, and these discoveries never come to an end. Hence the need for greater comfort does not exactly arise from within you directly; it is suggested to you by those who hope to make a profit from its creation.'[73] Where contemporary Marxists see advertising only as part of an 'irrational system' and a ploy to avoid economic stagnation by foisting consumption on the worker,[74] Marx views it as a necessary and progressive force which allows the worker 'his only share of civilization which distinguishes him from the slave.' The capitalist, says Marx, 'searches for means to spur [the workers] on to consumption, to give his wares new charms, to inspire them with new needs by constant chatter etc. It is precisely this side of the relation of capital and labour which is an essential civilizing moment, and on which the historic justification, but also the contemporary power of capital rests.'[75]

From this perspective, the development of consumer society actually reflects and strengthens the foundation of democracy and individual freedom in the external capitalist state. Competition between capitalists for the worker's purchasing power means that the capitalist relates to the worker *as an equal*. The capitalists' struggle for the worker's wages fragments their own class power and sets up a pluralistic network of competing social powers. '*It is the competition among capitals,*' writes Marx, 'which brings it about that the individual capital relates to the workers of the entire remaining capital *not as to workers* ... What precisely distinguishes capital from the master-servant relation is that the *worker* confronts him [the capitalist] as a consumer and possessor of exchange values, and that in the form of the *possessor of money*, in the form of money he becomes a simple centre of circulation – one of its infinitely many centres, in which his specificity as a worker is extinguished.'[76]

Money procures the worker a certain social power which he or she can exercise in the market place. The worker receives his or her wages 'in the shape of *money, exchange-value*, the abstract social form of wealth.' And this '*exchange-value, abstract wealth*' remains in the worker's 'mind as something more than a particular use-value hedged round with traditional and local restrictions. It is the worker himself who converts the money into whatever use-value he desires; it is he who buys commodities as he wishes and, as the *owner of money*, as the buyer of goods, he stands in precisely the same relationship to the sellers of goods as any other buyer.' Marx admits, of course, that the worker's means are limited and that his or her purchases are made 'from a fairly restricted selection of goods.' Nevertheless, 'some variation is possible as we can see from the fact that newspapers, for example, form part of the essential purchases of the urban English worker.' The worker, Marx insists, 'acts as a free agent; he must pay his own way; he is responsible to himself for the way he spends his wages.'[77]

Money is a social power that assures the worker's independence and freedom vis-à-vis the state. In earlier forms of society, the state's needs were supplied through coercive direct services so that the whole range of an individual's activity could be dictated by political authority. With money, however, the individual's skill and talents may be 'expressed in an external embodiment' which may then be taken by the state as a *thing*. Accordingly, government has little concern with how an individual earns the cash he or she hands over, just so long as the taxes are paid. Freedom, notes Hegel, is based on 'the principle that the individual's substantive activity – which in any case becomes something particular in content in services like those [required by the state] – shall be mediated through his particular volition. This is a right which can be secured only when the demand for services takes the form of a demand for something of universal value, and it is this right which has brought with it this conversion of the state's demands into demands for cash.'[78] Marx makes a similar point in the *Grundrisse*: 'In exchange value,' he writes, 'the social connection between persons is transformed into a social relation between things; personal capacity into objective wealth. The less social power the medium of exchange possess ... the greater must be the power of the community which binds the individuals together, the patriarchal relation, the community of antiquity, feudalism and the guild system.' But under capitalism, he continues, 'each individual possesses social power in the form of a thing.'[79]

Before 1917, the great mass of the Russian people lacked this autonomous power, this medium of exchange, and the institutions of Tsardom reflected its absence. In this society, individuals could make their collective will felt only by violence. 'In despotisms,' Hegel argues, 'where there are only rulers and people, the people is effective, if at all, only as a mass destructive of the organization of the state.'[80] The Soviet system that arose from the old regime's destruction failed to place any effective social power in the hands of the individual; instead all power went to the state in a vast effort of social development. The result was predictable: 'Rob [money] ... of this social power,' says Marx, 'and you must give it to persons to exercise over persons.'[81] Socialist republics, such as the USSR and China, are instances of societies in which there is, in Hegel's words, a 'public organization to provide for everything and determine everyone's labour.'[82] They are 'mono-organizational societies' controlled not by market relations but, as T.H. Rigby suggests, by 'hierarchies of appointed officials under the direction of a single overall command.'[83] The mono-organizational society also represents a form of class rule unanticipated by Marx – the dictatorship of Hegel's 'universal class', i.e. government bureaucrats or civil servants.[84]

Internally split along ownership lines, the business and agricultural classes in Hegel's system are defined in terms of their relationship to the system of needs. By contrast, the universal class is free of internal schisms based on property relations, while its consciousness and function are themselves aspects of state power. Civil servants, along with members of the state executive, 'constitute the greater part of the middle class, the class in which the consciousness of right and the developed intelligence of the mass of the people is found.' Because most of its members rely directly or indirectly on the state for their livelihood, the consciousness and function of the middle class as a whole are very close to those of the bureaucracy. 'The universal class', writes Hegel, 'has for its task the universal interests of the community. It must therefore be relieved from direct labour to supply its needs, either by having private means or by receiving an allowance from the state which claims its industry, with the result that private interest finds its satisfaction in its work for the universal.' The power of the middle class must be counterbalanced by the business class from below and also by the head of state from above. Only these forces 'effactually prevent it from acquiring the isolated position of an aristocracy and using its education and skill as means to an arbitrary tyranny.' The middle class, notes Hegel, is essential to the modern state for 'a state without a middle class must ... remain on a low level.' But it can be developed in a healthy state, 'only by giving authority to spheres of particular interests, which are relatively independent, and by appointing an army of officials whose personal arbitrariness is broken against such authorized bodies. Action in accordance with everyone's rights, and the habit of such action, is a consequence of the counterpoise to officialdom which independent and self-subsistent bodies create.'[85]

The socialist republics and many Third World countries are lacking the elements of civil society capable of countervailing the power of the educated middle class. The result is an arbitrary tyranny of the intelligentsia,[86] and since no one is less tolerant of the expression of divergent ideas than the intellectual, the free exchange of ideas in communist countries is severely curbed. Under Stalin, the strength of the middle class was continually decimated in order to curb its growing power. 'It was one of the effects of the purges,' Deutscher points out, 'that they prevented the managerial groups from consolidation as a social stratum. Stalin whetted their acquisitive instincts and wrung their necks.' The middle class was prohibited from becoming a possessing class, a business class: 'they could not start accumulating capital on their own account while they were hovering between their offices and the concentration camps.' Moreover, the middle class in the USSR is unlikely to develop into a possessing class, even without Stalin, since its 'privileges and power were bound up with the national ownership of productive resources.'[87] In the west, as Alvin Gouldner argues, Marxism itself tends to represent not the working class but rather the radical elements of the middle class acting as ostensible champions of workers and the poor.[88]

3 'BILDUNG' AND THE SOCIAL INDIVIDUAL

For Hegel, the external capitalist state is the sphere in which the 'particularity' of the individual 'is educated up to subjectivity'; capitalism constitutes a 'barrier' behind which the social individual matures until he or she 'overcomes it and attains' his or her 'objective reality in the finite'. Universal concerns are unknown to the individual in bourgeois society who looks after only purely personal and selfish interests. Even knowledge itself is treated as 'a mere means' to the satisfaction of needs, 'the pleasures and comforts of private life.' Adopting a broad definition of education, which he terms *Bildung*, Hegel views it as a product of experience in the work world as well as the school system. Education in civil society attains only the level of the understanding consciousness; and freedom remains abstract since capitalism 'is implicitly inimical to mind's appointed end, freedom.' Nevertheless, education teaches the consciousness of the individual that in society 'it has to do there only with what it has itself produced and stamped with its own seal.'

Bildung is the desperate struggle of work and self-realization; it is a *class struggle*, where the individual attains self-consciousness within the framework of his or her social role in the system of production. 'The final purpose of education,' remarks Hegel, 'is liberation and the struggle for a higher liberation still ... In the individual subject, this liberation is the hard struggle against pure subjectivity of demeanour, against the immediacy of desire, against the empty subjectivity of feeling and the caprice of inclination.' The product of education under capitalism, then, is the *social individual*, 'the infinitely independent free subjectivity,' an 'individuality' which is 'genuinely existent in its own eyes.'[89] In the *Grundrisse*, Marx repeats Hegel's observations on the educational movement of capital – the creation of the social individual. The result of bourgeois production, writes Marx,

is: the tendentially and potentially general development of the forces of production – of wealth as such – as a basis ... The basis as the possibility of the universal development of the individual, and the real development of the individuals from this basis as a constant suspension of its *barrier*, which is recognized as a barrier, not taken for a *sacred limit*. Not an ideal or imagined universality of the individual, but the universality of his real and ideal relations. Hence also the grasping of his own history as a *process*, and the recognition of nature (equally present as practical power over nature) as his real body.[90]

For Hegel, 'practical education acquired through working' in civil society 'consists first in the automatically recurrent need for something to do and the habit of simply being busy; next, in the strict adaptation of one's activity according not only to the nature of the material worked on, but also, and especially, to the pleasure of other workers; and finally, in a habit, produced by this discipline, of objective activity and universally recognized aptitudes.' He emphasizes the 'flexibility and rapidity of mind' developed by the worker in the labour process, the 'ability to pass from one idea to another, to grasp complex and general relations, and so on.'[91] Marx also stresses this development adding that the flexibility and versatility of the worker is most highly developed in North America. 'We can see this *versatility*, this perfect indifference towards the particular content of work and the free transition from one branch of industry to the next, most obviously in North America, where the development of wage-labour has been relatively untrammelled by the vestiges of the guild system, etc.'[92]

The versatility of workers in North America stems from the fact that *money*, rather than the satisfactions of work itself, is their absolute goal. If the capitalist is driven by desire for money, so is the worker; both share the same bourgeois value. The worker, writes Marx, is driven by 'the *compulsion* to *perform surplus labour* [which] implies also the necessity of forming needs, and creating the means of satisfying them, and of supplying quantities of produce well in excess of the traditional requirements of the worker.' The drive for profit under capitalism, then, also introduces vastly increased living standards for workers. Capital is infinitely versatile, and shows complete indifference to the type of production it finances, an indifference 'extended by capital to the worker. He is required to be capable of the same flexibility or *versatility* in the way he applies his labour-power.' As the worker loses interest in work itself, the influence of traditional crafts vanishes. No longer a shoemaker or a baker, the worker is motivated only by money and the '*leisure time*' required to develop his or her universal interests 'independently of material production.' 'Just as capital,' notes Marx,

views with indifference the particular physical guise in which labour appears in the labour process, whether as a steam engine, dung heap or silk, so too the worker looks upon the *particular content* of his labour with equal indifference. His work belongs to capital, it is only the use-value of the commodity that he has sold, and he has only sold it to acquire money and, with the money, the means of subsistence. A change in his mode of labour interests him only because every specific mode of labour requires a different development of his labour-power.[93]

Ambition spurred on by the capitalist mode of production forms a vital aspect of the worker's relationship to his or her children. 'The free worker is *in principle* ready and willing to accept every possible variation in his labour-power and activity which promises higher rewards.' Should higher rewards evade the worker's grasp, he or she will encourage the younger generation to increase *its* versatility and earning power in industry. If the worker's 'indifference to the particular content of his work does not give him the power to vary his labour-power to order, he will express his indifference by inducing his replacements, the rising generation, to move from one branch of industry to the next, depending on the state of the market.' The worker's versatility is expressed in the ability of capital itself to invade new areas of production and conquer new territory for the capitalist system. 'The more highly capitalist production is developed in a country, the greater the demand will be for *versatility* in labour-power, the more indifferent the worker will be towards the *specific content* of his work and the more fluid will be the movement of capital from one sphere of production to the next.'[94]

The traits Marx perceives in the worker are most highly developed in North America and may be at least partly responsible for the absence of socialism in the United States and its weak presence in Canada compared to Europe, where workers retain relatively strong craft and corporate loyalties. 'The fundamental character of the community,' Hegel observes, referring to the USA, is 'the endeavour of the individual after acquisition, commercial profit, and gain; the predominance of *private* interest, devoting itself to that of the community only for its own advantage.' But these traits are vital to the development of the independent self-consciousness of the social individual and, therefore, to the development of a new social order. As Hegel observes, 'America ... is the land of the future, where in the ages that lie before us, the burden of the World's History shall reveal itself.'[95] Marx's own observations on capital and labour in the United States, compared to Europe, are worth quoting in full because they emphasize the *identity* of the consciousness of the capitalist and the worker, an identity ignored by Marx's modern-day followers:

Nowhere does the fluidity of capital, the versatility of labour and the indifference of the worker to the content of his work appear more vividly than in the United States of North America. In Europe, even in England, capitalist production is still affected and distorted by hangovers from feudalism. The fact that baking, shoemaking, etc. are only just being put on a *capitalist* basis in England is entirely due to the circumstance that English capital cherished feudal preconceptions of 'respectability'. It was 'respectable' to sell Negroes into slavery, but it was not respectable to make sausages, boots or bread. Hence all the machinery which conquers the 'unrespectable' branches of capitalism comes from America. By the same token, nowhere are people so indifferent to the type of work they do as in the United States, nowhere are people so aware that their labour always produces the same product, money, and nowhere do they pass through the most divergent kinds of work with the same nonchalance.[96]

North America is important, not because capitalism is there about to enter its final death agony, but because a flourishing capitalist economy offers the best evidence for the inevitability and the future power of socialism. As Colletti suggests, 'in any genuine Marxist perspective, the United States of America should be the maturest society in the world for a socialist transformation.'[97] Marx argues that a socialist society is one 'in which individuals can with ease transfer from one labour to another, and where the specific kind is a matter of chance for them, hence indifference.' Labour is nothing but the means to create wealth, and a society where riches and gain are the paramount ambitions is also the most advanced society. There labour no longer dominates the individual, but rather the individual dominates labour; labour 'has ceased to be organically linked with particular individuals in any specific form. Such a state of affairs is at its most developed in the most modern form of existence of bourgeois society – in the United States.' Marx suggests that 'in France, owing to its peculiar social formation, many a thing is considered socialism that counts in England as political economy.'[98] With equal validity one could say that today many a thing that is considered socialism elsewhere counts as political economy in North America.

The modern worker's indifference to specific types of labour prepares the way with little resistance from the working class for the replacement of labour-power by machinery. The route to automatic processes, notes Marx, 'is ... dissection ... through the division of labour, which gradually transforms the workers' operations into more and more mechanical ones, so that at a certain point a mechanism can step into their places ... Labour no longer appears so much to be included within the production process; rather, the human being comes to relate more as a watchman and regulator to the production process itself ... He steps to the side of the production process instead of being its chief actor.' As will be discussed further below, automation undermines bourgeois production since the capitalist economy is based on exchange-values created by the worker. Where the worker no longer takes a direct role in production, and where the number of workers required to produce commodities is constantly diminished relative to the amount of production, then the capitalist may no longer have an adequate market for his or her commodities. At the same time, heavy reliance on advanced technology shows the absolute dependence of the capitalist on what Marx calls 'the social intellect.' Capital no longer appears as an achievement of assorted captains of industry, but rather as the collective achievement of society, or the social individual, as embodied in science and technology employed by the giant corporation. 'In the production process of large-scale industry ... just as the conquest of the forces of nature by the social intellect is the precondition of the productive power of the means of labour as developed into the automatic process, on one side, so, on the other, is *the labour of the individual in its direct presence posited as suspended individual, i.e. as social, labour. Thus the ... basis of this mode of production falls away.*'[99]

Marx's striking analysis of the development of automatic processes under capitalism, which shows how the *positive* movement of capital in a booming bourgeois economy leads to the suspension or transcendence of the capitalist mode of production, is taken from a similar discussion in Hegel's *Philosophy of Right*. 'The universal and objective element in work,' writes Hegel,

lies in the abstracting process which effects the subdivision of needs and means and thereby *eo ipso* subdivides production and brings about the division of labour. By this division, the work of the individual becomes less complex, and consequently his skill at his section of the job increases, like his output. At the same time, this abstraction of one man's skill and means of production from another's completes and makes necessary everywhere the dependence of men on one another and their reciprocal relation in the satisfaction of their other needs. Further, the abstraction of one man's production from another's makes work more and more mechanical, until finally man is able to step aside and install machines in his place.[100]

4   ON LAW AND JUSTICE

According to Hegel, work and industry in civil society creates a rational and self-dependent consciousness in the individual. This consciousness is shared by both the capitalist and the worker so that the bourgeois values of law, liberty, and individual freedom are no less the worker's than the capitalist's. 'In the business class,' notes Hegel, 'intelligence ... is the essential thing ... the individual is thrown back on himself, and this feeling of selfhood is most intimately connected with the demand for law and order. The sense of freedom and order has therefore arisen above all in the towns.'[101]

The notion of law and order has been criticized by Marx and his followers as a shibboleth for the defence of the privileges of the capitalist class. Indeed, in bourgeois society, where inequality and disparities of wealth and power are commonplace, the rule of law will naturally reflect these disparities. Notes Hegel:

That the citizens are equal before the law contains a great truth, but which so expressed is a tautology: it only states that the legal status in general exists, that the laws rule. But, as regards the concrete, the citizens – besides their personality – are equal before the law only in these points when they are otherwise equal *outside the law*. Only that equality which (in whatever way it be) they, as it happens, otherwise have in property, age, physical strength, talent, skill, etc. – or even in crime ... only it can make them ... equal in the concrete ... The laws themselves, except in so far as they concern that narrow circle of personality, presuppose unequal conditions, and provide for the unequal legal duties and appurtenances resulting therefrom.[102]

Law and order have certainly been employed as a means to combat the claims of the workers, yet, as Marx himself argues, it is also an essential element in the defence and development of proletarian interests. His discussion of the English Factory Acts in *Capital* provides an example of the fundamental importance of law and legislation for the working class:

Parliament passed five Labour Laws between 1802 and 1833, but was shrewd enough not to vote a penny for their compulsory implementation, for the necessary official personnel, etc. They remained a dead letter ... The factory workers, especially since 1838, had made the Ten Hours' Bill their economic, as they had made the Charter [which called for universal male suffrage and various electoral reforms] their political election cry. Some of the manufacturers, even, who had run their factories in conformity with the Act of 1833, overwhelmed Parliament with representations on the immoral 'competition' of their 'false brethren', who were able to break the law because of their greater impudence or their more fortunate local circumstances.

The victories eventually achieved by the working class were reflected in the work legislation enacted by Parliament. 'These highly detailed specifications, which regulate, with military uniformity, the times, the limits and pauses of work by the stroke of the clock, were by no means a product of the fantasy of Members of Parliament. They developed gradually out of circumstances as natural laws of the modern mode of production. Their formulation, official recognition and proclamation by the state were the result of a long class struggle.'[103]

As Marx points out, bourgeois *respectability, liberty*, and *law and order* are vital aspects of the consciousness of the modern worker. Like the capitalist the worker is anxious for law and liberty; he or she desires to have responsibility for the products of labour, and is keen to ensure that the commodities he or she produces are satisfactory to the consumer.

The free worker ... is impelled by his wants. The consciousness (or better: the *idea*) of free self-determination, of liberty, makes a much better worker of the [free individual] than of the [slave], as does the related feeling (sense) of *responsibility*; since he, like any seller of wares, is responsible for the goods he delivers and for the quality which he must provide, he must strive to ensure that he is not driven from the field by other sellers of the same type as himself ... [and] must maintain his own position, since his existence, and that of his family depends on his ability continuously to renew the sale of his labour-power to the capitalist.[104]

Hegel argues that the development of the United States in particular may be understood in terms of the shared values held by workers and capitalists concerning law, liberty, and individual freedom. The United States was colonized by 'industrious Europeans, who betook themselves to agriculture, tobacco and cotton planting, etc.' The interests of these individuals 'was given to labour, and the basis of their existence as a united body lay in the necessities that bind man to man, the desire of repose, the establishment of civil rights, security and freedom, and a community arising from the aggregation of individuals as atomic constituents; so that the state was merely something external for the protection of property.'[105]

Hegel's views on the United States are shared by Marx and Engels. 'Everything in America,' exclaims Engels, 'has to be new, everything has to be rational, everything has to be practical, consequently everything is different from the way it is with us.'[106] Marx is particularly fascinated with the national ethos of the United States – with what he calls, 'Yankee universality.' The USA, he writes, is

a country where bourgeois society did not develop on the foundation of the feudal system, but developed rather from itself; where this society appears not as the surviving result of a centuries-old movement, but rather as the starting-point of a new movement, where the state, in contrast to all earlier national formations, was from the beginning subordinate to bourgeois society, to its production, and never could make the pretence of being an end-in-itself; where, finally, bourgeois society itself, linking up the productive forces of an old world with the enormous natural terrain of a new one, has developed to hitherto unheard-of dimensions and with unheard-of freedom of movement, has far outstripped all previous work in the conquest of the forces of nature, and where, finally, even the antitheses of bourgeois society itself appear only as vanishing moments.[107]

The peculiar fascination exercised by law and civil liberties over the US national consciousness flows from the ethic of law, liberty, and freedom spawned by a bourgeois mode of production untrammelled by feudal remnants and given vast virgin territory over which to spread its wings. But capitalist jurisprudence, no less than bourgeois economy, is a product of the development of individual consciousness and rationality. If bourgeois production paves the way for communist production relations, bourgeois law has within it the elements of a rational or communist jurisprudence. The administration of justice under capitalism is essentially a process of struggle and education; it is through knowledge about the law and its application that men and women attain consciousness of their individual rights and freedoms, as well as their responsibilities. Without this necessary process of development, the transformation to a higher form of civilization is impossible. 'It is as a result of the discipline of comprehending the right that the right first becomes capable of universality.' Bourgeois law or right is far from perfect, and it is this imperfection which leads to the call for 'systematization, i.e. elevation to the universal, which our time is pressing for without limit.' But it is in that bourgeois society *par excellence*, the United States – especially after the great civil rights movement and anti-war struggle of the 1960s and 70s – that individual rights and freedoms, however abstract in content, have reached their highest attainment in the modern world, an achievement based on education about the rule of law: 'It is part of education, of thinking as the consciousness of the single in the form of universality, that the ego comes to be apprehended as a universal person in which all are identical. A man counts as a man in virtue of his manhood alone, not because he is a Jew, Catholic, Protestant, German, Italian, etc. This is an assertion which thinking ratifies and to be conscious of it is of infinite importance.'[108]

The first requirement of law, notes Hegel, is that it be known by the ordinary citizen. 'Law is concerned with freedom, the worthiest and holiest thing in man, the thing man must know if it is to have obligatory force for him.'[109] Law must be rational, and the mark of rationality is clarity and simplicity of expression. 'Thought is ... simply its manifestation; clearness is its nature and itself.'[110] He criticizes the tendency for 'knowledge of the law of the land [to be] accessible only to those who have made it their professional study.' The vulgar monopoly of the law exercised by a legal profession which 'makes itself an exclusive clique by the use of a terminology like a foreign tongue to those whose rights are at issue,' is one of the greatest shortcomings of the administration of justice in civil society. No mere frivolous restriction of trade, legal monopoly violates a citizen's most fundamental rights: 'the members of civil society ... are kept strangers to the law ... and the result is that they become the wards, or even in a sense, the bondsmen, of the legal profession. They may indeed have the right to appear in court in person and to 'stand' there (*in judicio stare*), but their bodily presence is a trifle if their minds are not to be there also, if they are not to follow the proceedings with their own knowledge, and if the justice they receive remains in their eyes a doom pronounced *ab extra*.'[111]

With the development of the universal interconnections of civil society, violation of the law comes to be seen as 'a danger to society and therefore the magnitude of the wrongdoing is increased.' Crime is no longer viewed as a violation of the person of a particular individual, but rather an abrogation of the rights of everyone. By contrast, in ancient times, 'the citizens did not feel themselves injured by wrongs which members of the royal houses did to one another.' Yet it is just because of the inner strength and universality of the mature civil society that punishment for crime is far less extreme than in earlier social forms. 'While it would be impossible for society to leave a crime unpunished, since that would be to posit it as a right, still since society is sure of itself, a crime must always be something idiosyncratic in comparison, something unstable and exceptional ... In this light, crime acquires a milder status, and for this reason its punishment too becomes milder.' The degree of punishment attached to a crime is a function of the consciousness of the social individual: the higher the level of general education, the lower the punishment. 'With the advance of education, opinions about crime become less harsh, and to-day a criminal is not so severely punished as he was a hundred years ago. It is not exactly crimes or punishments which change but the relation between them.' At the turn of the nineteenth century, when Hegel was writing, almost two hundred crimes on the English statute books called for the death penalty.

Just as the use-value of commodities in civil society is expressed as exchange-value, or money, the punishment of crime also takes on an abstract, universal value. The identity between crime and punishment 'is not an equality between the specific character of the crime and that of its negation; on the contrary, the two injuries are equal only in respect of their implicit character, i.e. in respect of their "value".' Thus prison sentences replace corporal punishment, and more barbarous forms of punishment, like flogging, amputation, torture, and so forth, disappear (or are reserved for surreptitious use against political prisoners). Eventually, as in most Western countries, capital punishment disappears or becomes 'rarer, as in fact should be the case with this most extreme punishment.'[112]

5 POVERTY, IMPERIALISM, AND THE EXTERNAL CAPITALIST STATE

If bourgeois society creates an abundance of consumer goods, raises living standards, fosters the interests of law, liberty, and (capitalist) private property, it also – and no less inexorably – produces an ever-increasing mass of the dispossessed and unorganized. 'In this same process,' writes Hegel, in an already cited passage, 'dependence and want increase *ad infinitum.*' Liberation in civil society, as Hegel observes, is 'abstract since the particularity of the ends remains [its] basic content.'[113] Private property constitutes 'the reality of the free will of a person, and for that reason [it is] ... for any other person inviolable'; it is the means whereby 'mind attains to a being-for-self, [and] the objectivity of mind receives its due.' Nevertheless, 'the full realization of ... freedom ... in property is still incomplete, still [only] formal.' If, as in the USA, individuals are motivated only by their own self-interest, and if self-interest is realized only in property, in external objects, then those who have no access to property are ignored, repressed, and humiliated. 'If you're so smart, why aren't you rich?' becomes a national slogan. The abstraction of value is concretely registered in money and theoretically achieved in the notion of God, a strange unity expressed on every greenback: 'In God we trust.'

Since the bourgeois conception of the state is the *'state external'*[114] – an institution devoted primarily to the protection of property – the universal interests of society are ignored in favour of the particularity of the individual. Consequently, in a society of abundance such as the USA essential social services are relatively starved and neglected. This contradiction, which as Mandel suggests is 'now admitted even by liberals'[115] was foreseen by Hegel as the inevitable outcome of a society that produces a great mass of poor on the one hand, and a nation of self-interested business-class individuals (capitalists *and* workers) on the other. Avineri declares that 'Hegel's paradigm of the burgher spirit cannot, of course, relate to the worker.'[116] But as I have argued, for both Hegel and Marx, this spirit does apply to the free worker, and it is a crucial mistake in any political analysis to overlook this fact.

The absolute tendency of bourgeois society is to create abundance, but an abundance divided unequally, which eventually breaks down into unparalleled wealth at one pole and misery at the other. Still the external capitalist state must eventually guarantee to each of its members, not only the safety of person and property, but also the right to work and a decent living; accordingly it begins to direct attention, however reluctantly, to its most glaring problem, that of poverty. The state is hamstrung in this effort, first because capitalism itself produces and reproduces poverty among those without 'skill, health, capital, and so forth,' and second, because the bourgeois economy is exposed to 'the danger of upheavals arising from clashing interests and to' periods of tension caused by the 'working of a necessity of which [the members of civil society] themselves know nothing.' The necessity Hegel refers to is the problem of over-production that arises within a system which profits from the use-value of human labour-power, but fails to provide the worker with the exchange-value required to purchase all the products of his or her labour.[117] This contradiction constantly creates a mass of surplus workers unable to find work or to provide for the means of subsistence. 'Only', writes Marx, 'in the mode of production based on capital does pauperism appear as the result of labour itself, of the development of the productive powers of labour.' The free worker is 'a virtual pauper' since 'the concept of the *free labourer*'[118] means that the worker relates to the means of production only accidentally, only through the mediation of the capitalist, of what Hegel calls 'the overlord to nothing.'[119] In periods of crisis, therefore, this relation is expressed as *unemployment*.

Capital by its nature, says Marx, 'posits a *barrier* to labour and value-creation, in contradiction to its tendency to expand them boundlessly. And in as much as it both posits a barrier *specific* to itself, and on the other side equally drives over and beyond *every* barrier, it is the living contradiction.' The result of over-production – the barrier to capital – is the *destruction of capital*,'[120] the wastage on a grand scale of raw materials, commodities, and human labour-power which continues until capital is once again ready to resume a new period of economic growth, accumulation, and increased employment. In periods of economic crisis, observes Hegel, 'it ... becomes apparent that despite an excess of wealth civil society is not rich enough, i.e. its own resources are insufficient to check excessive poverty and the creation of a penurious rabble.'[121] Hegel's observation is repeated by Marx in the *Communist Manifesto*: 'In these crises there breaks out an epidemic that, in all earlier epochs, would have seemed an absurdity – the epidemic of over-production. Society suddenly finds itself back into a state of momentary barbarism ... and why? Because there is too much civilization, too much means of subsistence, too much industry, too much commerce.'[122]

Although, as I have argued in Chapter 5, the *Communist Manifesto* is everywhere influenced by Hegel's discussion of civil society in the *Philosophy of Right*, Marx did not penetrate the secret of the distinction between use-value and exchange-value until ten years later, when, guided by Hegel's writings, he plunged into the study of classical political economy. 'By the way,' Marx writes in a letter to Engels in January 1858, 'things are developing nicely. For instance, I have thrown overboard the whole doctrine of profit as it has existed up to now. In the *method* of treatment the fact that by mere accident I again glanced through Hegel's *Logic* has been of great service to me.'[123] In 1857-58 Marx was labouring on the *Grundrisse*, a work which shows traces not only of the *Logic*, but of all three volumes of the *Encyclopaedia* as well as the *Philosophy of Right*. In the *Grundrisse*, Marx shows that classical political economy could not grasp the significance of economic crises and over-production because it did not distinguish between the use-value and (the much lower) exchange-value of labour. The bourgeois economists had adopted 'the standpoint of *simple exchange*' between capitalist and worker, a standpoint Hegel associates with the empty understanding which confuses ownership through use with the abstract ownership of capital. Since simple exchange involves no contradiction, classical economics imagined that over-production is impossible. 'The nonsense about the impossibility of over-production', writes Marx,

has been expressed ... by James Mill, in the formula that supply = its own demand, that supply and demand therefore balance, which means in other words the same thing as that value is determined by labour time, and hence that *exchange adds nothing to it*, and which forgets only that exchange does have to take place and that this depends (in the final instance) on the *use value* ... Too much and too little concerns not the exchange value, but the use value. More of the supplied product exists than is 'needed'; this is what it boils down to. Hence that overproduction comes from use value and therefore from exchange itself.[124]

Hegel's own analysis of over-production is regarded by most interpreters as the happy accident of a philosophical genius, who could not really be bothered with the mundane details of economics. Because most writers on Hegel are unaware that the *Logic* itself deals, as I have shown in earlier chapters, with the labour process and bourgeois production, they tend to under-rate the importance of economics in Hegel's system as a whole. In fact, however, the labour process is a component of ideality, itself the key concept in Hegel's thought. 'The mechanics of' Hegel's theory of economic crisis, declares Plant, 'are rather obscure.'[125] 'Hegel,' notes Plamenatz demurely, 'was not an economist ... He makes these suggestions' about poverty and economic crises 'merely in passing, and without attributing much importance to them. Were they suggested to him by what he had himself observed, or did he pick them up from someone else? I do not know. They are crumbs from his table, which become loaves in the social theory of Marx.'[126] Instead of being a dilettante in economics, as Plamenatz believes, Hegel accomplished the 'unique synthesis of the views of Ricardo and Sismondi,'[127] that virtually every scholar on the subject attributes exclusively to Marx. The social theory of Marx is therefore nothing but an encounter with Hegel. 'How ubiquitous Hegel is in Marx's work right up to the end,' exclaims Prawer.[128]

For Hegel, the contradiction between exchange-value and use-value lies at the heart of civil society, which is incapable of overcoming poverty and crises of over-production, even with the aid of the external state: for any attempt to assist the poor or to provide them with employment simply intensifies the contradiction between use-value and exchange-value. Besides violating 'the principle of civil society and the feeling of individual independence and self-respect in its individual members,' assistance to the poor would only re-create poverty by stimulating the economy and leading eventually to further crises of over-production. Direct job-creation by the state (a remedy favoured by many contemporary governments) would also provide no permanent cure for the same reasons. The unemployed, says Hegel, 'might be given subsistence indirectly through being given work, i.e. the opportunity to work. In this event the volume of production would be increased, but the evil consists precisely in an excess of production and in the lack of a proportionate number of consumers who are themselves also producers.' However inadequate, these measures are at least more humane than the solutions offered by the governments of Hegel's time: 'In Britain, particularly in Scotland, the most direct measure against poverty and especially against the loss of shame and self-respect – the subjective bases of society – as well as against laziness and extravagance, etc., the begetters of the rabble, has turned out to be to leave the poor to their fate and instruct them to beg in the streets.' The economic problems grappled with by Hegel and later by Marx were to be ignored by conventional economics until a century after Hegel's death. It required 'the Keynesian Revolution,' the establishment of the welfare state, and so on before bourgeois society began to take seriously the problem of poverty and the lack of 'effective demand.' This concern, reflected for example in the ill-fated US 'war on poverty', is anticipated by Hegel. 'Poverty,' he points out, leaves individuals 'more or less deprived of all the advantages of society, of the opportunity of acquiring skill or education of any kind, as well as of the administration of justice, the public health services, and often even of the consolations of religion, and so forth. The public authority takes the place of the family where the poor are concerned in respect not only of their immediate want but also of laziness of disposition, malignity, and the other vices which arise out of their plight and their sense of wrong.'[129]

A flourishing capitalist economy not only creates poverty and the conditions for future economic crises; it also dehumanizes and alienates the worker within the process of production. 'One side of the picture,' Hegel suggests, is the ever-expanding production of needs, commodities, and profit. 'The other side is the subdivision and restriction of jobs. This results in the dependence and distress of the class tied to work of that sort, and these again entail inability to feel and enjoy the broader freedoms and especially the intellectual benefits of civil society.'[130] If the division of labour under capitalism creates a free and versatile worker, capable of many tasks, and infinitely adaptable to all forms of labour, it also produces and reproduces a fractured, maimed, dehumanized, and alienated section of the working class. 'Factory work,' states Marx, 'exhausts the nervous system to the uttermost; at the same time, it does away with the many-sided play of the muscles, and confiscates every atom of freedom, both in bodily and intellectual activity.' The worker is turned into a slave of the machine 'which dominates and soaks up living labour-power ... The special skill of each individual machine operator, who has now been deprived of all significance, vanishes as an infinitesimal quantity [before] ... the system of machinery, which ... constitutes the power of the "master".'[131] The labour conditions described by Hegel and Marx have been brought to a fever pitch in modern times by the application of scientific management and Taylorism in both advanced capitalist and socialist economies.[132] And the impact of mass production on the worker remains the same as it was over a hundred years ago: 'Every sense organ is injured by the artificially high temperatures, by the dust-laden atmosphere, by the deafening noise, not to mention the danger to life and limb among machines which are so closely crowded together, a danger which, with the regularity of the seasons, produces its list of those killed and wounded in the industrial battle.'[133]

'Increasing mechanization of labour' in civil society, Hegel declares, swells the profits of the owners on one hand, and creates a mass of structural unemployment on the other.[134] These workers join what Marx calls, 'the sphere of pauperism ... the hospital of the active labour-army and the dead weight of the industrial reserve army' of the unemployed.[135] Both Marx and Hegel stress that these degraded poor are in no way a revolutionary force;

deprived of their livelihood and self-respect, they are more likely to turn to crime, gambling, and reactionary politics than to embrace progressive ideas and movements. 'Poverty in itself does not make men into a rabble,' Hegel explains; 'a rabble is created only when there is joined to poverty a disposition of mind, an inner indignation against the rich, against society, against the government, etc. A further consequence of this attitude is that through their dependence on chance men become frivolous and idle, like the Neapolitan *lazzaroni* for example. In this way there is born in the rabble the evil of lacking self-respect enough to secure subsistence by its own labour and yet at the same time of claiming to receive subsistence as a right.' Poverty is not a result of the evils of human nature or the inherent laziness of the poor, etc. 'Once society is established,' Hegel declares, 'poverty immediately takes the form of a wrong done to one class by another.'[136] Poverty is a form of class war.

(In a passage in the *Philosophy of Mind* (§499, 247), which few commentators realize is a discussion, among other things, of how poverty emerges from the bourgeois property relation, Hegel writes: 'the particular will sets itself in opposition to the intrinsic right by negating that right itself as well as its recognition or semblance. (Here there is a negatively infinite judgement ... in which there is denied the class as a whole, and not merely the particular mode – in this case the apparent recognition.) Thus the will is violently wicked, and commits a *crime*.')

Hegel's incisive analysis of what he calls 'the inner dialectic of civil society' leads him to formulate the theory of imperialism, which plays little or no role in Marx's work, and which was not fully developed until the turn of the twentieth century. In Hegel's view, the double pressure of over-production and poverty 'drives ... civil society ... to push beyond its own limits and seek markets, and so its necessary means of subsistence, in other lands which are either deficient in the goods it has over-produced, or else generally backward in industry, etc.'[137] After Hegel, J.A. Hobson and Lenin were the first to observe the connection between systematic colonization and the over-production endemic to a highly monopolized capitalist economy. Imperialism for them, as for Hegel, means more than the mere export of manufactured goods; it means expelling surplus population to the colonies, securing *captive markets*, monopolizing *raw materials* vital to industry, and also finding an assured field for the *investment of surplus capital*. 'Typical of the old capitalism, when free competition held undivided sway,' notes Lenin, 'was the export of *goods*. Typical of the latest stage of capitalism, when monopolies rule, is the export of *capital*.'[138]

When Marx wrote his major economic works, imperialism and colonization were generally considered to be antithetical to the development of capitalism. 'The colonies,' Disraeli declared in 1852, 'are millstones round our necks.'[139] Hegel, however, witnessed the first aggressively expansionist development of capitalism, which was followed, as Lenin observes, by the 'most flourishing period of free competition in Great Britain, i.e. [that] between 1840 and 1860.'[140] Hegel distinguishes 'systematic colonization' from the 'sporadic' form of colonization 'particularly characteristic of Germany. The emigrants withdraw to America or Russia and remain there with no home ties, and so prove useless to their native lands. The second and entirely different type of colonization,' he continues, 'is the systematic; the state undertakes it, is aware of the proper method of carrying it out and regulates it accordingly.' Under systematic colonization, surplus people, goods, and capital are pressed on the colonies opened up by trade and merchant adventure, and made accessible by the sea links which created 'commercial connexions between different countries': 'This far-flung connecting link affords the means for the colonizing activity – sporadic or systematic – to which the mature civil society is driven and by which it supplies to a part of its population a return to life on the family basis in a new land and so also supplies itself with a new demand and field for its industry.'[141] According to Lenin, imperialism is the highest stage of capitalism, it is 'capitalism in transition, or, more precisely ... moribund capitalism,' 'parasitic or decaying capitalism,' etc.[142] For Hegel, however, completion of the phase of active colonization would hardly exhaust the exploitative capacity of bourgeois society. 'Colonial independence,' he suggests, 'proves to be of the greatest advantage to the mother country, just as the emancipation of slaves turns out to the greatest advantage of the owners.'[143]

Overseas trade and imperialism, Hegel argues, are connected with the strengthening of the external state and the emergence of the corporation. The capitalist state is increasingly compelled to exert control over civil society in 'the form of an external system and organization for the protection and security of particular ends and interests *en masse*, inasmuch as these interests subsist only in this universal.' The contradictions which produce poverty and the concentration of wealth, as well as economic crises and over-production, force the external state to intervene in the economic realm. The furies of private interest militate against government intervention, but 'the more blindly [civil society] sinks into self-seeking aims, the more it requires such control to bring it back to the universal.' The state's presence is required to soften class conflicts and to shorten the period of extreme economic contraction and depression. Moreover, international business activity elicits further economic involvement by a state already expanded and developed through administration of colonial affairs: 'public care and direction are most of all necessary in the case of the larger branches of industry, because these are dependent on conditions abroad and on combinations of distant circumstances which cannot be grasped as a whole by the individuals tied to these industries for their living.'[144]

For Marx, government involvement in the economy, development of economic statistics, and so on, are 'efforts ... made to overcome ... alienation.' They reflect at once the fact that capitalist production is 'an *objective* relation which is *independent* of' individuals, and also the movement towards socialist relations of production. 'Although on the given standpoint, alienation is not overcome by these means, nevertheless relations and connections are introduced thereby which include the possibility of suspending the old standpoint.'[145] While he discusses government economic measures and the importance of legislation for the condition of the working class, Marx also details the work of the factory inspectors, the 'guardians' of the Factory Act who continued their 'legal proceedings against the "pro-slavery rebellion"' of the owners, even after the Home Secretary suspended the Act.[146] His account of the character of the factory inspectors is reminiscent of Hegel's description of the civil servant as 'dispassionate, upright and polite' in the *Philosophy of Right*.[147] According to both writers, the civil service is not simply a tool of the ruling class, but rather an active counterpoise to the despotism of capital. 'We should be appalled at our own circumstances,' notes Marx referring to the Germans and other Western Europeans, 'if, as in England, our governments and parliaments periodically appointed commissions of inquiry into economic conditions; if these commissions were armed with the same plenary powers to get at the truth; if it were possible to find for this purpose men as competent, as free from partisanship and respect of persons as are England's factory inspectors, her medical reporters on public health, her commissioners of inquiry into the exploitation of women and children, into conditions of housing and nourishment, and so on.'[148]

For Hegel and Marx, the state is essentially an instrument for self-education of the social individual; and its development parallels growth of the political consciousness of the worker. Accordingly, the organization of the state itself will determine the conditions leading to the overthrow of capital. 'In England,' declares Marx in the preface to the first edition of *Capital*,

the process of transformation is palpably evident. When it has reached a certain point, it must react on the Continent. There it will take a form more brutal or more humane, according to the degree of development of the working class itself.

Apart from any higher motives, then, the most basic interests of the present ruling classes dictate to them that they clear out of the way all the legally removable obstacles to the development of the working class. For this reason, among others, I have devoted a great deal of space in this volume to the history, the details, and the results of the English Factory legislation.[149]

If the state is essentially an aspect of the development of the consciousness of the social individual, and a means to counteract alienation imposed by an economic system that seems independent of the individual's will, the same applies to the emergence of the giant corporation. For Hegel, the corporation is as significant for constructing the rational or communist state as was 'the introduction of agriculture and private property in another sphere.'[150] As Marx suggests, the corporation 'is the abolition of capital as private property within the framework of capitalist production itself ... and hence a self-dissolving contradiction, which *prima facie* represents a mere phase of transition to a new form of production.' In the corporation, management is divorced from the function of the capitalist who now appears 'redundant' in relation to the process of production: 'the mere manager who has no title whatever to the capital, whether through borrowing it or otherwise, performs all the real functions pertaining to the functioning capitalist as such, only the functionary remains and the capitalist disappears as superfluous from the production process.'[151] Accordingly, even under the capitalist mode of production the work process is 'made rational instead of natural. That is to say, it becomes freed from personal opinion and contingency, saved from endangering either the individual workman or others, recognized, guaranteed, and at the same time elevated to conscious effort for a common end.'[152]

With the appearance of the corporation, domination of the worker by the arbitrary will of a single capitalist gives way to a system in which the worker has increasing authority and control over the conditions of work. Under capitalism, writes Marx, 'it remains true, of course, that the *relations of production* themselves create a ... relation of *supremacy and subordination* (and this also has a *political* expression). But the more capitalist production sticks fast in this formal relationship, the less the relationship itself will evolve, since for the most part it is based on small capitalists who differ only slightly from the workers in their education and their activities.' The various schemes put forward by modern-day corporations, in co-operation with labour unions, to reduce alienation at the work place, such as flexible hours, job-enrichment, involvement in management, and so on, are necessary products of the development of capitalism itself. However inadequate and illusory they may be, they spring from the fact that the form of work relations under advanced capitalism 'becomes *freer*, because it is objective in nature, voluntary in appearance, *purely economic*.'[153]

The corporation, Hegel argues, becomes a 'second family,' replacing the patriarchal family as the foundation of the modern state. It provides the means of technical education for the worker, attempts to protect him or her from the contingencies of the labour market, and so on. The individual within the corporation derives a sense of personal worth and stability – 'evidence that he is a somebody. It is also recognized that he belongs to a whole which is itself an organ of the entire society, and that he is actively concerned in promoting the comparatively disinterested end of this whole. Thus he commands the respect due to one in his social position.' The worker no longer has the aspect of 'a day labourer or ... a man who is prepared to undertake casual employment on a single occasion,' instead there is a place 'for the whole range, the universality, of his personal livelihood.'[154] Hegel, of course, is not referring to the actual *reality* of the corporation, but to its *historical tendencies*, tendencies reflected, however inadequately, in the modern corporation with its job protection and mobility schemes, retirement and health plans, and so forth.[155] These, along with the universal scope of the modern corporation, distinguish it dramatically from the narrow character of the early capitalist firm which denied absolutely the rights of the worker and offered little in return.

Commentators have expressed considerable doubt that the corporation in Hegel's theory bears any resemblance to the joint stock company Marx discusses or indeed to the modern multinational corporation. Bernard Cullen is typical in this respect: 'Hegel's *Korporation* has nothing at all to do with what we refer to today as corporations: industrial/financial conglomerates such as ITT, IBM and General Motors.'[156] As I argued earlier, however, Hegel's corporation certainly refers to incorporated business organizations, as may be determined by consulting his references to the corporation as a business licensed and regulated by the state.[157] Nor is there anything anachronistic in my interpretation. Berle and Means in their classic work on the subject observe that 'corporate enterprise is no new institution. From the days of the joint stock trading companies which built up the merchant empires of England and Holland in the Seventeenth Century, the quasi-public company has been well known.'[158] In the *Wealth of Nations*, which Hegel read closely, Adam Smith discusses the joint stock company at length, noting its suitability for banking, insurance, and public works, but doubting its usefulness in manufacturing and trade.[159] Despite Smith's misgivings, corporate bodies were well established in British manufacturing by the turn of the nineteenth century, and the first American manufacturing corporation was established in Boston in 1813. The Boston Manufacturing Company, write Berle and Means, 'was in many ways the prototype of the corporations of a later date. Though insignificantly small in comparison with the corporate giants of today this company had all their essential characteristics.'[160]

Although there were plenty of examples of incorporated businesses when Hegel published the *Philosophy of Right*, the corporation he envisions differs radically from them (and from the modern one) in several respects. The Hegelian corporation is a productive enterprise with an accordingly limited and particularistic scope, but it is also *a democratic political organization with direct links to the state*. As such it stands as the most important mediating institution between the isolated individual in civil society and the complex apparatus of government. Leading positions within his corporations are staffed through elections among their members, and subject to 'ratification by higher authority' in the state. Moreover, the atomistic tendencies Hegel associates with popular suffrage, which may result in government by an unrepresentative élite, are overcome by electing parliamentary representatives or deputies from within the corporations themselves.

Since these deputies are the deputies of civil society, it follows as a direct consequence that their appointment is made by the society as a society. That is to say, in making the appointment, society is not dispersed into atomic units, collected to perform only a single and temporary act, and kept together for a moment and no longer. On the contrary, it makes the appointment as a society, articulated into associations, communities, and Corporations, which although constituted already for other purposes, acquire in this way a connection with politics.

Individuals do not make their influence felt in government *qua* individuals but as members of a particular social class:[161] and the corporation is a political organization through which the business class of capitalists and workers is brought into the realm of the state. The business class, however, is a conflicted, divided class, broken into the antagonistic poles of worker and capitalist. The corporation's political linkages, therefore, are shot through with the same contradiction that characterizes the business class itself. As I argued in Chapter 6, the capitalist has formal ownership of the means of production while the worker is their possessor; the struggle for property rights between the two warring sides of the business class occurs within the corporation and is reflected in the democratic political institutions evolving from it.

'Possession is *property*,' writes Hegel, 'which as possession is a *means*, but as existence of the personality is an *end*.'[162] Although the worker in civil society takes possession of the means of production by using them, he or she gains no concrete property, only a subsistence wage. The poverty-stricken worker is without property, without the element of personality and mutual recognition between equals proper to concrete citizenship in the state. Lacking property – the external embodiment of his or her personality – the worker exists only as a *subjective* individual with no *objective* reality, a contradiction he or she must fight to overcome. 'For personality ... as inherently infinite and universal, the restriction of being only subjective is a contradiction and a nullity. Personality is that which struggles to lift itself above this restriction and to give itself reality, or in other words to claim that external world as its own.' It is on this basis that the corporation offers itself to the worker as the main arena of combat for property rights, the centre of educational struggle (*Bildung*) in civil society, and the foundation for full political participation in the state. 'The corporation mind, engendered when the particular spheres gain their title to rights, is now inwardly converted into the mind of the state, since it finds in the state the means of maintaining its particular ends.'[163]

Hegel did not miss the historical irony that corporations began as associations of workers and communities in ancient and feudal societies, only to take the form under capitalism of state-licensed enterprises and joint stock companies. He also noted that while establishing its own corporate bodies the bourgeoisie was systematically destroying what was left of the feudal guilds and blocking development of trade associations among the workers. Condemning these efforts to crush the proletariat, Hegel deliberately defines the corporation as a contradictory organization representative of the opposing interests of capitalists and workers. Thus if his corporation bears some resemblance to the giant businesses that straddle the economies of contemporary Western capitalism, it also corresponds to the opponents of the multinationals formed within big business itself – the labour unions. For he views organizations representing the workers as absolutely vital to the evolution of the rational state. 'It is of the utmost importance that the masses should be organized, because only so do they become mighty and powerful. Otherwise they are nothing but a heap, an aggregate of atomic units. Only when the particular associations are organized members of the state are they possessed of legitimate power.'[164]

For Avineri, as for most interpreters, Hegel is different from Marx 'since no radical call of action follows his harsh analysis of civil society.' Hegel, says Avineri, advocates only 'external control' of economic activity in civil society and does not urge intervention of the state into civil society as does

Marx. If Hegel had done so, his 'distinction between civil society and the state would disappear, and the whole system of mediation and dialectical progress towards integration through differentiation would collapse.'[165] Like Marx, however, Hegel is convinced that the corporation is a means through which capitalist society will pass into the rational state where common ownership of the means of production by the associated producers will prevail. It is through the external state and the corporation that 'the sphere of civil society passes over into the state.' The bourgeois state, in relation to the corporation, is just 'an external organization involving a separation and merely relative identity of controller and controlled,' but both these institutions 'find their truth in the absolutely universal end and its absolute actuality,' i.e., in the rational or communist state. In the rational state, 'the universal, which in the first instance is the right only' of private property, 'has to be extended over the whole field of particularity,' i.e., over the whole of civil society. Although the corporations change 'into a known and thoughtful ethical mode of life,' nevertheless they 'must fall under the higher surveillance of the state, because otherwise they would ossify, build themselves in, and decline into a miserable system of castes.' Both the external capitalist state and the modern corporation turn out to be the means whereby the individual in civil society is educated through class struggle to independent self-consciousness, to a 'form of thought whereby mind is objective and actual to itself as an organic totality in laws and institutions which are its will in terms of thought.'[166] This is the same transformation theorized by Marx:

In stock companies the function is divorced from capital ownership, hence also labour is entirely divorced from ownership of means of production and surplus-labour. This result of the ultimate development of capitalist production is a necessary transitional phase towards the reconversion of capital into the property of the producers, although no longer as the private property of the individual producers, but rather as the property of associated producers, as outright social property. On the other hand, the stock company is a transition towards the conversion of all functions in the reproduction process which still remain linked with capitalist property, into mere functions of associated producers, into social functions.[167]

8

Dialectic and the Rational State

1 THE DIALECTIC METHOD

If the Trinity is the principal mystery of Christianity, the dialectic is the chief mystery of modern western Marxism.[1] Much of the confusion is due to Marx's observation that the dialectic as it appears in Hegel's writing 'is standing on its head.' According to Marx, Hegel makes the Idea 'the creator of the real world' and fails to recognize that 'the ideal is nothing but the material world reflected in the mind of man, and translated into forms of thought.'[2] One of the conclusions of this study is that Marx fundamentally misjudges the Hegelian philosophy. He accepts uncritically Feuerbach's critique of Hegel, and fails to revise his own early and mistaken opinion about absolute idealism. Both Feuerbach and Marx fail to comprehend Hegel's distinction between the three levels of consciousness or ideology, although this distinction, as Hegel himself observes, is 'of capital importance for understanding the nature and kinds of knowledge.'[3]

Feuerbach remains confined to the first level of objectivity – the crude materialist celebration of sense perception, which takes the categories of thought to be merely a reflection of the external world. The second level is represented by Kant's transcendental idealism which holds that sense perception is guided and informed by the *a priori* categories of mind. Marx accepts Hegel's thesis that mind, understood as conscious human practice, is active rather than passive in relation to the outside world. But while he makes use of this third level of objectivity, he overlooks its application by Hegel to epistemology and the study of nature and society. Hence, he views the Idea as a form of thought, instead of what it really is – an expression both of the concrete reality of society and of the categories that create and correspond to that reality.

The basic principle of Hegel's thought, and of dialectic method as well, is the unity between subject and object of knowledge as achieved through ideality or revolutionizing practice. Conscious human practice or ideality 'cancels the antithesis between the objective which would be and stay an objective only, and the subjective which in like manner would be and stay a subjective only.' The nature of ideality, notes Hegel, has been presented in his philosophy 'often enough. Yet it could not be too often repeated, if the intention were really to put an end to the stale and purely malicious misconception in regard to this identity' of subject and object as obtained through practice.[4]

In the introduction to the *Grundrisse*, where Marx works out the elements of dialectic method, he observes that 'the economic categories ... express the forms of being, the characteristics of existence, and often only individual sides of this specific society, this subject.'[5] But if the categories express the relations of society, this is only because they also create them – through the mediation of concrete human practice. Ideas and knowledge – ideology – therefore, do not merely reflect, but are inseparable from, the object and manifestation of human thinking activity, or ideality. 'Mind,' writes Hegel, 'is only what it does, and its act is to make itself the object of its own consciousness.'[6] This dialectical relationship is applied by Marx to the notion of capital itself. 'The development of fixed capital,' he writes, 'indicates to what degree general social knowledge has become a *direct force of production*, and to what degree, hence, the conditions of the process of social life itself have come under the control of the general intellect and been transformed in accordance with it. To what degree the powers of social production have been produced, not only in the form of knowledge, but also as immediate organs of social practice, of the real life process.'[7]

Ernest Mandel argues that the economic categories studied by Marx 'are just forms of material existence, of material reality as perceived and simplified by the human mind.'[8] Mandel, however, refers only to the subjective side of the categories and forgets their objective side; he, along with most Marxist and bourgeois writers, ignores the unity of objective and subjective achieved through human practice, which is the most important aspect of the dialectic method. The economic category of labour, for example, which abstracts from the content of any particular type of work, 'is not merely,' states Marx, 'the mental product of a concrete totality of labours.' Rather, it refers to the 'indifference towards specific labours' characteristic of 'a form of society in which individuals can with ease transfer from one labour to another, and where the specific kind is a matter of chance for them, hence of indifference.' The United States – 'the most modern form of existence of bourgeois society' – is thus also the society where 'for the first time, the point of departure of modern economics, namely the abstraction of the category "labour", "labour as such", labour pure and simple, becomes true in practice.'[9]

The dialectic method as employed by both Hegel and Marx does not, of course, deny the objective reality of the external world. 'The sun, the moon, rivers, and the natural objects of all kinds by which we are surrounded,' states Hegel, '*are*. For consciousness they have the authority not only of mere being but also of possessing a particular nature which it accepts and to which it adjusts itself in dealing with them, using them, or in being otherwise concerned with them.'[10] Nevertheless, the categories of science, through which men and women interpret, explain, and utilize the objects of external nature and discover their laws, are products of human ideality and determine the relation of individuals to nature. Scientific categories are devoted not to the external manifestation of natural phenomena, but to their *inner connection* which can be grasped only through the power of thought. If the categories merely reflected natural objects, asks Marx, 'what need would there be of *science*?'[11] Dialectic method as employed by Hegel's philosophy of nature differs from natural science only because it 'brings before our mind the adequate forms of the notion in the physical world.'[12]

While the categories express and create through revolutionizing practice the social world of individuals, men and women do not consciously employ them in their everyday activities; the forms of thought are ideal determinations raised by science out of their merely implicit existence and manifestation in society. The pure economic category of labour, for example, does not determine the conscious practice of men and women in advanced capitalist society. It simply expresses what people *do*, not what they *think*. Before the categories of method in their pure form can be studied, they must exist in *implicit* or *unconscious* form in society. 'The stage of philosophical knowledge,' Hegel observes, 'is the richest in material and organization, and therefore, as it came before us in the shape of a result, it presupposed the existence of the concrete formations of consciousness, such as individual and social morality, art and religion.' The development of the categories of method – the 'objective thoughts'[13] of society, or what Marx calls 'the power of knowledge, objectified'[14] – 'must so to speak, go on *behind consciousness*, since those facts are the essential nucleus which is raised into consciousness.'[15] The men and women who emigrated to a new land in North America brought with them the bourgeois notion of *making money*, no matter how; they threw aside feudal conceptions of the identity of a person with his or her craft or trade, and plunged into a social world where labour is a means to an end, rather than an end in itself. The *theoretical* expression of their *practice* is the simple economic category, *labour.*

In his essay, 'Lenin before Hegel,' Louis Althusser draws attention to Lenin's aphorism that 'it is impossible completely to understand Marx's *Capital* ... without having thoroughly studied and understood the *whole* of Hegel's *Logic.* Consequently, half a century later none of the Marxists understood Marx!!'[16] But Althusser perceptively reverses this aphorism: '*A century and a half later no one has understood Hegel because it is impossible to understand Hegel without having thoroughly studied and understood "Capital"*!'[17] Althusser's remark points to a second major conclusion of this study: Marx's later work cannot be comprehended except as a dialogue with Hegel. By contrast, his early efforts constitute a humanist critique of society (and Hegelian philosophy) based on the crude materialism of Feuerbach. The mature Marx develops and concretizes many of Hegel's observations on bourgeois society, and utilizes his knowledge of Hegelian dialectic in the formulation of historical materialism. Marx's insights make it possible to grasp those aspects of Hegel which Marx himself overlooks or misinterprets. These include, as I have shown, Hegel's notion of ideality, which is identical with and much more developed than Marx's concept of revolutionizing practice, as well as Hegel's critique and analysis of religion, natural science, and bourgeois thought. Further, since Hegel had already worked out the essential distinction between use-value and exchange-value, this enables him to develop a profound critique of bourgeois private property, economic crises, and imperialism, which anticipates and, in some cases, goes beyond Marx. Also, he develops a theory of the state, social class, and the modern corporation that remains only implicit in Marx's writings, and which, as I argue below, provides the theoretical outlines of the new form of civilization which both thinkers see emerging from the capitalist mode of production.

In his essay 'The Three Sources and Three Component Parts of Marxism,' Lenin declares that 'the genius of Marx consists precisely in his having furnished answers to questions already presented by the foremost minds of mankind.' Marx, therefore, is 'the legitimate successor to the best that man has produced in the nineteenth century, as represented by German philosophy, English political economy and French socialism.'[18] Lenin's view is widely accepted, but it is mistaken. Before Marx, Hegel had already fused German idealism with British political economy and the ideals of the French Revolution. His influence was therefore pivotal in Marx's decision to study and criticize the classics of political economy[19] and the conclusions Marx drew from this study are identical with those of Hegel. Marx himself is well aware of his enormous debt to Hegel: 'You will understand, my dear fellow,' he writes to Engels in 1866, 'that in a work like mine [i.e., *Capital*] there must be many shortcomings in detail. But the composition of the whole, the way it all hangs together, is a triumph of German science and scholarship to which an individual German may confess since the merit belongs not to him but to the whole nation.'[20] Before Marx, of course, no one had contributed more to German science and scholarship than Hegel. In any case, Marx's letter repeats an observation Hegel makes about his own work: 'I could not pretend that the method which I follow ... is not capable of greater completeness, of much elaboration in detail; but at the same time I know that it is the only true method.'[21]

Although both theorists point to the value of dialectic method for their work many commentators are sceptical of these claims. Walter Kaufmann, for example, who provides a lucid introduction to Hegel, writes that 'I am not so much rejecting the dialectic as I say: there is none. Look for it, by all means ... but you will not find any plain method that you could adopt even if you wanted to.'[22] Kaufmann's difficulty in finding dialectic method is understandable since, as Hegel explains, 'it is not something distinct from its object and content ... it is the inwardness of the content, the dialectic which it possesses within itself, which is the mainspring of its advance.'[23] Among Western Marxists, Karl Korsch presents a thorough discussion of dialectic method, observing that it concerns 'the question of the *relationship between the totality of historical being and all historically prevalent forms of consciousness.*'[24] Lukács[25] and Gramsci[26] also approach the dialectic from this angle, assimilating it into a discussion of the class consciousness of the proletariat. 'The Marxist method,' declares Lukács, 'the dialectical materialist knowledge of reality, can arise only from the point of view of a class, from the point of view of the struggle of the proletariat.'[27] This account tends to degenerate into an élitist conception of history, according to which the developing consciousness of the workers is guided by an omnipotent party of middle-class intellectuals who provide the 'reasons' for the 'faith' of the workers.[28] As I have argued throughout this study, however, dialectic method ultimately concerns the consciousness not of a class, but of the social individual or the free worker. Thus for Marx, the defect of capitalist production is precisely that 'the growth of ... material wealth is brought about in contradiction to and at the expense of the individual human being.'[29] The role of civil or bourgeois society in the education and development, *through struggle*, of the social individual provides the historical justification for, and brings about the dissolution of, the capitalist mode of production.

For both Hegel and Marx, dialectic method can only be applied to a *given concrete reality*; its object 'is always what is given, in the head as well as in reality.'[30] Neither thinker is, in Marx's words, 'writing recipes ... for the cookshops of the future.'[31] The 'Objective Thoughts' – or social facts – studied by dialectical science are 'the *truth* ... which is ... the absolute *object* of philosophy';[32] and truth 'means that concept and external reality correspond.'[33] At the same time, dialectic method is not limited by what Hegel calls, the 'finite' categories of the understanding: these categories are finite because 'they are only subjective and the antithesis of an objective clings to them.' In other words, they cannot comprehend the dynamic unity of subject and object obtained through ideality or revolutionizing practice. Moreover, the categories of the understanding 'are always of restricted content, and so persist in antithesis to one another and still more to the Absolute.' The 'Absolute' is Hegel's term for the *rational state* in which reason and reality absolutely correspond. Fettered by the alienation and irrationality of bourgeois society, the understanding cannot come to terms with capitalism's transient character; thus it fails 'to point out how [its] categories and their whole sphere [i.e., the society to which they correspond: D.M.] pass into a higher.'[34] Accordingly, what Hegel means by the 'understanding' is just what Marx indicates with the term 'bourgeois.' This form of thought, Marx declares, 'views the capitalist order as the absolute and ultimate form of social production, instead of as a historically transient stage of development.'[35]

There are three aspects or moments of dialectic method. The first is *recognition* of the dialectic as it appears in the subject matter itself. 'The method,' Hegel declares, 'has emerged as the *self-knowing Notion that has itself* ... *for its subject matter* ... It is therefore not only the highest *force*, or rather the *sole* and absolute *force* of reason, but also its supreme and sole *urge* to find and cognize *itself by means of itself in everything*.'[36] The second aspect of dialectic method is *method proper*, which includes *the appropriation of the facts and laws of other sciences*.[37] The third moment of dialectic is *exposition* – the logical ordering and presentation of the movement of the object discovered through method. In the following discussion I will outline the first two moments of dialectic – *recognition* and *method*. The third, exposition, will be dealt with in the next, and concluding, section of this study.

The first moment – recognition – is the *basic presupposition of method* which Hegel calls, 'the consciousness of the form of the inner self-movement of the content,' or subject matter of science.[38] Marx refers to this presupposition in *Capital*: 'My standpoint [views] the development of the economic formation of society ... as a process of natural history.' Accordingly, society is seen as 'an organism capable of change, and constantly engaged in a process of change.'[39] Dialectic within the object of study constitutes the 'universal laws to which [its] life and changes conform.'[40] This might be called 'bio-dialectic'; and it is the bio-dialectic of bourgeois society that is studied by Marx in *Capital*. 'The ultimate aim of this work,' he affirms, is 'to reveal the economic law of motion of modern society.'[41] The presupposition of dialectic method may only be confirmed by the results achieved through it: 'The very point of view, which originally is taken on its own evidence only, must in the course of the science be converted to a result – the ultimate result in which philosophy returns into itself and reaches the point with which it began.'[42]

Dialectic method presupposes that society is inherently rational, or governed by laws; in this sense, society resembles nature, for it is constituted not by 'the formations and accidents evident to the superficial observer,' but – like nature – by laws which may be discovered by science.[43] There are, however, vital differences between the laws of society and those of nature. First, social laws can be discovered only through thought and theory; the sensuous methodology of natural science can play no part in their discovery. As Marx puts it, 'in the analysis of economic forms neither microscopes nor chemical reagents are of assistance. The power of abstraction must replace both.'[44]

Another distinction between the laws of nature and society is that the latter *originate* from the *conscious activity* of men and women and may also be *changed* by their activity.[45] Moreover, while natural laws are rigid and remain unaffected by knowledge, the transformation of social laws may be made possible, or, in any case, easier, by knowledge of them. 'Even when a society,' Marx observes, 'has begun to track down the natural laws of its movement ... it can neither leap over the natural phases of its development nor remove them by decree. But it can shorten and lessen the birth-pangs'.[46] The principle of law – whether of nature or society – involves '*an inseparable unity*, a *necessary inner connection*' between diverse phenomena: the law of gravity, for example, requires that all objects must fall to the ground at a given rate of acceleration; the law of value means that all commodities have exchange-value and use-value; criminal law states that all crimes involve punishment.[47] But legislative and criminal laws differ from those of nature and society because they are deliberately framed by individuals, while natural and social laws unfold outside the conscious intent of men and women.

There are two related, but incorrect, conceptions about what I have called the second moment of dialectic method – method proper. The first is that dialectic concerns the study of society as a *progressive series of stages*, one leading naturally to another; the second is that dialectic is essentially *nega-*

tive and *critical*. Both express only *one-sided aspects* of dialectic method. For Hegel, the belief that dialectic concerns the study of society 'as an issuing of the more perfect from the less perfect ... does prejudice to the method of philosophy.'[48] Dialectic method investigates the immanent or self-originating development of the social organism, i.e., of what Marx calls, 'the organic social body within which the individuals reproduce themselves as individuals, but as social individuals.'[49] And if an organism may be seen as a series of progressive transformations that ultimately reveal its mature form, it can also be envisioned as the explicit determination of what already implicitly existed in embryo or germ. In other words, the form of the new social organism is already contained in the old one. This is what Hegel refers to as the 'double movement' or 'doubling process' of the dialectic. The 'superficial thoughts of more imperfect and more perfect,' states Hegel, 'indicate the distinction' between each stage or form of consciousness and society from the next; they have nothing to do with its inner movement.[50]

A view of communist society as the next stage after capitalism is similar to Kant's notion of the 'good,' which Hegel characterizes as 'something which merely ought to be, and which at the same time is not real – a mere article of faith, possessing a subjective certainty, but without truth, or that objectivity which is adequate to the Idea.' This contradiction, he adds, 'may seem to be disguised by adjourning the realization of the Idea to a future, to a *time* when the Idea will also be.' Time, however, is merely 'a sensuous conception,' and does not remove the obligation of the theorist to prove what is held out to be true. *The only proof of the development of the new society lies in the present,* in the concrete, living actuality which science has for its object. 'The only way to secure any growth and progress in knowledge is to hold results fast in their truth.'[51] Consequently, dialectic method aims to disclose the rational elements within the present which presage the future. 'Rationality ... enters upon external existence simultaneously with its actualization, it emerges with an infinite wealth of forms, shapes, and appearances. Around its heart it throws a motley covering with which consciousness is at home to begin with, a covering which the concept has first to penetrate before it can find the inward pulse and feel it still beating in the outward appearances.'[52] The same idea is expressed in Marx's *Grundrisse*: capitalism, he writes,

the *most extreme form of alienation* ... is a necessary point of transition – and therefore already contains in *itself*, in a still only inverted form, turned on its head, the dissolution of all *limited presuppositions of production*, and moreover creates and produces the unconditional presuppositions of production, and therewith the full material conditions for the total, universal development of the productive forces of the individual.[53]

The supreme principle guiding dialectic method is Kant's notion 'that man ... alone is the final end and aim' of the natural and social order.[54] Thus Hegel's 'Absolute Idea,' which 'is the sole subject matter and content of philosophy,' is nothing else but the 'free subjective Notion that is for itself and therefore possesses *personality* – the practical, objective Notion determined in and for itself which, as person, is impenetrable atomic subjectivity – but which, none the less, is not exclusive individuality, but explicitly *universality* and *cognition*, and in its other has *its own* objectivity for its object.'[55] The growth of consciousness and society is a process in which the social individual who 'is implicitly rational ... must also become explicitly so by struggling to create himself not only by going forth from himself but also by building himself up within.'[56] This struggle, rather than a mere survey of the progressive stages of society, forms the object and content of dialectic method.

The result of dialectic, says Hegel, 'is the *individual*, the *concrete*, the *subject*.'[57] The individual is a *procession*, a *trinity*, of 'three in one and one in three'; he or she appears as the *individualization* of *knowledge* and *society*, the ideal and real community. What distinguishes capitalism from earlier social forms is that its principle of private property – especially the free ownership of one's labour-power – is the motive force behind the education and increased self-consciousness or rationality of the individuals within it. The struggle of the individual, which in civil society is necessarily *class struggle*, implies growing control over social forces even within the bourgeois mode of production, and is likely to turn aside all predictions of capitalism's imminent collapse. Capital itself, to use Marx's phrase, is a permanent revolution.[58] 'Every degree of the development of the social forces of production, of intercourse, of knowledge, etc. appears to it only as a barrier which it strives to overpower.'[59]

The transitory nature of capitalism results from its contradictory character which 'appears in such a way that the working individual *alienates* himself ... relates to the conditions brought out of him by his labour as those not of his *own* but of an *alien wealth* and of his own poverty.' But alienation is abolished within capitalism itself; in fact, abolition of alienation is a presupposition of the rational or communist state. 'The recognition' by the individual, says Marx, 'of the products' of labour 'as its own, and the judgement that its separation from the conditions of its realization is improper – forcibly imposed – is an enormous [advance in] awareness ... itself the product of the mode of production resting on capital, and ... the knell to its doom.'[60] The same notion is expressed in more abstract terms by Hegel: 'Everything that from eternity has happened in heaven and earth, the life of God and all the deeds of time,' he writes, 'simply are the struggles for Mind to know itself, to make itself objective to itself, to find itself, be for itself, and finally to unite itself to itself; it is alienated and divided, but only so as to be able thus to find itself and return to itself. Only in this manner does Mind attain its freedom, for that is free which is not connected with or dependent on another.'[61]

Individual self-awareness or rationality brings about the 'truth of necessity ... Freedom.' Under a mature form of capitalism, which is the point of transition to the rational state, 'it then appears that the members, linked to one another, are not really foreign to each other, but only elements of one whole, each of them, in its connection with the other, being, as it were, at home, and combining with itself. In this way necessity is transfigured into freedom – not the freedom that consists in abstract negation, but freedom concrete and positive.'[62] This is the same concrete and positive freedom advocated by Marx: 'Freedom ... can only consist in socialised man, the associated producers, rationally regulating their interchange with Nature, bringing it under their common control, instead of being ruled by it as by the blind forces of Nature; and achieving this with the least expenditure of energy and under conditions favourable to, and worthy of, their human nature.'[63]

Thinkers in the Marxist tradition believe correctly that the dialectic method is negative and critical towards existing society. 'The action of thought,' states Hegel, 'has also a *negative* effect upon its basis.'[64] Dialectical science, says Marx, 'does not let itself be impressed by anything, being in its very essence critical and revolutionary.'[65] Both theorists contend that the capitalist mode of production is arbitrary instead of rational; its cruel dialectic alienates the worker from his or her property and will, and contains the contradictions of wealth and poverty, over-production, imperialism, and dehumanization which propel bourgeois society towards the rational or communist state. 'It is the bad side,' writes Marx, 'that produces movement which makes history, by providing a struggle.'[66] Or, as Hegel puts it, 'For anything to be finite is just to suppress itself and put itself aside.'[67] The negative and critical aspect of dialectic, however, is only a part, and not even the most important one, of scientific method. 'The fundamental prejudice in this matter,' declares Hegel, 'is that dialectic has *only a negative result.*'[68] Rather than being purely negative, 'the result of Dialectic is positive, because it has a definite content.'[69] Marx also emphasizes that dialectic contains the 'positive understanding of what exists.'[70] Yet dialectic is not simply 'a subjective see-saw of arguments *pro* and *con*':[71] what Marx calls, referring to Proudhon's false dialectic, the 'petty-bourgeois point of view – composed of On The One Hand and On The Other Hand.'[72] *The dialectic method is ultimately a positive or affirmative approach to the study of consciousness and society.* 'To hold fast to the positive in *its* negative, this is the most important feature in rational cognition.'[73]

Dialectic studies *the process of becoming*, the progess of the, at first only implicit, rationality of the social individual. 'Enrichment,' notes Hegel,

proceeds in the *necessity* of the Notion, it is held by it, and each determination is a reflection-into-self. Each new stage of *forthgoing*, that is, of *further determination*, is also a withdrawal inwards, and the greater *extension* is equally a *higher intensity*. The richest is ... the most concrete and most *subjective*, and that which withdraws itself into the simplest depth is the mightiest and most all-embracing. The highest, most concentrated point is the *pure personality* which, solely through the absolute dialectic which is its nature, no less *embraces and holds everything within itself*, because it makes itself the supremely free – the simplicity which is the first immediacy and universality.'[74]

Capital, for example, is nothing but the objectified essence of the developing power of the social individual: 'real wealth is the developed productive power of all individuals ... The full development of the individual ... reacts back upon the productive power of labour as itself the greatest productive power.' Even the study of bourgeois political economy, therefore, presupposes that it is also the study of the organic development of the social individual: 'The final result of the process of social production always appears as the society itself, i.e. the human being itself in its social relations.'[75]

The process of becoming involves *absorption* and *transcendence* of all earlier stages of a developing and conscious organism by its most mature stage. 'In the absolute method,' says Hegel, 'the Notion *maintains* itself in its otherness ... at each stage of its further determination it raises the entire mass of its preceeding content, and by its dialectical advance it not only does not lose anything or leave anything behind, but carries along with it all that it has gained, and inwardly enriches and consolidates itself.'[76] Accordingly, the highest and most mature phase of the social organism – the communist or rational state – will contain within itself all the positive or rational aspects of earlier social forms, including capitalist society.

Recognition of the positive aspect of dialectic forms the 'epistemological break' which, as Althusser suggests, separates the work of the young from the mature Marx.[77] Before 1845, Marx was greatly influenced by Ludwig Feuerbach's criticism of the Hegelian 'negation of the negation' or 'true affirmation' which, Feuerbach claims 'restored ... theology ... through philosophy.' Hegel's writings conceal their reactionary content under a revolutionary guise: 'At first everything is overthrown, but then everything is put again in its former place.'[78] The young Marx applauds Feuerbach's '*serious, critical* attitude to the Hegelian dialectic,' especially his opposition to 'the negation of the negation,' which claims to be 'the confirmation of the true essence.' According to the young Marx, bourgeois society will destroy itself and a new communist society, 'positively self-deriving humanism,' will emerge from the ruins.[79] The same apocalyptic view, which contrasts strongly with his later ideas on the development of the social individual under capitalism, also appears in the *Communist Manifesto*:

The modern labourer ... instead of rising with the progress of industry, sinks deeper and deeper below the conditions of existence of his own class. He becomes a pauper, and pauperism develops more rapidly than population and wealth. And here it becomes evident, that the bourgeoisie is unfit any longer to be the ruling class in society, and to impose its conditions of existence upon society as an overriding law. It is unfit to rule because it is incompetent to assure an existence to its slave within his slavery, because it cannot help letting him sink into such a state, that it has to feed him, instead of being fed by him.[80]

For many commentators, Marx's dialectic method involves some type of reciprocity between the economic base and the ideological superstructure of society. Giddens, for example, suggests that the 'dialectical view' assumes 'reciprocal interaction of ... ideas with the social organisation of "earthly man" ... the active interplay between subject and object ... whereby the individual acts upon the world at the same time as the world acts upon him.'[81] Given this assumption, the problem becomes the degree to which the ideological superstructure (i.e., law, politics, religion, and so on) is influenced by the economic base and *vice versa*.

Hegel observes that dialectic method 'tries especially to show how the questions men have proposed ... on the nature of Knowledge, Faith, and the like – questions which they imagine to have no connection with abstract thoughts – are really reducible to the simple categories, which first get cleared up in Logic.'[82] The questions involved in interpretations of dialectic are no exception. The base/superstructure version is a regressive hybrid of the categories of reciprocity or functionalism, and causality; these categories, in turn, are the staple diet of the understanding or bourgeois consciousness.

Hegel provides a useful analysis of the category of reciprocity which reveals why so much difficulty is involved in determining the direction of the base/superstructure relationship. In the relation of reciprocity, the elements said to interact tend to disappear and dissolve into one another, so that instead of two interacting elements there turns out to be only one. 'Reciprocal action just means that each characteristic we impose [in this case, base or superstructure: D.M.] is also to be suspended and inverted into its opposite, and that in this way the essential nullity of the "moments" is explicitly stated. An effect is introduced into the primariness [i.e., the superstructure is said to have an effect on the base: D.M.]; in other words, the primariness is abolished: the action of a cause becomes reaction, and so on.'[83] The solution suggested for this dilemma by Engels, Althusser, and others (namely, that the economic base is determinant in 'the last instance') does one of two things. It either refers the relation between base and superstructure to the sensuous conception of time: i.e., the economy is the first (or the second-last) element in the relation of reciprocity, in which case nothing has been solved at all. Or it leads to the abandonment of the relation of reciprocity to the even less satisfactory category of causality: i.e., if the base, then the superstructure.

The base/superstructure version of dialectic assumes an *interaction* between the *conscious subject* and its *object*. Thus, for example, the laws or religion of a society result from the influence of economic activity on the minds of individuals within that society. But the assumption that consciousness depends upon and interacts with its object is false. Human consciousness is above all *active*; thinking, considered as ideality or revolutionizing practice, is not dependent on its object. 'We may be said to owe eating to the means of nourishment,' writes Hegel, 'so long as we can have no eating without them. If we take this view, eating is certainly represented as ungrateful: it devours that to which it owes itself. Thinking, upon this view of its action, is equally ungrateful.'[84] As Marx puts it in the *Theses on Feuerbach*: 'Social life is essentially *practical*. All mysteries which mislead theory to mysticism find their rational solution in human practice and in the comprehension of this practice.'[85]

The same conscious human practice that creates the ideological superstructure also creates the economic base. The reciprocal interaction of the two, which undoubtedly exists, is a result of the fact that they have an identical source. 'The true category,' Hegel observes, 'is the unity of all these different forms, so that it is one Mind which manifests itself in, and impresses itself upon these different elements.'[86] Hence, the bourgeois approximation to rationality (which turns out to be irrationality) is felt everywhere in capitalist society, from the organization of industry to the structure of the legal system. It is founded on a peculiar interpretation of human freedom (Hegel calls it 'an insanity of personality') according to which the individual is free to alienate the products of his or her own labour – which in fact are the property of the individual – and hand them over to the 'overlord to nothing,'[87] the capitalist. This relation makes possible the fantastic growth, the richness and complexity of bourgeois society, but the limit of the rationality of the capitalist property relation is also the limit of the capitalist mode of production itself.

The supreme importance of conscious human activity in dialectic method explains the prominence of the world-historical individual in the work of Hegel. For Hegel, world-historical individuals are *revolutionaries* who derive 'their purposes and their vocation,' from the underground principle of freedom which eventually bursts through the surface of society and overthrows the existing order. 'They are men, therefore, who appear to draw the impulse of their life from themselves; and whose deeds have produced a condition of things and a complex of historical relations which appear to be only *their* interest, and *their* work.' World-historical individuals are persons who, though unconscious 'of the general Idea they were unfolding,' nevertheless attained to 'an insight into the requirements of the time – *what was ripe for development*.' These individuals, these revolutionaries, expressed what was in the minds of all 'but in a state of unconsciousness which the great men in question aroused.' In other words, 'They are *great* men, because they willed and accomplished something great; not a mere fancy, a mere intention, but that which met the case and fell in with the needs of the age.'[88] Marx is also conscious of the individual's role in history, pointing out that 'acceleration and delay' in historical progress 'are very much dependent upon ... "accidents", including the "accident" of the character of the people who first head the movement.'[89] He argues, for example, that the French Revolution was not only a product of the struggle of great masses of people, but also of the deeds of heroes. 'Camille Desmoulins, Danton, Robespierre, Saint-Just, Napoleon, the heroes as well as the parties and the masses of the old French Revolution, performed the task of their time ... the task of unchaining and setting up modern *bourgeois* society.'[90] Nor does the role of the individual in history simply concern heroes. 'In the history of the United States,' he observes in 1862, 'and of humanity, Lincoln will take his place directly next to Washington! ... Lincoln is not the offspring of a people's revolution. The ordinary play of the electoral system, unaware of the great tasks it was destined to fulfill, bore him to the summit – a plebeian, who made his way from stone-splitter to senator in Illinois, a man without intellectual brilliance, without special greatness of character, without exceptional importance – an average man of good will. Never has the New World scored a greater victory than in the demonstration that with its political and social organization, average men of good will suffice to do that which in the Old World would have required heroes to do!'[91]

The actuality of a *nation* or *culture* is crucial to an understanding of the *ultimate object* of dialectic method: the *social individual*. 'The relation of the individual to' his or her nation, writes Hegel, 'is that he appropriates to himself this substantial existence; that it becomes his character and capability, enabling him to have a definite place in the world – to be *something*. For he finds the being of the people to which he belongs an already established, firm world – objectively present to him – with which he has to incorporate himself.' The ideality of the individual is fused with a particular spirit, a particular view of the world that permeates all facets of his or her culture. 'It is within the limitations of this idiosyncrasy that the spirit of the nation, concretely manifested, expresses every aspect of its consciousness and will – the whole cycle of its realization. Its religion, its polity, its ethics, its legislation, and even its science, art, and mechanical skill, all bear its stamp. These special peculiarities find their key in that common peculiarity – the particular principle that characterizes a people.'[92] Accordingly, Hegel's social and political theory is an account of the emergence and growth of the principle of individual freedom and its realization in the Western (or German) world.

Similarly, Marx's *Capital* is not just a study of the bourgeois mode of production in the abstract; it also concerns the life and spirit of that classic bourgeois society – England. 'What I have to examine in this work,' he writes, 'is the capitalist mode of production, and the relations of production and forms of intercourse ... that correspond to it. Until now, their *locus classicus* has been England. This is the reason why England is used as the main illustration of the theoretical developments I make.'[93] In like fashion, he connects the rapid development of the United States with the enterprising character of the individuals who settled there[94] and infused its spirit with what, in another context, he calls 'one of the delusions carefully nurtured by Political Economy':

The truth is this, that in this bourgeois society every workman, if he is an extremely clever and shrewd fellow, and gifted with bourgeois instincts and favoured by an exceptional fortune, can possibly be converted himself into an *exploiteur du travail d'autrui* ['Exploiter of others' labour'] ... But where there was no *travail* to be *exploité*, there would be no capitalist nor capitalist production.[95]

Whatever the defects of this American dream, it also contains a core of truth: 'In the usual formulation [of political economy], an industrial people reaches the peak of its production at the moment when it arrives at its historical peak generally. In fact. The industrial peak of a people when its main concern is not yet gain, but rather to gain. Thus the Yankees over the English.'[96]

In order to grasp the spirit of a nation or people, dialectic method investigates its supreme intellectual productions – the art, religion, science, and philosophy created within it; these are the *comprehension in thought* of society and represent 'the progression of the total actuality evolved.' The object of Marx's theoretical effort, therefore, is certainly capitalism, but capitalism as expressed in the *categories of bourgeois political economy*. A particular philosophy or scientific system represents the ideas of its creator, but also the entire richness of the social universe to which the thinker belongs. 'Everything hangs on this,' states Hegel, 'these forms [of science and philosophy] are nothing else than the original distinctions in the Idea itself, which is what it is only in them.'[97] Feuerbach and Kant, for example, express in thought the determinate categories and relations that constitute bourgeois consciousness and reality. Although science and philosophy are products of society, they are above it in *form*, since they place society 'in the relation of object.' The merely *formal* difference between theory and society, however, becomes an *actual* difference because it is through thought that 'Mind makes manifest a distinction between knowledge and that which is; this knowledge is thus what produces a new form of development.'[98]

The dialectical science of Hegel and Marx is a product of bourgeois society; but it also anticipates and expresses the development of the free and independent social individual who will find his or her concrete existence in the rational, communist state.

2 DIALECTICAL EXPOSITION AND THE RATIONAL STATE

Dialectical exposition – the presentation of the results of dialectic method – is not historical in character, although it is commonly (and wrongly) assumed to refer mainly to history. Putting aside the time-order of events related to the object under study, dialectical exposition deals with the object as a living organism which, as it were, unfolds itself from itself. 'In order to develop the laws of bourgeois economy,' says Marx, 'it is not necessary to write the *real history of the relations of production*.' To present society as an 'organic whole' means to represent it in a manner 'corresponding to its concept'[99] – or as Hegel puts it, in a manner corresponding to 'the immanent self-differentiation of the concept.'[100] The concept, in turn, like the processes within a living body, develops in all its parts, not historically or in a certain time-order, but *simultaneously*. 'The simultaneity of the process of capital in different phases of the process is possible only through its division and break-up into parts, each of which is capital, but capital in a different aspect. This change of form and matter is like that in the organic body ... the shedding in one form and renewal in the other is distributed, takes place simultaneously.'[101]

Dialectic *method* may, of course, be applied to history, but the *exposition* of historical development is different from dialectical exposition in its pure form.[102] Hegelian logic, for example, shows the movement of the categories in purely necessary, i.e., rational and non-historical, terms. In the history of philosophy, however, their appearance followed a particular time-order which differs in some respects from the logical one. Dialectical exposition in history, 'shows the different stages and moments in development, in manner of occurrence, in particular places, in particular people or political circumstances, the complications arising thus, and, in short, it shows us the empirical form.'[103]

Dialectical exposition must start from the most *abstract* form of the object under study, but also from its most *universal* and *necessary* aspect. 'The Idea,' writes Hegel, referring to both consciousness and society,

> must further determine itself within itself continually, since in the beginning it is no more than an abstract concept. But this original abstract concept is never abandoned. It merely becomes richer in itself and the final determination is therefore the richest. In this process its earlier, merely implicit, determinations attain their free self-subsistence but in such a way that the concept remains the soul which holds everything together and attains its own proper differentiation only through an immanent process.[104]

Since dialectical exposition begins with the simplest and most abstract conceptions, the sequence of the categories at some points may be similar to their appearance in history.[105] But in relation to application of dialectic method this similarity is purely fortuitous.

The absolute idea in Hegel's speculative logic – which, as I have argued, is the logical or theoretical expression of the relation of the social individual with the rational state – is the final category of logic. But it also includes being – the first category. The absolute idea, or rational state, is the richest and most developed form of (social) being. Accordingly, speculative logic concerns 'the knowledge that the idea is the one systematic whole.'[106] Similarly, the ultimate category in the *Philosophy of Right* – the rational state – includes the first category, i.e., 'the absolutely free will' of the social individual. 'In the state self-consciousness finds in an organic development the actuality of its substantive knowing and willing.'[107] Marx begins *Capital* with the commodity – the most abstract and universal category within capitalist society. The final chapters of *Capital* are concerned with the social relations developed around the commodity, i.e., private property *and* its abolition within the capitalist mode of production, first by the monopoly of the capitalist class, and then by socialist revolution.

Dialectical exposition presents the object of method in its *highest* or *ideal form*; in the same way, the *moments* or *aspects* of the object are displayed in their most extreme or purest configuration. This makes it possible to find in the object the means both to comprehend less developed forms and to anticipate future developments.[108] 'Our method,' says Marx,

indicates the points where ... bourgeois economy as a merely historical form of the production process points beyond itself to earlier historical modes of production ... These indications ... together with a correct grasp of the present, then also offer the key to the understanding of the past ... This correct view likewise leads at the same time to the points at which the suspension of the present form of production relations gives signs of its becoming – foreshadowings of the future.[109]

If the order of the categories in the *Philosophy of Right* has little to do with their historical succession 'in the *actual* world,'[110] this order is of supreme importance for understanding the Hegelian state: 'a philosophical division is far from being an external one.'[111] The concrete formations leading up to the rational state prove its dialectical necessity. Both the family and civil society – social categories that precede the *exposition* of the state (though not its *development* in history) – are 'stages or factors' which 'as actualities ... are yet at the same time to be viewed as forms only, collapsing and transient.'[112] Accordingly, Hegel examines the dissolution of the patriarchal family in civil society, along with the moments that lead to the '*splitting up*' and integration of civil society into the rational state.[113] The family and civil society are only the 'finite phase' of the rational state, a phase which is necessary 'only in order' for the consciousness of the social individual 'to rise above its ideality and become explicit as infinite actual mind.'[114]

'We should desire,' remarks Hegel, 'to have in the state nothing except what is an expression of rationality. The state is the world which mind has made for itself; its march therefore, is on lines that are fixed and absolute ... The state [is] a secular deity.'[115] The state Hegel refers to resembles Marx's communist society where social relations 'generally present themselves to [the individual] in a transparent and rational form,' and social production is 'under [the] conscious and planned control' of individuals.[116] But the rational society Hegel envisions has nothing to do with the abstraction of the 'withering away of the state.'[117] The notion that the state in communist society must eventually disappear is based on the bourgeois conception of the *external state*, according to which the state is *antithetical* and *antagonistic* to the interests of the individual. For Hegel, however, the state is the chief instrument of *self-education* and *freedom* for the social individual. In communist society, therefore, the state does not wither away; rather, the antagonistic sphere of civil society is *integrated with* and *rationalized by* the state.

Progress towards the rational state does not involve a complete departure from the governing institutions of capitalist society. The bourgeois order, states Hegel, is a 'battlefield,' where private interests oppose particular interests of general concern, and both of these are locked in struggle with the state and its more universal outlook. The major combatants on the battleground of a mature civil society are first, the business class, a class divided from within but at the same time approaching a unity of interest among its members based on joint ownership of the means of production; and second, the universal class, a class increasingly allied with those poor and dispossessed who are excluded from the corporations of the business class. A third combatant, the agricultural class, loses prominence in the struggle as its basis in the soil is undermined by the economic forces of civil society. The network of conflict and compromise which unites the contenders for power in bourgeois society constitutes the living core of the nascent rational state. With the development of the social state, classes as groups with unequal privileges and wealth disappear. But classes as groups of individuals organized in a corporate whole and performing varied and diverse modes of social labour will remain; in fact, within the rational state a person's social class is the mediating institution between the individual and government. Membership in any social class – which in the rational state will be either the class of civil servants or the business class – is completely open to the individual. Wealth and birth play no part in distinctions of class within the rational state.[118]

Transcending the class character of civil society by giving it a political form, Hegel's rational state sublates the alienated politics of the bourgeoisie into a democratic class politics. The result is a mode of government which resembles the liberal capitalist state in form but departs from it in content. In bourgeois political theory the state is composed of three main elements: the legislature or parliament, the judiciary, and the executive. Each element features a system of checks and balances on the powers of the other two. There are also three elements in Hegel's social state, but these are separate aspects of a unitary process of government rather than autonomous, conflicting powers. The judiciary is part of the executive instead of a separate entity; similarly, the government bureaucracy, the police, and the military, described by some writers as independent elements of the state, are actually aspects of the executive power. The three moments of the rational state are the *head of state*, the *executive*, and the *estates* or parliament. The executive and parliament correspond to the chief actors in civil society; members of the universal class make up the larger part of the executive, while the legislature mostly represents the claims of the business class and the corporations.

Organized as the state executive, the universal class of civil servants is responsible for the over-all guidance and administration of civil society; particular functions within the sphere of industry and production are carried out by the democratic corporations of the business class. The estates or parliament are formed by popularly elected representatives from the corporations. In this way, the electorate avoids the atomization and alienation intrinsic to the democratic set-up of the external state. Since deputies from the corporations are elected by the business or working class itself, they 'eo ipso adopt the point of view of society, and their actual election is therefore either something wholly superfluous or else reduced to a trivial play of opinion and caprice ... The interest itself is actually present in its representative, while he himself is there to represent the objective element of his own being.'[119]

Although parliament is usually seen strictly as a body of elected representatives, it actually brings together the three elements of the state in the process of government, a process identical with the trinity relation, the rational syllogism that unites the individual with society. Thus the head of state (the individual) is also head of the legislature (the universal) and has the power of ultimate decision. Similarly, the executive (the particular) – whose senior ministers are chosen by the head of state from elected representatives in the estates – belongs to the legislature in its capacity as an advisory body with specialized expertise and experience in areas of national concern.

Parliament guarantees general welfare and public freedom in the rational state as it is supposed to do in the liberal democratic one, but Hegel argues that the parliamentary guarantee is misconstrued by bourgeois political theorists, who believe the public has a deeper insight and knowledge of affairs than government bureaucracy. Accordingly, the estates are assumed to reflect the wisdom of the citizens and apply it to the problems of government. Hegel contends, however, that senior public servants and their professional and administrative personnel have a better understanding of the nation's organization and requirements than does the average citizen. Moreover, they are experienced and skilled in the mechanisms of government and are able to run it without parliament, which indeed they do when the legislature is in recess or otherwise engaged.

Parliament fulfils its role as guarantor of public freedom in the rational state first by virtue of the additional insight elected deputies offer bureaucracy and its ministers. The government learns how effectively its policies are applied and received at the local level through criticism and appraisal by the people's representatives, and it becomes aware of deficiencies and lacunae through the same process. Parliament also defends public freedom through its ability to influence the conduct of the bureaucracy; anticipation of criticism from the estates – and from elsewhere – induces officials to pay attention to their duties and administer programs in an efficient and responsible manner. The bureaucracy must expect criticism and discipline from parliament and the corporations and also from the head of state, who is anxious to maintain the legitimacy of his or her government.[120]

Hegel's rational state is suggestive for an analysis of contemporary liberal democratic society. The huge, modern bureaucracy, allied with state clients and public interest groups, may have its own class interests that could set it in opposition to dominant groups from civil society. Thus government initiatives in education, health, safety, and welfare may be seen as expressing the interests of the universal class and its constituency among the poor and unorganized (this is certainly how they are interpreted by the capitalist class in the United States). The Hegelian perspective also provides some powerful tools for understanding the complex relationship between government and the class structure of liberal democracy. If Hegel is correct, future political constituencies in liberal democratic society may be rooted in a functional rather than geographic network of representation, so that voters will elect candidates at the level of the business corporation, school, or government department. At the same time these organizations will be transformed through a process of conflict and struggle into organs of direct democracy and workers' control. The state apparatus itself will more and more become the self-conscious embodiment of the universal class and its allies, mediated at the top by the head of state and the upper levels of the executive, and from the bottom by corporations and parliament. In this form, the liberal democratic state could finally embrace the ethical principle Hegel called 'the final end of the state,' i.e., 'that *all* human capacities and *all* individual powers be developed and given expression in every way and in every direction.'[121]

Hegel is chiefly concerned with the state as it will exist in its *most concrete*, i.e., *rational, form*, but his theory results from an analysis of the affirmative aspects of already existing states. Accordingly, he is determined to justify the particular form taken by governments of his time, including the great influence wielded over the state by the class of landed property owners and the role of the monarchy. As I argued in Chapter 7, Hegel is convinced that the aristocracy's political influence will melt away along with its economic basis in civil society. Since positions of authority in the rational state are to be filled according to objective and rational criteria, rather than those of wealth or birth, the institution of primogeniture associated with aristocracy 'is nothing but a chain on the freedom of private rights, and either political meaning is given to it' – which, as Hegel makes clear, is out of the question in the rational state – 'or else it will in due course disappear.'[122]

Dialectic method deals 'with that which *is*'[123] and during Hegel's period, as he observes, 'in almost all European countries the individual head of the state is the monarch.' He is impatient with theorists who see nothing rational in the institution of constitutional monarchy, and who believe that a democratic republic is the only reasonable form of government. For Hegel, the question whether a republic or a constitutional monarchy is most to be preferred 'is quite idle,' precisely because 'such forms must be discussed historically or not at all.'[124]

The function of the constitutional monarch as outlined in the *Philosophy of Right* is actually consistent with that of any democratic national leader.[125] The head of state embodies the principle of individuality which runs through every democratic government and symbolically connects the leader's decision-making power with the will and rationality of each citizen. Personalization of political power, however, has nothing to do with despotic usurpation of authority; the power of the head of state is restricted simply to a choice of options offered by the state executive. As Hegel puts it, the monarch 'is bound by the concrete decisions of his counsellors, and if the constitution is stable, he has often no more to do than sign his name.' The appearance of power merely serves to disguise the leader's real subservience to the administrative mechanisms of government and ultimately to the organized will of every free citizen. Nevertheless, despite its illusory quality, the personal authority of the head of state 'as the final *subjectivity* of decision, is above all answerability for acts of government.'[126]

For Marcuse, along with many others, Hegel's rational state glorifies the Prussian monarchy and betrays 'his highest philosophical ideas. His political doctrine surrenders society to nature, freedom to necessity, reason to caprice ... Freedom becomes identical with the inexorable necessity of nature, and reason terminates in an accident of birth.'[127] But monarchy, constitutional or otherwise, will have no place in the rational state. When Hegel observes that the sovereign 'is raised to the dignity of monarchy in an immediate, natural, fashion, i.e. through his birth in the course of nature,' he is actually referring to the *finitude* and *transitory* character of the monarchy.[128] In a constitutional monarchy, '*birth* is the oracle – something independent of any arbitrary volition.'[129] But oracles of any kind are only required 'when men [have] not yet plumbed the depths of self-consciousness or risen out of their undifferentiated unity of substance to their independence.' The monarchy is a *flawed concept* because it lacks the character of rationality; it represents 'a single and natural existent without the mediation of a particular content (like a purpose in the case of action).' Princely power is only necessary as a counterpoise to the caprice and irrationality that characterize the development of civil society; it will disappear in the social state. The monarch, notes Hegel, 'is ... ungrounded objective existence (existence being the category which is at home in nature).'[130] But if this existence 'is at home in nature,' i.e., in the state of nature represented by the antagonisms and discord of bourgeois society, it will not be 'at home' in the rational state. Existence is a poor category since it refers to 'finite things' which 'are changeable and transient, i.e. ... existence is associated with them for a season, but that association is neither eternal nor inseparable.'[131]

Marx's mature work, as I have argued in this study, is devoted not only to the critical analysis of capitalism, but also to an investigation of the presuppositions of the rational or communist state. He explores the conditions for transcending bourgeois society that are formed within the capitalist mode of production itself. But he never went beyond the *economic* study of capitalism. In particular, he did not produce a comprehensive theory of the state; nor did he develop an aesthetic, or a critical examination of the history of thought. There is no confrontation with the categories of logic in Marx; and the reader will look in vain for a Marxist psychology or philosophy of nature or a system of law. Hegel, however, did produce a great deal of comprehensive work in all these subjects. Moreover, his efforts are informed by the same dialectic method that led Marx and him to identical conclusions about bourgeois political economy.

One reason for the superiority of scope and range in Hegel's thought over that of Marx is that Marx had no established income or position, and spent much of his life in unsettled conditions and strenuous political activity. Hegel had much more time, and the financial independence provided by state teaching and university posts, to devote his attention entirely to theory. But there is another, and perhaps more crucial, difference in their personal biographies. Hegel's was the age of the French Revolution and the incredible march of Napoleon's 'army of liberation' over the whole of Europe; Marx's was the age of Louis Bonaparte. Hegel's contemporaries formed the élite of classical German idealism, literature, and music: Kant, Schiller, Fichte, Schelling, Hölderlin, Goethe, Beethoven, and others were among his coevals, and some were his personal friends. Except for Heinrich Heine, Marx had only Engels, Feuerbach, and the other members of the Young Hegelians. However accomplished these thinkers were, they stood nowhere near the likes of Kant or even Schelling. Most of them are known today only through their association with Marx.[132] In England, of course, Marx was surrounded by the shallowest empiricism.

Marx was intensely aware of his isolation, an isolation made all the more bitter because he alone among the thinkers of his generation had a profound comprehension of Hegel. His grasp, as I have argued, was faulty; but without him, the mystery surrounding dialectic would, no doubt, be impenetrable. Marx did not transcend Hegelian philosophy; he merely developed and amplified ideas already available in the discussion of civil society in the *Philosophy of Right*. That he did so in a form and manner much more accessible to the intellectual climate of high capitalism than Hegel's more philosophical approach is self-evident.

The division commonly made between Hegel and Marx is illusory; the parallels between their theories are much more compelling than the differences. Based on the arguments in this book, there may be a large field of theoretical work and endeavour available to students of Marx. A new synthesis of Marx with Hegel might provide significant insights into diverse areas of theory and practice – insights that could transform contemporary Marxism and nourish the struggle for individual freedom and the rational state.

Abbreviations

A	Additions to *PR* drawn from notes taken at Hegel's lectures.
ACW	Karl Marx, *On America and the Civil War*, ed. and trans. Saul K. Padover (New York 1972)
Aesth.	*Hegel's Aesthetics: Lectures on Fine Art*, trans. T.M. Knox (Oxford 1975), 2 vols.
BW	Karl Marx and Friedrich Engels, *Basic Writings on Politics and Philosophy*, ed. Lewis S. Feuer (Garden City N.Y. 1959)
Cap., I	Karl Marx, *Capital: A Critique of Political Economy*, vol. 1, intro. by Ernest Mandel, trans. Ben Fowkes (London 1976)
Cap., III	Karl Marx, *Capital: A Critique of Political Economy*, vol. 3, ed. Frederick Engels, (New York 1967)
CCT	Karl Marx, *The Cologne Communist Trial*, trans. Rodney Livingstone (New York 1971)
CPE	Karl Marx, *A Contribution to the Critique of Political Economy*, ed. Maurice Dobb (New York 1970)
CPR	Karl Marx, *Critique of Hegel's 'Philosophy of Right'*, trans. Annette Jolin and Joseph O'Malley, ed., Joseph O'Malley (Cambridge 1970)
CR	G.W.F. Hegel, *The Christian Religion: Lectures on the Philosophy of Religion. Part III. The Revelatory, Consummate, Absolute Religion*, ed. and trans. Peter C. Hodgson (Missoula MT 1979)
CW	Karl Marx and Frederick Engels, *Collected Works* (New York 1975-82)
Enc. Logic	*Hegel's Logic, Being Part One of the Encyclopaedia of the Philosophical Sciences (1830)*, trans. William Wallace, with foreword by J.N. Findlay (Oxford 1975)

EPM   Karl Marx, *Economic and Philosophic Manuscripts of 1844*, ed. Dirk J. Struik (New York 1964)

ET   Karl Marx, *Early Texts*, trans. and ed. David McLellan (Oxford 1971)

ETW   G.W.F. Hegel, *Early Theological Writings*, trans. T.M. Knox (Chicago 1948)

EW   Karl Marx, *Early Writings*, trans. and ed. T.B. Bottomore (New York 1964)

GI   Karl Marx and Frederick Engels, *The German Ideology* (Moscow 1968)

GR   Friedrich Engels, *The German Revolutions: The Peasant War in Germany and Germany: Revolution and Counter-Revolution*, ed. Leonard Krieger (Chicago 1967)

Grund.   Karl Marx, *Grundrisse: Foundations of the Critique of Political Economy (Rough Draft)*, trans. Martin Nicolaus (Harmondsworth 1973)

Hist. of Phil.   *Hegel's Lectures on the History of Philosophy*, trans. E.S. Haldane and Frances H. Simson (New York 1974), 3 vols.

KM   *Karl Marx: Economy, Class and Social Revolution*, ed. Z.A. Jordan (London 1971)

LPH   G.W.F. Hegel, *Lectures on the Philosophy of World History. Introduction: Reason in History* trans. H.B. Nisbet, with intro. by Duncan Forbes (Cambridge 1975)

Phen.   *Hegel's Phenomenology of Spirit*, trans. A.V. Miller with analysis of the text and foreword by J.N. Findlay (Oxford 1977)

Phil. of Hist.   G.W.F. Hegel, *The Philosophy of History*, trans. J. Sibree (New York 1956)

Phil. of Mind   *Hegel's Philosophy of Mind, Being Part Three of the Encyclopaedia of the Philosophical Sciences (1830)*, trans. William Wallace with *Zusätze* trans. by A.V. Miller (Oxford 1971)

Phil. of Nat.   *Hegel's Philosophy of Nature, Being Part Two of the Encyclopaedia of the Philosophical Sciences (1830)*, trans. A.V. Miller, with foreword by J.N. Findlay (Oxford 1970)

Phil. of Rel.   G.W.F. Hegel, *Lectures on the Philosophy of Religion*, trans E.B. Speirs and J. Burdon Sanderson, ed. E.B. Speirs (New York 1962) 3 vols.

Pol. Writ.   *Hegel's Political Writings*, trans. T.M. Knox, with intro. by Z.A. Pelczynski (Oxford 1964)

PP   Karl Marx. *The Poverty of Philosophy: Answer to the 'Philosophy of Poverty' by M. Proudhon* (Moscow n.d.)

PR	*Hegel's Philosophy of Right*, trans. T.M. Knox (Oxford 1967)
R	Remarks: Explanatory notes added by Hegel to paragraphs in *Phil. of Nat.* and PR
RMP	Karl Marx, Frederick Engels, and V.I. Lenin. *Reader in Marxist Philosophy*, ed. Howard Selsam and Harry Martel (New York 1963)
SC	Karl Marx and Frederick Engels, *Selected Correspondence*, sec. ed. (Moscow 1965)
Sc. of Logic	*Hegel's Science of Logic*, trans A.V. Miller with foreword by J.N. Findlay (London 1969)
SW	Karl Marx and Frederick Engels, *Selected Works* (Moscow 1969), 3 vols.
System	G.W.F. Hegel, *System of Ethical Life (1802/3) and First Philosophy of Spirit (Part III of the System of Speculative Philosophy (1803/4)*, ed. and trans. H.S. Harris and T.M. Knox (Albany 1979)
z	*Zusätze*: Hegel's own lecture notes, and those of students who attended his lectures, along with other addenda annexed to Hegel's text by his editors. These appear in *Enc. Logic, Phil. of Mind*, and *Phil. of Nat.*

Notes

INTRODUCTION

1 See, for example, Jerrold Seigel, *Marx's Fate: The Shape of A Life* (Princeton 1978), and Fritz J. Raddatz, *Karl Marx: A Political Biography* trans. Richard Barry (Toronto 1978)
2 *Collected Works*, volume 38 (London: 1963)
3 Editor's Preface to 'Philosophical Notebooks,' 17
4 Trans. Ben Brewster, (London 1969)
5 Heiss's book was published in German. It was translated into English 12 years later as *Hegel, Kierkegaard, Marx: Three Great Philosophers Whose Ideas Changed the Course of Civilization*, trans. E.B. Garside (New York 1975), 172.
6 *The Young Hegel*, trans. Rodney Livingstone (London 1975), 358, 352
7 Martin Kitchen, *The Political Economy of Germany 1815-1914*

(Montreal 1978), 24-5, 27; Theodore S. Hamerow's standard work, *Restoration, Revolution, Reaction: Economics and Politics in Germany 1815-1871* (Princeton 1958), 3-4
8 Helmut Böhme, *An Introduction to the Social and Economic History of Germany: Politics and Economic Change in the Nineteenth and Twentieth Centuries* (Oxford 1978), 22
9 *Cap.*, I, 91
10 2 vols. (London 1767). Hegel's thorough examination of Steuart is discussed in H.S. Harris, *Hegel's Development: Toward the Sunlight* (London 1972), 434-6.
11 Kitchen, *The Political Economy of Germany*, 21; Böhme, *Social and Political History of Germany*, 18-19
12 *Cap.*, I, 97. See also E.J. Hobsbawm, *Industry and Empire: The Pelican Economic History of Britain*, vol. 3, *From 1750 to the Present Day* (1969), 94-5; E.P.

Thompson, *The Making of the English Working Class* (Harmondsworth 1963), 782.
13 Hobsbawm, *Industry and Empire*, 73; also Jacques Droz, *Europe between Revolutions 1815-1848* (Glasgow 1967), 87-8
14 *Jenenser Realphilosophie*, ed. J. Hoffmeister (Leipzig 1931), II, 257, quoted in Raddatz, *Karl Marx,*226
15 Quoted in P.A.W. Paur, 'Social Theories of the Industrial Enterprise in Germany: From the Early Nineteenth Century to the Present,' PhD thesis, University of London, 1978, 94-5
16 Ibid. 64-5, 154
17 Droz, *Europe between Revolutions*, 54.
18 *Critique of Practical Reason*, trans. Lewis White Beck (Indianapolis 1956), 110

CHAPTER 1

1 *Cap.*, I, 103, 102
2 Franz Mehring, *Karl Marx: The Story of his Life*, trans. Edward Fitzgerald (Ann Arbor 1969), 308. The anecdote comes from Heinrich Heine, who was a student of Hegel's in the early 1820s.
3 *Cap.*, I, 103
4 Practically alone among Marxists, V.I. Lenin makes a genuine contribution to the understanding of Hegel; the debt I owe to Lenin's commentary on Hegel in the 'Philosophical Notebooks' (*Col-*

lected Works, vol 38, Moscow 1963) will be readily apparent.
5 *Cap.*, I, 103
6 *Sc. of Logic*, 48
7 Ibid, 782-3; also *PR*, §22, 30
8 *Phil. of Nat.*, §298R, 135
9 *Sc. of Logic*, 44
10 Ibid
11 Ibid, 39
12 *Phil. of Nat.*, §245, 4; also *Sc. of Logic*, 742
13 *PR*, §189, 126
14 *Phil. of Nat.*, §245, 4
15 *Cap.*, I, 285
16 *Sc. of Logic*, 734
17 Ibid, 742, 757
18 Ibid, 746, 747
19 *Enc. Logic*, §211, 273
20 *Sc. of Logic*, 750
21 Ibid, 747
22 Ibid, 31
23 *Cap.*, I, 283-4
24 *Phen.*, 239-40
25 *Sc. of Logic*, 748
26 *Sc. of Logic*, 581, 583; *Enc. Logic*, §164, 229
27 *Aesth.*, I, 31-2; also *PR*, §7, 23-4, where ideality or the process of particularization is identified with the freedom of the will.
28 On this point see the insightful discussion in Czeslaw Prokopczyk, *Truth and Reality in Marx and Hegel: A Reassessment* (Amherst 1980), 69-79.
29 *Sc. of Logic*, 437
30 Ibid, 837
31 *Cap.*, I, 289-90
32 *EPM*, 177
33 *Reason and Revolution: Hegel*

and the *Rise of Social Theory*, sec. ed. (New York 1954), 127, 203. In his 'Philosophical Notebooks' Lenin remarks on the crucial importance of the dialectics of labour for the later Hegel. Lenin's insights are mentioned but not developed further by Georg Lukács in *The Young Hegel: Studies in the Relations between Dialectics and Economics*, trans. Rodney Livingstone (London 1975).

34 *Enc. Logic*, §§204-12, 267-74; *Sc. of Logic*, 734-54

35 A recent version of this interpretation, which offers an interesting comparison of Hegel and Marx, appears in G.A. Cohen's *Karl Marx's Theory of History: A Defence* (Princeton 1978), 1-27. The best corrective to this view remains J.N. Findlay's *Hegel: A Re-Examination* (London, New York 1958). 'As a philosopher,' writes Findlay (348), 'Hegel believes in no God and no Absolute except one that is revealed and known in certain experiences of individual human beings.'

36 A similar treatment of finite teleology occurs in *Enc. Logic*, §209z, 272-3.

37 *LPH*, 85-93

38 *Aesth.*, I, 183

39 *PR*, 11

40 *Enc. Logic*, §198, 264-5

41 The influence on Marx of Hegel's notion of the universal or social individual is emphasized by Jerrold Seigel in his excellent biogra-

phy, *Marx's Fate: The Shape of a Life* (Princeton 1978). 'Like Marx, Hegel had regarded the existence of some form of "universal individual" as the precondition for ending the abstraction and isolation of modern society, hence opening the way to a fully developed human life (189). Although Seigel relies on the classic interpretation of Hegel as an idealist prone to 'speculative excesses,' and pays too little attention to Hegel's social theory, he nevertheless presents a fresh and inspired account of Marx's relationship with Hegel.

42 *PR*, §207z, 271; §207, 133; §308R, 200-1

43 *Hegel* (Cambridge 1975); *Hegel and Modern Society* (Cambridge 1979). 'Feuerbach and Marx,' writes Taylor, ' "anthropologized" Hegel's Spirit. What replaced Hegel's *Geist* was man, generic man. For Hegel, on the other hand, man must come to see himself as a vehicle of a spirit which was that of a broader reality, whose total embodiment was the universe. So that even at the summit of his development man remains in the presence of something greater than himself.' *Hegel*, 160

44 Joseph O'Malley, editor's introduction to *CPR*, xi-xii

45 They are included in *The Fiery Brook: Selected Writings of Ludwig Feuerbach*, trans. with an

introduction by Zawar Hanfi
(New York 1972), 153-246

46 'Preliminary Theses,' 154

47 CPR, §262, 7-8, 9

48 PR, §144, 105

49 Phil. of Mind, §482, 239-40

50 PR, §31, 34-5. In his classic analysis of the Hegelian theory of the state, Bosanquet remarks on the importance of Hegel's complete system for an understanding of Hegelian political theory. 'Hegel's Philosophy of Right (or of Law), though published by him as an independent work, is essentially an expansion of paragraphs which form one sub-division of his Philosophy of Mind, itself the third and concluding portion of the Encyclopaedia of Philosophy, of which the two earlier portions are the Logic and the Philosophy of Nature.' The Philosophical Theory of the State, sec. ed. (London 1958), 234

51 Sc. of Logic, 42

52 Phil. of Mind, §486, 243

53 Sc. of Logic, 31-7

54 Ibid, 757-8

55 Enc. Logic, §25, 46

56 PR, §264, 163; §258, 157

57 Ibid, §29R, 33

58 Hist. of Phil., III, 402

59 PR, §21, 29-30

60 Ibid, §11, 25

61 Phil. of Mind, §§521-2, 256

62 In Hegelian terminology, civil society also includes two other moments: the administration of justice, and institutions concerned

with integrating the individual into the community: government or public authority and the corporations. As discussed below, Hegel makes a sharp distinction between government as it appears in civil society and the state as an object of theory.

63 Hist. of Phil., III, 402

64 PR, §21, 29

65 Ibid, §28, 33; §27, 32

66 'Philosophy,' writes Hegel in the Phil. of Mind, 'awakes in the spirit of governments and nations the wisdom to discern what is essentially and actually right and reasonable in the real world ... for thought makes the spirit's truth an actual present, leads it into the real world, and thus liberates it in its actuality and in its own self.' §552, 285-6

67 LPH, 150-1

68 Ibid, 130

69 Phen., 111-19; Phil. of Mind, §§430-9, 170-8

70 LPH, 131 (italics removed from original).

71 See, for example, the discussion in Seigel, Marx's Fate, 203-5. Seigel observes that 'neither the fact of class struggle, the nature of the classes involved, nor even the prospect of a future order free of conflict and exploitation, were novel ideas when [Marx and Engels] began to employ them.'

72 This point is made also by Duncan Forbes in his introduction to LPH, vii-xxxvi. 'Since Hegel's

philosophy is not the "idealist" photographic negative, which Marx thought he was developing into a true picture, and since "civil society," which incorporates what Hegel called "the system of needs," is an essential aspect of the "Idea" of the modern state, and therefore of freedom properly conceived, Hegel's philosophy of history, in principle at any rate, incapsulates and postulates a materialist or economic interpretation of history,'(xxii).

73 PR, §194R, 128
74 Ibid, §28, 38
75 LPH, 69-70 (italics removed from original). See also Sc. of Logic, 821-3 and Enc. Logic §§233-5, 290-2
76 The parallels between the analyses of capitalism put forward by Hegel and Marx are emphasized in Robert Heiss's Hegel, Kierkegaard, Marx: Three Great Philosophers whose Ideas Changed the Course of Civilization, trans. E.B. Garside (New York 1975). A less satisfactory account appears in Shlomo Avineri's Hegel's Theory of the Modern State (Cambridge 1972)
77 E.g., Phil. of Mind, §533, 262-3
78 PR, §194, 128; §199, 129-30
79 Grund., 161
80 PR, §194, 128
81 Grund., 409
82 Lukács, for instance, refers to Hegel's 'resolute rejection of any thorough-going democracy, his

failure to recognize the productive energies in the lower classes.' The Young Hegel, 369. Similarly, Avineri: 'One looks in vain for [the working] class in Hegel's system of estates.' Hegel's Theory of the Modern State, 109

83 PR, §§197A 197, 270, 129; §§193-4, 128; §187R, 125
84 'Educational struggle,' says Hegel, is the means through which 'the subjective will ... attains objectivity within.' (PR, §187R, 124-5). As a moment in the development of self-consciousness this process occurs in the Philosophy of Mind under the rubric 'Self-consciousness Recognitive,' and concerns 'a life and death struggle' which 'ends in the first instance as a one-sided negation with inequality ... the status of master and slave' (Phil. of Mind, §§430-3, 170-3). Hegel's discussion of education in civil society in PR deliberately refers back to these paragraphs in the Philosophy of Mind.
85 PR, §243-4, 149-50
86 Although the dual structure of the agricultural class is recognized by most commentators, it is far from being accepted that Hegel's business class includes the proletariat. My arguments for this position appear below in Chapter 6, section 2.
87 Referring to the three classes of civil society as estates, a term which emphasizes their political as well as economic significance,

Hegel underlines the mutually antagonistic aspect of classes in a
passage which later found an echo
in the first lines of the *Communist
Manifesto*: 'Where civil society,
and with it the State, exists, there
arise the several estates in their
difference ... The history of constitutions is the history of the
growth of these estates, of the legal relationships of individuals
to them, and of these estates to
one another and to their centre'
(*Phil. of Mind*, §527, 258). In
a letter to me, Professor Tom Sea
observes regarding Hegel's use
of the term estates that 'The German word is "Stände", and ...
it includes a far broader array of
connotations and implications
than just the political and economic. "Stände" when used to refer to the representative institutions
of the German states is definitely
political, but "Stände" when used
to describe social groups refers
to status – social, political, economic, cultural, etc. The transla-
tors of Weber's *Wirtschaft and
Gesellschaft* chose 'status-group'
as a more appropriate equivalent
for this usage, and I would be
inclined to think that it was in this
broader sense that Hegel was
using the word.' Hegel refers to
the two different meanings of
Stände in *PR*, §303R, 198.

88 E.g., *Phil. of Mind*, §§488-91,
   244-5; *PR*, §71, 57
89 *PR*, §195, 128; §209, 134

90 Ibid, §§59-61, 49-50; §62, 50;
   §62R, 51
91 Ibid, §62R, 51
92 *Phil. of Mind*, §527, 258
93 *PR*, §§199-200, 129-30; see in
   addition, *Phil. of Mind*, §434,
   174, where the master-slave relation is shown to result in the
   creation of 'a *permanent* means
   and a provision which takes care
   for and secures the future.'
94 *PR*, §204, 132
95 *Phil. of Mind*, §527, 258
96 Ibid, §434, 174
97 *PR*, §203, 131
98 *Phil. of Mind*, §528, 258
99 *PR*, §238, 148
100 *Phil. of Mind*, §529, 259-60
101 *PR*, §203R, 132. In his criticism
    of Hegel's theory of the state,
    Marx makes much of the large
    role in government which Hegel
    assigns to the landed nobility
    and its principle of primogeniture.
    However, the whole force of He-
    gel's analysis suggests that the
    material foundation of the aris-
    tocracy crumbles with the devel-
    opment of bourgeois society; and
    with the death of its material
    life the aristocracy is likely to lose
    its political existence as well. I
    deal with this argument further in
    Chapter 7, section 2.
102 'It is quite clear that Hegel's con-
    ception of the universal class was
    founded on an academic model,
    and that he saw no clear separa-
    tion between the professoriat and
    other government functionaries ...

Thus it is the enlivening symbiosis of the academy and civil life that provides a key to the Hegelian notion of bureaucracy and the cultivation of the universal class.' George Armstrong Kelly, *Hegel's Retreat from Eleusis: Studies in Political Thought* (Princeton 1978), 215

103 *PR*, §§291 294 296, 190, 193

104 *CPR*, 72, 45

105 'Marx ... formulates the basic features of his own social and political theory through a systematic rejection of the agencies for social-political unity offered by Hegel.' O'Malley, 'Editor's Introduction,' *CPR*, li

106 *PR*, §§270R 288, 169, 189; §250, 152

107 Ibid, §290A, 291

108 Hegel's use of the word 'police' in this context has often been cited as yet another instance of his supposed Prussianism. But the meaning of the term in Hegel's day was much broader and far more positive than it is now, as evidenced by the following quotation: 'The purpose of policing is to ensure the good fortune of the state through the wisdom of its regulations, and to augment its forces and its power to the limits of its capability. The science of policing consists, therefore, in regulating everything that relates to the present condition of society, in strengthening and improving it, in seeing that all things contribute to the welfare of the members that compose it. The aim of policing is to make everything that composes the state serve to strengthen and increase its power, and likewise serve the public welfare.' Johann von Justi, *Eléments généraux de police* (1768), quoted in Jacques Donzelot, *The Policing of Families*, trans. Robert Hurley (New York 1979), 7

109 *PR*, §340, 215

110 *Phil. of Mind*, §523, 256-7; also *PR*, §§157 183, 110, 123

111 *PR*, §256, 154; *Phil. of Mind*, §532, 262

112 *Aesth.*, I, 48; also *Phil. of Mind* §539, 265-8

113 *PR*, preface, 10

114 The structure of the Hegelian state – which follows the syllogistic mode, individual, particular, universal, with these terms representing, respectively, the monarch, the executive and civil service, and the legislature – does not concern us here since it is dealt with in detail in Chapter 8. But it is worth mentioning that the role of the monarch, which has generated considerable criticism of Hegel, is not at all inconsistent with that played by democratically elected heads of state. Hegel is merely demonstrating the rationality of personal leadership, not of monarchy *per se*. See, for example, Bernard Bosanquet, *The Philosophical Theory of the State*, 264; Kelly, *Hegel's Retreat from*

Eleusis, 221; and Forbes, 'Introduction,' *LPH*, xxxiv
115 *PR*, §279, 182
116 *PR*, §270A, 283; *Phil. of Mind*, §502, 248; *PR*, §260, 161; §258R, 156
117 *Cap.*, I, 173
118 *Phil. of Mind*, §537, 264
119 *PR*, §270, 165
120 Ibid, §§297 255A, 193, 278
121 Ibid, §267, 163

CHAPTER 2

1 *Marxism and Hegel*, trans. Lawrence Garner (London 1973), 10, 25
2 *The Secret of Hegel: Being the Hegelian System in Origin, Principle, Form and Matter*, I (London 1865), 144
3 Herbert Marcuse, *Reason and Revolution: Hegel and the Rise of Social Theory*, sec. ed. (New York 1954), 167
4 Carl J. Friedrich, 'Introduction' (unpaginated) in *Phil. of Hist.*
5 Ibid
6 *Reason and Revolution*, 155
7 Ibid, 167
8 *Marxism and Hegel*, 19
9 *Hist. of Phil.*, II, 1, 96
10 Ibid, 21
11 Ibid, 2
12 Ibid, I, 439
13 Ibid, 291
14 Ibid, II, 13, 14
15 Ibid, 10
16 *The Open Society and Its Enemies*, vol. I: *Plato* (London 1957)
17 *Hist. of Phil.*, II, 9; I, 430; II, 96
18 Ibid, II, 25, 99
19 Ibid, 19
20 Ibid, I, 88; II, 19
21 *Hegel* (Cambridge 1975), 389
22 *Hist. of Phil.*, II, 20
23 Ibid, 30-1
24 Ibid, II, 31, I, 434
25 *LPH*, 126-7
26 *Phil. of Rel.*, I, 79
27 *Hist. of Phil.*, II, 24
28 See Walter Kaufmann, *Hegel: A Reinterpretation* (Notre Dame 1978), 271-2
29 *LPH*, 105
30 *Hist. of Phil.*, II, 24; also *LPH*, 81
31 *Hist. of Phil.*, II, 115; also *LPH*, 70-5
32 *Hist. of Phil.*, II, 24
33 Ibid, 97
34 *PR*, §274, 178-9
35 *Hist. of Phil.*, II, 97-8
36 Ibid
37 H.S. Harris, *Hegel's Development: Towards the Sunlight 1770-1801* (Oxford 1972), 63, 114
38 *Hist. of Phil.*, II, 30
39 *PR*, §203R, 131-2
40 *Hist. of Phil.*, II, 34
41 *Enc. Logic*, §67, 102-3
42 *Hist. of Phil.*, II, 34
43 Ibid, 37
44 *Marxism and Hegel*, 27
45 *Hist. of Phil.*, II, 36
46 *Enc. Logic*, §147z, 209; §181z, 245; §95, 139
47 *PR*, §7R, 23; *Hist. of Phil.*, II, 103, 75
48 *Hist. of Phil.*, I, 323-4

49 *Enc. Logic*, §95, 139
50 *PR*, §257, 155
51 *Hist. of Phil.*, II, 43, 44
52 *SW*, I, 14
53 *Hist. of Phil.*, II, 40-1
54 *PR*, §123A, 252
55 *Man and Society: A Critical Examination of Some Important Political Theories from Machiavelli to Marx*, vol. II (London 1976), 178
56 One of the best of these is Emil L. Fackenheim's *The Religious Dimension in Hegel's Thought* (Bloomington, IN 1967).
57 John Edward Toews shows that these splits already existed during Hegel's lifetime, in *Hegelianism: The Path toward Dialectical Humanism, 1805-1841* (Cambridge 1980), 141-99.
58 William J. Brazill, *The Young Hegelians* (New Haven 1970), 47
59 David McLellan, 'Introduction' to *ET*, xiv
60 Brazill, *The Young Hegelians*, 30
61 McLellan, 'Introduction,' xxi
62 Brazill, *The Young Hegelians*, 143
63 Ludwig Feuerbach, 'Preliminary Theses on the Reform of Philosophy' in *The Fiery Brook: Selected Writings of Ludwig Feuerbach*, trans. with an introduction by Zawar Hanfi (New York 1972), 168
64 *PP*, 186; *CCT*, 64; *PP*, 103
65 *From Hegel to Marx: Studies in the Intellectual Development of Karl Marx* (New York 1976), 15
66 *EPM*, 184

67 *CW*, IV, 192
68 *SW*, III, 340, 346. An interpretation of Hegel's attitude to religion similar to that of the later Marx and Engels is put forward by the French theorists Alexandre Kojève in *Introduction to the Reading of Hegel: Lectures on the 'Phenomenology of Spirit,'* ed. Allan Bloom, trans. James H. Nichols Jr (New York 1969), and Jean Hyppolite in *Genesis and Structure of Hegel's 'Phenomenology of Spirit,'* trans. Samuel Cherniak and John Heckman (Evanston, IL 1974).
69 'Philosophical Notebooks' in *Collected Works*, vol. 38 (London 1960)
70 *Politics and History: Montesquieu, Rousseau, Hegel and Marx*, trans. Ben Brewster (London 1972)
71 *SW*, I, 15
72 §234z, 291
73 *Reason and Revolution*, 161
74 'Philosophical Notebooks,' 104
75 *SW*, III, 340
76 'Philosophical Notebooks,' 248
77 *Hist. of Phil.*, I, 65, 9-10, 49
78 Ibid, I, 49, III, 402, 409
79 *CPR*, 137
80 *From Hegel to Marx*, 78
81 The uneasy relationship between Hegel and his followers and the Prussian censors is thoroughly documented in Toews, *Hegelianism*.
82 *Hist. of Phil.*, III, 480
83 Quoted in Georg Lukács, *The Young Hegel: Studies in the Rela-*

tions between Dialectics and Economics, trans. Rodney Livingstone (London 1975), 462
84 Ibid.
85 *Hist. of Phil.*, II, 22
86 Ibid, 11
87 *Phil. of Mind*, §573, 313
88 *Hist. of Phil.*, I, 91, 94
89 *Phil of Rel.*, I, 200
90 *Hist. of Phil.*, I, 73; III, 148
91 *EW*, 52-3
92 *Hist. of Phil.*, III, 159
93 *EW*, 52
94 Eugene Kamenka, *The Philosophy of Ludwig Feuerbach* (New York 1970), 117
95 *SC*, 151
96 *EW*, 44
97 Kamenka, *Feuerbach*, 94. As Marx W. Wartofsky observes, the 'substance ... and leading idea' of Feuerbach's critique 'is simple and even ancient: that man created the Gods and that the Gods embody man's own conception of his own humanity, his own wishes, fears, needs, and ideals.' *Feuerbach* (Cambridge 1977), 197
98 Kamenka, *Feuerbach*, 62, 37
99 *Hist. of Phil.*, I, 38
100 *Phil. of Rel.*, I, 41-2, 78
101 Ibid, 78-9
102 Shlomo Avineri, *Hegel's Theory of the Modern State* (Cambridge 1972), 30
103 *Hist. of Phil.*, III, 50
104 *PR*, §270R, 165, 167
105 *Cap.*, I, 493-4
106 *SW*, I, 14
107 *EW*, 202-3, quoted in Colletti,

Marxism and Hegel, 222
108 *CPE*, 20
109 *Hist. of Phil.*, II, 99; I, 55. See also Colletti, *Marxism and Hegel*, 255-7
110 *Phil. of Mind*, §573, 304
111 *The Works of Heinrich Heine*, vol. V, 'On Germany' (London 1892), 109
112 *Enc. Logic*, §24z, 42
113 *Hist. of Phil.*, II, 376, 375
114 Ibid, 376, 234, 235, 376-7
115 *Phil. of Hist.*, 308-9
116 *Hist. of Phil.*, III, 2-3
117 *Phil of Hist.*, 329-30
118 *Phil. of Rel.*, II, 323
119 *Phil. of Hist.*, 324
120 *Enc. Logic*, §194z, 260-1
121 *Hist. of Phil.*, II, 377
122 Ibid, II, 378; III, 40-1
123 Ibid, II, 380
124 *BW*, 168-9
125 *Phil. of Hist.*, 333, 328
126 *CR*, 194-5; *Phil. of Rel.*, III, 79-80
127 *Hist. of Phil.*, III, 3
128 *Phil. of Rel.*, I, 79-80
129 *Hist. of Phil.*, III, 4
130 *Phil. of Hist.*, 324; also 248-50
131 *Hist. of Phil.*, III, 4, 5
132 *Phil. of Rel.*, I, 244
133 *SW*, I, 14
134 *Hist. of Phil.*, III, 7-8
135 Ibid, 8
136 *Phil. of Hist.*, 331
137 *Hist. of Phil.*, III, 10
138 *Phil. of Rel.*, I, 17
139 *Phil. of Mind*, §482, 239-40
140 *From Hegel to Marx*, 47, 37
141 *Phil. of Mind*, §482, 240; *Phil. of Hist.*, 335

142 Hegel's dark vision of the decay
and death of Christianity occupies
the last pages of his *Lectures on
the Philosophy of Religion* (III,
149-51). See also *CR*, 294-7. Peter
C. Hodgson offers a valuable
commentary on these pages in his
notes and appendix to *CR* (309-
11, 346-8).
143 *Hist. of Phil.*, I, 81
144 *Cap.*, I, 173
145 *Phil. of Mind*, §482, 240; also
Phil. of Hist., 334
146 *Phil. of Hist.*, 334
147 *Hist. of Phil.*, III, 21-2
148 *Phil. of Hist.*, 335
149 *Hist. of Phil.*, III, 22, 105

CHAPTER 3

1 'Preliminary Theses' in *The Fiery
Brook: Selected Writings of Ludwig Feuerbach*, trans. with an
introduction by Zawar Hanfi
(New York 1972), 157
2 Eugene Kamenka, *The Philosophy
of Ludwig Feuerbach* (New York
1970), 62
3 *The Essence of Christianity*, trans.
George Eliot (New York 1957),
255
4 *SC*, 423
5 *Hist. of Phil.*, III, 13-14
6 *Phil. of Rel.*, I, 28
7 *Cap.*, I, 494
8 *Phil. of Rel.*, I, 2-3 'As soon as
theology ceases to be a rehearsal
of what is in the Bible, and goes
beyond the words of the Bible,

and concerns itself with the character of the feelings within the
heart, it employs forms of thought
and passes into thought.' Ibid, II,
343; *CR*, 23-4
9 *Enc. Logic*, §§36z, 57; 194z, 261
10 *Hist. of Phil.*, III, 50-1
11 Ibid, 51. The 'absolute result' of
the Crusades is 'the conviction
that man must look within himself
for that *definite embodiment* of
being which is of a divine nature:
subjectivity thereby receives absolute authorization, and claims
to determine for itself the relation
[of all that exists] to the Divine.'
Phil. of Hist., 393
12 *Hist. of Phil.*, III, 43
13 *Hegel* (Cambridge 1975), 494,
481
14 *Phil. of Rel.*, I, 70; *CR*, 137; *Phil.
of Rel.*, III, 51
15 *Hegel*, 571, 481
16 *Phil. of Mind*, §564, 298
17 *Hegelianism and Personality*
(Edinburgh 1892), 196, 242
18 *Phil. of Rel.*, I, 205
19 *Phen.*, 348
20 *Phil. of Rel.*, I, 7
21 Ibid, 2; *CR*, 78; *Phil. of Rel.*, III,
11
22 *Enc. Logic*, §159, 222
23 *Phil. of Hist.*, 445
24 *Hist. of Phil.*, II, 115
25 *Phil. of Rel.*, I, 228; also *Phil. of
Hist.*, 443
26 *Hist. of Phil.*, III, 53-4
27 Ibid, I, 92
28 *Phil. of Hist.*, 380
29 *Hist. of Phil.*, III, 41-2

30 Ibid, 42, 98
31 *Phil. of Rel.*, I, 7-8
32 *Phil. of Hist.*, 355
33 *Phil. of Rel.*, I, 9
34 Ibid.
35 *Phil. of Mind*, §389, 33
36 *Phil. of Rel.*, I, 10
37 Ibid, II, 13, 15
38 *RMP*, 240
39 *Phil. of Rel.*, I, 30, 36
40 *CR*, 82, 219; *Phil. of Rel.*, III, 25, 99
41 *Phil. of Mind*, §571, 301
42 *CR*, 13; *Phil. of Rel.*, II, 335
43 *Phil. of Mind*, §568, 300
44 *Phen.*, 325-6
45 *Phil. of Mind*, §§436 436z, 176
46 *CR*, 187; *Phil. of Rel.*, III, 83
47 *CR*, 144-5; *Phil. of Rel.*, III, 57
48 *Phil. of Hist.*, 407
49 *Phil. of Mind*, §§569-70, 300-1
50 *Hist. of Phil.*, I, 105, 100, 99, 97
51 *BW*, 480. This well-known passage is strikingly similar to Hegel's description of Oriental despotism in the *Philosophy of Right* (§355, 221-2).
52 *Phil. of Mind*, §377z, 2; 384z, 20; also *PR*, §356, 221
53 *Grund.*, 110
54 *Enc. Logic*, §147z, 211; §50, 83-4
55 *Phil. of Mind*, §384z, 19-20
56 Ibid, §381z, 9
57 *Hist. of Phil.*, II, 382-5
58 *Phil. of Mind*, §381, 8
59 *Phil. of Rel.*, I, 30
60 *Enc. Logic*, §92z, 137
61 *Phen.* 467
62 *Marxism and Hegel*, trans. Law-rence Garner (London 1973), 269
63 *Principles of the Philosophy of the Future*, trans. Manfred H. Vogel (Indianapolis and New York 1966), 24, 30
64 *Enc. Logic*, §71f, 106
65 *Phil. of Mind*, §573, 304
66 Ibid, §573, 313, 304, 305
67 *Hegel*, 349
68 *Phil. of Mind*, §573, 312
69 *Marxism and Hegel*, 12, 19
70 *Phil. of Mind*, §573, 311
71 Ibid, §443z, 185-6
72 *Sc. of Logic*, 150
73 *Enc. Logic*, §95, 140; also *Sc. of Logic*, 154-5
74 *Sc. of Logic*, 138
75 *Hist. of Phil.*, II, 381
76 *Enc. Logic*, §42z, 69
77 *Marxism and Hegel*, 19
78 *Enc. Logic*, §96z, 141
79 Ibid, §98z, 145; §92z, 137
80 Ibid, §115, 167-8
81 *Sc. of Logic*, 159
82 *Enc. Logic*, §115z, 168; also 'Self-consciousness is ... the nearest example of the presence of infinity.' *Sc. of Logic*, 158
83 *Enc. Logic*, §119, 172
84 'Philosophical Notebooks,' *Collected Works*, vol. 38 (London 1960), 190
85 *Hist. of Phil.*, II, 148-9
86 Aristotle, 'Metaphysics', in *The Philosophy of Aristotle*, introduction and commentary by Renford Bambrough, trans. J.L. Creed and A.E. Wardman (London, Cambridge 1962), 126-8
87 *Hist. of Phil.*, II, 183; (Aristotle,

'Psychology,' in *Philosophy of Aristotle*, 247); 163 (Aristotle, 'Physics,' in *Aristotle: The Physics*, vol. I trans. Philip H. Wickstead and Francis M. Cornford (London 1957), 199)

88 *Hist. of Phil.*, II, 147. 'The cause of an *act* is the inner disposition in an active subject, and this is the same content and worth as the outer existence which it acquires through the deed.' *Sc. of Logic*, 561

89 *Hist. of Phil.*, I, 24, 26

90 *Cap.*, I, 287

91 Ibid, 532-3

92 *Enc. Logic*, §206, 270; §209, 272

93 *Cap.*, I, 284

94 *Enc. Logic*, §208, 272

95 *Sc. of Logic*, 746-7

96 *Phil. of Hist.*, 241

97 'Philosophical Notebooks,' 189

98 *Sc. of Logic*, 747

99 *Enc. Logic*, §208, 272

100 *Phen.*, 118. This discussion is summarized in *PR* (§§56-7, 47-8) and *Phil. of Mind* (§§430-5, 170-6).

101 *Phen.*, 240

102 *Cap.*, I, 283

103 *Phil. of Hist.*, 239

104 *Enc. Logic*, §209, 272-3, quoted in *Cap.*, I, 285

105 *Cap.*, I, 285. Compare Marx's account of the labour process with the following quotation from the *Enc. Logic* (§209, 272): 'Purposive action, with its Means, is still directed outwards, because the End is also *not* identical with the object, and must consequently first be mediated with it. The Means in its capacity of object stands, in this second premiss, in direct relation to the other extreme of the syllogism, namely, the material or objectivity which is presupposed. This relation is the sphere of chemism and mechanism, which have now become the servants of the Final Cause, where lies their truth and free notion. Thus the Subjective End, which is the power ruling these processes, in which the objective things wear themselves out on one another, contrives to keep itself free from them, and to preserve itself in them. Doing so, it appears as the Cunning of reason.' See also *Phil. of Nat.*, §245z, 5.

106 Herbert Marcuse, *Reason and Revolution: Hegel and the Rise of Social Theory* (sec. ed.), (New York 1954); Colletti, *Marxism and Hegel*

107 *From Hegel to Marx* (Ann Arbor 1976), 37

108 *Hegel*, 326. J.N. Findlay's account of finite teleology makes more sense than Taylor's, but Findlay also does not see the connection between teleology and the dialectics of labour. *Hegel: A Re-Examination* (London, New York 1958), 248-52. Nor does W.T. Stace who complains, as does Findlay, that there is 'no real deduction' or transition between the three moments of teleology and confesses

'that Hegel's meaning is here
obscure to me, but I doubt
whether it was clear to himself.'
The Philosophy of Hegel (New
York 1955), 275

109 *Enc. Logic*, §209z, 273
110 Because ideality has the power to
transform its object in accordance
with its own purposes, the object
itself is rendered a mere 'ideal.'
'The notion is this immediate
power; for the notion is the self-
identical negativity, in which the
being of the object is characterized
as wholly and merely ideal.' 'In
the fact that the End achieved is
characterized only as a Means
and a material, this object, viz. the
teleological, is there and then put
as implicitly null, and only
"ideal".' (*Enc. Logic*, §§208, 212;
271, 274) Similarly, 'the ego determines itself in so far as it is the
relating of negativity to itself.
As this self-relation, it is indifferent to this determinacy; it knows
it as something which is its own,
something which is only ideal,
a mere possibility ...' (*PR*, §7, 23)
111 *Sc. of Logic*, 740
112 *Enc. Logic*, §212, 274
113 *PR*, §28, 32-3
114 *Enc. Logic*, §213, 275
115 Ibid, §213z, 276
116 *GI*, 198
117 *Enc. Logic*, §214, 278
118 *Phil. of Mind*, §§377 377z, 1
119 *Enc. Logic*, §194, 261
120 Trans. Talcott Parsons (New York
1958); originally published 1904-

5)
121 *Hist. of Phil.*, III, 106. Compare
with Weber's thesis also Hegel's
observations on Protestantism's
propensity to make 'men ... the
victims of a tormenting uncertainty as to whether the good
Spirit has an abode in them,' a
factor that made it 'indispensable
that the entire process of spiritual
transformation should become
perceptible to the individual himself.' *Phil. of Hist.*, 425
122 *Phil. of Mind*, §377z, 2
123 *Phil. of Hist.*, 37, 413, 407
124 *Hist. of Phil.*, III, 114
125 Ibid
126 *Phil. of Hist.*, 417-18
127 *Karl Marx and World Literature*
(Oxford 1976), 316
128 *Hist. of Phil.*, III, 114, 150
129 *Phil. of Rel.*, I, 249
130 Ibid, 245
131 *Phil. of Hist.*, 420; also *PR*,
§204A, 270-1; §256R, 154-5
132 *Cap.*, I, 152
133 *Phil. of Rel.*, I, I, 81; also *Phil. of
Mind*, §459, 213-18
134 *Hist. of Phil.*, III, 150
135 *GI*, 42, 504
136 In fact, Hegel anticipates Engels'
own analysis of the German rebellion. The peasant revolt at
Münster showed, he writes, in
Phil. of Hist., 419, that 'the world
was not yet ripe for a transformation of its political condition as
a consequence of ecclesiastical reformation.'
137 *GR*, 46

138 *The World Turned Upside Down:*
Political Ideas during the English
Revolution (Harmondsworth
1975), 139, 142, 148
139 *Hist. of Phil.*, I, 87
140 John Plamenatz, *Man and Society:*
A Critical Examination of Some
Important Social and Political
Theories from Machiavelli to
Marx, vol. II, (London 1976),
209-11
141 *Grund.*, 106
142 *Hist. of Phil.*, III., 158, 152. See
also *Phil. of Hist.*, 415
143 *Hist. of Phil.*, III, 154, 157, 158
144 *Phil. of Hist.*, 402
145 *Hist. of Phil.*, III, 159
146 *Cap.*, I, 247
147 *Hist. of Phil.*, III, 159, 148-9
148 Ibid, 160-1
149 'Enlightenment,' writes Hegel, 'is
caught up in the same internal
conflict that it formerly experienced in connection with faith,
and it divides itself into two parties. One party proves itself to
be victorious by breaking up into
two parties; for in so doing it
shows that it contains within itself
the principle it is attacking, and
thus had rid itself of the one-
sidedness in which it previously
appeared.' *Phen.*, 350-1
150 *KM*, 77
151 *Enc. Logic*, §133z, 190
152 *Hist. of Phil.*, III, 177
153 *Prolegomena to Any Future Meta-*
physics, ed. Lewis White Beck
(New York 1950), 66
154 *Phil. of Mind*, §573, 311

155 *Hist. of Phil.*, II, 155
156 *Karl Marx and World Literature*,
315
157 *Enc. Logic*, §130, 186
158 *Cap.*, I, 433, 165
159 'Second Part: Critique of Teleological Judgement,' in *Critique of*
Judgement, trans. James Creed
Meridith (Oxford 1973), 24
160 *Critique of Practical Reason*,
trans. Lewis White Beck (Indianapolis 1956), 8
161 *KM*, 80
162 *Critique of Judgement*, 22
163 *Enc. Logic*, §24z, 44; see also
PR, §56R, 147; §189, 126; §196,
128-9; *Phil. of Nat.*, §245, 4-5
164 *Phil. of Mind*, §389z, 34
165 *KM*, 79-80
166 *Hist. of Phil.*, III, 163-5
167 *SW*, I, 13
168 *Hist. of Phil.*, III, 166
169 *SW*, II, 13
170 'Philosophical Notebooks,' 191,
212-13
171 *Hist. of Phil.*, III, 167
172 Ibid, 167-9. Like Marx, Hegel
had reason to believe that admission to 'academies of learning'
is 'outwardly determined.' As
Walter Kaufmann observes, Hegel
'had not found it easy to fit into
the social structure of his time:
while a great many mediocrities
were appointed Professors of Philosophy, he was thirty-eight when
he settled down to his first decent
job – as headmaster of a boy's
secondary school – and he was
forty-six when he finally obtained

an academic chair.' *Hegel: A Reinterpretation* (Notre Dame 1978), 292

CHAPTER 4

1 *CPE*, 20
2 *SW*, I, 398
3 Louis Althusser, *Essays in Self-Criticism*, trans. Grahame Locke (London 1976), 95
4 Ibid, 94, 99, 178, 97
5 *For Marx*, trans. Ben Brewster (London 1969), 115
6 *Political Power and Social Classes*, trans. Timothy O'Hagan (London 1973), 12-13
7 *For Marx*, 115, 102
8 *PR*, §21A, 232; also §44R, 41-2
9 Geraldine Finn offers a provocative and unsettling argument for a direct relationship between Althusser's materialist theory and his personal practice in her polemical article, 'Why Althusser Killed His Wife,' *Canadian Forum*, Sept.-Oct. 1981
10 *Grund.*, 106
11 *PR*, 10; §21A, 231
12 *Grund.*, 460-1
13 *PR*, 10
14 *Grund.*, 483
15 Roman Rosdolsky, *The Making of Marx's 'Capital,'* trans. Pete Burgess (London 1977), 415
16 *Principles of the Philosophy of the Future*, trans. Manfred H. Vogel (Indianapolis and New York 1966), 36

17 *EPM*, 188
18 *Principles*, 70-1
19 *Phil. of Hist.*, 24, 20, 22
20 *SW*, I, 14
21 *PP*, 110-11; my emphasis
22 Manfred H. Vogel, Introduction, ix, in Feuerbach, *Principles*, 51
23 *KM*, 75, 72
24 *Principles*, 51
25 *SW*, III, 348
26 *Principles*, 64-5, 62-3. Feuerbach's doctrine requires 'that sensibility be *passive*, that it give what is there, that it not reflect or intrude consciousness upon the given, but that it deliver up the given *tout court*, as *really other*.' Marx Wartofsky, *Feuerbach* (Cambridge 1977), 348
27 Sebastiano Timpanaro, 'Considerations on Materialism,' *New Left Review*, 85 (1974), 7
28 *ET*, 124
29 *Principles*, 10, 68
30 Georg Lukács, *The Young Hegel: Studies in the Relations between Dialectics and Economics*, trans. Rodney Livingstone (London 1975), 533
31 *Philosophical Foundations of the Three Sociologies* (London, Henley, Boston 1977), 171
32 *SW*, I, 13
33 Sydney Hook, *From Hegel to Marx: Studies in the Intellectual Development of Karl Marx* (Ann Arbor 1976), 285
34 Dominique Lecourt, *Proletarian Science? The Case of Lysenko*, trans. Ben Brewster (London

1977), 104
35 *Principles*, 16-17
36 *From Hegel to Marx*, 267
37 Ludwig Feuerbach, 'Preliminary Theses on the Reform of Philosophy,' in the *Fiery Brook: Selected Writings of Ludwig Feuerbach*, trans. with an introduction by Zawar Hanfi (New York 1972), 172
38 *KM*, 73
39 Ibid, 84
40 *Principles*, 16-18
41 Ibid, 69-70
42 The young Marx is not so certain that mere sensation is above intelligence and will, but *EPM* contains many passages reminiscent of Feuerbach's sensationalism. The following one is characteristic: man 'is affirmed in the objective world not only in the act of thinking, but with *all* his senses ... The *forming* of the five senses is a labor of the entire history of the world down to the present ... Thus, the objectification of the human essence, both in its theoretical and practical aspects, is required to make man's *sense human*, as well as to create the *human sense* corresponding to the entire wealth of human and natural substance.' (140-1)
43 Anthony Giddens, *New Rules of the Sociological Method: A Positive Critique of Interpretive Sociologies* (London 1976), 15, 160
44 *KM*, 84
45 *Grund.*, 542

46 *PR*, §52, 45
47 *Enc. Logic*, §46, 74
48 *Phil. of Mind*, 377z, 1; 381z, 11
49 *PR*, §44, 41-2
50 *Phil. of Mind*, §381z, 13, 12
51 Ibid, §386, 22
52 *Phil. of Nat.*, §248R, 17
53 *Phil. of Mind*, §386, 22
54 *Cap.*, I, 164-5
55 Ibid, 165-7; my emphasis
56 Ibid, 167
57 Ibid, 173-5
58 *Phil. of Mind*, §386, 22
59 *Grund.*, 158, 159
60 Introduction, *Principles*, ix
61 *Enc. Logic*, §99z, 147; §104, 153. Also *Sc. of Logic*, 212-13
62 *Enc. Logic*, §104z, 154; also *Sc. of Logic*, 214-15
63 *Hist. of Phil.*, II, 150
64 *Ideology and Utopia* (London 1936), 165
65 *Sc. of Logic*, 53
66 Paul Feyerabend, *Against Method: Outline of An Anarchistic Theory of Knowledge* (London 1978), 302
67 *PR*, §52R, 46
68 *Compact Edition of the Oxford English Dictionary*, vol. I, (1971), 55
69 *Cap.*, I, 1056, 1061
70 Ibid, 1058, 1053
71 *Grund.*, 462
72 *Enc. Logic*, §§148-9, 211-12
73 *Cap.*, I, 1054, 990
74 *Marxism and Philosophy*, trans. Fred Halliday (London 1970), 97
75 *Grund.*, 712
76 *Cap.*, I, 982, 1055

77 *Marxism and Philosophy*, 129
78 *Enc. Logic*, §62, 96
79 *Principles*, 1xxiii, 45
80 *KM*, 79
81 *Enc. Logic*, §38z, 63-4; also *PR*, §52R, 45
82 Karl R. Popper and John C. Eccles, *The Self and Its Brain* (London 1977), 6-7
83 *Enc. Logic*, §38, 62
84 *Hist. of Phil.*, III, 433-6; also *Phil. of Nat.* §§254-61, 28-44
85 *Enc. Logic*, §26, 47. This 'reflection theory of thought' became the mainstay of dialectical materialism as it was developed from Engels through to Lenin and Stalin (Z.A. Jordan, *The Evolution of Dialectical Materialism* (London 1967) and survives outside the Soviet Union in much of the writings of Western Marxism. Writing in 1930, Korsch observes that this ' "philosophical" outlook was ... dispensed from Moscow to the whole of the Western Communist world. Indeed it formed the basis of the new orthodox theory, so-called "Marxism-Leninism".' *Marxism and Philosophy*, 122-3
86 Immanuel Kant, *Prolegomena to Any Future Metaphysics*, ed. Lewis White Beck (Indianapolis 1950)
87 *Phil. of Mind*, 400, 73
88 *Critique of Pure Reason*, trans. J.M.D. Meiklejohn (London 1893), 46
89 *Enc. Logic*, §23, 36
90 Ibid, §38z, 64

91 *Cap.*, I, 1006
92 *Grund.*, 159
93 *Enc. Logic*, §19z, 28-9
94 'The weaknesses of the abstract materialism of natural science, a materialism which excludes the historical process, are immediately evident from the abstract and ideological conceptions expressed by its spokesmen whenever they venture beyond the bounds of their own speciality.' *Cap.*, I, 494
95 The emerging feminist assessment of natural science as a sexist ideology that emphasizes dominance, control, and violence is redolent of the Hegelian critique and presents some of the best evidence for the reactionary character of the hard sciences. See, for example, Geraldine Finn, 'Women and the Ideology of Science,' *Our Generation*, vol. 15, no. 1 (winter 1982), 40-50; Brighton Women and Science Group, *Alice through the Microscope: The Power of Science over Women's Lives* (London 1980); Carolyn Merchant, *The Death of Nature: Women, Ecology and the Scientific Revolution* (New York 1980); Susan Griffin, *Women and Nature: The Roaring inside Her* (New York 1978)
96 Karl R. Popper, *Conjectures and Refutations: The Growth of Scientific Knowledge* (London and Henley 1976), 100, 102
97 *New Rules*, 137; also Thomas Kuhn, *The Structure of Scientific*

Revolutions, sec. ed. (Chicago 1970), 24-5
98 *Sc. of Logic*, 49
99 *Hist. of Phil.*, I, 4-5
100 Benton, *Philosophical Foundations*, 141
101 *Hist. of Phil.*, I, 379.
102 *Enc. Logic*, §121z, 176; §38, 61-2; also *Phil. of Nat.* §261R, 42
103 *New Rules*, 137-8
104 *Cap.*, I, 1055, 959, 966, 967
105 *New Rules*, 140
106 *Hist. of Phil.*, I, 10, 56
107 *Cap.*, I, 1063, 998

CHAPTER 5

1 George Lukács, *History and Class Consciousness: Studies in Marxist Dialectics*, trans. Rodney Livingstone (Cambridge MA 1971), 111
2 Immanuel Kant, *Critique of Pure Reason*, trans J.M.D. Meiklejohn (London 1893), 210-11
3 Karl R. Popper, *Conjectures and Refutations: The Growth of Scientific Knowledge* (London and Henley 1976), 191
4 *Enc. Logic*, §47, 75
5 *Phil. of Mind*, §386, 22
6 *Cap.*, I, 167
7 *Conjectures and Refutations*, 181
8 *Prolegomena to any Future Metaphysics*, ed. Lewis White Beck (Indianapolis, 1950), 27
9 *Cap.*, I, 167
10 *Enc. Logic*, §60, 38; also *Sc. of Logic*, 595
11 *Cap.*, I, 174

12 Ibid, 477
13 *PR*, §189A, 268; §189R, 126-7
14 Lucio Colletti, *Marxism and Hegel*, trans. Lawrence Garner (London, 1973)
15 Ted Benton, *Philosophical Foundations of the Three Sociologies* (London, Henley, Boston 1977)
16 Lucio Colletti, 'A Political and Philosophical Interview,' in *Western Marxism: A Critical Reader*, ed. New Left Review (London 1977), 325
17 *Enc. Logic*, §86z, 125-6
18 *Sc. of Logic*, 61
19 *Enc. Logic*, §22z, 35
20 *Prolegomena*, 29-30
21 *Sc. of Logic*, 589
22 *Enc. Logic*, §41z, 67
23 *Critique of Pure Reason*, 82, 90-1, 308-9
24 *Sc. of Logic*, 589
25 'Interview,' 326-7
26 R.G. Collingwood, *The Principles of Art* (London 1975), 214
27 *Prolegomena*, 47
28 *Phil. of Mind*, §398, 66
29 *Marxism and Hegel*, 121
30 *Enc. Logic*, §42z, 71; *Phil. of Mind*, §437z, 178
31 *Cap.*, I, 174
32 'The possibility of a culture of the intellect which leaves the heart untouched, as it is said, and of the heart without the intellect – of hearts which in one-sided way want intellect, and heartless intellects – only proves at most that bad and radically untrue existences occur.' *Phil. of Mind*,

§445, 188

33 Ernest Mandel, Introduction, to *Cap.*, I, 16-17
34 *Grund.*, 101
35 *Enc. Logic*, §37z, 60
36 *Hist. of Phil.*, II, 13
37 *Grund.*, 101
38 *Enc. Logic*, §42z, 69-70; *Sc. of Logic*, 588-9
39 *SW*, III, 347
40 *History and Class Consciousness*, 131-3
41 See Susan Meld Shell, *The Rights of Reason: A Study of Kant's Philosophy and Politics* (Toronto 1980), 142
42 *Enc. Logic*, §82z, 120. See also *Phil. of Mind*, §442, 183-4.
43 'Philosophical Notebooks,' *Collected Works*, vol. 38 (London 1960), 219
44 *Phil. of Mind*, §443z, 185; §445z, 191; also §444, 186; §444z, 187
45 *Ibid*, §467z, 227; §465z, 224; §§467z 468, 227
46 'Philosophical Notebooks,' 213
47 *Phil. of Mind*, §469, 228; §469z, 229; §481, 238
48 *Enc. Logic*, §82, 120-1
49 *Sc. of Logic*, 31-2
50 *Enc. Logic*, §25, 46
51 *Ibid*, §22z, 35; §60z, 94; also *Sc. of Logic*, 25, 595
52 'Interview,' 327
53 *Enc. Logic*, §44, 72; §22z, 35; also *Sc. of Logic*, 121, 593-4
54 *Ibid*, §43z, 71; §50, 81. Ironically, the Hegelian critique of Kant's thing-in-itself includes the original version of a phrase Marx later used against Hegel's dialectic: 'It must be inverted, in order to discover the rational kernel within the mystical shell.' *Cap.*, I, 103
55 *Aesth.* I, 116
56 *Enc. Logic*, §43z, 71; §244, 296; also *Sc. of Logic*, 782
57 *Ibid*, §19z, 28; §13, 18
58 Karl Korsch, *Marxism and Philosophy*, trans. Fred Halliday (New York and London 1970), 59
59 *Enc. Logic*, §9, 13
60 *Phil. of Mind*, §426, 167
61 *Conjectures and Refutations*, 326
62 *Marxism and Philosophy*, 94
63 *Phil. of Mind*, §423z, 164; also *Sc. of Logic*, 414
64 *Sc. of Logic*, 489
65 Immanuel Kant, *Critique of Practical Reason*, trans. Lewis White Beck (Indianapolis 1956), 15, 68, 45
66 *PR*, §135R, 89-90; §135A, 254
67 *Critique of Practical Reason*, 30
68 *Enc. Logic*, §54, 87; also *PR*, §§135 135R, 89-90; §135A, 254
69 *Critique of Practical Reason*, 32, 33-4
70 *Enc. Logic*, §§54 54z, 87-8; §60, 93; also *PR*, §§135 135R, 89-90; §135A, 254
71 *Phil. of Mind* §440z, 180-1; also *Sc. of Logic*, 821
72 'Philosophical Notebooks,' 218-19
73 *Critique of Pure Reason*, 242
74 *Conjectures and Refutations*, 317
75 *Critique of Pure Reason*, 212

76 *Enc. Logic*, §48, 77; also *Sc. of Logic*, 423-4
77 *Conjectures and Refutations*, 327
78 *Enc. Logic*, §46, 74; §48, 77
79 *Hist. of Phil.*, III, 444-5
80 *Critique of Pure Reason*, 223
81 *Hist. of Phil.*, III, 448
82 *Cap.*, III, 817
83 *Enc. Logic*, §60, 92
84 *Cap.*, III, 819
85 *Sc. of Logic*, 440
86 *Phil. of Mind*, §426z, 167; §427z, 168; also *Enc. Logic* §60, 92
87 Ibid, §428, 169, §§430-5, 170-6; also *Phen.*, 111-19
88 *Enc. Logic*, §60, 92
89 *KM*, 143
90 *Enc. Logic*, §60, 92
91 *Phil. of Mind*, §431z, 171-2
92 *Cap.*, I, 414
93 *Phil. of Mind*, §433, 173
94 *PR*, §201A, 270
95 *Phil. of Hist.*, 258-9, 284-6, 85-6
96 *Phil. of Mind*, §434, 174
97 *SW*, I, 108
98 *Grund.*, 885
99 *PR*, §200, 130
100 *Phil. of Hist.*, 145
101 *Enc. Logic*, §58, 90; §57, 89; §24, 43. See also *Phil. of Nat.*, §§249 249R 249z, 20-2
102 *PR*, §200R, 130
103 *Enc. Logic*, §24z, 45
104 'On the Common Saying: "This May Be True in Theory, but It Does Not Apply in Practice",' in Hans Reiss, ed., H.B. Nisbet, trans., *Kant's Political Writings* (Cambridge 1970), 78; also, *The Philosophy of Law: An Exposition of the Fundamental Principles of Jurisprudence as the Science of Right* (Edinburgh 1887), §46, 167-8
105 *PR*, §§42R 43R, 40-1
106 *SW*, I, 111
107 *PR*, §238, 148
108 *SW*, I, 111
109 *PR*, §239, 148; §239A, 276
110 *SW*, I, 123-4
111 *PR*, §175, 117; §175A, 265
112 *Philosophy of Law*, §§22-3, 108-9; also Shell, *The Rights of Reason*, 150-1
113 *Phen.*, 275
114 *PR*, §166, 114; §164, 263
115 Ibid, §166R, 115; §238, 148
116 *Phil. of Mind*, §522, 256; *PR*, §176, 118; §238, 148
117 *Grund.*, 245
118 *PR*, §199, 129-30
119 *Grund.*, 158
120 *Phil. of Mind*, §423z, 164
121 *PR*, §41, 40, §56, 47
122 *Phil. of Mind*, §§436z 437, 176-7
123 *Grund.*, 831
124 *Phil. of Mind*, §437z, 178
125 *PR*, §44R, 42
126 *Phil. of Mind*, §469z, 229
127 *SW*, I, 127
128 *Grund.*, 245-6
129 *Cap.*, I, 256, 976
130 *PR*, §199, 130
131 *Cap.*, III, 815
132 *Cap.*, I, 977
133 *Grund.*, 247-50
134 *Cap.*, I, 980, 951
135 *Enc. Logic*, §115, 166
136 *Cap.*, I, 982

137 Ibid, 125
138 *Enc. Logic*, §118z, 171
139 *Cap.*, I, 126
140 Ibid, 102-3
141 *PR*, §63, 51-2
142 *Phil. of Mind*, §§493-4, 245
143 *Phen.*, 236-52. Earlier, less complete discussions appear in *System* 119-27 and 249-50.
144 *Phil. of Mind*, §494, 245
145 *PR*, §63, 52
146 Ibid, 51
147 *Lenin and Philosophy and Other Essays*, trans. Ben Brewster (London 1971), 87, 91
148 *Enc. Logic*, §§115z 116z, 168-9; also *PR*, §59, 49; §63, 51
149 *PR*, §63, 51; also *Enc. Logic*, §150, 213
150 *Cap.*, I, 128
151 Ibid, 129-30
152 *PR*, §67, 54
153 *Cap.*, I, 271
154 *PR*, §67, 54
155 *Cap.*, I, 272-3
156 *PR*, §195, 128
157 *Cap.*, I, 1006, 273
158 Ibid, 274-5
159 *PR*, §244, 150; §244A, 277
160 *Cap.*, I, 275-6, 782-3
161 *PR*, §244, 150
162 *Cap.*, I, 1069
163 Ibid, 270; also *PR*, §196, 128-9; *Phil. of Mind*, §524, 257
164 *Cap.*, I, 278, 280

CHAPTER 6

1 *Grund.*, 164
2 *PR*, §63A, 240; §192, 127;

§192A, 269
3 *Cap.*, I, 1063
4 *Grund.*, 652, 464
5 Immanuel Kant, *Critique of Practical Reason*, trans. Lewis White Beck (Indianapolis 1956), 68
6 John Plamenatz, 'History as the Realization of Freedom,' in *Hegel's Political Philosophy: Problems and Perspectives*, ed. Z.A. Pelczynski (Cambridge 1975), 30
7 *PR*, §15, 27; §16, 28
8 Ibid, §15A, 230
9 *Enc. Logic*, §145z, 206
10 *Pol. Writ.*, 313, 316, 325, 310, 312, 325
11 Shlomo Avineri, *Hegel's Theory of the Modern State* (Cambridge 1972), 163
12 Gareth Stedman Jones, 'Engels and the End of Classical German Philosophy,' *New Left Review*, 79 (1973), 35
13 *Pol. Writ.*, 317
14 *PR*, §311R, 202-3
15 *SW*, II, 221
16 Ralph Miliband, *The State in Capitalist Society: The Analysis of the Western System of Power*. (London 1969), 162
17 *Pol. Writ.*, 318
18 *Phil. of Hist.*, 452
19 *Pol. Writ.*, 318-19
20 *Practical Reason*, 57, 103, 44, 28, 30
21 *PR*, §36, 37
22 Ibid, 135A, 254
23 *Hist. of Phil.*, III, 461; also *PR*, §29R, 33
24 *Practical Reason*, 87

25 *Phil. of Mind*, §385, 22
26 *Hist. of Phil.*, II, 98
27 Anthony Giddens, *Capitalism and Modern Social Theory: An Analysis of the Writings of Marx, Durkheim and Max Weber* (Cambridge 1971), 222
28 *PR*, §72, 58; §65A, 241
29 M. Kalecki, *Theory of Economic Dynamics: An Essay on Cyclical and Long-Run Changes in Capitalist Economy* (London 1965), 45-7
30 *Cap.*, I, 1064
31 Ibid 93, 90
32 *PR*, §276A, 287
33 *Cap.*, I, 101
34 Ibid, 102, 101, 92
35 *From Hegel to Marx*, 74-5
36 *Cap.*, I, 175
37 *Grund.*, 708, 711
38 *Cap.*, I, 1024
39 *Phen.*, 21
40 *Enc. Logic*, §§81 81z, 116-18; 82z, 120
41 *PR*, §195A, 269
42 *Karl Marx and World Literature* (Oxford 1976), 298
43 *Cap.*, I, 102-3, 100
44 Ibid, 254-5, 738
45 Ibid, 432, 439
46 Ibid, 914
47 *Hist. of Phil.*, III, 159
48 *Cap.*, I, 915
49 Ibid, 735, 986, 448, 1037
50 *PR*, §140, 100
51 *Cap.*, I, 1038
52 *Grund.*, 289
53 *Enc. Logic*, §119z, 173-4; §120, 175; §91z, 135; see also *Sc. of Logic*, 435-8
54 *Cap.*, I, 1005-6
55 *PR*, 2
56 *Modern State*, 109
57 'Hegel and Political Economy, II,' *New Left Review*, 104 (1977), 106
58 After admitting that Hegel 'probably wishes us to take it for granted that the class of wage-labourers is a part of the manufacturing class,' Bernard Cullen perversely concludes that 'Hegel has failed to integrate the working class into his system of classes.' *Hegel's Social and Political Thought: An Introduction* (New York 1979), 108
59 *PR*, §80B(3), 63, also §67, 54; §204, 132
60 *Enc. Logic*, §121z, 175-8
61 *Cap.*, I, 980
62 *Enc. Logic*, §213, 274-5; also *PR* §8, 24; §56, 47; §59, 49
63 *Cap.*, I, 284
64 *Enc. Logic*, §212, 273
65 *Cap.*, I, 1007
66 Ibid, 982, 1024, 1019, 1016, 1039
67 Ibid, 1039, 1006
68 Ibid, 1001, 994, 289
69 *PR*, §196, 128-9, my emphasis
70 *Cap.*, III, 615
71 Herbert Marcuse, *Reason and Revolution: Hegel and the Rise of Social Theory*, sec. ed. (New York 1954), 189
72 *Grund.*, 465
73 *PR*, §§54-6, 46-7
74 Ibid, §58, 47-8; §41A, 235-6

75 Ibid, §46R, 42-3; 41A, 236
76 Ibid, §57, 49; §67, 54; §192, 127; §41, 40
77 Ibid, §47, 43; §48R, 44; §47R, 43; §48R, 44; §96, 68
78 *Grund.*, 500-1
79 *PR*, §57R, 48; §168R, 116
80 *Hist. of Phil.*, I, 99-100
81 *PR*, §57A, 239
82 *Grund.*, 501
83 *PR*, §49A, 237; §49R, 44
84 *Cap.*, I, 177
85 *Reason and Revolution*, 194
86 *PR*, §59A, 239; also §59, 49; §60, 49
87 Cf. *Sc. of Logic*, 747
88 *PR*, §§61-2, 50
89 *Enc. Logic*, §212, 273; §140, 197
90 *PR*, §62R, 50
91 *Cap.*, I, 1002
92 *PR.*, §40R, 39-40
93 *Cap.*, I, 1002
94 *Phil. of Mind*, §406Z, 115; §408Z, 128
95 *Cap.*, I, 1003-4
96 *PR.*, §49R, 44; §76A, 242-3; §63, 51; §77R, 59; §63, 51; §77, 59. Hegel's analysis of capitalist private property appears also in *Phil. of Mind* where he argues that in civil society 'the external *recognition* of right is separated from the right's true value; and while the former only is respected, the latter is violated. This gives the wrong of *fraud* – the infinite judgement as identical – ... *where the nominal relation is retained, but the sterling value is let slip.'* (§498, 247; my emphasis)

97 *Cap.*, I, 300, 302, 991
98 *Modern State*, 98-9, 109
99 Similarly, Bernard Cullen demonstrates a painful ignorance of the Hegelian unity of opposites: 'it seems strange that Hegel should expect us to believe – after the descriptions he himself has given us of the conflicts *within* the manufacturing class of civil society, between those who work for a wage and those who own the productive property – that the working *Klasse* could just be integrated into the manufacturing class ... quite naturally; or, indeed, that they really have a place in any of the *Stände* in civil society.' *Hegel's Social and Political Thought*, 112
100 *Reason and Revolution*, 183
101 'Political Economy,' 113
102 *PR*, §62R, 51
103 Ibid.
104 *Cap.*, I, 929-30

CHAPTER 7

1 Herbert Marcuse, *Reason and Revolution: Hegel and the Rise of Social Theory*, sec. ed. (New York 1954), 211
2 *PR*, §183, 123
3 *Phil. of Mind*, §523, 256-7; also *Phil. of Hist.*, 84
4 *PR*, §258, 156
5 Immanuel Kant, *The Philosophy of Law: An Exposition of the Fundamental Principles of Juris-*

prudence as the Science of Right, trans. W. Hastie (Edinburgh 1887), 164; cf. Susan Meld Shell, *The Rights of Reason: A Study of Kant's Philosophy and Politics,* (Toronto, Buffalo 1980), 153

6 *SW,* I, 110-11

7 *PR,* §124R, 84; §184, 123; §186A, 266

8 *Cap.,* I, 990

9 *Phil. of Mind,* §502, 248

10 *PR,* §184, 123; §32A, 233

11 Ibid, §263A, 281; §185, 123; §243, 149

12 *Cap.,* I, 1045, 742

13 *Enc. Logic,* §211, 273

14 *Cap.,* I, 742

15 *System,* 171

16 *Cap.,* I, 990

17 *PR,* §§251-2 253R 253, 152-4

18 *Cap.,* III, 436-7

19 *PR,* §253, 154

20 John Scott, *Corporations, Classes and Capitalism* (London 1979), 175-6

21 'Classwide Rationality in the Politics of Managers and Directors of Large Corporations in the United States and Great Britain,' *Administrative Science Quarterly,* 27 (1982), 222

22 *Cap.,* III, 438

23 *PR,* §232, 146; §234, 146; §234A, 276

24 *PR,* §§236 235, 147; §236A, 276

25 *SW,* I, 123

26 *Pol. Writ.,* 306-9

27 *PR,* §258A, 279; also *Sc. of Logic,* 799-800

28 There has been a revival of interest in developing a Marxist theory of the state. But the debate has not got much beyond rather Talmudic analyses demonstrating that the state *is* civil society, i.e. that it may be comprehended entirely in terms of its function in maintaining the capitalist order. After a concise and stimulating review of this debate Theda Skocpol writes, 'so far, virtually all Marxists continue simply to assume that state forms and activities vary in correspondence with modes of production, and that state rulers cannot possibly act against the basic interests of a dominant class ... The result is that still hardly anyone questions this Marxist version of the enduring sociological proclivity to absorb the state into society.' *States and Social Revolutions: A Comparative Analysis of France, Russia, and China* (New York 1979), 28; see also my 'The Corporation and the External Capitalist State: The Political Theory of Hegel and Marx,' paper presented at the Canadian Sociology and Anthropology Association Meetings, Saskatoon, June 1979.

29 *PR,* §268A, 282

30 V.I. Lenin, *Selected Works in Three Volumes* (Moscow 1971), II, 294

31 Leon Trotsky, *The Revolution Betrayed: What is the Soviet Union and Where is It Going?* trans. Max Eastman (New York

1970), 58; see also Skocpol, *States and Social Revolutions*, 215, 284-6
32 *PR*, §297A, 291
33 Fernando Claudin, *The Communist Movement: From Comintern to Cominform*, trans. Brian Pearce and France MacDonagh (Harmondsworth, Middlesex 1975), 86
34 Ibid, 117
35 *SW*, I, 479
36 *PR*, §201, 130-1
37 *Phil. of Hist.*, 420
38 *PR*, §206, 132; §203, 131
39 Isaac Deutscher, *The Prophet Armed: Trotsky: 1879-1921*, I (New York 1965), 321
40 'Record of a Discussion with Heinrich Brandler,' *New Left Review*, 105 (1977), 55, 53
41 *PR*, §207, 133; also §7, 23-4; *Enc. Logic*, §§163-5, 226-30
42 *Phil. of Hist.*, 399, 402, 429-30, 446-7
43 *Phil. of Mind*, §529, 259-60; *PR* §238, 148
44 *PR*, §203R, 132. As will be seen in the concluding chapter, these changes in the form of the agricultural class also have implications for its role in the state.
45 *Phil. of Hist.*, 385; also *PR*, §204, 270-1
46 *PR*, §200, 130; §206, 132
47 *Phil. of Hist.*, 144, 147; *PR*, §206, 132-3
48 *Cap.*, I, 1032
49 *PR*, §206R, 133
50 *Cap.*, III, 885-6
51 *Cap.*, I, 797
52 *PR*, §20, 29; §187R, 125-6
53 *Enc. Logic*, §81z, 116
54 *Cap.*, I, 1007-8
55 *Grund.*, 165, 332
56 *Cap.*, I, 1041
57 *Grund.*, 88
58 *PR*, §270A, 283
59 *Grund.*, 325
60 *PR*, §187R, 126
61 *Grund.*, 409-10. Marx's use here of Hegel's term for the bourgeois economy, i.e., the 'system of needs,' is not just another instance of his employment of Hegelian terminology; it also indicates that in these passages he is reflecting directly on the relevant paragraphs of *PR*.
62 *PR*, §192, 127, §209R, 134; §190R, 127
63 Ibid, §191, 127; §194, 128
64 *Grund.*, 409
65 Paul A. Baran and Paul M. Sweezy, *Monopoly Capital: An Essay on the American Economic and Social Order* (New York 1966), 141
66 *The Revolution Betrayed*, 57-8. Trotsky's remarks are reminiscent of Hegel's observation that the invention of another kind of consumption good – gunpowder – 'was one of the chief instruments in freeing the world from the dominion of physical force and placing the various orders of society on a level. With the distinction between the weapons they used, vanished also that between lord and serf.' *Phil. of Hist.*, 402

67 *PR*, §193, 128
68 The massive distribution of universal credit cards hardly qualifies modern capitalism as Marx's ideal society. Nevertheless, 'unlike paper money or coin' a credit card 'does not possess a definite number. Its use requires thought and self-control and the credit obtainable through it depends on the individual's credit rating. The parameters to the cards' use are qualitative not quantitative ... of course, the system must still rest on the quantities of money involved but this quantitative element becomes slightly obscured and the individual has more to contribute to the monetary relations he engages in.' Simon Smelt, 'Money's Place in Society,' *British Journal of Sociology*, XXXI, no. 2 (June 1980), 221
69 *Grund.*, 159
70 *PR*, §190A, 269
71 *Cap.*, I, 1033
72 Ernest Mandel, *Late Capitalism*, trans. Joris de Bres (London 1978), 398
73 *PR*, §191A, 269
74 E.g., *Monopoly Capital*, 128-31
75 *Grund.*, 287
76 Ibid, 420-1
77 *Cap.*, I, 1033; also *Grund.*, 287
78 *PR*, §299R, 194-5; also §236R, 147
79 *Grund.*, 157-8
80 *PR*, §302A, 292
81 *Grund.*, 158
82 *PR*, §236R, 147
83 'Stalinism and the Mono-Organizational Society,' in Robert C. Tucker, ed., *Stalinism: Essays in Historical Interpretation* (New York 1977), 53
84 *PR*, §205, 132. The Hegelian notion of the bureaucracy as a distinct class was revived after the Second World War by writers in the socialist states of eastern Europe. See, for example, Milovan Djilas, *The New Class: An Analysis of the Communist System* (London 1957).
85 Ibid, §297, 193; §205, 132; §297A, 291
86 Cf. George Konrad and Ivan Szilenyi, *The Intellectuals on the Road to Class Power: A Sociological Study of the Role of the Intelligentsia in Socialism*, trans. Andrew Arato and Richard Allen (New York 1979)
87 Isaac Deutscher, *The Prophet Outcast: Trotsky: 1929-1940*, III (London 1963), 306-7, 305
88 *The Future of Intellectuals and the Rise of the New Class* (New York 1979)
89 *PR*, §§187 187R, 125-6
90 *Grund.*, 542
91 *PR*, §197, 129
92 *Cap.*, I, 1034
93 Ibid, 1026, 1013
94 Ibid, 1034, 1013-14
95 *Phil. of Hist.*, 85-6
96 *Cap.*, I, 1014
97 Lucio Colletti, 'A Political and Philosophical Interview,' in *Western Marxism: A Critical Reader*

(London 1977), 347

98 *Grund.*, 104, 885

99 Ibid, 704-5, 709

100 *PR*, §198, 129

101 Ibid, §§203A 204A, 270

102 *Phil. of Mind*, §539, 266

103 *Cap.*, I, 390-5. Colin Sumner offers an incisive critique of current Marxist views on law and a penetrating discussion of Marx's position in 'The Rule of Law and Civil Rights in Contemporary Marxist Theory,' *Kapitalistate: Working Papers on the Capitalist State.* (San Francisco 1981), 63-92

104 *Cap.*, I, 1031

105 *Phil. of Hist.*, 84

106 Quoted in Yvonne Kapp, *Eleanor Marx, 2: The Crowded Years (1884-1898)* (London 1976), 278

107 *Grund.*, 888, 884

108 *PR*, §211A, 271-2; §209R, 134

109 Ibid, §215A, 273

110 *Hist. of Phil.*, I, 89

111 *PR*, §228R, 145

112 Ibid, §218R, 140; §218A, 274; §96A, 246; §101, 71; §100A, 247

113 Ibid, §195, 128

114 *Phil. of Mind*, §385Z, 21-2; §523, 257

115 *Late Capitalism*, 587

116 *The Modern State*, 109

117 *PR*, §237, 148; §236R, 147-8; §245, 150

118 *Grund.*, 604

119 *PR.*, §62R, 50

120 *Grund.*, 421, 446

121 *PR*, §245, 150

122 *SW*, I, 114

123 *SC*, 100

124 *Grund.*, 424, 423, 424

125 Raymond Plant, 'Hegel and Political Economy, II' *New Left Review*, 104 (1977), 112

126 John Plamenatz, *Man and Society: A Critical Examination of Some Important Social and Political Theories from Machiavelli to Marx*, 2 (London 1976), 247, 249-50

127 Roman Rosdolsky, *The Making of Marx's Capital*, trans. Pete Burgess (London 1977), 459

128 S.S. Prawer, *Karl Marx and World Literature* (Oxford 1976), 310

129 *PR*, §§245 245R, 150; §241, 149

130 Ibid, §243, 149-50

131 *Cap.*, I, 548-9

132 Harry Braverman, *Labor and Monopoly Capital: The Degradation of Work in the Twentieth Century* (New York: 1974)

133 *Cap.*, I, 552

134 *PR*, §253R, 153, §244, 150

135 *Cap.*, I, 797

136 *PR*, §244A, 277-8, *SW*, I, 118

137 *PR*, §246, 151

138 *Selected Works*, I, 715

139 Quoted in ibid, 728

140 Ibid.

141 *PR*, §248A, 278; §248, 151

142 *Selected Works*, I, 766, 764-5

143 *PR*, §248A, 278

144 Ibid, §249, 152; §244, 150; §236, 147-8

145 *Grund.*, 161

146 *Cap.*, I, 349, 401

147 *PR*, §296, 193

148 *Cap.*, I, 91

149 Ibid, 92

150 *PR*, §253R, 153
151 *Cap.*, III, 436, 438, 387-8
152 *PR*, §254, 154
153 *Cap.*, I, 1027-8
154 *PR*, §§252-3, 153
155 For a critical discussion of these aspects of the giant corporations, see R. Edwards, *Contested Terrain: The Transformation of the Workplace in the Twentieth Century* (New York 1979)
156 *Hegel's Social and Political Thought: An Introduction* (New York 1979), 91-2
157 *PR*, §§251 252 253 253R, 152-4
158 Adolfe A. Berle and Gardiner C. Means, *The Modern Corporation and Private Property* rev. ed. (New York 1968), 11
159 *An Inquiry into the Nature and Causes of the Wealth of Nations*, ed. C.J. Bullock (New York 1909), 480-5
160 *The Modern Corporation*, 11
161 *PR*, §255, 154; §288, 189; §§308 308R, 200
162 *Phil. of Mind*, §489, 244
163 *PR*, §40, 38; §39, 38; §289R, 189. See also *Phil. of Mind*, §§488-91, 244
164 *PR*, §255A, 278; §290A, 290-1
165 *Modern State*, 151
166 *PR*, §256, 154; §229A, 275; §255A, 278; 256R, 155
167 *Cap.*, III, 437

CHAPTER 8

1 Sidney Hook, *From Hegel to Marx: Studies in the Intellectual*

Development of Karl Marx (Ann Arbor 1976), 60
2 *Cap.*, I, 103, 102
3 *Enc. Logic*, §20, 29; also *PR*, §21R, 29-30
4 *Enc. Logic*, §204, 269; §193, 258
5 *Grund.*, 106
6 *PR*, §343, 216
7 *Grund.*, 706
8 Introduction, *Cap.*, I, 22
9 *Grund.*, 104-5
10 *PR*, §146R, 106
11 *SC*, 191
12 *Enc. Logic*, §24, 40
13 Ibid, §25, 45-6
14 *Grund.*, 706
15 *Enc. Logic*, §25, 46; also *PR*, §343, 216. 'Reflection on the forms of human life, hence also scientific analysis of those forms, takes a course directly opposite to their real development. Reflection begins *post festum*, and therefore with the results of the process of development ready to hand.' *Cap.*, I, 168
16 'Philosophical Notebooks' in *Collected Works*, 38 (London 1960), 180
17 *Lenin and Philosophy, and Other Essays*, trans. Ben Brewster (London 1971), 109
18 *Selected Works in Three Volumes* (Moscow 1971), I, 66
19 *CPE*, 20
20 Quoted in S.S. Prawer, *Karl Marx and World Literature* (Oxford 1976), 369
21 *Sc. of Logic*, 54
22 *Hegel: A Reinterpretation* (Notre

Dame 1978), 160
23 *Sc. of Logic*, 54
24 *Marxism and Philosophy*, trans. Fred Halliday (London 1970), 133
25 Georg Lukács, *History and Class Consciousness: Studies in Marxist Dialectics*, trans. Rodney Livingstone (Cambridge MA 1971)
26 Antonio Gramsci, *Selections from the Prison Notebooks*, trans. Quinton Hoare and Geoffrey Nowell Smith (New York 1971)
27 *Class Consciousness*, 21
28 Gramsci, *Prison Notebooks*, 339
29 *Cap.*, I, 1037
30 *Grund.*, 106
31 *Cap.*, I, 99
32 *Enc. Logic*, §25, 45
33 *PR*, §21A, 231
34 *Enc. Logic*, §25, 45; §16, 22
35 *Cap.*, I, 96
36 *Sc. of Logic*, 826
37 *Enc. Logic*, §12, 18
38 *Sc. of Logic*, 53
39 *Cap.*, I, 92-3
40 *Sc. of Logic*, 51
41 *Cap.*, I, 92
42 *Enc. Logic*, §17, 23
43 *PR*, 4
44 *Cap.*, I, 90
45 *PR*, A, 224
46 *Cap.*, I, 92
47 *Phil. of Mind*, §422z, 163
48 *Enc. Logic*, §159, 221
49 *Grund.*, 832
50 *Enc. Logic*, §241, 295; §159, 221; also *Hist. of Phil.*, I, 22
51 *Enc. Logic*, §60, 91; §89, 133
52 *PR*, 10-11

53 *Grund.*, 515
54 *Critique of Pure Reason*, trans. J.M.D. Meiklejohn, (London 1893), 251
55 *Sc. of Logic*, 824
56 *PR*, §10A, 229
57 *Sc. of Logic*, 837
58 *SW*, I, 179
59 *Grund.*, 541
60 Ibid, 541, 463
61 *Hist. of Phil.*, I, 23
62 *Enc. Logic*, §§158 158z, 220; *PR*, §§23 27, 30-2
63 *Cap.*, III, 820
64 *Enc. Logic*, §50, 81
65 *Cap.*, I, 103
66 *PP*, 116
67 *Enc. Logic*, §81, 116
68 *Sc. of Logic*, 832
69 *Enc. Logic*, §82, 119
70 *Cap.*, I, 103
71 *Enc. Logic*, §81, 116
72 *SC*, 157
73 *Sc. of Logic*, 834; also *Enc. Logic*, §82, 119
74 *Sc. of Logic*, 840
75 *Grund.*, 708, 711, 712
76 *Sc. of Logic*, 840; also *PR*, §§343-5, 216-17
77 Louis Althusser, *For Marx*, trans. Ben Brewster (London 1969), 34-5
78 *Principles of the Philosophy of the Future*, trans. Manfred H. Vogel (Indianapolis and New York 1966), 33-4
79 *EPM*, 172, 187
80 *SW*, I, 119
81 Anthony Giddens, *Capitalism and Modern Social Theory: An Analy-*

sis of the Writings of Marx, Durkheim and Max Weber
(Cambridge 1971) 210
82 Enc. Logic, §25, 46
83 Ibid, §156, 218
84 Ibid, §12, 17
85 SW, I, 15
86 Hist. of Phil., I, 50
87 PR, §62R, 50
88 Phil of Hist., 30-1; also PR, §348,
   218
89 SC, 264
90 SW, I, 399
91 ACW, 222
92 Phil. of Hist., 74, 64
93 Cap., I, 90
94 GI, 90-1
95 Cap., I, 1079
96 Grund., 86-7. In this passage,
   Marx reproduces a discussion by
   Hegel, where the latter also refers
   to the British nation: 'A Nation
   is moral – virtuous – vigorous –
   while it is engaged in realizing
   its grand projects, and defends its
   work against external violence
   during the process of giving to its
   purposes an objective existence.
   The contradiction between its
   potential, subjective being – its
   inner aim and life – and its actual
   being is removed; it has attained
   full reality, has itself objectively
   present to it. But this having been
   attained, the activity displayed
   by the Spirit of the people in
   question is no longer needed; it
   has its desire. The Nation can still
   accomplish much in war and
   peace at home and abroad; but

the living substantial soul itself
may be said to have ceased its activity. The essential, supreme interest has consequently vanished
from its life, for interest is present
only where there is opposition.'
Phil. of Hist., 74; also PR, §347,
217-18
97 Hist. of Phil., I, 33, 34-5; also
   Enc. Logic, §25, 45-6
98 Hist. of Phil., I, 55; also PR,
   §343, 216. 'Philosophy awakes in
   the spirit of governments and
   nations the wisdom to discern
   what is essentially and actually
   right and reasonable in the real
   world ... thought makes the spirit's truth an actual present, leads it
   into the real world, and thus
   liberates it in its actuality and in
   its own self.' Phil. of Mind, §551,
   285-6
99 Grund., 460, 100, 885
100 PR, §33R, 36
101 Grund., 661
102 'A capital misunderstanding ... is
   that the natural principle or the
   beginning which forms the starting point in the natural evolution
   or in the history of the developing
   individual, is regarded as the truth,
   and the first in the Notion.' Sc.
   of Logic, 588
103 Hist. of Phil., I, 29-30; also PR,
   §32, 35
104 PR, §32A, 233
105 Hist. of Phil., I, 30; also Grund.,
   102
106 Enc. Logic, §242, 296
107 PR., §34, 37; §360, 222-3

108 *PR*, §32, 35; *Phil. of Mind*, §380, 7-8
109 *Grund.*, 460-1
110 *Phil. of Mind*, §408z, 130; also *PR*, 32R, 35
111 *PR*, §33R, 36
112 *Enc. Logic*, §147, 208
113 *Phil. of Mind*, §408z, 130
114 *PR*, §262, 162
115 Ibid, §272A, 285
116 *Cap.*, I, 173
117 E.g. *SW*, III, 147
118 *PR*, §289, 189; §308, 200-1
119 Ibid, §§272R 273, 174-6; §§288-9, 189-90; §308, 200; §311R, 202
120 Ibid, §§272-3, 174-6; §§300-3, 195-8; §§300-1A, 292
121 *Aesth.*, I, 48
122 *PR*, §258A, 279, §203R, 132; §306A, 293
123 *Phil. of Hist.*, 87
124 *PR*, §329, 296; §273, 177
125 This point was made long ago in Bernard Bosanquet's classic, *The Philosophical Theory of the State*, sec. ed. (London 1958), 264
126 *PR*, §297A, 288; §284, 187
127 Herbert Marcuse, *Reason and Revolution: Hegel and the Rise of Social Theory*, sec. ed. (New York 1954), 218, 217
128 *PR*, §280, 184
129 *Phil. of Hist.*, 428
130 *PR*, §§279 280R 281, 184-5
131 *Enc. Logic*, §193, 259
132 I owe these observations to a conversation with Professor Donald G. MacRae.

Index

Absolute, 75-6, 79, 83, 139
Absolute idea, 117, 140, 244, 252-3.
See also Idea; Freedom; Rational
State; Social individual
Absolute idealism, 51-4, 65, 71-84, 90,
141. *See also* Dialectic method;
Idealism; Unity
Absolute mechanism, 19
Absolute mind, 68-9, 119
Abstraction: in capitalist system, 167-
74; God as, 79; and Kant's moral
philosophy, 75; matter as, 126; not
a quality of Hegelian absolute, 76;
in Roman rule and Jewish religion,
62-3; ruling principle of bourgeois
society, 190; of thing-in-itself, 142-3.
See also Universality
Actuality, 21, 111, 119, 207. *See also*
Idea; Objectivity; Rationality
Advertising, 210-11
Agricultural class: consciousness of,
99-100, 202-5; decline of, 254, 257,
269n.101, 289-90n.66; dual
structure of, 181, 212, 268n.86;
Hegel's theory of, 30-8. *See also*
Class consciousness; Class, social
Agriculture, 48, 99-100
Alexandrian school, 102
Alienation, 46, 72, 84, 100; in
bourgeois property relation, 123-6,
173, 190-1; in capitalist mode of

production, 157-8, 164, 230, 243-4;
as characteristic of understanding
consciousness, 118-22, 136; most
extreme form of, 142; in natural
science, 123-31; and natural will,
66-8; reduction in work place, 231-
2; relation of capitalist and worker
to, 197; and religion, 58-60, 72-4,
76, 79-82, 99; and sale of labour-
power, 153-4
Alteration, 88
Althusser, Louis, 53, 175, 248, 279n.9;
on relationship of Hegel and Marx,
4-5, 110-15, 162, 239, 246-7
Appearance, 196
Aquinas, Thomas, 72
Anglican Church, 200-1
Anselm, 76
Antipater, 91
Aristocracy, *see* Agricultural class
Aristotle, 56, 89-93
Art, 16
Atheism, 52-8, 73, 85
Athens, 89
Automobile, 21, 45-6, 95, 209
Avineri, Shlomo, 5, 169, 193, 234-5;
no working class in Hegel's system,
181, 268n.82

Bauer, Bruno, 52
Becoming, 86, 246

Giddens, Anthony, 117, 129-30, 173
God: and concept of ideality, 84-97; is
  dead, 56, 66; Enlightenment concept
  of, 77-8; as the human individual,
  57, 65-7, 72-4, 79-84, 102; as
  pictorial conception, 44, 74-5;
  proofs of existence of, 39-43, 76,
  127
Gouldner, Alvin, 213
Gramsci, Antonio, 4, 240
Greece, 25-6, 61-8, 100, 176; class
  struggle in, 151, ideality and the
  Greek spirit, 89-94; mythology of,
  82, 101-2, 118; state in, 40-3
Gunpowder, 102, 289-90n.66

Head of state, 213, 255-8
Hegel, G.W.F.: analysis of labour
  process, 13-20, 26-32, 89-97, 124-5,
  157, 181-94, 276n.105, 277n.110;
  assessment of Kant, 116, 133-48,
  153-7, 168-73, 244; atheism of, 52-
  8, 266n.35; on Aristotle, 89-93;
  British model used for social and
  political theory, 6-9; business class
  includes capitalist and worker, 30-2,
  180-2; 268n.82; 268n.86, 286n.58,
  287n.99; compared with Weber, 97,
  277n.121; concerned with individual
  freedom, 18, 250; criticism of
  bourgeois democracy, 169-71, 233,
  255-7; critique of bourgeois property
  relation, 29-31, 184-94, 286n.58,
  287n.96; as a 'dead dog,' 177, 193;
  denies pantheism, 84-6; on distinction between use-value and
  exchange-value, 161-3, 239; distinguishes labour from labour-
  power, 163-4; on 'final end of the
  state,' 257; and French Revolution,

42, 48, 55, 128, 239, 259; fuses
  German idealism, British political
  economy, and ideals of French
  Revolution, 9, 134, 239-40; life of,
  5-9, 48, 55-7, 258-9, 272n.81, 278-
  9n.172; materialist theory of history
  in, 26-7, 65, 93, 149, 176, 267-
  8n.72 et passim; on machinery, 197-
  8, 217-18, 227-8; on 'moment of
  liberation' in civil society, 207-12;
  on negative aspects of Christianity,
  60; performs his own transformative
  critique, 21-2; philosophy based on
  ideality, 90; on Plato, 39-51; and
  political economy, 7, 9, 134; his
  'Protestant bias,' 101-2; provides
  theoretical basis for socialism, 9;
  rejects accepted notion of dialectic,
  16-17; on Rousseau's political
  theory, 23-4, 55, 66-7, 75; on
  supremacy of the state, 200; theory
  of imperialism, 228-30; theory of
  over-production, 223-8; on the USA,
  216, 220; use of religious language,
  48; versatility of the worker, 214-18
Heine, Heinrich, 56, 62, 259
Heiss, Robert, 5
Hephaestus, 91
Hill, Christopher, 101
Hiroshima, 137
Hitler, Adolf, 188
Hobson, J.A., 228
Hook, Sidney, 52-3, 55, 68, 95, 115,
  175
Hume, David, 78, 127, 134, 136-7
Hyppolite, Jean, 5

Idea, 20-7, 39-51; a priori basis of
  nature and mind, 143-4, 149;
  communism as abstract, 243;

slave from free worker, 164, 210-11, 220, 229; and private property, 100, 184-8
Materialism, 4-5, 51, 103-7, 112-17, 122-31
Mathematics, 122-3
Matter, 104-6, 114, 123, 126-7
Means, G., 232-3
Means of production: in bourgeois property relation, 181-3, 189-94; in the labour process, 13-20, 89-97, 167-8, 185, 197, 277n.110; struggle over, between capitalists and workers, 30-1, 194, 233-5, 254
Mechanism, 92-7, 175
Mehring, Franz, 11
Metaphysics, 12, 127, 129, 136
Middle class, 32-3, 213. *See also* Universal class
Mill, James, 120, 225
Monarchy, 257-8, 270-1n.114
Money: as absolute goal of worker and capitalist, 206-8, 215-18, 238; which begets money, 158-9; as social power for the worker, 211-12; as universal equivalent, 119-20, 156, 167, 181
Mono-organizational society, 212
Mueller, Adam von Nittersdorf, 8
Muenzer, Thomas, 101

Nagasaki, 137
Napoleon I of France, 6, 72, 249, 259
Nation, 250-1, 294n.96
Natural science, 40-1, 73, 77, 99; as alienated structure of thought, 123-31, 281n.94; and classical political economy, 120-1, 148-9; Feuerbach's attitude towards, 115-17; finite character of, 103-5, 134; Kant's

program for, 136; method of, 242; use of, 96, 218
Nature: and agricultural class, 32; attitudes towards, 62-4, 82; autonomous reality of, 12-13, 77, 87-8, 98, 126, 145, 238; bondage of, 187-8; in concept of the Trinity, 79; evolution of, 152; and individual, 117-18; interchange with, under communism, 245; in the labour process, 13, 92-3, 116-19, 208; laws of, 104, 139, 174-5, 179, 242; and Logic, 104-6, 142-4
Necessity, 75, 77, 106-7, 124-5, 190, 224
Negativity: as aspect of identity, 162-3; characteristic of individual, 88, 150; in Christianity, 40, 64, 79-84; destroys the thing, 160; and dialectic method, 242-3, 245-6; effect of thought on its object, 143; in labour process, 15, 17, 93, 119, 189, 277n.110; to negate the negation, 86-7; and poverty, 228; and slavery, 187
Neo-Platonism, 62-4
Newton, Isaac, 41
Nixon, Richard Milhous, 204
North America, 199, 216-17
Notion: and dialectic method, 241, 251-3; as ideality, 83-6; as the Individual, 16, 97, 157, 244, 246; as self-consciousness, 73-6; as the state, 19, 23; as subjectivity, 119; as theoretical knowledge, 40-3, 104; as worker in the labour process, 92, 182, 277n.110
Noumena, 136
Number, 122-3